FRITH
ON
CRICKET

HALF A CENTURY OF WRITING BY DAVID FRITH

FOREWORD BY JOHN WOODCOCK

GREAT NORTHERN

Great Northern Books
PO Box 213, Ilkley, LS29 9WS
www.greatnorthernbooks.co.uk

Photo acknowledgements: PA Photos; Philip Brown; David Knapp;
rear cover photograph by Julianne Frith-Orr

ISBN: 978 1 905080 72 4

Design and layout: David Burrill

CIP Data
A catalogue for this book is available from the British Library

BOOKS by DAVID FRITH

Runs in the Family (with John Edrich) 1969

"My Dear Victorious Stod": a Biography of A.E.Stoddart 1970 and 1977

The Archie Jackson Story 1974 and 1987

The Fast Men 1975

Cricket Gallery (ed.) 1975

Great Moments in Cricket (as 'Andrew Thomas'; with Norman Harris) 1976

England v Australia: A Pictorial History of the Test Matches Since 1877
(12 editions between 1977 and 2008)

The Ashes '77 (with Greg Chappell)

The Golden Age of Cricket 1890-1914 1978

The Illustrated History of Test Cricket (ed. with Martin Tyler) 1978

The Ashes '79

Thommo (with Jeff Thomson) 1979

Rothmans Presents 100 Years England v Australia (co-editor) 1980

The Slow Men 1984

Cricket's Golden Summer: Paintings in a Garden (with Gerry Wright) 1985

England v Australia Test Match Records 1877-1985 (editor)

Pageant of Cricket 1987

Guildford Jubilee 1938-1988

By His Own Hand 1990

Stoddy's Mission: the First Great Test Series 1894-95 1995

Test Match Year 1996-97 (editor)

Caught England, Bowled Australia [autobiography] 1997

The Trailblazers: the First English Cricket Tour of Australia 1861-62 1999

Silence of the Heart: Cricket's Suicides 2001

Bodyline Autopsy 2002

The Ross Gregory Story 2003

Battle for the Ashes 2005

The Battle Renewed: the Ashes Regained 2006-2007

Inside Story: Unlocking Australian Cricket's Archives (with Gideon Haigh) 2008

The David Frith Archive Catalogue 2009

The Stoddart biography and *Pageant of Cricket* and *The Ross Gregory Story* each won the annual Cricket Society Book Award; *Bodyline Autopsy* was Wisden's Book of the Year and runner-up in the William Hill Sports Book of 2002, and early in 2010 Cricketweb.net named it as Cricket Book of the Decade; DF was British Magazine Sportswriter of the Year 1988 (Sports Council) and Wombwell Cricket Lovers Society's Cricket Writer of the Year 1984; *Inside Story* won the Australian Cricket Society's 2008 Cricket Book of the Year award. He alone had five titles in The Fifty Best Australian Cricket Books of All Time (Ronald Cardwell and Roger Page, 2006). Two years later only he had as many as four books in Cricinfo's Top 45 of all time, a list compiled by Suresh Menon.

CONTENTS

FOREWORD

by JOHN WOODCOCK, OBE
former Times cricket correspondent and editor of Wisden

NO-ONE CAN have steeped himself in cricket more assiduously or with more singular intent than David Frith. Indeed, there is no-one else quite like him in the game. Although not a lot is seen of him, in the way it is of those who do the daily round of cricket reporting, he has built up a remarkable collection of famous cricket friends and acquaintances. Most of these have come from England and Australia, many from long ago, and all of them have yielded at some time or other to David's probing for information, much of it for the edification of his readers.

He is an eminent cricket historian, the leading authority on cricket films, a past editor of *The Cricketer*, the founding editor of *Wisden Cricket Monthly*, the author of numerous cricket books, and the creator of an exceptional and highly personalised cricket archive.

Being very much his own man, David writes without fear or favour, and his hobby is the pleasure and practice of research. No other cricket writer I have known would have had the urge – let alone submitted to it – to put so much work into a comprehensive study of cricketers who have committed suicide. Happily, *By His Own Hand* would need much less updating today than if it had been written sixty or seventy years ago.

No life is real without heroes and opinions, and David Frith rejoices in both. He is equivocal only when it comes to his allegiance during an Ashes series. Having been born in London, he was brought up in Australia before returning at the age of twenty-seven to England. In later years, once he could afford it, he spent part of each winter back in Australia. Hence the ambivalence over his identity, which he dismisses by saying that he supports whichever side he thinks is the more deserving, or, on other occasions, more in need of the Ashes.

In other matters there is no such hesitancy. David's pursuit of the legendary and reclusive Australian all-rounder of the 1920s, Jack Gregory (*Mr Gregory, I Presume?*), and of the only aboriginal to have made a mark on the game in remotely "modern" times (*The Oblivion of Eddie Gilbert*) shows him in his role as a kind of cricketing archaeologist.

At the same time, he does not hold back when expressing disaffection, such as for what he considered to be the undue ruthlessness with which West Indies achieved their supremacy under Clive Lloyd and Vivian Richards (*An Unappetising Tour*).

There is, perhaps, about David Frith a trace of Addison's "touchy, testy, pleasant fellow". The testiness and the touchiness have tended to hamper relationships, particularly with his magazine proprietors, as well as to command respect; the pleasantness is correspondingly and amply rewarding.

This selection of his writings is sure to win him new admirers, among other things for the amount of ground it covers, the facts it uncovers, the personalities it discovers, and the commitment which imbues it.

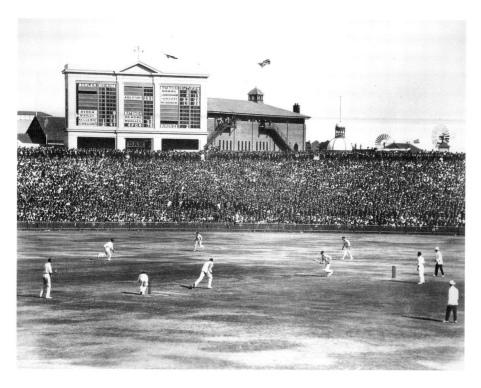

The author's spiritual homes: Sydney Cricket Ground and Lord's

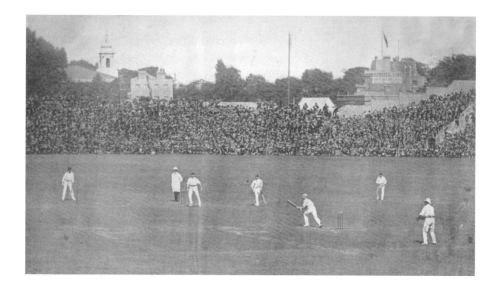

PREFACE

GLANCING THROUGH this collection – from the school essay of 1952 through to the reflections on the gripping Ashes Test match at The Oval in 2009 – conveys a certain truth to me. With the passing years, an early sense of cosiness and innocence has been overtaken occasionally by solemnity and concern, the reaction to disservices to this beautiful game by some who have run it, some who have played it, and even some who have written about it. Once installed in an editorial chair, I accepted the inherent responsibility as I watched with sadness and sometimes anger the suffering that cricket had to endure because of administrational greed and negligence.

Cricket has long been my currency, and I am in some debt. It is a good world in which to live. It has delivered a cavalcade of great spectacles and much travel, friendship and emotional seesaws, all underpinned by the calming effect of cricket in film and on television and in the better books and the treasured acquaintance of many good people, history-making cricketers among them.

And all that time I was clattering away on old typewriter keyboards, graduating to the convenient word-processor. The ambition was to enlighten, or to share the pleasure and excitement as well as the recurring indignation at the bruises inflicted on cricket by the greedy and the uncaring whose duty it is to protect the game. Many of them now refer to cricket as a "product", a term which makes the flesh creep. Insecurity is one of the major curses pressing down on this age. All around us is tacky celebrity, with money the obsession. Seemingly there is never enough of it, and commercial sponsorship, like a gaudy great armchair, has long been propping up cricket, manipulated by (as Mary Russell Mitford put it almost two hundred years ago) "people who make a trade of that noble sport".

There are advantages and drawbacks to having twin cultures. My first eleven years were lived in a London suburb, half of them in wartime. The next fifteen were spent in Sydney. Since then I have bobbed about like a cork in the ocean, with cricket and family the lifelines. J.M.Kilburn called one of his books *Thanks to Cricket*, just beating me to it. Only once in a while have I had cause to speculate on whether I might have spent my life more usefully.

Family and friends know that I seldom care to gaze into the future. My preferred aspect is backwards. But there is one matter in which I may perhaps claim to have been a bit of a visionary: through my burning desire to see the end of injustices in the field of play. For many years now umpires' costly errors could easily have been rendered a thing of the past by utilising whatever clear evidence was shown in video replays. Administrators' duty is to keep cricket healthy and solvent (and, most important of all, *pleasing* to cricket-lovers) until such time as it becomes the responsibility of their successors. But for years, pandering to the resistance of vain, myopic and seemingly stupid umpires and others, they have lacked the gumption to employ the obvious solution.

The International Cricket Council maintains an iron grip on some aspects of the game: such as spending millions on trying to spread cricket to places like China, for reasons which elude the average cricket-lover. At the same time the ICC has continued to be befuddled by the video replay phenomenon. Recently I watched a Test at Adelaide where a bad decision was swiftly put right after a "challenge" by the fielding side. But half-an-hour later I watched highlights of the concurrent Mumbai Test in which Dilshan was given out lbw by a so-called "elite" umpire (an Australian who always looks so pleased with himself). Replays showed the ball missing the stumps by a vast distance. Alas, the countries involved in this match had been allowed to reject the system, so the batsman left the field, understandably looking aggrieved.

Now, at long last, the crusade by someone who is, after all, a *traditionalist* is on the verge of fulfilment as the referral system is adopted. When umpiring blunders never again derail an important match, it's a better world by far.

If certain themes recur in this collection, it is no accident. It merely reflects the frustration caused by administrators' dilatoriness in safeguarding cricket's welfare. Further examples were the slackness in dealing with the brutal excesses of bouncers, and then, in Britain, the game was sold to satellite television, leaving several million youngsters and loyal oldtimers who couldn't afford the subscription with no more live Test or one-day cricket at their disposal in the land where the game began. Greed had triumphed again, and certain administrators were congratulating themselves on the financial bonanza, while boasting that heaps of money was going to "grass roots" cricket.

Enough complaining (for the time being). As for a writer's personal (unsponsored) output, when informed that E.W.Swanton had written eight million words on cricket during his career, John Arlott is said to have groaned: "And without leaving one memorable sentence." While having been responsible for nothing like as prolific an output as "Jim" Swanton's, I hope to escape an indictment like that one. By virtue of the nature of their work cricket writers are probably prone to tetchiness at times. To judge from his (warmly appreciated) foreword to this volume, that superlative writer John Woodcock seems to think so – though he may not altogether appreciate the problems which befell me while working for certain magazine proprietors. I'm glad of this chance to acknowledge just how much John's support meant to me over the years.

Naturally enough there is much here from *Wisden Cricket Monthly*, a magazine I founded in 1979 and ran and edited for a long time: seventeen years. Before that there were six years as editor of *The Cricketer*. Elsewhere, even allowing for much work which could not be accommodated here, the range is pretty broad, leaving the writer himself surprised at how many outlets there have been for someone so keen to expound on anything concerning cricket and its people. Book extracts sit alongside newspaper and magazine articles, opinions alongside discoveries, the reflective, the personality studies, reviews, obituaries, occasional protest alternating with delight, the historic, the unexpected. We have gone easy on match reports. There have been too many of them and many were lengthy. My special heroes are nonetheless duly indulged.

That first school essay, penned close to sixty years ago, was the work of a hopeful boy. This retrospective is the work of a slightly tired but still keen and very grateful septuagenarian, whose gratitude is extended to Barry Cox and his team – principally David Burrill – at Great Northern Books, and to Duncan Hamilton for having assessed the potential (during a Wisden dinner, of all occasions); illustrations have come from the author's collection, with my thanks also to Philip Brown, PA Photos, and David Knapp; and with acknowledgement to all the publications, mine own and others, which have provided the space for my (some way short of eight million) words.

DAVID FRITH
Guildford, Surrey; January 2010

THE SEED IS SOWN
1952

My first essay on cricket was composed in 1952 for Mr Fergus Cloran, my English master at Canterbury Boys' High School, Sydney (alma mater to the great left-hand batsman Arthur Morris and Australian Prime Minister John Howard). The kindly Mr Cloran was a source of encouragement, and my first experience of what might be termed sub-editing came from his gentle hand. To my embarrassment, the first correction became necessary at the very second word – in the title itself. I'd mis-spelt "influential". Just as well that my numerous cricket magazine contributors in the years ahead, as they saw their offerings modified or corrected, knew nothing of their editor's own clumsy beginning. Nonetheless, Mr Cloran awarded me an encouraging 16 out of 20 for this composition and marked it "V.good". With that, all thoughts of becoming a barrister or an architect or a film-maker evaporated.

An Influential Personality

WHEN I met Alec Bedser my final doubts as to my future occupation were dispersed. The meeting showed to me the attractions of journalism – the interest and thrill of interviewing visiting personalities. There is a unique exhilaration about speaking to a person upon whom the eyes of the world are continually focussed.

When the MCC [1950-51 team] were in Sydney, having just completed the 3rd Test, I was standing outside the Hotel Australia when the two giant Bedser twins came down the steps and stood talking to each other. The street was crowded, yet, surprisingly, no-one looked at them for as much as a second time. Two men of such proportions would warrant a stare at most times, whether Test players or not. However they seemed rather perplexed, and I humbly offered assistance.

They wanted to know which tram to catch for Bondi (they were going for a surf). I was not quite sure myself, and just then my young brother came out of the shop on the corner and joined me.

"This is Alec and Eric Bedser," I said, and he immediately reached for his pocket to get his autograph book. It was at this stage that Alec noticed my Wembley Speedway badge, and realised that I was a Motherlander.

He spoke with the famed Cockney accent and straightaway made for conversation. Then and there, as he spoke, I wondered over the thousands of times this man's name had appeared in print; and here was I calmly chatting to him as if I had known him for years. I am afraid I was the more garrulous, questioning him on England's future prospects in the Test cricket field. How were the injured members of the team? Was Denis Compton returning to form or not? So we talked for about 20 minutes, with him asking me how I liked the change in climate – apparently he didn't – and how I had enjoyed the Test match.

How I certainly had enjoyed the Test match; and it was there that I realised that here was a man to be admired. In that Test he bowled 345 balls [*344 shown in most records*], and even now I cherish a vivid mental picture of him plodding to the bowling crease with his shirt wringing wet with sweat, and with the merciless sun beating down on us from above (though I was on the Hill wearing a spacious sun-hat).

This meeting left a tremendous impression on me, and indeed, upon my brother, though he doesn't say so, and since then I have met several other personalities, just briefly, but nevertheless long enough to see that it is enthralling to bring news to the reading public – and these people make the news.

Now, Alec Bedser is back in England, sharpening his claws for the coming Anglo-Australian Test series. He will be world news again. In four or five years' time I may be assigned to write a coverage on a Test match, and I have this man to thank for inducing me to become a writer.

It is seldom that one person can influence another to the extent of indicating his future occupation. True, a boy very often will become a sailor for the simple fact that his father before him was one. This is a case of environment. But the idea which came to me through talking to Bedser, Mr R.G.Menzies [in the SCG car park], and other identities has pulled from out of the blue the job which best suits my taste.

Alec Bedser (left) with Jim Laker and the author at the launch in 1977 of the latter's illustrated history of the Ashes Tests, the first thousand-picture cricket book.

A small matter of fifty-odd years later, having known Bedser – now Sir Alec – for much of that time, I found myself doing a sound recording with him for the Imperial War Museum. His war had been quite as eventful as his cricket career. When shown the above school essay he seemed characteristically unimpressed.

EARLY OFFERINGS
1959-1972

Years later came a couple of non-cricket articles in the school magazine and then some bylined reports of soccer matches for the local newspaper, stories which sometimes posed a frustrating challenge to modesty, for I had played in most of the matches under review. By the early 1960s, having had a couple of cartoons published in Sydney newspapers, I decided to seek a cricket opening in the land of my birth. Local newspapers in Surrey and The Cricketer magazine became infrequent takers for enthusiastic offerings, besides which there was some weekend agency work and the odd letter to a newspaper. A collaboration with John Edrich brought my first efforts at book authorship, soon followed by a biography of the wondrous late-Victorian Middlesex and England batsman and rugby player A.E.Stoddart. But it was not until 1972 that full-time employment in my chosen field came at long last as editor of The Cricketer. The following scraps are from these years of patience, hope, endeavour and frustration, starting with the opening paragraph of a football report which reveals an uncanny foretaste of a passionate pioneering campaign which I was to launch in an editorial many years later, urging the introduction of a video review system to eliminate umpires' errors on the cricket field.

ON A soggy pitch which made ball control difficult, St George lost an exciting game against highly-rated Neerlandia at Prince Edward Park last Saturday. A series of questionable decisions by the referee had much to do with the result, and a draw would have been a fairer reflection on the performances of the two teams.

St George Call, April 30, 1959

Spofforth – the Demon Bowler

FROM BALMAIN, Sydney, to Long Ditton, Surrey, is a daunting distance. F.R.Spofforth, in a lifetime's creation of history on a multitude of cricket fields, covered the distance over the course of his 72 years.

But the distinguished gentleman who moved into quiet retirement at Ditton Hill Lodge in 1919 to lavish care and pride on his chrysanthemums bore scant resemblance to the brash 24-year-old who had landed in 1878 with Dave Gregory's Australian team. "The Demon" then was tall and lean and had fire in his belly. His cause was to show the English that the "Colonial" cricketers were not only literate white men, but had grasped more than just the rudiments of the game.

His hour came on May 27. The Australians arrived practically unrecognised at Lord's, which was squelching from recent rains. W.G.Grace and Hornby opened the MCC innings, and after two wickets, including the Doctor's, had fallen early, a stand looked like developing. Gregory called up the towering, moustachioed Spofforth.

In 23 balls the Demon took six wickets for four runs, including a hat-trick, and the eminent MCC side had been scythed down for an irreverent 33.

The Australians had to struggle when they batted, and midway through this hectic afternoon their innings had folded up for 41. WG once more strode to the middle with Hornby to hold these devastating newcomers at bay. Spofforth, building a reputation with every ball, had WG missed first ball, bowled him with the next, and bowled Webbe first ball. The bearded Boyle also took two swift wickets and a wicked ball from Spoff sent Hornby from the field in pain. MCC had one run on the board with five men back in the pavilion.   A stand of 16 ensued, but shortly after 5 o'clock MCC had been dismissed for 19: Boyle 6 for 3, Spofforth 4 for 16.

The Australians made the necessary 12 and this sensational match was over but a few hours after it had begun.

Frederick Robert Spofforth was made. His hostility, his cunning, his sheer speed – word of his powers thundered across the cricket world. He was very tall and swung his arm high; his countenance could be fearsome, terrifying; and his aim was to destroy every English wicket that came before him.

During this year of 1878 he bagged the incredible tally of 764 wickets at 6 apiece at home, in England, and in the United States on the return trip.

The year 1879 began auspiciously too, with 13 wickets at Melbourne in "Spofforth's match", when he took the first Test hat-trick. The astounding analyses piled up one on the other and his reputation preceded him everywhere, claiming some proportion of his wickets for him. But by now this perceptive man was taking into his repertoire all the expertise and guile of the top English bowlers.

He became more than a fire-breathing express bowler. He varied his pace and trajectory, cut viciously from the off, flung down the yorker, held the next ball back. With the supreme Blackham behind the stumps and Boyle unprecedently close on the leg side, Spoff was the most formidable enemy in the world to batsmen however skilled.

It took a strong man to stand up to him. Jim Phillips, the great umpire, clashed with him over his dragging. Spoff once held the ball as Phillips called "No-ball". "Sorry, Jim. My foot slipped," Spoff explained with an evil grin.

Phillips regained his composure and barked out "No-ball!" to the next delivery, legitimate though it was. Spoff turned on him. "Sorry, Spoff. My tongue slipped!" Phillips explained blandly.

He came on the second of his five tours of England in 1880, but it was two years later that he performed his most historic feat. It was at The Oval, late in August, and it is known as the "Ashes match". For the first time, England at full strength were beaten in a home Test – and by a hair-raising seven runs. Spofforth blasted out 14 batsmen for 90 runs and all England wept as her cricketing body was cremated.

England regained those Ashes at Sydney the following year, but it was hardly Spofforth's fault. He took 4 for 73 and 7 for 44. The 1884 tour of England brought him over 200 wickets, including an astounding 7 for 3 at Birmingham, and at the end of the year he played an important part in Australia's two home wins in the first five-match Test rubber.

The 1886 series went resoundingly to England, but Spoff's 16 Test wickets were almost as many as the other Australians took between them. He seemed affected, though, by damage to his right hand from a hefty drive by Lord Harris.

That summer he married a Derbyshire girl and took her back to Australia with him. The following January he played his final Test, the thrilling 13-run win by England at Sydney.

And so his career at the highest level was at an end: 18 Tests, 94 wickets. But there was plenty more cricket in the Demon yet. England had grown on him and his early antagonism was mellowing unexpectedly. In 1888 he left his position as bank manager in Melbourne and sailed for the Old Country, this time to settle. A few days out from Melbourne his wife gave birth to a baby, and the family Spofforth were given a Derbyshire welcome that July.

He saw out the two-year county qualification, managing two games against Yorkshire in 1889 and taking 15 wickets in one of them. Yet his county career was short: one season as co-captain, taking 42 wickets at 11.36 – top of the averages, where he had always belonged.

In 1891 he moved to London and began playing club cricket with star-studded Hampstead, whose doyen was the great Stoddart. Soon MacGregor, England's wicketkeeper, had joined them, and with a host of Middlesex players at their disposal Hampstead became perhaps the strongest club side London has ever known. From the start Spofforth was irresistible. In 1893 he exceeded 100 wickets and staggered everyone with an innings of 155, and the next year exactly 200 victims fell before him. Never again was he quite as prodigious, but he was now 41. Till he was 50 he averaged 50 wickets a year for Hampstead; the final domestication came with his election to vice-presidency of the club.

Retirement came at the end of 1905, when a new era of cricket was in full bloom. He prospered as a tea merchant; the Great War cast its ugly shadow; and in a reshaped world the great cricketer left Ashley Cottage in Walton-on-Thames and took up residence at Ditton Hill Lodge.

The year 1926 was a stirring one for English cricket. In the Oval classic the Ashes were regained by Chapman's immortals on August 18, but the aged warrior was not there to see it. He had never fully regained his health after a bout of ptomaine poisoning, and on June 4 he died at home. He left £164,000.

Lord Hawke, Archie MacLaren and Clem Hill were among those who attended the funeral at Brookwood cemetery, and wreaths came from MCC, Surrey, the Australians, Hampstead CC, and Thames Ditton CC.

Today, Ashley Cottage and Ditton Hill Lodge stand no more and there is only the red granite memorial at Brookwood; but the robust glory of one of the district's surprise celebrities will live on for ever more in book and legend.

Esher News and Advertiser, August 25, 1967

F.R. "Demon" Spofforth, an early lookalike for Dennis Lillee: similar Australian fast-bowling scourges a century apart.

Another cricketer with local connections was H.H.Stephenson, who was born in Esher. Little could I have foreseen, as I wrote about him in 1967, that just over thirty years later I would be compiling a book (The Trailblazers) on the first English cricket tour of Australia, led by Stephenson in 1861-62. There is not room here to reproduce the early Stephenson feature.

Two articles on an off-beat subject were published in The Cricketer in the late 1960s. This, the second of them, looks at the final resting places of some further long-forgotten cricketers:

The Great Departed

IF, AFTER having browsed through some of cricket history's endless pages, you venture out into the winter drizzle, this, I am sure, is the most evocative time at which to pay tribute by the graveside of any of our departed cricket champions.

Apart from the sport's literature and the photographs which remain, often formal and inanimate, there is no other tangible link between ourselves and those colourful cricketers once so vibrant and three-dimensional, now transmogrified eternally to the printed word with its severe limitations. No other tangible link, that is, except the stone memorials marking the sites of their mortal remains.

There, tranquil under the yew trees, your thoughts drifting to appropriate moments in cricket's past, your imagination is free to roam. It need not be an occasion of sadness. I commend it.

The homage sometimes is, understandably, sadder than others, as when youth has been cut down, or when depression has driven a cricketer to end his own life. Albert Trott was one such. A strand of tragedy ran through his life. There was the cricket tragedy – minor in perspective – of his omission from the 1896 Australian touring side despite a sensational Test debut. He "defected" instead and for years was the most potent all-rounder in county cricket.

Yet his hit over the Lord's pavilion and its seductive after-effects, together with increasing ill-health and a weakness for the bottle drove him into miserable retirement. In the summer of 1914 at his digs in Denbigh Road, fifteen years but a day after his historic blow at Lord's, a shot from a Browning pistol ended it all. His grave at Willesden is unrecognised, a pathetically overgrown mound identified as P613 and half a world away from the bushland of Victoria.*

A.E.Stoddart, after four visits to Australia perhaps more popular there than in St John's Wood, if that were possible, died just as tragically the following year. It was a surprise even to the local people to find that the red granite memorial, obscured by tall grass, its cross shattered by Luftwaffe bombs, marked the final repose at Radford Churchyard, Coventry, of the ashes of one of England's finest Victorian sportsmen.**

His great professional compatriot Arthur Shrewsbury, a suicide also, lies at Gedling, Nottingham, where a noble tombstone of marble, dedicated to "a renowned cricketer", stands by the gateway to the Saxon church.

It is here also, of course, that Alfred Shaw is buried – more than a pitch length away, as it happens, and a good deal more than Shaw's additional crafty five-pace run-up. Perhaps on some of the warmer summer nights a ghostly cricket ball does float from one corner of the churchyard towards the gas-lamp by the gate, to be met by a straight and heavenly bat.

Canon Watson told me of the strange sight which greeted him one winter morning four years ago. Where Shaw's large cross of Cornish granite had once stood there was a gaping hole in the ground. A well, long since filled in, had collapsed and the consequent subsidence had taken the monument with it – an alarming situation remedied in due course by the Church and the County Club who sank a supporting concrete pier. Now, presumably, the shadowy net practice continues in the hush.

George Parr and Richard Daft, great men of Notts, lie thirty-five yards apart at Radcliffe-on-Trent cemetery, the latter beneath a huge horizontal marble cross which will survive years aplenty. By his side lie twin sons who died in infancy, and, nearer the pathway, Butler Parr, unrelated to George.

George Parr [leader of the first English cricket tour overseas, to North America in 1859] died in 1891, when a branch from his famous elm was placed on the coffin and a descriptive and picturesque headstone set in position.

The restless spirit of Sammy Woods surely flits yet across the West Country he loved so well, despite the cacophony of traffic along the Exeter Road. A fittingly hefty granite memorial stands over his grave at St Mary's cemetery, Taunton. Who will ever know how many bottles of ale remain hidden and unclaimed in Somerset fields, planted for future refreshment by this whimsical Anglo-Australian?

Archie MacLaren's grave is near the parish church at Warfield, Berkshire, where it is quiet and still and the mellow green downs roll away to infinity. Closer to London, at Shirley, near Croydon, powerful and aggressive Walter Read, another England captain, lies at rest in the rather populous churchyard. There a commanding white cross remembers a great batsman, although, as so often, there is no mention of the game that monopolised his years.

Gregor MacGregor, double international and double facially for Charlie Chaplin, was buried at Hampstead in 1919 after a sad and rapid decline. A reassuringly stout cross of granite ensures lasting remembrance of a great wicketkeeper.

Two of Surrey's finest players are buried at Richmond: the mighty Tom Richardson, whose memorial depicts a broken wicket, and Billy Brockwell – whose last nights on earth were spent on straw in a barn so near the cottages in Ham which he had once owned – bachelor gay*** Brockwell, who with three of the best Australian wickets in a couple of overs once swung a Test match, his final resting place an unmarked plot carpeted with fine grass.

And at Elmers End rests the Champion, W.G.Grace, his tomb rightfully restored to pristine dignity and now a regular point of homage for serious cricketers who might be well advised to plan their visit during licensing hours****, with a pub near at hand named after the supreme cricketer.

* The revelation eventually prompted some action: Middlesex CCC had a neat headstone erected some years after this article appeared.
** In an odd reversal of Trott's case, "Stoddy's" memorial was removed years later because of persistent vandalism in that churchyard.
*** This word employed at a time when it still meant nothing more than "happy, carefree".
**** Written when pubs' opening times were sensibly limited.

The Cricketer Spring Annual 1968

Looking back is usually a rich source of enjoyment, amazement and fulfilment, even when the retrospective is but seven years, as in these reflections on a nocturnal listening brief, an intimate glimpse of life after dark in the Frith household in an outer suburb of Sydney in 1961:

A Test Match by Night

THE RECENT Australian tour has been full of all the old excitement and tensions for us all, but there was a time for me when Test matches in England had to be followed at a lonely distance. The memorable Old Trafford match of 1961, one day of which I recorded in personal notes, was rather an uncomfortable affair. Come back with me seven years; the scene is a living-room in Sydney.

The sun, they tell us, is shining down on Old Trafford, and the ground is fresh and green in the morning air. But all around me it is dark as I lie before the kerosene heater, staring at the flickering shadows on the ceiling and listening to the voice of a commentator on the crackling wireless by my side.

It is 8.30pm and there is a bottle of port wine by me, for there is a long day's Test cricket ahead. I move an inch closer to the heater, pulling the rug around my buttocks to protect them from the creeping cold air as solidly as Lawry is going to protect his stumps against the English bowlers.

Now – everything set? Wireless tuned precisely, and not too loud for the sleeping children and the half-sleeping wife? Is the bread and jam near at hand in case the fingernail diet becomes tedious; and the record book for some later dark inquisitive hour when I may want to know how many Trueman needs for his 200 wickets?

The old player winds up his introduction, knowing full well that the two scheming teams down there will soon expose him as a totally unrealistic dreamer. Then the excitement hits me and time is forgotten.

I don't feel tired; just relaxed. Soon my eyes are forced shut by the sharp heat; the upper lids are heavy and slide down like automatic pink curtains. And then the picture forms. I am wafted halfway across the universe and lowered into the best position on the ground. In fact, as the inclination comes, I am actually standing at cover, watching the England captain direct his field.

I examine each fieldsman in turn, sip some port, and watch the tall thin figures of Booth and Lawry stride to the centre. How relaxing this is, especially when I recall the tiresome routine of the past week. I could never have withstood the pressure but for the lovely anticipation of the Test match. The thought sustained me through the day just as the port will sustain me through the night.

A wicket falls! And the muscles in my stomach tighten, proving once again that I haven't really got the temperament for Test cricket. I soon recover, but the innings doesn't. Davo gets a blob and the tail folds up tamely.

I look towards the venetian blinds, seeking a reason for the collapse; and they hang there in the gloom, probably asleep, as all sane things should be.

Now I am hovering magically over the arena again as England start to bat, and the commentator roars that Davidson imparted huge swing to that last ball. I picture it: heading for third slip then veering back ten feet or so to touch the edge of the bat. Must have swung a lot, or am I getting sleepy already? No, the storyteller said it swung a long way, and he should know; enviably he is actually on the spot.

Noddy Pullar hits a four and I find myself acclaiming it softly, gazing into the flames and murmuring "This is good stuff!" Perhaps it would be even more pleasing from the pavilion balcony, or sitting by the ropes? No! That would mean the distraction of people either side, and I can't help recalling the old fellah in the faded cricket cap who sat by me on the Hill last summer and mumbled crazily to himself about Macartney from lunch till tea non-stop. And of course there is no getting-home-after-the-match problem when you're in your own lounge room.

The clock ticks steadily and eventually Subba Row is out just on lunchtime, when many of my acquaintances will retire to bed. The boss, for one, will probably pack it in then. He can't afford to be bleary-eyed in the morning; yet he runs the risk of missing the most intriguing part of the day's (or night's) play. It usually happens that way.

The comments of the oracles are worth listening to; but it *is* a pity they can't share this port, it's so beautiful. So is the glow of the fire now; the experts could hardly be warmer. Apart from my toes, alone and rather chilled in the darkness. The commentator shouts into the microphone and I am just about to commemorate the fall of a wicket with a small toast when he informs us it was "not out". I pour myself the toast all the same and the players troop off for lunch. The light clicks on.

Well, what a different world this is: Sydney, at 10.30pm, with forty minutes to fill in, and the house cold as a freezer locker. This is the all-night listener's testing time, when he must resist the warm temptation to go to bed. After all, there will be a morning summary, and then the newspapers. Yet if that had been my inclination I would have missed the drama of the Watson-Bailey stand in '53 and Benaud's 97 and Laker's memorable massacre in '56, to say nothing of Dexter's scintillating 180 a few weeks back.

No enthusiast does things in half measures, and I know from the start, fatigued or not, I'll see the thing out.

Clif Cary, Harold Larwood and John Dease have a studio discussion that threatens to become quite violently international. Better get up and start the blood circulating. A peep through the blinds at the moon, bright and blue, flooding the dozing district with eerie light. Now for a look in at the boys, both sleeping so peacefully. One day I'll tell them all about this, and they can stay up and listen to the Test with me. That will be when Bob Simpson is middle-aged (and I won't be so young myself).

A book rests on the sideboard and I glance through it, but it is irrelevant and uninteresting, so it slips from my fingers; I head for the refrigerator instead. A slab of bread, a crisp apple, milk, a banana and a few biscuits. The MCC president himself could hardly be dining more delectably at that very moment.

For an idle minute I do my own summing-up and conclude that the match is evenly balanced. England can't afford to lose, or the Ashes would stay with Australia (though I'd have to go to London to see them) and much of the interest would drain from the series.

Yet the final Test always commands attention, even if the rubber has been decided. There is always something poignant about the final game – the sad realisation that the fun has ended for several years. As the players walk off for their champagne the man in the street (or the man in the dressing-gown, sitting stunned by the fire) experiences an indescribable sorrow.

I reflect on the action packed into the previous weeks – catches, cover-drives, criticism – I've digested the lot from my secret vantage point. And now all is history. All that will remain will be the tour diaries.

But don't fret, Frith, for it is still only the fourth Test, and even if your wife wishes it were the last of the series and of all time for that matter, there is still plenty of fun in store: if I can stay awake.

And now these blessed critics in the studio are arguing again about pitches and negative bowling and things, so I check the children once more and catch sight of the bottle of port next to the heater. Better not leave it there to explode; better drink it.

The game is resumed and McKenzie has Dexter caught, which prompts that strange vacillating roar from the crowd. England consolidate, and the urgent atmosphere subsides. They must certainly miss Cowdrey. I turn the fire up a little and close my eyes again in an endeavour to picture the cricket field, wondering whether the sun is still out at Manchester. Does Peter May realise there are anxious ears this far away listening to his performance? And how many others are listening in the Australian darkness at that moment?

May bats serenely, confidently, we are told; and so I drowse. The flames burn steadily and another cricket story is slowly written. And the bottle of port, hidden by shadow, is at last forgotten.

The broadcast comes through in patches; only the howl of applause which greets a boundary restores consciousness. The immaterial is missed; I am absorbed in the general theme of it all. The floor seems to have hardened, but it would be most unwise to lie down or give way finally to the temptation to creep into bed with the transistor. Sleep would come faster than a Trueman thunderbolt. Experienced night observers of Test matches develop an immunity to discomfort.

The runs come, with Pullar and his captain batting comfortably. What first-innings lead will England need? Two hundred, perhaps? Or two-fifty? Australia may collapse as they did at Leeds. Who knows? There may be a few shocks still to come.

The tea interval is welcome, for I feel peckish: the packet of cheese, resisted at lunch, meets its inevitable fate. So does the tomato. Then I drift tiredly back into the lounge, bowling an exquisite imaginary leg-spinner at the unconscious television set, settle down again and switch to some music. It is pleasing but distracting, so back to the critics and, eventually, the Test for the final session.

Now I am weakening, for less than two overs after resumption I droop badly with fatigue. All of a sudden the drowsiness is uncontrolled. One moment May and Pullar are both 33, but a few seconds later May is 90 and Close 14 ! What ever happened to Pullar? Two hours have flown by in a matter of moments. There was no-one to jab me in the ribs and keep me awake. The cricketers, unaware of my oblivion, have continued playing. And now it is all over. Stumps are drawn. While consciousness slipped away and my back was turned, so to speak, the Aussies got rid of Pullar, and May hit another 50-odd.

How tragic that I lost the fight against sleep. Luckily nothing momentous had happened, but what if there had been a collapse! Indeed, the only thing to collapse was me, and I'm rather shame-faced about it, although I can always read the details of play in the *Herald*.

England are well placed, so I myself become well placed under the blankets at last, lying pensive for a while then sliding into semi-sleep, waking at the sound of the milkman trotting down the path, then dreaming again and finally, at an hour unknown, whilst England awaited her sunset, finding complete peace.

The Journal of the Cricket Society, Volume 4 Number 1, Winter 1968-69

Although written in 1968 as an exercise, the following memoir was not published until 1989, when it found a home in a Lord's Taverners anthology. It is a passage that marks the end of yet another age of innocence:

Ashes Classic at The Oval

TEST CRICKET is documented in great detail thanks to newspaper reports, radio tapes, video recordings, and books of players' memoirs. There seems, therefore, little that might be added to this mass of data, especially in the case of the more famous matches. However, on the extraordinary final day of the England v Australia Test match at The Oval in 1968, although I was there only in the capacity of dogsbody for a news agency, I kept scribbling down notes, just for something to do. Twenty years on, they give an unconventional view of a famous event. Pieces of the raw material assemble to give a picture of a day's cricket still unsurpassed for high drama:

WE RAN through all the emotions during that last day. Our sense of justice was badly offended when the torrential downpour at lunchtime seemed to have rescued

Australia yet again, giving them a series which England deserved to share and probably to win. I shall never forget the hysterical laughter which issued from the Australian end of the Press-box. It continued loud and long, and did nothing to assuage our disappointment as we watched the fat and furious globules of water crash into the newly-formed puddles and trickle down a wall of the Press-box. The lightning flashed and the thunder rumbled, and it really seemed that the gods were having a go at us. "Send her down, Huey!" shrieked the Aussies, and one of them led the way by cabling home confidently that the match was washed out, and the series thus went one-nil to the tourists.

The score was 86 for 5, Inverarity and Jarman in, and Australia 266 runs away from victory. I went on schedule to the telephone room. Through the rear window I saw a newspaper placard: Princess Marina Dead. The bell rang and the *Birmingham Mail* copy-typist said unemotionally, "When you're ready, dear." Bill Wanklyn's lunchtime story concluded with the cruellest irony: "It only looked like being a light shower." People were scuttling from awning to awning, newspapers held protectively, many retreating through the Hobbs Gates, hailing cabs, jumping into buses, and diving down into the tube station at the end of the road.

I spent most of this Test match seated beside Jack Fingleton, whose moods varied, but seemed to improve hardly at all. The inane chatter of the GPO telephonists behind us didn't help.

During the match I had phoned through Sir Learie Constantine's story and Brian Scovell's report for the *Daily Sketch*, and dashed into Fleet Street to deliver J.M.Kilburn's handwritten story to the *Yorkshire Post*. Among the writers I had spoken with, Lyn Wellings had been interesting. He said there was precious little money in writing books, considering the time and labour involved. Ian Wooldridge later agreed that it is sometimes an essential enterprise if one is to promote one's capabilities. John Edrich, whose book I was writing, had batted all through the opening day for 130 not out. I would like to think my wife and I played our part by arranging to mind little Cathryn, allowing Judy Edrich to be at The Oval to give a touch of wifely support.

Frank Tyson sat puffing one cigar after another, thinking up his four-syllable words. Bill Bowes, who must have pinged down a fair ball in his day, talked entertainingly. Bobby Simpson, recently retired, sat grim-faced throughout. Denis Compton was rarely seen, except in the Press refreshment room before play. Richie Benaud was busy, from microphone to typewriter to telephone and back again. The big story on Saturday had been E.W.Swanton's conjecture that Basil D'Oliveira would be chosen for the South Africa tour, that South Africa would object, and that MCC would cancel the tour.

Several million Englishmen wanted to cheer an England win over Australia. It last happened in London fifteen years ago, and that is a frightfully long time. The skies were fairly innocent on the final morning, with a forecast of showers late in the afternoon. Australia, with Lawry and Redpath out, needed a further 339 for victory.

I parked my car off Fentiman Road, and in response to the raucous overtures of the urchin protection gang I mumbled something that sounded like "I'm a policeman, and don't need my car minded, thank you." I prayed the warning would work.

The placards pleaded with us to read Constantine in the *Sketch*, Arlott in the *Guardian*, Peter Wilson in the *Mirror*. Touts asked for spare tickets near the Oval tube entrance and offered them for sale further on. The flags fluttered from the gas-holders and the crowd was building up. By the main [Hobbs] gates people stood and gazed at the arriving cars, scrutinising every passenger as they drew up.

During the morning session England secured three more wickets, and things were going quite according to plan. Underwood trapped Ian Chappell and issued a warning to the rest by making one ball kick and another shoot. Walters bowed out of a disappointing series with a single. Darting from place to place, I found myself on the top tier of the pavilion when Sheahan clipped Illingworth to midwicket and Snow scooped up the catch. Within minutes the staircase was crowded with mournful members as the rain cascaded down and the radio commentators lamented the passing of the game as the puddles widened.

In the Long Room bar men gloomily drank their beer and munched their veal-and-egg pies. John Edrich seemed resigned to the abandonment. That was it, his shoulder shrug seemed to say. Now for South Africa.

Bob, an old mate, cried for a while on my shoulder. Young Gordon went home, in company with many others. The bars did huge business. Someone reckoned Bill Lawry had been seen with a sumptuous grin on his aquiline face. John Thicknesse looked startled, as is his custom. Keith Miller looked pensive.

The rain eased, but what a dreadful sight The Oval presented for the faithful who had remained. An official abandonment had still to be announced, but the first faint sign of hope was the appearance of Cowdrey, in England blazer, tiptoeing around the puddles to examine the pitch and surrounds. There was much consultation and stroking of chins, but the groundstaff worked feverishly as the sun broke through. Volunteers gathered quietly in the outfield and began thrusting the spiked poles into the ground to let the water away. Scores of sacks were laid and rolled and squeezed into reservoirs outside the boundary rope, which had been lost from view when the flood was at its highest. People wandered aimlessly and looked at each other bemusedly. It dawned on some that there might after all be more cricket, however restricted. We had to adjust our thinking again.

Times were suggested. Five o'clock, a quarter to, even half-past four. In the Press-box copy had ceased to flow. Most of us wandered and wondered. The turf in front of the pavilion was moist but hard underneath, a hot week having left the undersoil craving water. The heavy accumulation was sinking fast, absorbed by a thirsty earth.

As things were quiet – positively desultory – in the England dressing-room I took my *World of Cricket* in to get some more signatures. Tom Graveney had his dark-brown eyes fixed on the crossword. Ray Illingworth, despite his troubles with Yorkshire, was in pleasant mood. D'Oliveira willingly signed too. Colin Milburn, his left shoulder still hurting from a blow that morning, chuckled his way through a few lines. Colin Cowdrey was as serene as ever. John Snow sat alone, boyish and glum. Another of the younger element, Alan Knott, was stretched out on the seating. He said five wickets were too many to get in so short a time (a 4.45pm resumption had been announced, tea having been taken), and the pitch would be a pudden. Edrich, who knows it better than most, agreed. Derek Underwood wanted to sign the book near the Beckenham CC entry, where apparently he had been given a mention. I steered him to the Kent chapter instead. By the day's end he had earned an entry under Heroes.

The sun was beaming down now, and excitement was building up as the players emerged, an unforeseen miracle. The close fielders crowded in, but the only disturbance to the peaceful scene for some overs was the occasional crow-like call of Inverarity or Jarman as a run was stolen.

Forty of the available seventy-five minutes had actually passed before England broke through. D'Oliveira got one through Jarman, and there it was: a bail on the ground. He was bowled. When umpire Arthur Fagg stood chatting with the England players as Jarman left the field, Fingo said it was a disgrace. An umpire should remain alone and aloof at all times.

Underwood replaced D'Oliveira at the pavilion end. Mallett, who had batted some time in the first innings, propped the first ball into David Brown's eager hands horribly close at forward short leg. McKenzie survived only to the last ball of the over, when Brown caught him too, off bat and pad. The jubilation in the centre and among the sparse gathering of spectators was special.

Gleeson came in, a comic figure, with about 25 minutes to see out and only Connolly to come after him. There would probably be eight more overs, so quickly did the field change over and so smartly did the bowlers walk back. Illingworth was kept out by Inverarity.

We saw the single-prevention process at the end of the over, but Gleeson, far from being trapped, swept Underwood to the unguarded boundary, and aimed other mighty blows through the infielders, who can only have been drunk with anticipation. There was a very loud appeal last ball of the over, but Charlie Elliott, low over the bails, turned it down.

Gleeson slammed Illingworth straight at Dave Brown, who was crouching only seven feet from the bat, and he doubled up in pain. Slowly he got to his feet, ready for the next round. The knockout would surely be his if he could stay on his feet. The next ball was edged at catchable height, but Cowdrey was not fine enough at slip: 120 for 8, and the field dispersed for Inverarity. Gleeson at the other end faced Underwood again, hemmed in all round by stooping Englishmen.

Edrich, four feet from the bat, caught a bump-ball. A ball fizzed through. The next was padded away, to a great chorus of shouting. A single off the last ball was strategically refused.

What can happen in 30 balls? Knott ripped off the bails, but an Australian foot remained in its territory. Illingworth bobbed in again, and another ball was safely repelled. There was much patting of the pitch, the wide smears of sawdust a constant reminder of what had happened earlier in the day. A threatening black cloud had now wandered off beyond the gas-holders.

Quarter-of-an-hour left. Underwood to Gleeson, and the second ball really leapt. Underwood changed to around the wicket. Gleeson was not in line to the next one, and over went his off stump, to another outburst of hysteria.

Alan Connolly loped down the steps to the biggest crisis of his life. There were catcalls, but he was wasting no time. It was 5.50pm as he took guard and swept the pitch clear, with sarcastic handclapping echoing round the ground. He played the last ball to leg. Inverarity, close to carrying his bat through the innings, took a single off the fourth ball of the next over, exposing Connolly. The Victorian contrived four leg-byes fine, and kept out the last ball.

Despite later statements that victory came six minutes from the scheduled end of play, my watch, and I'm certain the clock at the Vauxhall end too, showed 5.57pm when Inverarity fell. He played the first ball to Edrich at suicide point; pushed the next off the back foot back to the bowler; and thrust a defensive pad across to the third ball. He was not considered clear of off stump, and the urgent appeal was granted. Inverarity was leg-before for 56, Australia all out 125, England winners by 226 runs almost on the final bell. It was some time later that I caught up with Underwood's figures: 31.3-19-50-7.

Twenty-four hours later England's unlikely victory was submerged by the news of D'Oliveira's omission from the MCC team to South Africa. Quite as sad was the overlooking of jolly "Ollie" Milburn.

Tales from Around the Wicket (Graham Tarrant/David & Charles, 1989)

Patriotic fervour: spectators help remove surplus water at The Oval in 1968. Their efforts enabled the Test match to be resumed just in time for an England victory.

Stoddy Hits 485

I could not comprehend why so little was known about the much-admired Andrew Ernest Stoddart (1863-1915), successful Ashes captain in the 1890s, skipper of England also at rugby, a highly likable and popular man who was the sporting toast of his country. Perhaps it was his suicide that caused a curtain quietly to be drawn. I decided to research into his life and produce a book. A couple of major publishing houses declined the chance to publish it so I raised the finance to publish it myself in a limited edition of 400 copies at £2.25 including postage. It won the inaugural Cricket Society award, and copies of that original edition now fetch around £75. One of the most awesome of "Stoddy's" many sporting achievements was a world record score of 485 in a match for Hampstead when he was already a Middlesex cricketer and England wing three-quarter:

IN THE Hampstead pavilion on August 2, 1886, A.Russell Parker was presented with a gold watch to commemorate twenty years with the club. He expressed his thanks and his pride in "the best club, the best ground, and one of the best men in Middlesex", referring unmistakably to Stoddart.

A match against Stoics was programmed for the Wednesday upon the Hampstead ground so worthily praised by Russell Parker in his speech; and on Tuesday night Stoddart and some of his friends went dancing and afterwards got to playing poker "just for half an hour". It was after midnight when they commenced, and when the well-dressed young stockbroker (now sometimes called "The Masher" for his elegance) found himself winning an appreciable amount of money he played irresistibly on, mesmerised perhaps by the pattern of play, reluctant to leave the table with his friends' losses. He gave them generous time to recover: one round of jackpots followed another and his play grew wilder each hand, but he kept winning. As dawn broke they decided stumps ought to be drawn.

There was hardly any point in going to bed this fine summer morning, so it was warm baths all round then a cab to the swimming baths to freshen up. Stoddart usually did rise early (except on the day of a big match, when he often saved himself by rising almost when it was time to take the field) but this was bordering on absurdity. He always was slow and meticulous about his toilet, and he always ate a late breakfast; and this great day, after a hearty meal, it was a case of ambling straight down to the ground, where the wicket was pitched in the centre of the expanse.

"Stoddy" padded up and took Marshall with him to the wicket at 11.30. Marshall was soon bowled, and "Daddy" Besch walked out to join the erstwhile gambler. After an hour's murderous assault Hampstead were 150 for one wicket, and after Besch had gone two short of a century and Smith-Turberville had been bowled for 5, Swift came in and helped thump the total to an incredible 370 at lunch after two and a half hours' play.

Lunch took an hour, then Stoddart and Swift resumed their tempestuous fun and finally achieved 383 runs together. Russell Parker came in and, possibly mindful of the security of his gold watch, was caught for only 4. Doyle and then Dollar supported Stoddart in his furious rampage. His Magic brand bat sent the ball singing to the edges of the ground with power drives born of muscular forearms and a middleweight's shoulders. The afternoon sun blazed down as he hurtled through the 300s and, at about 5 o'clock, reached 400. Everyone was wide-eyed.

The highest score ever recorded, 419 not out made a year previously by J.S.Carrick at Chichester, was just a few strokes away. Heroically the Stoics bowlers kept to the task, but the Hampstead champion took the world record, and immediately gave the sole semblance of a chance: at 421 he drove screamingly to mid-on, who failed to hold it, and two runs were taken.

Past 450, and the umpire, probably amused as well as fatigued, urged him to make sure of his half-thousand.

At 485, when the stoical trundlers and fielders must have been looking desperately to their only salvation, the clock, Stoddart miscued a hit to leg off Renny and sent the ball swirling high into the wind. It was said they ran almost three, "Stoddy" quoting 100 to 1 on the ball, before it plummeted into the hands of Kelly, the tall and inexhaustible fast bowler grazing at deep point.

Hampstead's final tally of 813 (not a wide bowled throughout) was the highest total ever in a one-day match, and one report stated academically that Stoics did not bat; there was no declaration law then, and though many may have wondered down the years why the Hampstead men did not throw their wickets away around, say, 400, the innings did at least make a fruity talking point, and, more pertinently, it gave a memorable fillip to the career and reputation of A.E.Stoddart.

It was once suggested that this must have left him feeling very anxious to get some sleep, to which he replied, "Well, perhaps I was, but we had a lawn tennis match, a four, on that evening, so I had to play that. Then I had another tub, and had to hurry too, because we had a box at the theatre and a supper party afterwards. But after that I got to bed all right, and it wasn't nearly three!"

> *"My Dear Victorious Stod": A Biography of A.E.Stoddart*
> *(Frith, 1970; Lutterworth, 1977)*

Stoddart stroked 207 against Blackheath three days later, fell to a W.G.Grace long-hop at 98 for Middlesex at Gloucester on the Monday, then registered his maiden century for Middlesex at the end of the week: 906 runs in four innings over ten days.

Drewy Stoddart, the beau ideal of the Victorian sportsman: captain of England at cricket and rugby, briefly holder of the highest score in cricket history and for eighty years the highest by an England captain in a Test in Australia: but his life ended in tragedy.

Encounters with old cricketers invariably warm the heart, but there was something special about sitting with a man who had bowled to W.G.Grace and to Don Bradman and who had left figures in the good book which will always stand supreme:

A Pilgrimage to Rhodes

WILFRED RHODES of Yorkshire and England has never really given up playing cricket. One can sense the eternal involvement as he places his wrinkled fingers around an imaginary seam, or as he implores batsmen everywhere to position the 'springboard' back foot with care. That a man of ninety-three, without sight, should be so wedded to the game while young men retire from it when still in their prime is a poignant paradox.

He seems happy in his darkness. He chuckles frequently – something he rarely did in his playing days, if we are to believe his contemporaries. His memories of players and places are clear, particularly those of the earlier days, when he joined battle with M.A.Noble, whose fast one he foresaw by the finger grip ("That's being observant, isn't it?") and Arthur Shrewsbury (the "nice little fellow") and WG, who made him slightly nervous but drew out the best in him.

And he made surely one of the most remarkable statements ever to come from a bowler: "*I wanted to get at Victor Trumper*"! The context was a Darling-Trumper partnership, and the reasoning was faultless in that the left-arm bowler wanted the right-hand batsman, and Schofield Haigh [bowling at the other end] wanted left-hander Darling. But the pronouncement was still as remarkable as it was intrepid.

To visit cricket's senior citizen is to feel as John Mitford must have felt in 1833 when he went to Tilford to seek out Silver Billy Beldham. There is no blackened bat to press reverently to one's lips, but there are historic cricket balls aplenty: the one which bowled Australia out for 36, the one with which Rhodes took some of his 15 wickets in a Melbourne Test match, the one which gained him a wicket first ball in Australia sixty-seven years ago. There is, too, a small ball of Bulli soil, hard as musket shot, to remind him of the strips on which he toiled during periods of drought.

Though one may vow to steer wide of figures, it is almost impossible to spare them and yet convey his greatness. His 16 "doubles" and lifetime haul of 4187 wickets will probably never be exceeded, as much because first-class cricket will be curtailed in forthcoming seasons as that the bowler who stays in it until he is fifty-three will stand out as a freak of the first order.

So now the grand old man sits with his memories, proud at having contained Trumper during his 185-run blitz at Sydney, sad at having had Bradman dropped first ball in 1930. His judgments are set from decades of reaffirmation. Who was his pick of slow bowlers? Would it have been Blythe or Grimmett or Jack White or Hordern (who once told him between overs that he only enjoyed bowling at England's last six)? None of these. Gloucestershire's Charlie Parker was his pick.

Rhodes's batting, we have come to understand, was his sore point. He made 58 centuries, and his happy days at the crease were innumerable (even when he made 199 against Sussex, when Haigh ran him a short run only minutes before his downfall). But people were always trying to persuade him to reject this faculty. He was a bowler, and should not flirt with batting!

Stewart Caine, who was to succeed Sydney Pardon as editor of *Wisden*, was perhaps the first to taunt Rhodes in this way. And even after his opening stand of 323 with Hobbs at Melbourne, Reg Duff accused him of having only one stroke. ("That was all I needed on that hard ground, with five men on the fence!") He was

*Young Wilfred Rhodes, many years before the interview, by which time he was
sightless but awash with memories*

prepared to excuse the Australian, who had been propping up the bar most of the afternoon, but the comment obviously stung: "I might not have had a lot of strokes, but I must have had good defence, [pause] mustn't I?" [Rhodes's memory failed him in the detail: Duff had died two months previously. But he had probably made his cute remark on another occasion.]

His old friend S.F.Barnes could bat a bit too, he was quick to point out.

Wilfred Rhodes is our last witness to much cricket folklore: the "Let's get 'em in singles" legend at The Oval in 1902 was "some pressman's invention"; Clem Hill was clearly run out at Sydney, when the crowd grew hostile; the Ashes triumph of 1926 was assured from his first over, when he and Strudwick agreed that they had seen enough – the match would most certainly be won in due course.

He lived for over forty years in a cottage in Marsh, near Huddersfield, and across the street lived a lad named James Mason, who was later to become something of a film actor. "They had a French governess. I can see her now, walking with her bag under her arm, tight-fitting bodice, or what-they-call-it." But he rejects the idea of a small plaque being attached to the former Rhodes residence.

Of modern times – the South African problems: "It's a pity. I don't want to say much about it, but isn't it so all over the world? Didn't our amateurs come out of the middle of the pavilion, and the professionals come out of their holes? Didn't they? Isn't that apartheid? Perhaps it isn't apartheid: it's an old English custom."

Underwood in Australia? "He might find things not so bad now. He's very determined, isn't he? And he can carry on a long time." Rhodes had proved Ranjitsinhji's sombre predictions false in 1903-04, and he wants our greatest young hope to do the same to his Jeremiahs in 1970-71.

Recently an admirer in Ceylon sent Wilfred Rhodes a fifteen-page summary of his performances in first-class cricket. With proud professional thoroughness Rhodes already knew most of the statistics by heart. He thought the compilation, read to him by his daughter, was a very fine opus, and he seemed pleased at this further reminder that he was far from forgotten; yet, though it had taken a month to assemble, what was it to the thirty-three years of batting and bowling that made it possible?

Our conversation drew to a halt, not through his bidding though his voice was husky by now. He came to the door and explained the easiest way to the main road.

"It's all curves, is Bournemouth." An apt remark from the master slow bowler. Then quickly, as if he had spotted a flaw in a batsman's defence and had to get the information to his skipper, he shook hands and felt his way back into the house.

Playfair Cricket Monthly, February 1971

Cricket always seems to be struggling with a range of concerns about its well-being. The game itself is pure and enchanting. The problem often is the kind of people who seize the power to control its immediate destiny. The situation almost forty years ago was worrying enough to inspire a look at just how underprivileged boys had coped over the previous hundred years:

Where Have All the Lamp-Posts Gone?

SPRING BRINGS fresh hope as we emerge from a winter of Test cricket reports – principally bitter – and of edited videotapes with an incredibly unimaginative visual introduction, and of catching up on cricket books that deserved earlier reading.

The winter's climax came on February 17, when the Ashes changed hands: English men and boys who listened through the night to the fall of the last five Australian wickets were prepared to admit that not even man's landing on the moon for the first time had set the nocturnal pulse-rate so high.

Now, with winter receding, one's thoughts broaden. Spring is bringing fresh inspiration; England's frustration, for the moment, has been overcome (in cricket, at least); soon it will be time to wipe the dust off the bat. Boys everywhere will be imitating their new heroes: Snow, Knott, Luckhurst – and in the North: Boycott.

Or will they?

A friend remarked a few months ago that kids were not playing in the streets any more. The lamp-posts are still there, tennis balls are cheap, and today's imported cricket bats are not only reasonably priced but they are sized for boys of all ages. No modern lad need suffer the incursions of a cut-down bat: tired wrists and bruised breastbones.

So I became more vigilant, and took note of a chalked wicket on a brick wall in Battersea. There was no little fellow in front of it saying "You blokes be England and I'll be Victor Trumpet [*sic*]", but there *were* several juvenile *footballers* by the crossroads. And this was August!

It has been widely held that street, or "lamp-post", cricket has given hordes of boys their first steps to cricket stardom. It follows that if the combined effects of heavy traffic and all-year soccer reduce the numbers of little lamp-post cricketers the game will be the poorer ten years from now.

The portent sent me dipping into my books during the cold months in some sort of survey of cricketers' beginnings. The greatest of all cricketers, William Gilbert Grace, enjoyed rather a privileged upbringing among animated brothers and sisters, model parents, and a doting uncle who saw to it that WG played with a straighter bat than that of his elder brother EM, who had got into bad cross-bat habits because the only weapon available to him had been a heavy full-size bat. The father had chopped down some trees and laid out a pitch. A canvas sheet served as wicketkeeper, and a retriever and two pointers augmented the fielding side. The Graces practised joyously as long as weather and daylight allowed.

Contrasting with this, and proving that devotion may sometimes overcome deprivation, is the picture of young Arthur Mailey spinning his orange in the hessian-walled dining room, relieving the gloom of a depressed household where his five bob a week earned at seam-pressing helped keep the family on soup bones and bread. His dreams were of Trumper and art. Grinning mischievously most of the time, he spun his way into Test cricket and the affections of all who knew him.

Men like Larwood and Trueman must have reflected often enough on the cricket bug that bit them as lads. Their almost inevitable lifetimes in the coal-pits did not materialise. Perhaps the diminishing ranks of coalminers will mean fewer fast bowlers with the ability to heave away all day at the batsmen.

The fact that both Ray Lindwall and Frank Tyson bowled their hearts out as boys in an effort to strike oil-drum wickets with their fast bowling may argue that the three wooden stumps really are too undramatic. More children might be attracted to the game if the wickets were to be musical and otherwise more alluring!

Television probably has had much to do with the falling-off in street cricket. If a certain podgy boy in Burnopfield had been tempted away twenty years ago by 'Jackanory' in colour, cricket might never have known the sublime exhilaration of Milburn in full cry. Apparently at the age of nine he had nothing better to do than to carry his overnight score of 340 to well over 500!

Ken Barrington grew up in wartime, with only cigarette-cards of pre-war players to inspire him. But his loving soldier-father gave him a rough bat, and at the barracks nets the gentle bowling of other Tommies set him off on the long trail which ended thirty years later with the bombardment by Hall and Griffith.

News of Basil D'Oliveira's 100 against New Zealand at Christchurch on what must have been a very difficult wicket served as a reminder that he, too, learned to bat firstly in the street then on primitive matting wickets around Cape Town. He developed the same sort of resourcefulness that the young Bradman needed at an early age as he waged his lonely battle against a flying golf ball with merely a cricket stump.

Jack Hobbs also used a stump when, at the age of twelve, he played with a tennis ball on a gravel patch at Jesus College, Cambridge (where his father was groundsman). He felt that his scratch cricket actually assisted his development as a maker of correct strokes, but it must surely also have bred an instinct for split-second adaptability.

If ever a cricketer's adult qualities were displayed ahead of time it must have been in the case of Len Hutton. From tea-time till dusk, evening after evening, he and his chums played in a corner of the Pudsey ground during the late 1920s. Many a Hutton innings stretched through consecutive evenings, and many a time in later years as he held the fort for England must he have pondered his boyhood dreams.

Walter Hammond, like Barrington, grew up in a military environment. His was in Malta, and although he had the abundance of sunshine so useful to a growing lad, the conditions were less than luxurious. He had to salvage bats smashed by the garrison troops; the ball was indescribable; the wicket was chalked on the door of a gun-shed. Hammond the adult was to write that "I am of the opinion that it does a boy no harm to learn a sport in that way".

Fathers quite naturally provide the most outstanding influence in attracting a boy to cricket. Wilfred Rhodes was supplied with bat and ball by his sire very early in life, and his dedication followed as a matter of course. As he approached manhood his determination knew no bounds: for ages in solitude in a barn he taught himself the craft of spin bowling. His anxiety to play cricket cost him a career in the railways. He never had cause to regret it.

Neil Harvey and his five brothers had a novel way of sharpening their reflexes. They played on a strip of concrete and, using a cut-down bat, they bowled a glass marble at each other! Which helps explain how he played Tyson so well.

A recently-published cricket history [by Rowland Bowen] predicts that the game must lose its popularity except as a pastime for boys. It is a sobering forecast which cricket, in its present insecurity, can shrug off but unconvincingly. Will today's children when they are full-grown have great matches to which to take *their* sons?

My conviction is that they will, though the form will have changed – as it has always been changing. Cricket gets in the blood. Certainly boys give up fivestones long before they leave school – but that is hardly the same game.

Playfair Cricket Monthly, April 1971

In the next thirty-odd years cricket had more change inflicted upon it than the unsuspecting author, or any of his contemporaries, could possibly have forecast. And despite the brazen claims of those who have run the game in the first decade of the new century, fewer and fewer youngsters now seem to be playing it seriously. This is a predictable consequence of the disappearance of live cricket from a great proportion of television screens in Britain after the awarding of the lucrative contract to BSkyB satellite service. Now only the wealthier minority can afford to watch cricket on television. Many elderly folk too, having loved cricket all their lives, now find it beyond their means. The perpetrators of this moneygrubbing exercise – certain politicians as well as cricket administrators – will surely be found by future generations to have damaged cricket in the UK more than any other person or group in the game's recorded history. As for the wickets painted on walls or provided by street lamp-posts, the streets of England are now crawling with young footballers, even in midsummer.

A favourite childhood haunt provides an excuse for an unusual piece of research:

Cricketers in Wax

WHEN Madame Tussaud brought her waxworks exhibition to Marylebone in 1835 the champion cricketer of the day was Alfred Mynn. But it was to be over fifty years before any cricketer was glorified in the world-famous galleries: the eventual inclusion of W.G.Grace, A.E.Stoddart and Arthur Shrewsbury in the display was one of the many signs that cricket unarguably had become a popular part of English life.

WG has been in and out of the exhibition ever since. He was delighted at his original conclusion, though not, perhaps, at the remark of the little girl who had failed to find his effigy.

"What! How did you miss me? I am there as large as life."

"Well, sir, to tell you the truth, it cost sixpence extra to go into the Chamber of Horrors."

In 1892 it was planned to take the figures of Shrewsbury and several other celebrities, including [Alfred] Lord Tennyson, to the Chicago Exhibition, where they were to be housed in "a magnificent Moorish palace, with a glorious garden of palms in the centre".

As far as can be verified, cricket – ironically – was only lightly represented during the Golden Age. Shrewsbury was withdrawn in 1894, Australia's Joe Darling was featured in 1899 at the end of his successful tour, and Stoddart lingered on till 1905. But the archives reveal no Ranjitsinhji, no Trumper, no Jessop. Jack Hobbs was cast in 1923 and remained, apparently continuously, until 1955 – setting up yet another record. Herbert Sutcliffe also had a long innings – seventeen years from 1930.

Wyatt, Jardine and Hammond all took their places in the 1930s, as did Woodfull and Bradman, prompting one to echo that the only bowler to be honoured was Sir Francis Drake over in the Grand Hall. Alec Bedser finally broke the batsmen's monopoly (as was his custom) when the calipers were put over him in 1954. That was a time for heroes: Len Hutton was there, and Trevor Bailey, and Peter May, having joined the (figurative) giants of 1947, Compton and Edrich. Norman Yardley was disassembled at this point, but cricket now had its finest representation.

The sculptor's photographs and measuring charts reveal statistics such as *Wisden* has never recorded. How many cricket followers knew, for instance, that Bill Edrich's zygomatic arch measures 5¾ inches – the same as the distance between his chin and his tragus? Don Bradman's chest in 1934 was 38 inches and his waist 34. He is due for a comeback in 1972, principally to evoke a sigh or two from the expected influx of Australian visitors during Ashes year.

Jim Laker was modelled in 1957, presumably on the strength of something he had done at Old Trafford the previous summer, and Ted Dexter arrived in 1962, a year ahead of Frank Worrell. Mike Smith was briefly on show in 1966. Colin Cowdrey's recent withdrawal from exhibition might bring some personal relief to him. His injury and illness of the past two years must have left him wondering if there are one or two pin marks in the wax. For the moment only Garry Sobers is left, glistening under the arclights with fellow champions of lesser sports.

The Cricketer Winter Annual, November 1971

Never ageing: at the mercy only of meltdown: fairly recognisable models of Herbert Sutcliffe, W.G.Grace, Wally Hammond, Don Bradman and Jack Hobbs at Tussaud's waxworks exhibition in London in the 1930s.

The four months spent in Australia in 1971-72, searching for a fresh direction in life, proved fruitless apart from some thrilling meetings with legendary cricketers from the old days. The first was with a gentleman (the word is used with emphasis) who modestly and rather reluctantly confirmed the details of a glittering career:

Mr Elegance: Alan Kippax

IN THE season of 1925-26 Alan Kippax confirmed his standing as a major Australian batsman by making 448 runs for New South Wales at an average of 112. His last innings was 271 not out against Victoria, and all his runs were made with fair speed and great charm. Yet at the end of the season he was a shock omission from the Australian team to England. It was generally considered a sinful blunder, and the public outcry reverberated for years afterwards.

Kippax's first impulse was to throw himself over the nearby Gap at Watsons Bay. Instead, he set up the NSW Sports Store with Herb Geldard. In their first year they almost went out of business through excess patronage! They could not keep up with the demand as cricketers and clubs all over the state inundated the Martin Place, Sydney shop with orders, many of them accompanied by votes of confidence in the stylish batsman generally regarded as Victor Trumper's legatee. The business still flourishes, and might serve as an inspiration to any disappointed young hopefuls in 1972.

Not that Alan Falconer Kippax was young by Australian batting standards. He turned twenty-nine that year, and felt it was his final chance to stake a lasting right to Test match honours. He was not to know that two tours of England lay ahead.

Reflecting on it all in the office of his shop forty-six years later, he felt 1926 marked the natural peak of his career. Thereafter he modified and curbed his style.

England's supreme batsman, Jack Hobbs, had discerned his class: "Take him to England," he had advocated. But Kippax had to outgrow a generation of cricketers before making the trip as one of Bill Woodfull's hopefuls in 1930. By then he had written himself into the record books and into the hearts of the crowds at Sydney and Melbourne, batting with such enchanting elegance that anyone today who saw him for even half-an-hour will sigh and nod knowingly at the mention of his name.

He speaks wistfully, if not readily, of those far-off seasons which brought him over 12,000 runs and 43 centuries – forceful statistics in the context of the lighter programmes of the day. His 6096 runs (at *70* per innings) for NSW should remain a record total for the state for some time yet. [*This aggregate was eventually overtaken in December 2000 by Michael Bevan, who was born two years before this article was written.*] These statistics need to be stated, even though it is as faulty to make final judgment on them as to assess Gainsborough's elegant art by the number of brushstrokes.

Alan Kippax regards as his finest performance a 68 against Victoria at Melbourne on a sticky wicket, "Dainty" Ironmonger and Ted McDonald bowling with unnatural menace. With established Test batsmen falling all about him the junior man played his innings of a lifetime.

There were other more spectacular achievements: 315 not out against Queensland, several double-centuries against Victoria, his Test hundred against England when he hooked Harold Larwood fearlessly, and the innings which placed his name indelibly in the annals of cricket: his 260 not out against Victoria when, with Hal Hooker, he added 307 for the last wicket.

NSW, chasing 376, were nine for 113 when Hooker joined Kippax, who had 20. They batted throughout Christmas Day 1928, Hooker quite uninterested in runs and his skipper driving Jack Ryder and the Victorians to distraction with his strokeplay and tactical singles. The freak stand extended to over five hours. It gave NSW a first-innings win and the Sheffield Shield, and it left the two batsmen with one of the most whimsical of records – certainly a delightful conversation piece.

Kippax recalls using the new ball in his first match for NSW in 1918, when M.A.Noble was captain, and had he been courageous enough to appeal when he rapped the pads of the formidable "Big Ship", Warwick Armstrong, he would have gained an illustrious wicket (or so umpire Bob Crockett told him later).

He once took five wickets for NSW against MCC, bowling leg-breaks. But batting was to bring him his fame. Anyone who recorded Trumper's runs in an exercise book and joined him at the nets before the serious practice began – as did the boy Kippax – simply had to become a batsman.

It has been said of him that he carried Trumper's glorious torch after the Great War, and that the same torch passed to the ill-fated Archie Jackson. It is long since extinguished.

He made his first-grade debut for Waverley at the age of fifteen while still at Cleveland Street School. Two great Australian veterans, wicketkeeper Sammy Carter and the ageless Syd Gregory, were still playing, and Kippax addressed them as "Mr", a mark of respect that he regretfully feels has perished along with other courtesies.

After the interruption of war he settled into first-class cricket, attracting unusual notice in 1922-23 with innings of 170, 68, 51 and 197; but it was 1925 before his opportunity came in Test cricket. He shared a debut with Clarrie Grimmett against England at Sydney, making 42 and 8, and adding 105 with Ponsford to save Australia's first innings. Also in 1924-25 he scored 212 not out in the most important match of the domestic season, NSW v Victoria.

The 1926 rebuff followed, and then he played his part in the rebuilding of NSW and Australian cricket. His young, inexperienced team fielded out to a Victorian world record total of 1107 in December 1926, and in the return match at Sydney they accomplished the most remarkable table-turning of all time when they dismissed a weakened Victoria for 35, McNamee taking 7 for 21. Kippax scored 217 not out in less than four hours for NSW.

He played in all five Tests against Percy Chapman's 1928-29 England side, making a modest 311 runs in 10 innings, one of which ended in controversy. A widish ball from Geary was adjudged by square-leg umpire Elder to have bowled Kippax, though there were those who felt the ball could only have rebounded from George Duckworth's pads. His century in the next Test was deeply satisfying.

In 1930 he realised his ambition to tour England. He was thirty-three. He remembers the hospitality wherever the Australians went and the delights of touring in an age that knew no television or acute traffic congestion or cheap sensationalism. With Vic Richardson he enjoyed a royal welcome at the Yorkshire village of Kippax, and the team was received at a host of still private stately homes and showered with more theatre tickets and social invitations than it could possibly handle.

But Kippax's mission was to make runs, and this he did – not least when the going was rough. He made a splendid century against Middlesex at Lord's when the ball was flying, and in the first Test his unbeaten 64 out of 144 was an exceptional display of sticky-wicket technique. At last English crowds were sampling the supple, wristy gracefulness, the sparkling strokeplay.

In the Lord's Test he made 83 and added 192 with the wondrous Bradman, and at Leeds they added 229, with Bradman reaching 334. Kippax is the chief witness in judging the quality of Bradman's innings that day, for he faced the same Maurice

Tate pounding down the same swerving deliveries. He pays awed tribute to the manner in which The Don whisked the ball away to the midwicket boundary, re-enacting the stroke and rolling his own educated wrists: "He saw the ball so quickly!"

Tate had more success in the Sussex match, but Kippax stood out with two hundreds, and was to make 250 four years later on his second tour (his only century). He wrily claims he enjoyed Hove's salty air.

Home again in 1930-31, he was proud to make the first-ever Test century for Australia against West Indies: 146 at Adelaide. But on the same ground against South Africa the following season he was run out without facing a ball after failing to complete what would have been the 200th run for Bradman, who finished 299 not out.

Now came another ugly setback. Playing up-country at Grenfell, where a matting wicket had been laid over wet turf, he was hit in the face by a ball that kicked off a buried iron peg. No sooner had he recovered from the resultant broken nose than disaster struck again at Brisbane. He had been hooking aboriginal fast bowler Eddie Gilbert with his customary ease, though one bouncer he missed hit the sightscreen on the full. But against less pacy "Pud" Thurlow he hooked too early and his temple was gashed. A mere half-inch meant the difference between life and death. Six stitches were inserted, he spent three days in hospital, and the scar is visible today.

The following season brought Douglas Jardine's English "bumper squad". The Bodyline campaign proved more repugnant to Alan Kippax than to many Australians – and would have been so even if he had not recently suffered head wounds. He played only in the first Test, taking a knock from Voce and falling to Larwood for 8 and 19. In company with everyone present he marvelled at the heroic 187 not out by Stan McCabe.

At the end of that turbulent series he produced in collaboration with E.P.Barbour a book entitled *Anti Bodyline* wherein he vehemently condemned intimidatory bowling and suggested that public opinion alone ought to kill it off. He expressed alarm at the increase in accidents in park cricket at that time. The crisis passed, though it took more than public opinion to stabilise matters. A measure of safety had to be legislated into the game. It was some comfort for the walking wounded.

In 1933-34 Kippax was back among the runs, especially at Sydney. He and Bradman added a record 363 for the third wicket in only 135 minutes against Queensland, and he further entertained his home crowd with scores of 128, 44 and 111 not out. It led him sweetly into his second tour of England, where he averaged over 50 again, though playing in only one Test and falling foul of influenza. At Manchester he and Chipperfield were isolated as diphtheria suspects.

That tour was the end of the international road for Kippax. Golf began to take more of his time, becoming the fourth sport to bring him honours. He had been an interstate and All-Australian baseball pitcher and second baseman, and he later represented NSW at bowls.

There was much to look back on: the serious tours, the missionary tours, the light-hearted tours. The missionary tours had taken him to North Queensland, where turf pitches had been laid out and pavilions built from the funds raised, and to New Zealand, which he feels continues to deserve Australian support in exchange for providing inexperienced players with a sample of English-type pitches.

The most unusual of his tours was to North America in 1932. With a twinkle in his eye he recalls that much of the cricket was almost as bizarre as the Hollywood parties given by Boris Karloff, Leslie Howard, Tom Mix and Norma Shearer.

Alan Kippax and Bert Oldfield were awarded a joint testimonial in 1948-49, and the battering that Lindsay Hassett endured in that match is remembered with genuine respect and gratitude. It was not a Test match: with the ball bumping so viciously Australia's diminutive captain-elect might have been excused for being easily satisfied. But he was determined to battle it out, thus lengthening the match in the interests of the beneficiaries. Hassett was paying a deliberate, painstaking tribute on behalf of pre-war cricket-lovers everywhere. A.F.Kippax, softly-spoken, silver-haired former NSW captain, still treasures the memory of Hassett's gallantry.

Australian Cricket, February 1972

Alan Kippax died later that year at the age of seventy-five.

Smooth run-maker: Alan Falconer Kippax.

Calling to see perhaps the greatest demon bowler of the 20th Century turned out to be a rewarding social occasion:

Harold Larwood: Reviled and Revered

THE SHOULDERS are identifiably wide, the arms long, and the lips disconcertingly tight. But the grey-blue eyes twinkle with a certain kindliness from behind the glasses. He was once the most feared fast bowler on earth – respected, reviled, revered. Now he lives a mile from the Sydney Cricket Ground. And he lives on his memories.

Harold Larwood came to this neat brick cottage in this quiet street over twenty years ago after Jack Fingleton's mischievous newspaper item* had set him thinking in his Blackpool sweet shop (where cigarettes and stock were so hard to come by in post-war England) that life in Australia might be preferable. Fingleton's emigration myth became fact, and the kindness and consideration of the Australians were evident from the earliest moments: Larwood, his wife Lois, their five daughters and young man paid £16 for full board while awaiting the house. It seemed cheap, and the explanation leaked out in due course. Prime Minister Chifley, ever an admirer, had paid the other half of the guesthouse tariff.

It was many years after his exit from first-class cricket that Larwood was persuaded to write THE story of his life. He felt unsure about it. He had no wish to revive the fury and the hatred, but finally he opened his suitcases of cuttings and telegrams. Fresh photographs were taken of him with his trophies – cricket balls surprisingly unbloodied but marked with small silver shields, illuminated addresses, team photographs, the silver ashtray "from a grateful skipper [Jardine]", and, most cherished of all, a telegram of congratulation from the dying Archie Jackson.

The book was popular, as was a television feature in 1970. Now he seems never to tire of talking over old times, seeing them in an uncomplicated way and relishing the memories with no trace of regret, as a 67-year-old should, sitting (but more often standing) in his comfortable lounge room with its English-style fireplace such as is not built any longer despite increasingly cool winters.

He remembers his Nottinghamshire "work-mates", Bill Voce, Fred Barratt, Sam Staples. He remembers his adversaries, Don Bradman, Stan McCabe, Bill Woodfull. He seems a happier man having had the chance in later life to shake hands with schoolmaster Woodfull, whose suffering during the Bodyline series and whose integrity throughout his life were equally renowned.

Harold Larwood can still exchange hearty laughter with Lois at the recollection of being caught for 98 in a Sydney Test match – by the world's worst fieldsman at that.

He sees most of his cricket through television nowadays. The newspapers still quote him avidly. When the latest marvel, Dennis Lillee, burst into the headlines with some decidedly hostile bowling against the World XI he was asked his opinion of the newcomer, and he was generous in his assessment.

On the whole he is unimpressed with contemporary cricket standards: "The fast bowlers are pampered. They take 'em off after half a dozen overs. Why, at Melbourne in 1928 I sent down 34 overs, Maurice Tate bowled 62, and George Geary 81. And we had some fine so-and-so batsmen to bowl at!"

Paradoxically he has been heard both to curse the Bradmans, Ponsfords and Woodfulls, and to thank the fates for serving them up, thus giving his performances an unexcelled hallmark. He is not the only ex-Test player with strong views on modern quality – or lack of it – and some of his reasoning defies argument.

Even in a caricature there was something menacing about Harold Larwood, the world's fastest and most accurate bowler. In his mild later years he welcomed many visitors to his home on the other side of the world, including the author's son Johnny (over).

He is, as ever, a working man, and he has always responded to being in Australia, where the working man is accorded a unique and time-honoured esteem. He recalls with an abiding disbelief the function arranged by D.R.Jardine during a business trip to Sydney twenty years ago. A number of old Test cricketers gathered at the table leaving one vacant place. It was filled in due course by Prime Minister Menzies. No-one stood; familiar respects were exchanged casually all round.

"You wouldn't have had that with a British Prime Minister, would you!"

He and Lois visited England in 1968, and he found himself generally apprehensive about asking after old cricketers and friends for fear they had passed on. It contributed to their peace of mind to discover that they felt no considerable regret at having left England behind in 1950. When the time came they were content to return to the "openness" of Sydney – a long way in time and space from Langton Colliery and Nuncargate.

Ray Robinson tells a nice story of "Lol" Larwood. When a computer "Test" was "played" at Lord's last winter the machine callously accorded him nought for plenty. "Ah well," said Larwood, "my feet aren't what they used to be."

* Fingleton took exception to this wording and went as far as to deny that he'd written anything of the sort. It was a splitting of hairs. Harold Larwood confirmed that the Australian had visited him in his shop and had then put the idea of emigration into his head by writing that he might actually have been considering such a move already. Fingleton's former Bodyline nemesis remained forever grateful for the notion.

The Cricketer, April 1972

The rarest of interviews followed, with a reclusive Australian all-rounder from the 1920s who was the Keith Miller of his day. The problem was that he never spoke to journalists:

Mr Gregory, I Presume?

JACK GREGORY, First AIF, New South Wales, and Australian fast bowler who made even Walter Hammond blanch, scorer of the fastest-ever Test century, arguably the greatest of slip fieldsmen, was not discernibly pleased to see me.

He has stolidly resisted interviews for half a century, and my diffident announcement through the fly-screen door that I had driven 200 miles down from Sydney expressly to see him left him quite unmoved.

It was an important day for the world at large: on the kitchen table a portable television was displaying an instantaneous picture of President Nixon stepping off the aircraft at Peking. It was a significant moment for me too: here at last I beheld the most elusive and evasive of cricket's illustrious living – the massive, dynamic sporting doyen of Australians during the 1920s.

The chief pretext of my call was a small pile of books for the autograph treatment, and as we seated ourselves and listened to the American anthem and commiserated with each other on the humidity, the man who would never "talk" began to "talk".

"When we passed through America it was Prohibition. Somebody organised some King George IV [whisky] for us through a bootlegger!"

What had determined him never to write or submit to interviews? The explanation was surprisingly simple. A Sydney newspaperman had cornered him (some physical achievement!) outside the dressing-room and asked if he knew why Charlie Kelleway had been dropped from the Australian side. "I said 'Blowed if I know', and next day the paper ran a story: "Gregory cannot understand why Kelleway was dropped"!

A pity. Jack Gregory's memoirs would have been worth reading. He took only 38 Sheffield Shield wickets, but 85 Test batsmen succumbed to his bouncing dam-buster bowling. He was clearly Australia's major fast bowler between Cotter and Lindwall, and had his right knee not given way in 1928 he would have played a key role in yet one further series at least.

"I'm finished, boys" was his oft-quoted exclamation as he limped from the field. I had put the smell of liniment down to imagination as I climbed up to the house that day. But there was the tube – on the table. He saw me peering at it. "My knee's like a barometer. I had to put some of that stuff on. It's going to rain soon."

A cartilage had been removed in 1922, when the operation was anything but routine. The treatment served him well until the breakdown. "That was the first Test played at Brisbane [at the Exhibition Ground, not the Gabba]. Bradman's first, my last."

Did he watch much cricket these days? "I didn't bother going up for the Rest of the World match. Those coves didn't seem to be putting themselves out." He looked intently at the TV screen through the glasses perched on his slightly retrousse nose.

"By jove, I like that 50-overs stuff!" he reflected. "They have to get on with it. I liked to hit hard myself, because I loved the game and I tried to amuse the public. They like to see bright cricket."

I told him of the restricted bowler's run-up operating in the English Sunday League. "That would've suited me. I took twelve paces – fifteen yards." I contemplated whether the front-foot law might have set him problems with his famous kangaroo leap.

The room was quiet apart from the Nixon-in-China noises. Ordinarily it would have been time for me to leave; but I bought more time by enquiring after the local activities. "I fish from the boat – caught six bream yesterday. A friend landed a nine-pound flathead this morning. (Pause). I play bowls."

How long had he lived down here? "My wife [a former Miss Australia] died nine years ago, and I stayed with my daughter for a while. I retired early. Thought it was the best thing. The company [K and E] I belonged to was taken over. The shares were paid out in cash."

Another silence, and I wondered if a yorker or a bouncer was coming next from this white-haired seventy-seven-year-old. There was no material sign about the place that a cricketer lived here: no books, no trophies, no bats or balls.

Emerging from his meditation, he spoke again. "There was a Gregory in the Australian Test team right up to the time I finished." (Actually there was an interval of twelve years between bearded Dave and tiny Syd, who himself missed very few Tests in the course of twenty-two years. The family tradition is nevertheless remarkable.)

Jack, who has a sister aged ninety-eight, was one of six children of Charles S.Gregory, one of the mighty brotherhood of seven that included Australia's first Test captain, Dave (buried, incidentally, without any sort of monument at Gore Hill cemetery, Sydney)*.

The first of the line had emigrated very early in Australia's history. When he was a lad Jack unearthed some family letters dated 1795. His mother was Edinburgh-born, and his middle name is her maiden name, Morrison.

"Plum Warner gave me my chance, you know. It was the name that did it. He found out I was Syd's cousin."

"Are you sure it wasn't because of your performances?"

"No. I went to England from my artillery outfit in France, and when Warner heard there was a Gregory in the AIF team he started the ball rolling for me. I was a batsman then."

Gregory is not necessarily the first player the uninitiated would choose if asked to name the scorer of the fastest Test century (119 v South Africa at Johannesburg in 1921 – in stunning contrast to C.N.Frank's 152 in 8½ hours later in the match). "I didn't know it was a record till my son told me some time later. Seventy-five minutes."

"Seventy. Jessop's was seventy-five."

"Yes, well, I just enjoyed batting. Never bothered about records."

What did he feel about his old Sydney grade club [and mine] Paddington going out of existence? His response was as unsentimental as his thunderbolt bowling in the old days (". . . when we finished Test matches in two or three days"): "Oh, I played for lots of clubs – North Sydney, Manly, Paddington, Waverley, Randwick, Sydney."

For Jack Gregory the past seems well and truly shut away in its place. Names thrown up enticingly brought at best a laconic comment. "Jack Ryder, we always said, ran faster than he bowled!" The 1971 reunion? "Yes, I met some of the chaps. Hadn't seen many of them for donkey's years – 'Nip' Pellew, Clarrie Grimmett, Bill Whitty."

Did he know that his old adversary Frank Woolley, who had made two heroic nineties against him in the 1921 Lord's Test, had married recently? "Hmm," he muttered to himself, "companionship."

J.M.Gregory, Garbo-like in his autumn years, gives the impression of needing little more that the comfort of Nature's companionship. I wondered, as I drove along the banks of the Wadonga River past the oyster leases and up into the wooded hills, whether it really could have been a Test cricketer whose remembrances I had been probing.

*Attention having been drawn here to a lamentable oversight, a monument was erected some years later after public subscription.

The Cricketer, May 1972

Jack Gregory died the following year, a week before his seventy-eighth birthday.

Batting fearlessly, if inadvisedly, without gloves, Jack Gregory blazes away, as was his preference. Inset: the quick snapshot sneaked by the author half-a-century later.

The Oblivion of Eddie Gilbert

THE QUEENSLAND aboriginal cricketer Eddie Gilbert, famed for his bursts of express bowling during the 1930s, had not been heard of for so long that I took it upon myself when in Brisbane to track him down.

An oldtimer in the suburb of Red Hill, where Eddie was last seen, thought he had died about five years before. We checked in the general store run by a cricket fan of some sixty summers: "I'd just about swear to it. Old Eddie went right out of circulation and we never heard nothin' of him for ages. I reckon he must've died ten years back at least. They had him in Goodna for a while."

I drove out to the psychiatric hospital along the Ipswich Road in the hope of establishing the truth of the matter. The superintendent, barely concealing his surprise at my questions, led me through to the records office, where he produced Eddie Gilbert's hospital history card: "Eddie was admitted on December 8, 1949. His age was shown as thirty-seven."

I thought he would have been slightly older than that; perhaps the paperwork was completed hastily that sad day.

"If you're writing about him," the superintendent volunteered, "I can tell you a few things. He took six wickets in his last game for Queensland. Terrific bowler – only ran half-a-dozen steps. He got the knack from boomerang throwing. Some reckoned he chucked, but I never thought so. It was just his funny wrist action. Wish we had somebody like him right now."

Some weeks earlier Bill Hunt, the pre-war New South Wales player, had been in no doubt about it: "Eddie threw *me* out! By cripes, yeah! And later on I deliberately did the same to him. And d'you know what he said? I'll tell you. He put his arm round my shoulder and said, 'Well bowled, Bill. That was a beauty!' So you see, the little fellah couldn't tell a bowl from a chuck anyway! Nice chap, but."

It was Hunt's contention that Stan McCabe, whose name will live for three classic Test innings, himself considered his best hand to have been a 229 not out against Queensland at Brisbane in 1931 after Eddie Gilbert had served Don Bradman with "the luckiest duck I ever made".

The lithe black man that day, bowling with horrifying hostility on an under-prepared pitch, had New South Wales in ribbons at 31 for 3, with Alan Kippax in hospital after a dreadful blow on the temple from a mis-hook off Thurlow. At that point McCabe took command.

So long ago. Now here was I seeking to trace the conclusion of a life story. The superintendent glanced up from the history card. "He was married at the time he came here. Nobody's visited him for ages. He used to be violent occasionally, but he's all right now – no trouble. But he's bottled right up within himself. You won't get him to talk. We've tried everything. He'll never change. Just as well perhaps. If he went out again he'd be back among the plonkies down at the Adelaide [pub] in no time."

"You're telling me he's here – alive?"

He nodded. "As I say, he's completely withdrawn. It's impossible to get through to him. He walks the grounds all day – he's content in his own private world. We've tried to interest him in some kind of recreation: his reflexes are still sharp. But when we put a cricket ball in his hand he just stared at it."

The rarest of shots of Eddie Gilbert in an institution in the twilight of his life.

It came as a shock. Eddie – still ticking after all! Even the locals had seemed so certain. I had fallen into line with them and quietly and briefly mourned their popular hero of long ago, the fast bowler to whom they had bellowed encouragement to "give Jardine a taste of his own bodyline medicine".

In *That Barambah Mob*, David Forrest's amusing blend of fact and fantasy, Eddie has already been immortalised: on the top of Henry Stulpnagel's head was imprinted (in reverse) " . . . nufactured in Austra . . . ", a living souvenir of a Gilbert bumper. "When that ball hit the concrete," he exclaimed, "she'd smoke!" Mr Stulpnagel also knew why Eddie never became a Test cricketer: "He made an ape of Bradman, and he was black, and he was born in Queensland, and they didn't like the look o' that whippy wrist of his."

I made my reverent plea to the superintendent: "I'd like to see Eddie."

"It's no use. He won't talk."

I pressed him. I had to see the historic cricketer.

He picked up the phone and asked the attendant at the appropriate wing to "find Eddie". We walked across the sunlit lawns, past slumbering patients, small-talk lost in the insistent buzz of insects. The coolness in the outer block was a relief.

Eddie was some time in coming. Sitting in the office, I scanned the grounds through the open window. Suddenly a male nurse was standing at the door, and behind him, reluctant to advance, was a thin man in a maroon T-shirt and black shorts. His hair was white and close-cropped, his skin glistening ebony. It was unmistakably Gilbert.

He shuffled into the room, head to one side, eyes averted, impossible to meet. His physique would have been insignificant beside Tom Richardson, Miller or Trueman, yet he was not the midget legend has depicted. Five feet eight, with long arms: the devastating catapult machine he must once have been was apparent.

"Shake hands, Eddie," his attendant urged kindly. The hand that had propelled the ball that had smashed so many stumps was raised slowly; it was as limp as a dislodged bail. He was muttering huskily and incoherently, gently rocking his head side to side.

"Want a fag, Eddie?" the nurse asked softly. Eddie grunted, watched the cigarette begin to smoulder, and puffed at it. His legs, typically of his race, were thin. He turned on them restlessly. He was an outdoor man; a room was a cage.

When I asked the nurse if Eddie could write his name for me he coaxed him to pick up the ball-point. At the end of an agonising minute Eddie backed away, leaving only a tortured 'E' on the paper. His squinting eyes, deep-set and bloodshot, flashed briefly across all of us.

I thought then of what Archie Jackson, Australia's batting genius, had written about Eddie Gilbert in 1933: "The adulation he has received has not affected his mental equilibrium. Such a player is an ornament to the game; may he continue to prosper!"

Eddie walked off, still breathing his wheezy monotone; he wandered through the meal hall, and the last I saw of him was as he drifted, a desolate individual, across the parched grass.

The Cricketer Winter Annual, November 1972

Eddie Gilbert died in January 1978 and was buried in the cemetery at the Cherbourg settlement, where a fitting memorial was not erected until almost thirty years later. It was then revealed that his full name was Harold Edward Gilbert.

A light piece for my friends who put together match programmes for matches at Queensland's Woolloongabba ground:

Cricketers and Film Stars

ONE OF my weaknesses is that I continue to see facial likenesses between cricketers and film stars. The other evening William Lundigan was playing the piano in a Hollywood musical and for a moment I thought it was Richie Benaud. The Marx Brothers season has also just been with us, and when Groucho in *Duck Soup* (*not* a cricketer's film) walked across a room I could not help thinking of Slasher Mackay. No facial resemblance admittedly, but, my goodness, how they walk alike. Bob Massie looks like taking over Slasher's place in flatfootedness.

I can't decide whether Jardine or Dexter more resembled Basil Rathbone. Here the facial likeness went with a similarity in manner – a Sherlock Holmes haughtiness which, while it may not have reflected the real person, was all that the general public got for its money.

Then there was a Scot who kept wicket for England in the 1890s: Gregor

MacGregor. He looked like Charlie Chaplin some years before the beloved tramp had himself reached manhood, and the "twinship" was taken up in the 1920s by Percy Fender, whose receding chin also gave him something in common with the character Miles Malleson.

A movie was once proposed on the life of Don Bradman, with Ron Randall to star; but if ever a film biography of Denis Compton is made then surely Ray Milland would have to take the part.

There have been other resemblances, many of which I suppose are to my eyes alone: Herbert Sutcliffe looked so like Robert Cummings; Vic Richardson like another swashbuckler, John Barrymore; Ray Lindwall faintly like Edmond O'Brien; and could Douglas Fairbanks have had a closer double than Arthur Gilligan?

In Keith Miller I always saw Gary Cooper, and Tom Graveney showed flashes of that comic David Tomlinson. A recent photo of Test captain turned businessman Bobby Simpson might well have been of tough-guy Broderick Crawford, and when Bruce Francis strolls across the outfield he proves one thing: that Jack Benny's walk is not his alone.

Archie Jackson at times looked like another gay* young man, Michael Wilding; and in Neil Hawke there was something of Victor Mature. Among the oldtimers, Alfred Shaw is exactly like Sebastian Cabot (more often seen on television), and the cricketer who looks so much like Marlon Brando in the picture of the 1902 Australian Test team is actually Jack Saunders.

Arthur Mailey, I always thought, had something of George Arliss about him, and Arthur Morris and William Holden, apart from hair styles and colouring, were almost interchangeable facially and in their calm demeanour.

Colin Milburn's resemblance to Fatty Arbuckle was too obvious, yet his pals named him "Ollie" after the stouter half of Laurel and Hardy. He might also have existed in an earlier comic-book life as Billy Bunter, bless him.

How about the silent-screen idol John Gilbert for "Chuck" Fleetwood-Smith? Or Dustin Hoffman for Brian Taber? I believe also that Jeff Hammond has some Jack Palance potential. M.J.K.Smith has that Glenn Miller look; but who wouldn't in those glasses? Mike Procter, on the other hand, is a slightly smaller version of the husky Jon Voigt and would bring *Midnight Cowboy* to the cricket field if ever he batted with Taber.

It's an absurd pastime, I realise, and many of the similarities I see will doubtless prove elusive to others; but it helps during dull sessions and also adds another dimension to movie-watching. Several of the 1972 Australian Test players, for instance, got the message by growing Omar Sharif moustaches. But next time you see an old C.Aubrey Smith film such as *Little Lord Fauntleroy*, don't worry if the moustachioed gentleman seems to resemble a 19th Century Sussex cricketer who captained England in the first Test match against South Africa. It's one and the same man!

* Repeating that this is a word which at this time meant nothing more than simply "carefree and happy".

Queensland Cricket Association programme

MAGAZINE PIECES ETC
1973-1978

A brave cricketer whose book I had helped write five years previously was a willing interviewee at one of the several turning points of his splendid career:

Captain Edrich of Surrey

JOHN EDRICH has not been seen to smile often during the past few seasons, but there is a fresh light in his eyes now. He has been made captain of Surrey at precisely the point in his career when he was running out of ambitions. Now, apart from the beckoning landmark of a hundred centuries, he has his penetratingly blue eyes trained on one key target: a trophy for Surrey.

It has not always been easy playing cricket in the wake of Surrey's Championship-winning era, 1952 to 1958. The club's followers have been somewhat impatient (except in 1971) at the drought which has followed the years of plenty.

Playing at The Oval, where, says Edrich, "there is never quite the local support you find at places like Old Trafford and Bradford", the players are still striving to imprint themselves over the silhouettes of May, Bedser, Laker, Lock, Barrington, Surridge.

Like Lord's, it is one of the better grounds to play on if you are a visiting player (particularly now that the aforementioned giants are in retirement). This is because, apart from any supposed variations in demeanour among citizens of different counties, The Oval is far removed from the heart of Surrey. On Sundays – at Byfleet or Guildford or Leatherhead – the Surrey cricketers, in contrast, sense an estimable crowd support.

But the ghosts of the 1950s and the geographical hardships are facts of life, and Mr Edrich, successor to Messrs Fender, Jardine, Surridge and Stewart – has always been disposed to face facts fairly and squarely. "I want 100 percent effort. I'm not interested in glamour or so-called star quality. Give me eleven triers any day. Look at Leicestershire. Theirs was a team effort. Fighting all the way."

He is an outstanding example himself of how endeavour and steady application can bring greater rewards than have accrued to certain more gifted batsmen. He bisects his smile with a churchwarden pipe: this is not the man who was losing sleep over his cricket, who used to wake at two in the morning and stare ceilingwards in the darkness. He knows the tensions of first-class cricket are not at an end for him and that certain difficulties will always present themselves, but in an extraordinary way his load seems to have been lightened.

"It's given me a new lease on life," he says. "We've got some very good youngsters coming along, and I'm going to give them all the help and encouragement I can. Another thing: I don't think we at Surrey have yet come to terms with limited-overs cricket. But we will."

Many of his players are abroad this winter. Three are with MCC in the East; Younis is in South Australia; Dudley Owen-Thomas ("a real good'un – he's just got to adjust to the nitty-gritty of county cricket after the University") is in Kenya, Jackman in Rhodesia; Intikhab is leading Pakistan in Australasia.

But those who were available were summoned to a get-together (not a "meeting" – too formal) at Edrich's home. Ideas were exchanged and aims discussed. The staff is now eighteen, and may conceivably increase. The feeling of impending renascence is inescapable.

"I've played about 60 times for England – against all the Test countries in fact [*there were then seven*] – and I've made a few runs, mostly, I hope, when they've been needed. I've had to cut out all risks during the past few series because England have had no Graveney or Barrington to follow; it would have been great to have had Peter May waiting padded up every time. So you see, I was just playing along, and the only way to go was down. Now I'm rejuvenated, revitalised, what you like."

He makes no secret of his intense admiration for Ray Illingworth, whose right-hand man he has been for three years in the England team. Between them they have hardly more flamboyance and affability than a pair of Russian field marshals, but their combined strategy has won and retained the Ashes against odds surprisingly heavy when they are considered carefully.

Are his Test match days past? "Who can say? I'd certainly like to earn more caps, but we'll have to see."

He thinks that Dennis Lillee is not quite as fast as Wes Hall at his peak, but that his change of pace is his best weapon. He pays tribute to Lillee's stamina too: he was inexhaustible, like Hall. Next time England meet him he should be an even greater obstacle.

It was the recollection of the last day of the last Test of 1972 that drained his face of its composure. "When Illy went off injured and I swung the bowling around a lot – you remember: Arnold, Snow (who was pretty sick), Parfitt (Illy would have used him), Greig and Underwood (Dolly was injured too) – I learnt later that I'd come in for some terrible stick in the radio commentary.

"The phone kept ringing that evening. The former Test player who was doing the summary obviously had no idea of Snowy's trouble for one thing. And we needed two wickets immediately for no runs, so what could anyone have done! I was assured of some sort of an apology, or at least a public explanation. But it never came."

Edrich is a disciplined cricketer, and the misery of that day will be filed out of sight when he leads his side out in April.

"I've been away a great deal on Test duty over the past few years," he says, knitting those heavy Norfolk eyebrows. "Now I really want to do something for Surrey."

The Cricketer, January 1973

Number 33 in the Gallery series, this spotlight on a very special Australian batsman tracks his progress through the first few years of rich promise:

Greg Chappell

WHEN, IN March 1970, Lawry's Australians sorrowfully disembarked after their disastrous tour of South Africa, Australian cricket was just about out on its feet. Perhaps the biggest disappointment – if the invoice of 333 runs for McKenzie's sole Test wicket be overlooked – was Ian Chappell, who had been flagrantly billed by his captain at the start of the series as "the world's best batsman". The Springboks shattered that daring claim in a whirl of bouncers and yorkers and signalised with a bewildering four-nil victory what can now be seen as their last contest before banishment from international cricket.

Australia was stunned. The end was nigh.

But the worriers should have known better. History's pattern is there, like an alluvial meadow, producing crops from hidden seeds after even the hardest winter.

Although Australia next opposed England – and lost – the beginnings of a revival were soon apparent. Chappell's younger brother, Greg, was brought into the side for the second Test of the 1970-71 series, and he was prompt in writing his name into the record books and inside his green cap – in indelible ink.

He walked to the crease at Perth when Australia were 107 for 5 in reply to England's 397. In four and a half hours he scored 108, and with Redpath, who made a stoic 171, Chappell added 219. He fought very hard for his half-century, but in the evening as shadows lengthened and the bowlers' feet ached he plundered his last fifty in an hour. He was twenty-two years of age and the toast of his country.

He had entered first-class cricket at eighteen and registered his first century that same season (1966-67), a gritty innings played in Brisbane's cloying heat and humidity and with the painful after-effects of a poisoned foot. With a college-boy freshness but uncompromising mien he had passed through the extra-mural examination of county cricket with Somerset, developing month by month, making the first Sunday League century, bowling at medium pace well enough on one occasion to take 7 for 40 against Yorkshire (having earlier been a leg-spinner) and broadening both his experience on wet wickets and his philosophy with a "pair" at the hands of Geoff Arnold (balanced within months by two centuries in a match for South Australia against Queensland).

His most satisfying innings was a century on a slow turner at Weston-super-Mare against Middlesex.

He failed in his second Test match (the Sydney debacle), missed out again at Melbourne, and fell to Peter Lever without scoring at Adelaide Oval, the home ground of his grandfather, Vic Richardson, and now, with younger brother Trevor having joined Ian and Greg (all products of Prince Alfred College) in the South Australia side, the Chappells' own paddock.

Then came the decider, the seventh Test, at Sydney. And after Greg's three-hour 65 had helped Australia to a first-innings lead of 80 they needed, with five wickets in hand, 100 runs for a victory which would have levelled the series and saved the Ashes.

That fifth day opened with Greg Chappell and Rod Marsh in possession. One can only say in support of their increased stature today that had it been the 1973 models Chappell and Marsh the result would have been a foregone conclusion and Australia should have been safe. As it was, Marsh fell through inexperience and an Illingworth kicker left Chappell stranded. England finished two up and Australia were left wistful and with vengeful eye.

Those in opposition who saw Greg Chappell as a growing threat in future years searched for weaknesses and concluded that he was too on-sided. But he was a growing man, a Test centurion, the most exciting prospect his country had had since Walters. The leg-sidedness would doubtless take care of itself.

And it did. By 1972 he was an all-round batsman, playing positively through the covers, through mid-off, and, to the relief of those who earlier had enjoyed his on-side play, the original crack off the toes was there in all its glory. He was a charm to watch: confident and unruffled, a lesson to all from within his cocoon of concentration. Until he was dismissed Australia always stood a chance. When he *was* out, England relaxed just a shade.

Tall, with an upright almost Edwardian stance, he makes, when he drives, a characteristically strong commitment to the front foot; the body bends forward over the fulcrum of the braced left leg, giving him such a commanding airborne view of the oncoming ball that it is the plainest formality that it should be dispatched with

Greg Chappell: no more classy batsman has played Test cricket in our time.

power and certain placing all along the ground. And the manner in which the right foot kicks high behind the stroke is nothing less than arrogant. There is little in his style to suggest his teenage inspirations Neil Harvey and Bob Simpson.

Somerset did try to entice him back at a salary larger than any previously offered but Chappell declined, believing that so much continuous cricket could be detrimental in the long term

During the season which separated the two Anglo-Australian rubbers Australia took on the Rest of the World XI, and for the home side's batting the two Chappells with Stackpole bestrode the series – after Greg had sat out the first two matches as twelfth man. He re-entered international competition with 115 not out at Melbourne, 197 not out at Sydney, and 85 at Adelaide, and sudden doubts about his inclusion for the tour of England were forgotten.

In 1972 Chappell, with the bat, and Lillee, with the ball (with Chappell either crouching menacingly at short leg or grasping everything within reach at third slip), were, with Stackpole's valiant consistency at Number 1, Marsh's redoubtable form, and Massie's surrealist performance at Lord's, the main forces in Australia's implicit dominance of an ideal Test series.

Greg, having made a technically admirable 131 at Lord's – the innings of the series – came near to earning the freedom of London by scoring another hundred at The Oval in the fifth Test. This time brother Ian also reached three figures as coolly and undemonstratively they constructed a stand of 201 for the second wicket. Incredibly it was only the second time they had added a hundred in tandem, but it revived thoughts of the Woodfull-McCabe, Bradman-Ponsford, Barnes-Morris brand of batting dependability.

The match was won, the series squared, and the team went home; but not before the captain had paid public though subtle tribute to his brother's standing. He suggested that he himself would never be the accomplished batsman that Greg now was, but he was careful not to damn him with claims too lavish. He remembered how that could rebound.

Some months later the brothers were making masterful centuries against Pakistan. Such is the new dynasty. Gregory Stephen Chappell, it may be reflected, came into the world just a week before Bradman's scoreless final Test, in 1948, which nevertheless was a good year for Australian cricket. Now there are some who would say it was a wonderful year for Australian cricket.

The Cricketer, February 1973

By the time of his retirement ten years later Greg Chappell had established himself in the minds of many as the second-best batsman Australia had produced.

Keen to show that I was a hands-on editor and no mere pen-pusher, I gained permission to train with 1972 county champions Warwickshire – and filled a page in the magazine at a somewhat punishing price:

How the Champions Prepared

LATER IN the day, when the track-suits had been removed and the Warwickshire cricketers were looking more like cricketers and less like footballers, I had difficulty in finding one among them willing to accept that my mid-morning illness was a result of waking before dawn and driving three hours non-stop to Birmingham – and *not* of the frantic exertions on the recreation area behind the stands.

It was not, perhaps, the most comfortable way of investigating how hard county players prepare for the season, but it was to be convincing. Ask any of them, anywhere in the country, and the response is likely to be the same: "It's not like the old days, you know. We don't just roll up for the first match. We train, and train hard."

How might this pitch of fitness compare with the physical trim of a professional soccer player though? There can be no valid comparison, considering the differing rhythms of these games. Senior coach Alan Oakman is of the opinion that, assuming lungs and muscles are as they ought to be, batsmen need to bat and fast bowlers need to build up their speed and slow bowlers need to work for automatic command of length and direction. Wicketkeeper Barry Flick was doing his bit too – standing with nowhere to retreat to as Dave Brown thumped them down the net at Neal Abberley.

All this came later. The day began, as had the previous few for the unprotesting players, with a steady jog-trot. Led by the long-legged Brown and Bob Willis, we slapped on more pace after a few laps, and then started hopping sideways and spinning round and swinging arms skywards. Then some leapfrog, when Dennis Amiss almost literally lost his head. Then on the sun-kissed grass Sar'Major Oakman had us reaching for our toes and "cycling" in thin air.

Frith to Jameson, with coach Oakman keeping an eye on things. (Ken Kelly)

My excuse for stopping was that I wished to observe.

Half-a-dozen more laps, with the Editor safely at the back of the line with burly John Jameson. So far so good.

Now for some reflex diving and catching. Fun at first, then the back muscles and breathing system begin to send up little messages of protest. The pace increases: into pairs we go, and one tosses two balls while the other leaps about to catch and lob them back. Innocent in theory, punishing in practice.

"Gentle jog," says Mr Oakman, and the smart navy track-suits resume the disciplined file and soon it is time for the puffing observer to stop to make more notes.

The *coup de grace* comes with a daft exercise where a man runs between two stumps twenty yards apart while another lobs a ball *almost* out of reach. A lunging catch brings applause. Five minutes of this brings an ominous tightening to the upper reaches of the diaphragm. While the good men of Warwickshire cross the field to start a relay – presumably to improve their wind and their running between wickets (remembering the Gillette final? [they lost three men to run-outs in the loss to Lancashire in 1972]) – the dismal Frith waits for photographer Ken Kelly to unload his camera before retching inconspicuously on the grassy bank.

Soon we were back in the changing-rooms, guzzling glucose drink and putting on more familiar attire. The ensuing four hours of net practice, split by a handsome lunch, saw the ritualistic unfolding of another cricket season. The four West Indies Test stars [Gibbs, Kallicharran, Kanhai, Murray] were otherwise engaged thousands of miles away, but for the rest each ball sent down epitomised hope, each stroke a promise of more to come when the action grew more serious.

"Mic" Rouse whistled a ball through John Whitehouse and clipped the leg stump. Norman McVicker slammed Peter Lewington for "six". Willis measured out his full run and did his mesmeric knees-up all the way to the crease. "One of his limbs will fly off some day," cracked one of the perspiring players.

Dennis Amiss, fresh from his triumphs in Pakistan, batted coolly and elegantly and prompted the conviction among the seniors that he is now more inclined to back-footed play.

No-one was idle. The slips cradle took a pounding.

As the afternoon wore on it came Frith's turn to bat. He was soon wondering why A.C.Smith (who topped Warwickshire's bowling last summer) had bothered keeping wicket at all when he could bowl these swinging cutters. Bill Blenkiron bowled a mean length and line as well, and when it was all over, and Alan Oakman looked across enquiringly, Frith was bound to shrug resignedly, too breathless to say with the sincerity intended that it had all been a pretty impressive workout.

Amiss's Eastern suntan made us, by comparison, look very pink in the shower room. Amid the jumble of suitcases plastered with MCC markings a mildly soporific feeling descended. Dave Brown patted his overheated feet and rejected the suggestion that he was due for a retread. What was the mortar-board doing on the clothes peg? That, said grinning Alan Smith, was for wearing during the reading of the Riot Act on occasions when they lost by ten wickets or worse. Since this last happened in August 1971 it was hardly surprising that the headpiece was laden with dust.

As the captain has stated: "Being realistic, it may well be that we shall have to wait a year or two before seeing great success again." I am satisfied of one thing: if they *are* in for a thin time – and this probably applies to any county cricket side in the 1970s – it cannot be blamed upon lack of preparation for the season's rigours.

The Cricketer, June 1973

Warwickshire finished seventh in 1973. This article prompted an impatient response from pre-war Leicestershire and England batsman E.W.Dawson, who pointed to the rigorous net sessions endured by his contemporaries in pre-season preparations.

What a different range of sounds flowed from our radio and television sets during the summers of the 1970s. Here is the response to an invitation to summarise them:

Commentators XI

THEIR LARYNXES exude the cricket news all summer long through wirelesses and transistor sets on factory benches, in office desk drawers, old folks' homes, outposts of the Commonwealth, often even to lounging television viewers, which is grossly unfair to the handicapped television commentators, whose prime oath is never to talk too much.

We grow used to their voices and favourite phrases as the seasons and the cricketing generations slip past. We grow tired of them, as we tire of a favourite uncle's monologue – only to await his next visit, a vitality of summer.

Some have been performing a long time, others longer still, and they are, without exception, men of stolid maturity, with not a screamer among them. This, more than anything, separates them from most other sports broadcasters, and may even be a restraining force on cricket's thrust into the pop era (dreaded by the faithful).

They normally function in twenty-minute shifts: Alan Gibson, slightly nasal and beautifully precise, sometimes impish, almost mischievous, winding his way through sentences that can only be extempore yet sound carefully scripted; the good-natured Brian Johnston, of the delightful schoolboy spirit, unquenchably optimistic, even when the stands are on fire at Port-of-Spain; John Arlott, with heavy mileage in both talking time and topography, relaxed, or seemingly so, and seeking the humour around the nub. Only the other day he saw New Zealand fast bowler Richard Hadlee's "sinister" run-up as reminiscent of Groucho Marx chasing a waitress. The voice of English summer, uninterrupted since Hitler died.

Between overs comes the strident assessment of Trevor Bailey, who made himself into a Test batsman; who made legions of spectators think carefully before watching him; who converted himself into a broadcaster; who usually has the state of the match diagnosed and parcelled up. His communiques during the battle are often awe-inspiring as their accuracy is confirmed. He has been known to get excited, even agitated, at, for instance, unpredictable captaincy or a slow over rate. It is widely assumed that his soul was cleansed at a confessional at the termination of his own first-class playing career.

The end-of-play summaries are pronounced by E.W."Jim" Swanton, once described as the man with the seal-skin voice. No nonsense here either. He has covered, in one journalistic capacity at least, 250 international cricket matches and displays admirable forbearance in resisting the common urge to reminisce. A thousand days and more is an almost indigestibly long time to have one's eyes trained on Test match cricket. His reading of a match, like Bailey's, is thorough in its understanding, yet conditional in its recognition of the numerous possibilities. Beware the adamant cricket critic.

Norman Yardley, having made a comeback to Test broadcasting, restores the dialectical link with the top end of the country and lessens the watchdog image of the commentary box not one jot. Shrewd, wry, and at the microphone a trifle critical at times (vide Close, Old Trafford, 1961*), as a cricketer terribly useful (refer D.G.Bradman).

Indeed, life in the box can be torrid. Even the inoffensive Bill Frindall, the BBC's "keeper of records", under whose torrent of computerized memoranda the commentary team is frequently submerged, was hooked lustily (metaphorically) by Jack Fingleton only last season after innocently informing the nation that "we need 2.6 an over". With a snarl that listeners must almost have seen, Fingleton addressed the keeper of records with a withering "Who's *we*?"

Now to turn the sound up on television: the man of the hour is the droll, kindly Laker. Jim, formerly the emperor of off-spin, has seated himself as easefully beside the cameras as ever he bowled a ball indirectly into his leg trap. Laconic, always well-informed (as, for that matter, are all the fraternity), he is the antithesis of the hysterical and high-pitched story-teller, describing the scene, as he does at times, in a confidential, almost intimate murmur.

The anchor-men, Peter West and Frank Bough, ubiquitous televisionaries and smooth craftsmen both, have some prize commentary material at their disposal here. Ted Dexter, dry-throated as Gene Kelly, sartorially so interesting, still conveys that impression of being a cricketer first and foremost. There has been a fairly widespread frustration that Dexter is observing instead of participating. Any of several individuals could fill the number three spot in the television commentary team; there are precious few endowed to bat three for England.

So be it, however, and no such impatience plagues the audience as it watches and listens to the chummy communication of Denis Compton, folk hero of a rather earlier age. His views are customarily plain. The absence of complication is endearing. Only occasionally is there a tinge of dogma, but somehow he almost never invites the viewer to prove him wrong and to rub it in. He must have been one of the nicest fellows by whom to be run out.

The all-star Eleven is completed as Richie Benaud wings in, bringing as astute a brain as was ever applied to the frolic of cricket. His manner before camera is idiosyncratic: a half-squint direct into the lens, a rare smile to disarm the retreating viewer, then the delivery of a throaty, economical statement defying all contradiction. As captain of Australia ten years ago, he so often had to implore his key bowler Alan Davidson to bowl another over and another. His persuasive powers are now laid bare for all to appreciate.

The living-room can be a clamorous place at Test match time when the addict, in slippers and tieless and with beer and sandwiches at his elbow, has both radio and television turned to almost full volume.

"My goodness," Brian Johnston exclaims on Radio 3, "that ball did turn!" "It pitched in the footmarks, Brian," Trevor Bailey retorts. "Interesting," Peter West breathes. "We ought to see some turn now, on the fourth day," Richie Benaud explains. "Can't you turn it down?" the addict's wife pleads. "I couldn't be so rude to friends," the addict says.

* Yardley, as I recall, was very harsh on-air in his criticism of Brian Close after his dismissal, caught by an out-of-position O'Neill as he swept, trying to regain the initiative for England. Yardley was a Test selector at the time.

The Times, June 21, 1973

All gone now, and yet remembered, some of them, for their professionalism, which has largely been lost in a modern age in which star-struck producers employ only ex-England captains and others who happened to be passing, some of whom have truly dissonant voices which are an insult to the listener's ear. It's an offshoot of the ghastly celebrity culture of today.

One of the finest ever to represent England, and once a world record-holder too, casts his mind back to so many momentous days:

George Geary at Eighty

"I AM not much of a hand at writing these days," wrote George Geary. "My right arm and hand feel as if I have bowled them out."

That was not all. He had recently had a new left hip fitted, made of plastic, a relief from the increasing immobility which still cannot keep him in his armchair when there are strokes to illustrate and tales of the Maharaja of Patiala's fighting ram to act out.

He is eighty on July 9, and justifiably proud of it. Only he and Gordon Salmon remain of those who played for Leicestershire before the First World War; the days of activity seem very far behind him now.

He toiled for his county from 1912 until his retirement in 1938; he carried England's colours in South Africa and Australia and at home, starting the 1927-28 series (after three earlier Tests in England) with Barnes-like effect on the matting pitch at Johannesburg, taking 12 wickets – only to throw his elbow out at Newlands during the second Test and miss the rest of the series. In Australia a year later he headed England's Test bowling and established a record with a gallant stint of 81 overs in an innings. More of that anon.

George Geary, son of a shoemaker, was one of sixteen children ("I used to be a bit embarrassed about that"), ten of whom survive. They were a close-knit family, and proud when George, the eldest, went from the village, Barwell, to play for the county in 1912. He had never seen a first-class match in his life.

Those were the days when Leicestershire played at the Aylestone Road ground, which, during the Second War, was host to the Fire Service, American troops, and a high-explosive bomb. Now it supports an electricity generating station.

After coming perilously close to emigrating to Canada with two pals, George made rapid progress before the First War, playing, albeit without distinction, in a Test trial at Lord's in his second full season, 1914. It was the Lord's Centenary match, and the record shows that S.F.Barnes withdrew with a strained leg. George remembers otherwise: "When he heard he was to be paid just the standard wages for this game he was annoyed. He went down to the nets before the start and came back limping. I was very disappointed not to see him bowl."

Six weeks later Europe was at war, and somewhere in Kent young Aircraftman Geary was put out of the war effort by someone's negligence in leaving an aircraft engine "live" when he was preparing to spin the propeller. The blade slashed him across the left shoulder and down the thigh. "I was black for weeks," he recalls with a wince. "They said I was finished with cricket. I was offered a pension of three-and-six a week!"

In the two-day Championship matches of 1919 he found the going heavy, and in 1920 he played league cricket with Nelson, taking 95 wickets cheaply. He was found "a bit of a job – they made me into a civil servant in an office. I was no use – hopeless." Leicester invited him back, and his career gradually progressed.

By the mid-1920s he was regularly at the top of his county's bowling, cutting the ball at fast-medium to a perfect length off a model action and displaying a tirelessness remarkable in one who had been so brutally injured.

He was given his first England cap in 1924, but rain at Old Trafford restricted play against South Africa to less than three hours. That winter he toured South Africa for the first time with Tennyson ("Great fun. It was honestly"), taking 86 wickets and emerging as a considerable slip fieldsman.

In 1925 he made his first century for Leicestershire – 122 against Kent – the first of seven for the county, though he tends to remember a 99 against Cambridge better than any of them. In 1934, in Jack Hobbs's final Gentlemen v Players match, Geary made 109 at Folkestone. But he regards himself unpretentiously as having been a bowler whose batting feats were incidental.

His first great Test match occasion was at The Oval in 1926, when England regained the Ashes after fourteen years' deprivation. Earlier in the series he and Macaulay had valiantly added 108 for England's ninth wicket at Leeds to save the follow-on and, as it transpired, the match and the series.

"Carr, the captain, whispered to me, 'Stick it. Don't bother about runs.' So, of course, George Macaulay had several goes and came off with it. Poor old Struddy came in and got out straight away – but we'd saved the follow-on."

Geary had been but a few feet from Carr when the England skipper dropped Macartney off the fifth ball of the match. It was an infamous error. Australia would have been 2 for 2, but Macartney raced to a century before lunch, Australia to almost 500. In view of the juxtaposition of the fieldsmen I could not resist asking what was Carr's reaction: "Unprintable, I'm afraid!"

Geary's precious 35 not out was backed by only two wickets, and he was left out at Manchester; but he was reinstated for the historic Oval match and made his mark with his catching.

"I don't want to swank about it, but the two off Larwood must have been coming at about eighty. They bruised the *back* of the hand. Woodfull and Macartney. [No need to look it up.] They were out before they were in after that. When they put me on to bowl the last man out I couldn't feel the ball! I couldn't cut it, couldn't do anything with it."

There was another recollection: "Before we went down on the last morning someone got into the bedroom and pinched all my money."

This was the season when his bowling was so potent that in the space of eight innings in June he dismissed 39 batsmen, 14 each at Southampton and Ashby de la Zouch.

He was to gorge himself to the extent of 10 for 18 three years later at Pontypridd (a world record until Verity's 10 for 10 in 1932). Glamorgan had needed only 84 to win, but on a sporty wicket Geary was unplayable, reacting characteristically to Maurice Turnbull's suggestion from the non-striker's end that he was only bowling "straight'uns" by clean bowling him with a leg-cutter.

Talking of leg-cutters, he suddenly recalled having passed on to Alec Bedser something about the craft when that future England champion was a young man in the 1940s.

After the 1926 summer he went off to India with Arthur Gilligan's side, and has no trouble locating a photograph of G.Geary with rifle under arm and foot on slain tiger to remind him of some exhilarating days. That was when Patiala's fighting ram also came into the story, and the vision of the fleeing Maharaja toppling into a pond and of the English cricketers trying to maintain straight faces was too much for either of us.

So we turned again to the 1928-29 series, when Percy Chapman led one of England's greatest teams to victory over an Australia that was finding itself between playing generations. The tour began catastrophically for George Geary. On a lively Perth wicket Ron Halcombe brought one up off a length and smashed his nose. He collapsed onto the stumps, but was adjudged "retired hurt". "They carried me off on a door. They hadn't got a stretcher."

Months later, back in England, he had two bones removed from his nose: "They gave them to me in a bottle. Best operation I've ever had – it improved my sense of smell. The smell around Piccadilly! I've never smelt anything like it!"

With Sam Staples injured and unable to play at all and "Tich" Freeman not making the Test side, the full weight of the attack fell on the manly shoulders of Tate, Larwood, White and Geary. Only once did England have an appetising wicket on which to bowl: at Brisbane, and Australia were wiped out for 122 and 66. This was the one Geary missed. For the remaining four contests: "I don't think I turned a ball in all the lot. I don't mind saying that when I got a wicket it wasn't my fault. It was the batsmen who made mistakes." Appalling modesty.

He thought wistfully of the sticky wicket at Melbourne when England won their third match by making 332 runs. "Larwood and I – we were a bit tired, you see – we sat outside the hotel. You could see the scoreboard. Every time they hit a run we could see it. I said to Lol, 'It's time we went'. We sat behind the pavilion for a while, then one of the lads shouted, 'George, Lol, where are you? You're in next!'"

Geary went in at the fall of the sixth wicket (Chapman) and set about getting the four needed for victory. He drove Ryder straight to Bradman at mid-on and Tate charged down the pitch. "He lost his head. We only wanted four to win – *four to win!* Duckie [Duckworth] came in and said to me, 'For God's sake get this four. They're all in the lavatory and they won't come out!' 'You don't want to get excited,' I said. I never got excited. I couldn't."

"Ryder couldn't have given me one better. Braddie [Bradman] knew I could hit fairly straight, so he came a little bit straighter. And this one pitched round about leg stump and I gave it such a wallop and Braddie couldn't get to it. 'Run!' says Duckie, 'run!' Not me. I could see it was going for four easy."

And there was a sequel. Geary had borrowed a bat from Ernest Tyldesley, who told him he could keep it if he won the match. Now Geary was offered, and accepted, £10 for the bat. "Jack Hobbs told me I'd have got £250 for it in London – the bat that won the Ashes!"

How did he feel after his marathon of 81 overs at Melbourne in the fifth Test (101 in the match for 136 runs)? "Oh, I didn't feel too bad. There's nobody ever bowled as many in Australia. Someone or other bowled more when Hutton beat Bradman's record."

In the Adelaide Test, during which he made a vital contribution of nine runs off 101 balls, his bowling was restricted by cramp – "a helluva big lump". The captains allowed him off for massage. "My word, you've got a bad one there," said the attendant. Then an Australian official came into the dressing-room and said he would not be allowed back on the field after treatment. "I didn't know who he was. I offered to snap him through bloody window. Later on a taller man came in, but I wasn't afraid. Syd Barnes used to do it. He even went off for a bath sometimes when he felt like it!"

What about Don Bradman? "A very level-headed sort of chap. And he meant it – he *meant business*. He meant to break all the records there were to break. I spoke to him quite a lot when he first started. The other boy died. Archie Jackson. I told our fellows there'd be some leather-hunting with these two.

"But I don't think there was ever a better cricketer than Wally Hammond. I don't. He *was* a great player – when he meant it. I liked him. We used to get on very well together. He could cut 'em off his knees. I mean, that showed his strength."

Other highlights came to mind. The Leeds Test of 1930 (Bradman, "meaning business", 334). "A doped wicket!" Abiding memory? G.Geary, run out, 0. A shocking decision. Old umpire Bestwick spent the interval in the toilet. A famous stand with Patsy Hendren at Trent Bridge four years later, when George, almost forty-one, made his second and final Test fifty: "I could see O'Reilly set his teeth. It made me set mine." The stand of 101 again saved a follow-on, but not the match.

Here he dismissed Bradman (29) for the third time in Tests, having already bowled him with a perfect leg-cutter in the Leicester match. The next encounter, "Verity's match" at Lord's, was Geary's only Test there, and his last. He was reluctant to play, for his knee was painful. Thus ended on a low key a staunch offering for king and country.

Four more years of yeoman service to Leicestershire; a second benefit in 1936, when he took 7 for 7 and 6 for 20 against Warwickshire at Hinckley, Dempster getting his side home by one wicket and Geary pocketing a princely £10 from the match; then, from 1938, two decades coaching at Charterhouse and one at Rugby. "I really enjoyed coaching the boys. I used to tell them what a grand game is cricket. Several I could have picked out from different schools that could have played county cricket, but the fathers couldn't afford to let them go as amateurs."

One did go on – P.B.H.May. "I told them: 'He won't only play county cricket; he'll play for England.' I wanted to give him confidence. Confidence! I used to make him pick his bat up as high as he possibly could." That bat made 85 centuries, 13 for England, and when Peter May finally put it away he wrote to his old coach and thanked him "for everything".

George, a widower, attends few matches now. He has moved to a modern house and, because of the discomfort of travelling, receives his cricket through television. The England cap which once hovered six feet and half an inch above the turf of Manchester and Melbourne now hangs from the corner of a picture frame which houses the image of its owner shaking hands with "the old king" (George V). The frail newspaper cuttings are dog-eared; the contents of the photo albums are slowly yellowing.

As George Geary wrote when he accepted my request to visit him: "How tempus fugits!"

The Cricketer, July 1973

There was one further visit to George Geary. By now he was in a nursing home. He greeted me with the same beaming smile, but conversation was now impossible. Dementia had drawn a curtain to isolate him from the world. He died in 1981, aged eighty-seven.

The Ashes-winning England XI of 1926, with George Geary standing third from right back row. The others are (standing) Harold Larwood, Maurice Tate, Greville Stevens, Herbert Sutcliffe, Patsy Hendren; front: Herbert Strudwick, Jack Hobbs, Percy Chapman, Wilfred Rhodes, Frank Woolley. The author had the privilege of knowing seven of them, and corresponded with Hobbs.

Following a dreadful car crash, England's popular heavyweight batsman Colin Milburn tried desperately hard to retrieve his career as a cricketer:

Colin Milburn fights on

HE IS just about the friendliest man in cricket, and there is plenty of him. The "Colin" gave way to "Ollie" some seasons ago, when this rotund, flannelled Oliver Hardy made many a bowler look as feeble as Stan Laurel. Then his exciting career came to a shocking halt in May 1969 when, as the result of a car accident, he lost his left eye and some of the vision from his right. A wave of grief swept through cricket, and there followed much speculation (which became tedious) as to the likelihood of his returning to the game. He gave in to the pressure a year later and tried himself out at the nets, only to establish that it was hopeless. During 1971 and 1972 he slipped back into the obscurity from which he had first sprung in 1959, and his name bobbed up only spasmodically and sadly whenever England's periodic batting inadequacy was debated. Then in January this year he decided to have another try – quietly – at the indoor nets at Northampton.

"The lads were great. They gave me a lot of encouragement, and I felt it was genuine." After seven or eight sessions the next step was to move outdoors. The glimmer of hope was fanned into a tiny flame, and Milburn discussed with secretary Ken Turner the possibility of a return to the county.

Turner made it clear to Derbyshire before that first "friendly" match that Milburn wanted no condescension from the bowlers. He got none – not even from express bowler Ward. In later matches Snow and McKenzie were both called up as soon as he came in. That was the way Ollie wanted it.

Injuries to Jim Watts and Peter Willey created an unanticipated opening in the side, and Milburn, after thinking in terms of half a season in the Second XI, was suddenly pulling on his outsize flannels and "laughing with the lads" again in the Northants dressing-room.

It took him five first-class matches to pass 20, and at first a two-hour stint in the field hurt his ankles, despite all the squash he had played. Then a 36 against Essex was followed by 34 against Gloucestershire, 44 against Sussex and, as the season drew to a close, 41 in the first match against Leicestershire and 44 in the second. These scores, with lowly punctuating innings, are perhaps unremarkable . . . until one recalls the battered figure that emerged in the early summer of 1969 from Northampton General Hospital, where he had so far given no serious thought to the future: "I've been too busy enjoying myself in hospital!" . . . until one recalls the chilling finality of various statements that apparently wrote off all chance of our seeing him bat again in top company.

The final match, which decided second place in the 1973 Championship, was at Guildford, against Surrey, the side he was due to face the morning after the accident. Ollie was bowled by Arnold in the first over of the innings. He tried to cut a ball too close to him. Sympathetic applause was involuntarily offered, though the batsman could have done without it. What outgoing, scoreless batsman ever did relish it? Better than silence, perhaps. Almost anything is better than silence.

It was a remarkable day, that one: for two hours later Northants were following on. There was an unuttered dread , surely universal among the comprehending, that Milburn might make a "pair". The pitch was still "doing a bit", and Arnold and Jackman could sniff a two-day victory and with it the Championship runners-up honours. (Runners-up may be nowhere compared to champions, but third place is

Still giving the ball a whack after the loss of an eye, Colin Milburn tried so hard to pick up his career after the dreadful car accident.

even less than nowhere – though this time £1000 was at stake.)

They bowled, and Milburn and Virgin batted. They batted without great discomfort, except when Ollie turned his broad back on a couple of second runs that might just have been there. Milburn pushed the ball through midwicket, cracked it square to the boundary with the short forearm jerk that is his very own, and eventually uncorked the vintage bottle of them all with a swatting pull off a fractionally short one from Jackman that landed the ball in a neighbouring flower-bed.

He reached 50, to ecstatic applause, and then fell, for 57, to Intikhab, bowled round his legs as he tried to sweep. The ball turned a lot. It needed to.

Now he is in Perth, Western Australia, playing for Mount Lawley as captain/coach, broadcasting, selling cars in between times. He has no idea whether he will make the Sheffield Shield side. He would like to. He will not be heartbroken if he doesn't. He hopes the brighter light will make sighting the ball that much easier. It was batting at number six earlier this year that made things difficult. When he moved up to open the innings – against the shiny new ball – he felt much more in control. One suspects it better suited his temperament too.

He has not consciously cut out any strokes, nor does he fret at the limitations so savagely imposed on Milburn Mk II. He claims he was never darkly depressed during the four years. "I was just bored. I couldn't picture me behind the counter of my sports shop every day."

Many people liked his humour and his direct approach to television commentary. Was it his decision to give it up? "No, they just didn't want me." He used to sum up a Wes Hall bumper with exactly that sort of simplicity.

He became engaged in July, but he has no firm idea when he will marry Vicki. He proposed in the early hours of the morning in a nightclub. He drives a car still, but never at night. The £19,000 from his testimonial is in trust. On his own admission it would have been "chaotic" to have given him the lump sum.

So, like an aspiring schoolboy, Milburn – maker of 23 centuries, the last against Leicestershire, the one before that in his last innings for England, against Pakistan at Karachi – is once more searching eagerly, determinedly, for his first hundred.

The Cricketer, December 1973

Colin Milburn's return to first-class cricket went no further. He remained on the scene, crooning loudly in a bar or in my car or as a tour escort on the Jolly Roger in Bridgetown Harbour. The cricket world was saddened more deeply than is customary when this universally popular man died after a heart attack in February 1990.

Cricket's Meaning at a Time Like This

CRICKET MEANS many things to many people. County cricketers have occasionally been heard to express hopes for weather interference, enabling them to escape from their sporting labours; conversely I know men who, buoyant in summer, become morose and spiritually shrivelled in the off-season.

Can the allegations ever be refuted that addicts of cricket, which inflicts a kind of widowhood upon countless women, are inadequates? Do its addicts – more kindly called enthusiasts – really even care about this charge?

There are those who enter scores daily into notebooks, who telephone for the latest score each time the boss turns his back, who are members of three or four county clubs. At another level there are those who claim aggressively never to have watched cricket since Compton and Edrich retired (what they have missed!), or who insist with compelling sincerity that there is nothing worth looking at outside club or village or school cricket. Some find satisfaction only in debating theory, not always concerned whether or not the listener is willing as they air their intricate prescriptions for the cure of all cricket's supposed ills. And who hasn't met that particular worshipper who all his life sings the praises of the specific hero of his boyhood? Then there is the one who eyes his victim seriously and proclaims cricket to be an escape, a near-religion, *a religion*. I have done so myself, and sometimes almost convinced.

Seldom has the escape concept been more clearly silhouetted than in recent weeks. The 1973 season closed, the second bumper summer in succession, and was forgotten too soon simply because the news bulletins grew gloomier each day. As December groaned along, the lights were dimmed during the power crisis, at least giving us a glimpse of an evocatively shadowy London – as Alfred Mynn or any other pre-neon passer-by must have known it. Petrol became scarce to the point of panic, and there were no hansom cabs and at times few trains to replace the immobilised motor car. Supplies of electricity, meat at acceptable prices, sunshine, and even newsprint were diminishing. Hard times – an expression of which might have been the recent demolition of a church in my own town; its replacement a bank.

The Great Powers continued to glare at each other, political confidence was crumbling in several lands, terrorists and kidnappers stalked this good earth, sterling trembled, and even the soporific effect of television was punitively denied us after 10.30pm.

Beyond this, most English cricket followers seemed oppressed by the team's prospects in the Caribbean. Those who were not blessed with the anticipation of seeing in the flesh some of the Test series in West Indies were left to prop whatever scaffolding around their morale that they could find, such as indoor nets, indulging in long, pathetic sessions of "do you remember?", or simple prayer for the speedy arrival of the English summer of 1974, bringing with it the familiar, reassuring sight of an inhabited cricket ground.

I once proved, in contradiction of a long-held suspicion, that it is possible to exist without a devotion to cricket. But it is, on the whole, better to have it. So long as the volume is carefully adjusted. If only the hyper-enthusiast were more moderate he might well win over more disciples. We might go so far as to suppose that if the average daily reporter watched less cricket he might transmit greater feelings of love and care. This is not to say that Fleet Street sports editors are giving the game all the mileage it deserves. Far from it. Apart from well-known exceptions, the dailies have failed dismally to recognise cricket's new appeal and vitality, preferring both in and out of the football season to project something space-consuming out of relatively trivial football matches and managers. And we are now threatened with the possibility of football until June!

In contrast there seems never enough of the summer game during the winter. Rather like a slice of toast with all the marmalade at one end.

During such time we may turn, like the harassed cavaliers of old, to the simple sporting pastime. This, in its present vicarious form of reading books and attending cricket dinners, looking through tears on a soundless-clapping host, will get men through, determination mounting all the time that next summer's open fields and cricket companionship will be savoured more than ever before. Unless even these things somehow are denied us.

The Cricketer, February 1974

Any perceived incipient nervous breakdown failed to materialise. Thirty-five years on, some of these assertions still hold true, while some of the laments are now dated. Round-the-clock television coverage is now available, if the premium can be afforded and the viewer can put up with the new breed of non-stop clattering commentary. And that unbeautiful game, football, continues to spread its tentacles across the sporting calendar.

Sir Donald Bradman visited England for the final time in 1974, and won over even more admirers:

The Don Comes to Town

"MY FIRST visit to England, in 1930," said Sir Donald, "was during the Depression. When I look at the Financial Times Index at the moment I think perhaps my timing hasn't improved!"

"The Don", the most consistent run-maker in cricket history, was speaking at the Anglo-American Sporting Club's special dinner at the London Hilton on May 13. The visit to Britain, his first since 1961, was arranged by the Lord's Taverners, some of whose members joined with those of the Anglo-American – over a thousand attended – in according to him, as he prepared to respond to Sir Alec Douglas-Home's happy welcoming toast, a standing ovation. It was an even better reception, quipped Sir Donald, than he received at The Oval in 1948 (his final Test). "It didn't help me much then!" (He was bowled second ball by Eric Hollies without scoring, having needed only four runs to retire with a Test average of 100 – assuming Australia had no need to bat a second time. It will be recalled that England made 52 and 188, Australia 389.)

Sir Donald, a Lord's Taverner himself, saw a significance in the evening's twin theme of boxing, mentioning that he was born in 1908, the year of the Johnson/Burns fight at Sydney. Surrounded by members of the 1948 England team and other distinguished guests from many walks of life, he lamented the absence of friends now passed on, such as Lord Birkett and Harry Altham. He mourned also the disappearance of the original Tavern at Lord's: "But at least the Long Room still stands. My boots are preserved there – inside Maurice Tate's!"

He recalled that in 1948, at a Cricket Writers Club reception to his team, when England's selectors were looking for fresh talent – "as they usually seem to be" –

the Duke of Edinburgh's name was put forward. The advice, as we all know, was ignored!

The Don was relaxed and in fine form. He tickled his audience with light touches ("They tell me a geriatric is a German who takes three wickets in three balls"); he cut into Taverners history in acknowledging the new president, Alf Gover, and recalling a favourite past-president, Sir Robert Menzies; and he drove home the need for "freedom under the law" as defined by Lord Birkett at Nuremberg, the need for honesty, sincerity, integrity, humanity. "Otherwise the pitch will become unfit for play."

Again, a standing ovation. The diners, under the chandeliers and the veil of cigar smoke, had their memories of an historic speech, preceded by the showing of newsreel film of the 1930 and 1934 Test matches. Bradman's double- and triple-centuries were applauded yet again.

Sir Donald, for his part, had an audible reminder of the affection in which he is held in England. He had, too, a permanent reminder: a crystal decanter, presented by the Earl of Westmorland, president of the Anglo-American Sporting Club, inscribed "for his unique and unforgettable contribution to cricket". Later Sir Donald made as if to stand on his chair to receive a further presentation from six-foot-four-inch Alf Gover. The members loved it.

What is a Test blazer worth? An Australian blazer? Bradman's? Vintage 1936-37? Seven hundred guineas, said Geoffrey Platt of Hertfordshire, whose bid was final. Henry Cooper's boxing shorts fetched £200; Graham Hill's helmet, covered in autographs, £150; a bat signed by the 1961 Australians, 100 guineas; another signed by England and Australia, 1948, a staggering £450. The original of Roy Ullyett's menu cartoon was bought for £800. Some of these values may seem far from rational, but it was essentially a charity gala, which should explain all.

During the week preceding the banquet The Don emerged from his secret hideout to hold a press conference at the Hilton, answering with keenness and courtesy a dozen tired old questions that must have been put to him a thousand times before. Asked by a female reporter from a magazine which caters for "senior citizens" whether he felt as fit as he looked, Sir Donald chirped: "Perhaps not as fit as I look. But I'm grateful to be as well as I am." To what did he owe his fitness? "Good living over the past sixty-five years!"

Has he retired from business? "I can't afford to!" At which his old friend Alex Bannister, of the *Daily Mail,* chuckled, "How can you say that with a straight face!"

As for the apparent growth in verbal aggression, there has been, he said, a considerable amount of it over the years, though in 1932 (the year of Bodyline) it was a much worse form of aggression he and his fellow batsmen had to withstand! And what of the forthcoming series in Australia? The 1974-75 rubber between Australia and England will be evenly fought, said Sir Donald Bradman, "though loyalty compels me to go for Australia."

The Cricketer, July 1974

A review of Dennis Lillee's sizzling book Back to the Mark:

Confessions of a Rib-Cracker

OVER THE past couple of years Dennis Lillee's back has had quite as much publicity as Fred Titmus's toes or Raquel Welch's chest. The poor fellow has been X-rayed, manipulated, and locked in a plaster cast. Through it all he has remained determined to get back to big cricket. Now, at last, he is "back to the mark", and the entire world of cricket congratulates him. Whether he deserves plaudits for his "autobiography" is a separate matter.

It has happened before that cricketers have not been completely familiar with their written life stories – where a collaborator is involved – as it goes to press. But we must take it on face value and accept that the words are Lillee's.

So, we now know that he regards batsmen as being "like thieves, desperately trying to steal from me the ascendancy I believe is mine".

Fair enough.

"I treat them like faceless, meaningless thieves."

Well, okay.

"I try to find something about the faceless batsman that really annoys me, then I build on that until it becomes a sort of hatred that burns in my guts until I get him out."

Steady on!

"I'm just so pent up against the batsman that I let him have a bit of my tongue as he goes."

So we've noticed.

"I try to hit a batsman in the rib-cage when I bowl a purposeful bouncer, and I want it to hurt so much that the batsman doesn't want to face me any more."

Dennis, Dennis! In one page of print all my visions of a reincarnation of the great and gallant Tom Richardson are destroyed.

Lillee believes in "winning at all costs", and it seems his saving clause is that there is no trauma in cricket that cannot be healed over a few evening beers. All this makes ironic reading so soon after his references in Chapter 2 to early sources of inspiration such as Wes Hall, Graham McKenzie and Fred Trueman – grand sportsmen all three. "That was the way I wanted to bowl, it was the way I wanted to be regarded – fiery and aggressive, take no liberties with him, you never know what's coming next."

I happened to be sitting with Trueman when he first set eyes on Lillee in action. After two balls he said, observant as ever, "He sidesteps just before his final stride." Of this feature alone Fred disapproved. Come to that, so did Lillee's backbone, for he was eventually to go down with three stress fractures.

Forced by weak ankles to wear special boots as a boy, Lillee prophetically knocked Geoff Boycott's cap off with the first ball he bowled against an English team. This was at the start of two years of continuous cricket. Against the Rest of the World, at Perth, he took 8 for 29. In 1972 he was again magnificent, taking 31 Test wickets, a record for Australia in England*. The wear and tear eventually brought him down.

He owes much to Tony Lock, his early state captain, and to Ray Lindwall. He has also had some typically sound advice from Sir Donald Bradman, including an early suggestion to forget about any "bumper war". That was before Jeff Thomson came along.

Lillee makes some interesting observations: that the one-day internationals should be between Test matches, avoiding the risk of anti-climax, and allowing the tourists to leave immediately after the final Test; that counties should qualify to play against the Australians, i.e. bottom clubs excluded; that Australian cricketers are grossly underpaid; that Ian Chappell (who has generated such tremendous team spirit) and his men were "cheated" by the Leeds pitch in '72.

The book has its humorous moments too: when Lillee, as nightwatchman, batted successfully through to the close of play at Sydney in 1971, a straightfaced Chappell told him next morning that he had done his job well and could now go back to number 10 in the order. He was green and he took his captain seriously. But when he was missing as England took the field, the joke was on the anxious Aussie skipper. It says something for Lillee that he can tell that one against himself.

* Bettered by Lillee himself: 39 wickets in a six-Test series in 1981, when Terry Alderman took an overall Australian Ashes record of 42. In the 1989 series Alderman took 41 wickets in the six Tests.

The Cricketer, February 1975

A first visit to Pakistan resulted in a special audience with the legendary A.H.Kardar:

Dictatorship with Democracy at Heart

ABDUL HAFIZ KARDAR, president of the Board of Control for Cricket in Pakistan, former Oxford Blue and Pakistan captain, knows exactly where Pakistan cricket is going – or, more precisely, where he would like to take it. With an unshakeable grip on the wheel he has driven his views across to the presidents of MCC and the Boards of India, Australia and New Zealand.

He wants to "democratise" the International Cricket Conference* by scrapping the veto powers held since inception by England and Australia, and he wants ICC meetings to be held in rotation in member countries rather than always at Lord's. He wants Sri Lanka to have full Test match status, and he begrudges Israel even associate membership of ICC because he feels they are not strong enough. He walked out of last year's Conference in protest.

Pakistan's avuncular attitude towards Sri Lanka has expressed itself in their sending a touring team there without financial guarantee, and investing 50,000 rupees (just over £2000 – big money in context) in hosting Sri Lanka on a return tour. Yet all Pakistan's hopes for and belief in Sri Lanka – so important to the development of cricket in Asia – could crumble if the island's team disappoints in the Prudential World Cup in England in June. Indeed, it would be the most classic of ironies if Pakistan themselves were to humiliate their "ward" in the match at Trent Bridge on June 14.

Worthily, Mr Kardar has Pakistan taking the lead in strengthening cricket in Asia, since none of the other Test countries are able to do so. India are apparently not wealthy enough. The game, as Pakistan Board secretary Zafar Altaf wrote recently, is in danger of dying in Asia; it must not be allowed to die.

Is there not a danger that world blocks will form? Mr Kardar hopes not. England and West Indies in the west should assist Canada, the USA and Bermuda. The large Negro population of America, he feels, is ripe for induction into the game. Pakistan's community feelings extend well beyond Sri Lanka. They wish to help cricket in Malaysia, Singapore, Hong Kong, Papua-New Guinea, and Burma. The grand vision extends even to Australasia. Invitations were recently sent to New Zealand, who promised to discuss the matter of their joining the Asian Cricket Conference at their next Council meeting, and Australia, from whom a reply is overdue.

Fate meanwhile fights relentlessly to keep India and Pakistan apart on the cricket field. Resumption after fifteen years was planned, but since Pakistan insist that it is India's turn to travel (their profit on Pakistan's visit in 1960-61 was probably at least a million – well-remembered – rupees), and that five Tests should be played, India's insistence on three Tests only, with an immediate reciprocal visit by Pakistan, has restored the stalemate.

Pakistan reminded India of the reciprocal guarantee thought to have been agreed at the Asian Cricket Conference at Lahore in December. The difficulty is that India would not accept the minutes of Conference, believing them to be unfaithful to reality.

Behind all the negotiation and counter-negotiation there would appear to be a desire for a deliberately slow normalisation process between Pakistan and India. Test match competition between them will have to stay in the decompression chamber until such time as the politicians see fit to unbolt the door.

The trouble with the Indian Board, Mr Kardar believes, is that it is too cumbersome, with perhaps thirty members. Pakistan itself used to have twenty-odd, but this has now been pruned down to seven. The "beauty" of it is that the seven were not elected. Mr Kardar chooses his officers on merit. Furthermore it proves expedient for him to make many of the less important decisions himself without consultation.

He explains away the apparent inconsistency of the life ban on Younis Ahmed for playing with Derrick Robins's XI in South Africa on the one hand and the mere carpeting of Mushtaq Mohammad for associating with the same team (incredibly dubbed "racialist" by some Asian sportswriters) by stating that Mushtaq will never be appointed to the captaincy or vice-captaincy of Pakistan. Meanwhile his apology to the Board has enabled him to continue to play for his country – and to make a match-saving century at Lahore against West Indies.

As for, say, Jeff Thomson's playing with the Robins' XI in South Africa, this would bring a ban on him from entry into Pakistan in any capacity except that of a member of an official Australian touring team. Australia have been invited to tour next season now that their tour of South Africa has been cancelled. Even at a minimum charge of six rupees for admission the grounds should fill to see the Chappells and Lillee and Thomson.

Pakistan's line on South Africa is clear. While apartheid exists there will be no contact or recognition. There seemed little interest in cricket circles at what small headway is being made towards multi-racial cricket in South Africa.

* Now the International Cricket Council.

The Guardian, April 4, 1975

What a difference thirty-five years can make. Indian cricket not wealthy enough? The game dying in Asia?

Mr Kardar, in whose presence most people seemed to be completely overawed, would probably not have been best pleased had he known that my next exploratory visit was to be to South Africa:

Flight to Johannesburg

WHAT CAN one learn of South Africa in a mere week? More than by not going at all, at least. The streets of Johannesburg, ingrained with gold-dust as they well may be, convey a multitude of Blacks and Coloureds, almost all of whom *looked* contented. There was no jostling or barging, hardly a resentful glare. That was impression number one. Did I see the shanty towns? Only passingly. But I have seen the shanty towns of Naples and Panama and Brisbane and Lahore . . . and London.

In cricketing circles there is much optimism that South Africa, after these years of ostracism, will re-enter Test cricket before much longer. It may not, perhaps, be based on tangible pointers: rather it may be secured to a belief that what they consider to be such "persecution" cannot last indefinitely.

"We have fallen over backwards to please the outside world," said former South Africa batsman Eric Rowan. "And the outside world just tells us to get stuffed. I tell you, there is a great deal in this country that would be the envy of most other nations. Some of the people who grew fat from Africa are now its sternest critics."

"Grand" apartheid holds its course, but "petty" apartheid has shown signs of crumbling. The Transvaal Cricket Union is moving towards mixed club cricket, and mixed Curric Cup competition before long is not beyond the bounds of possibility. A problem of some duration has been the intractability of the Coloured cricket body, SACBOC. Under Hassan Howa and now Rashid Varachia they have consistently refused aid and resisted attempts at conciliation.

Meanwhile the Black cricketers and their leaders strive onwards. Don Wilson, Yorkshire and England slow left-arm bowler, has been for several years the TCU's head coach with special responsibility for Black cricketers. His team comprises Barry Stead and Phil Carrick (looking after Soweto, the Black city with a population of one million) and Richard Lumb and Ashley Harvey-Walker (in charge of the all-White schools). Rohan Kanhai joined them for a while this summer.

Wilson recently took an all-Black side on a tour of Rhodesia. Twelve players were chosen from the John Passmore Week tournament in December. They came from all over South Africa, and ten of them had never flown before, eleven had never entered a hotel. Perhaps the greatest ordeals were the cocktail parties. Eleven came from the Xhosa tribe and the other from the Suto.

Wilson saw improvement in their bowling and fielding during the tour, though their batting – on turf for the first time – understandably was a little disappointing. In the two-day match against the President's XI, which included seven Rhodesia players, Paddy Clift and Peter Carlstein among them, Edward Habane, still in his teens, scored 60-odd. The tourists lost by 100 runs, but were not disgraced.

Two days later the Black XI played Derrick Robins' XI and lost only off the final ball. From there the next step was Langa, where Habane made 54, with five sixes and four fours. Opening bowlers Nontshinga and Njokweni took four wickets each. Don Wilson continues to feel happy, though not complacent, about progress to date.

Attendances at Transvaal's match with the Robins XI were poor, the causes supposedly being dull weather, Transvaal's lowly position in the Currie Cup, and, most of all, the absence of Jeff Thomson. The local Press had given him the big build-up, and his late decision not to join the Robins XI created much bitter disappointment. As one Johannesburg scribe put it, Thomson would fill the Sydney Opera House just by standing on stage polishing the ball.

In a cricket-starved land it was hard to understand why the ground wasn't full, especially on the Saturday. It was on that second morning that Tony Greig arrived, like fifteen cubic feet of sunshine, direct from the MCC side in Hong Kong.

Other memories that will abide include conversation into the early hours with Brian Close, Ken Barrington and Terry Jenner, with the skipper [Close] not unexpectedly holding the floor most of the time (a floor, incidentally, spread with Close's gift zebra skin – until he lost patience with those of us who persistently spilt our coffee and other drinks over it – on purpose, he said). It was pleasant, too, to talk with Willie Watson, still looking fit, as becomes a double international, and John Waite, now a successful sports shop proprietor, and Lee Irvine, captain of Transvaal, erstwhile of Essex.

An afternoon in the beautiful city of Pretoria began at Johannesburg railway station, where once stood the original Wanderers cricket ground (it stretched the imagination to be standing on concrete under which once flourished grass and Victor Trumper's bat) and almost ended on the platform at Pretoria when, cutting it fine, I had to scuttle past all the Non-Whites carriages to reach a "Net Blankes" carriage as the train began to pull out.

South African life continually throws up reminders of another time. First there was the newsreel at the cinema – remember the newsreel? Only an hour or so earlier I had seen and heard my first steam engine for many years. It was good to peel back "progress" if only for a short while.

So many South African players – Ali Bacher chief among them – have retired early since Test cricket became a contest only for other nations. Eddie Barlow's continuing performances are marvelled at – and appreciated no end. As poignant a case as any is that of Clive Rice, who joins Nottinghamshire this season. In 1971 he was chosen in South Africa's side for Australia. It became a "ghost team" whose members went only as far as to have blazer measurements taken. With minor adjustments Rice had the garment tailored initially for Tiger Lance for the 1970 England-tour-that-never-was. Now he looks towards county cricket. If he does well South Africans will be proud. But in a sad sort of way.

The Cricketer, May 1975

Much has been – and could still be – written about the colourful Fred Trueman. A limited offering was called for late in 1975:

Fred Down Under

ONE OF the greatest disappointments of my youth was not being able to watch Fred Trueman in Australia in 1954-55. He did not tour. Nor did Tony Lock: and both these aggressive young Englishmen represented the revival, free from all inhibition, of the cricket of the Old Country.

There were other exciting new players too, of course, such as May, Cowdrey and Graveney; but these two bowlers, having made their marks against Australia in 1953, were the *claws* of the post-war Lion. Their very lack of discretion and their ceaseless belligerence had something to do with their omission from the highly successful side which Len Hutton led, and probably their presence would, in any case, have added little to England's dominance.

But their absence took some absorbing for one who had been promoting their prowess to friends and acquaintances for months beforehand.

Eventually they came – four years later, when the tide had turned. Unlucky. It was a most miserable tour for England, with nothing to compare with it until this winter just passed. All the same, Fred's reputation had preceded him faithfully, and he was the man the crowds looked for every time MCC or England took the field. He took a wicket with his first ball in Australia and soon became famed for his play-acting – scowling, hands on hips; gesturing to the crowd; great value for money when batting too, missing with a swipe and peering, hand shading eyes, into the distance; holding bat as Tommy gun and "shooting" bowler or fielder.

It all endeared him to Australian crowds in perhaps the last season out there when

70

goodwill towards Englishmen was still widespread and spontaneous (it was a winning year for Benaud's Aussies, and Britain had yet to begin courting Europe). Fred was not stuffy, not reserved, not supercilious. They liked that. He must be a fellow who viewed life as they – and not Poms – customarily viewed it.

He is supposed to have retorted, when invited to admire "our Bridge", that it was "not *your* bloody Bridge – Dorman Long of Yorkshire built it, and you haven't paid for it yet!" Or something like that.

But this oft-repeated retort didn't dent the image. With his status in the land, he of all people could get away with that. He has been back several times since, latterly for double-wicket contests and charity matches. At forty-four he is still a great drawcard.

The Twelfth Man (Wombwell Cricket Lovers' Society, 1975)

"It won't come out, son!" said Fred Trueman as the author took this shot at the Sydney Cricket Ground in January 1959. For once he was wrong.

Three Old-Timers

MIDST ALL the urgent clamour of a World Cup, a Test series and assorted other cricket events it has been wonderful to glance backwards in the company of three grand old cricketers of many years ago. Frank Woolley and his delightful American wife recently made a brief visit to England from Canada, Martha in the hope of gathering material for a book on Frank's early life, and he, the Pride of Kent, now eighty-eight, to meet some of his countless friends. With a trendy hair length and twinkling eyes, Frank Woolley was still able to raise himself fully if slowly to his magnificent height.

At Edgbaston, it was pleasant to meet again E.J."Tiger" Smith, England's oldest Test veteran at eighty-nine, whose long and crystal-clear memory is the source of kaleidoscopic reminiscence. Dennis Amiss, in this dark hour of his, would be fully aware of old Tiger's technical acumen.

And finally, what a pleasure it was to welcome H.L.Hendry and his wife. "Stork" was last in England with the 1926 Australians. At eighty he is still able to play straight in a game of back-garden cricket, and to recall with gusto some of the fun of pre-war cricket. They don't get fun out of it today, he seems to believe. And it was not easy to contradict him.

The Cricketer, September 1975

Long before Test match grounds became awash with blazered officials and security men wearing gaudy flak jackets and stoney stares, freedom of movement was taken for granted. Hence the mission into the Australians' dressing-room at the end of the 1975 Ashes series to say goodbye and ruminate on the unfurling era of coarse behaviour:

Not the Sweetest of Opponents

"WHAT'S ALL this garbage you've been writing about us, Dave?" Ian Chappell challenged me when I called in during the Oval Test to bid bon voyage (or whatever it is you bid your friends when they are about to step into a great airworthy metal tube) to Bertie, the General, Fot, Bacchus, Fitter'n, Rowdy, Roscoe, Maxie, Two-up, Gus, etc, etc.*

Ian was referring to something I wrote in the September *Cricketer*: that his team had not been "the sweetest of opponents" in recent years. "Out there," he said, pointing to the middle, "is no place to be amicable." Point taken – up to a point.

There seems to have developed during the 'Seventies a conviction – in many walks of life – that courtesy is alien to masculinity; ergo, those jealous of their manliness need to be impassive except when "needling" opponents.

Lately there have been illustrations of this from almost every cricketing country in the world, and while it might – just *might* – be allowable at international level, since this is a branch of showbusiness (close to the theatre of mime), it will, and indeed has, spread to other areas. I learned last week that there were frequent instances of verbal abuse in the middle during Surrey Clubs Championship matches last season.

If these fellows had possessed reasonable self-control all their lives, why has their behaviour changed now? Are they apeing their betters? Surely the field of *club* cricket at least *is* a place to be amicable? Why, to pose one further question, are so many people saying that football means practically nothing to them any longer? There is almost certainly a causal connection.

An Australia v West Indies series is coming up, and the six Test matches between two strong and very attractive teams should provide much to interest a vast worldwide following. Yet perhaps the most fervid hope should be for the series to be played in the player-induced climate of chivalry as was that memorable contest fifteen years ago in Australia by Benaud and Worrell and the sides they led.

The numerous newcomers to Australia's cricket grounds last year deserve to see something a little less one-sided than the Tests of 1974-75 and they deserve to experience international cricket of high quality and free of petulance and childish "niggles".

If they see this kind of cricket, I promise – no "garbage"!

* Ian Chappell, Rick McCosker, Dennis Lillee, Rod Marsh, Alan Turner, Ashley Mallett, Ross Edwards, Max Walker, Jeff Thomson, Gary Gilmour.

The Cricketer Winter Annual, November 1975

A tribute to a brilliant and popular little cricketer – and to his "clan":

Mushy: a Joy to Behold

WHAT IS almost thirty feet long, smiles a lot, travels the world, has made about 60,000 runs, and has the proudest cricket mother of all? Answer: the Mohammed family of five brothers – Wazir, Raees, Hanif, Mushtaq, and Sadiq.

Amir Bee, their mother, has, in a sense, given more to cricket than anyone else in history, though Martha, mother of W.G.Grace and his wonderful brothers, is a strong challenger. Her big, bearded son became the most famous figure in all England and made cricket a national game. Yet even he and his brothers could not lay claim to having appeared – one or other of them – in every Test match played by their country. The seven Fosters of Worcestershire were an impressive lot, but Reginald alone played for England. The Hearnes of Kent were rather thick on the ground too, but no-one would seriously put them up as rivals to the mighty Mohammeds. There are three talented brothers Hadlee in New Zealand, and a trio of Chappells in Australia (where, incidentally, brotherhood has been big business in cricket, as witness the Archers, the Bannermans, the Benauds, the Giffens, the Gregorys, the Harveys, the McLeods, the Trotts, and the Trumbles). But nowhere – just nowhere – have a father and a mother struck such a dramatic jackpot as the late Shaikh Ismail and his former All-India badminton champion wife Amir Bee. Their pride and the pride of Pakistan has been enough to fill not only the stands of Karachi and Lahore but of many others around the cricket world.

It so happens that I have seen a good deal more of Mushtaq Mohammed than of his brothers. Early in 1975 I watched him sweat through a century in a Test match at Lahore when Pakistan had everything to lose against West Indies. A few months later, in conditions far less tense, I saw him make a hundred for Northamptonshire against Surrey at Guildford. This time the match wasn't saved, but the feeling was the same: that if the side had had *two* Mushtaqs they might have won. To be greedy, with *three* Mushtaqs they might have won by an innings!

One of the attractions of his batting is that he is often so obviously fighting his natural instinct to hit the ball – every ball – hard, while knowing that his wicket is next to indispensable. Some batsmen sit on the splice and give every impression that they enjoy doing so. Not "Mush". And when he is throwing himself into all his virile strokes he is a joy to behold.

There is more to him, of course, than batsmanship. Though he is underemployed with it for much of the time, he is an enchanting purveyor of wrist-spin. He once began to explain to me how a top-spinner was not conceivable by design. His argument, though typically genial, was involved and had me beaten just as surely as if I had tried to repulse his googly with a real bat.

Another point I recall was his mentioning that at fifteen, when he became the world's youngest-ever Test cricketer, he was too "green" to feel any pressure. He didn't really know where he was or what he was doing, except that he was playing cricket – something he'd been given to understand he did well – for his country. He grew up and he grew to realise what "pressure" really is. He handles it well, and could serve as a living example for England of the belief that if a young man has Test potential then he should not be kept waiting too long, for he will almost certainly grow each day more and more into an ordinary club or county player. Dip him in it the moment that first chance presents itself!

Mushtaq was thirteen when he first played first-class cricket, fifteen years and 124 days when he appeared in a Test match, and seventeen years and 82 days when he became the youngest maker of a Test hundred – records all defiant and challenging. Now, as an old man of thirty-two, Mushtaq Mohammed, nine years a Northants capped player, applies himself to a benefit, with all the hard work that this entails. He will be alive to the pressures this time, but I do so hope he feels, when he contemplates the outcome, that it was very worthwhile, for he does deserve to do well.

Mushtaq Mohammed Benefit Year 1976

A Pre-Vision of Batsmen's Helmets

IF ADDICTIVE smokers can be cured by being forced to watch colour film of charred lungs, and if drunken car-drivers found guilty of causing fatal road accidents can be punished by viewing gory films and by touring casualty wards, what can we do for the fast bowlers who dispense bouncers with gusto and to excess – at tailenders as well as top men?

The "quickies", we know, are a breed apart. Most of those who have inflicted near-fatal injuries upon batsmen have managed to recover their composure in an astonishingly short time. "Sugar Ray" Robinson and Emile Griffith – to take two notable examples from the ring – forged on with their professional careers after accidentally killing opponents – at what cost to their peace of mind few of us will ever know. None of the fast men that I can recall has turned thereafter to gentle off-breaks or some such after bouncing a batsman into the intensive-care ward.

There must be a parallel between hostile bowling and car-driving. Does not a motorist consciously slow down – for a mile or an hour or a day – after passing a crimson-flecked wreck by the roadside, with its attendant rescue workers and ambulancemen? Soon, if not forgotten, the spectacle is placed firmly into an obscure corner of the mind. The speed creeps up again; the attention may begin to wander. "It can't happen to me" – one of the oldest self-comforts in the book. Caveman Fred probably muttered it to himself after Caveman Bert was taken by a dinosaur.

This very season a county batsman has been knocked cold, and I listened to the still-shocked recollections of those awful moments by members of the fielding side:

"His eyes rolled up, and all you could see was the whites." "Blood was coming from his nose." "After a while his legs started twitching. It was terrible." "I couldn't go over to him," said another player, who happened himself to be a batsman. "It wasn't my scene."

It is nobody's scene. Yet it happened, has happened often, and will continue to happen. Cricket has its dangers, and only the use of a tennis ball will eliminate them. Realistically, these dangers *must* be reduced to a minimum. The topic of intimidatory bowling is inescapable in cricket conversation today. The suggested treatments are more varied than the cures for warts.

A line across the pitch is clearly impractical since pitch-pace and bowlers' lift vary enormously. A ration of one or two bouncers per over – quite apart from the problem of deciding what is a bouncer and what is a long-hop – with any subsequent bouncer being called "no ball", plays too far into the batsman's favour. Yet here perhaps we are getting close, if umpires were to unite in the practice of applying what would be an amended Law 46 (vi) by no-balling all short-pitched fast balls *the instant a reasonable number has been bowled*. But what a weighty responsibility to add to the already heavily-laden umpire. Only the very best could be expected to apply the control to the majority satisfaction.

I think we can discount the suggestion that fast bowlers and their captains have consciences which will serve as safety governors. This may be so, but it has not prevented a long, long catalogue of head and chest injuries. We are examining fear. Facing fast bowling stripped of its physical threat – whether by conscience or legislation – is as Queensberry rules to bareknuckle, to return to the boxing idiom. The fast men utilise fear, and it would still be worth a fast bowler's while to concede the occasional penalty run (or runs) to remind a batsman that he should not take any liberties . . . unless infringement meant banishment from the bowling attack for the remainder of the innings. Law 46 now allows for this. A Buller or Egar might well have implemented it by now, but it seems there are no umpires of that sensibility and calibre of courage in Australia or West Indies, areas where the tightest control is needed.

Even so, we may see firm umpiring (particularly *a propos* suspected intimidation) this very summer, even on England's snoring Test pitches.

Beyond all this are the opinions of top batsmen. It could be argued that theirs is the only opinion that really matters. Tony Greig believes protective headgear would overcome the problem, reducing the peril, increasing confidence for the hook stroke, eliminating fear as a fast bowler's weapon. David Steele thinks likewise, adding that when a fast bowler switches to around the wicket and drops one short, the umpire *must* see this as intimidation. Rod Marsh of Australia has seen enough from his strategic position behind the stumps also to advocate "crash hats". Intikhab Alam, who was once knocked flat by Andy Roberts from around the wicket, believes heavy run penalties would be the answer.

Perhaps a combination of measures will dispel the growing anxiety. Crash-hats with visors are a repugnant prospect, but if some batsmen decide to wear them, for the sake of their wives and children, no-one will have the power to stop them. A new problem will be when to put them on or to remove them. Even Pat Pocock once cheekily bowled a bouncer, and Chandrasekhar's is none too pleasant. Let us pray good sense prevails.

The Cricketer, June 1976

A couple of years later helmets came in, even in club and school cricket, and the age

75

of watching batsmen whose faces were fully visible had passed. As usual, it took the authorities far too long to get to grips with the sinister question of excessive bouncer bowling. Eventually, to the sound of squeals from fast bowlers around the world, a specific ration was imposed.

A momentous occasion for women's cricket in a summer of exceptional drought was their first-ever match on the sacred turf of Lord's:

Tweed Skirts and Bobbed Hair

THE VARIATIONS in the shapes and flavours of cricket never cease to amaze. In the passage of a month I have seen the game at its ugliest and prettiest, at its most eager and at its most abhorrently cynical. After the infamous final eighty minutes on the Saturday of the Old Trafford Test, when cricket came close to blood sport [West Indies fast bowlers mounted a sickening attack on England batsmen Close and Edrich, uncurbed by the umpires], it was refreshing to watch schoolboys in action. The occasion was the (attempted) final of the London Schools *Cricketer* Trophy, but the irony was that with only a dozen overs bowled, an enormous blue-black cloud set course for the ground and bombed it with something I believe is called "rain". That was that for the day, except that during the casual conversations ensuing it was interesting to hear a father's views upon cricket as an occupation. His eighteen-year-old son has just been signed by a county. He will support the boy – if and when his wages prove inadequate – for two years. By then, father and son both calculate, there would still be time to seek a career outside the game. One's heart goes out to them both.

The magnificent Test match at Leeds restored much of the lustre previously lost. For days of mighty cut and thrust spilt over to a final day of truth. West Indies are the better side – Tony Greig was quite prepared to acknowledge it – and it was something of a delusion to suppose that England were going to draw level. Still . . . what if the second innings had had a sound foundation? Cricket is sometimes a game of delusions, and occasionally even the delusions are delusions, as Gertrude Stein might have said.

Miss Stein was not at Lord's on August 4, but hundreds of ladies with tweed skirts and bobbed hair were. There were schoolgirls and old gentlemen too, and more non-cricket journalists than cricket journalists. For this was women's cricket's greatest day – the "final bastion" falling, the "last male preserve" scuttled, and all that trite stuff. It was decorous, even genteel. The ball seemed to hang in the air when bowled, though we were assured that these were the faster bowlers in action. The strokes were mainly textbook, but featherweight. The fielding was clean, the throwing weak. One of the aficionados suggested that the girls were overawed by their surroundings. Sharon Treadrea of Australia wasn't. Here was a genuine turn of brisk medium-pace – after she alone had hit the ball with a heavy sound, finding the boundary rope often and with conviction. Chris Watmough of England later matched her forcefulness.

There was a slightly grotesque "Press conference" during lunch, in – of all sites – the Lord Harris Gardens. Someone had a wry sense of humour. Rachael Flint dealt superbly with the slick and well-worn questions, and her opposite number, Anne Gordon, smiled, ducked, or played dead-bat. Then the bell rang, and suddenly it seemed less unnatural to see white-skirted cricketers walking out through the pavilion gate (though that may be anything but a unanimous view). An historic day indeed, and not simply because this journal's Editorial Director [E.W.Swanton] was hugged in the Long Room by the England captain.

In all the play that goes on hour after hour, season after season, generation after generation, there are precious few moments of true destiny. That first ball sent down in Test cricket by Shaw to Bannerman, English home invincibility shattered in 1882, Bradman's last Test innings (or his first, for that matter), Bosanquet's first googly victim. I hope male readers won't think the suggestion too fanciful (and I know female readers won't) that when June Stephenson bowled that opening ball to Lorraine Hill at Lord's on that Wednesday in August, something more than a game of cricket had started. MCC will naturally welcome the women cricketers back only as and when a busy annual fixtures programme allows. But the ladies will be patient. They have shown their patience already.

What might be their next target? One from their ranks in a men's county side? Then perhaps into the England XI? Remember how Tom Spedegue, bowling his stratospheric "dropper" onto the bails, played for Bishops Bramley one week and England the next! Enid Bakewell and Lynne Thomas could be the answer to England's opening batting problem. Roberts and Holding would surely be too chivalrous to bounce them at girls! (Let one who is often taken too seriously explain that the suggestion is hardly full-bodied.)

The Cricketer, September 1976

How could one ever have foreseen that Marylebone Cricket Club would one day open its membership to women? As Jonathan Swift wrote almost three hundred years ago, vision is the art of seeing things invisible.

The Centenary Test match in Melbourne in 1977 and the celebrations that surrounded it remain easily the most spellbinding event in the long history of cricket:

The Greatest Gathering

Friday, March 11

PURRED BACK into Australian air space five years almost to the day since leaving it. An unceremonious return, since dawn is still a few hours away and everyone aboard this cosy Qantas 747 Jumbo – except aircrew, I trust – is sleeping. First light reveals again what an awesomely vast country that 18th Century Yorkshire captain claimed in the King's name. Excitement at last begins to rise in me at the prospect of this massive nation playing the little island I left yesterday at cricket.

Melbourne around lunchtime. One of the first sights is a golden tram, illuminated, with cricket motif all over, flying the Australian flag fore and aft. Hot, humid, blustery. Book in. Shower, rest ten minutes. Then curiosity gets the better of me and I head for the Melbourne Cricket Ground. This colossal empty salad bowl should be filled with 100,000 grains of rice tomorrow (it wasn't – the media were blamed for frightening many away), but now it echoes to the footsteps of the few – buying souvenirs at the trestle table, gazing at the canvas name-placards clinging to the walls: Trumper, MacLaren, Hobbs, Hill, Bradman, Compton, Woolley, Gregory and dozens more. An inspired touch from the organisers. At last a welcome familiar face: Stork Hendry. This evening I meet and talk with an old captain, Norm O'Neill, for the first time since 1953. I feared this was going to be the greatest name-drop operation in the history of cricket.

Saturday, March 12

DAY ONE of the Centenary Test match is heralded in with a televised champagne breakfast at the Hilton. Newsreels are projected and old players are interviewed. The scene is set. At the MCG all is chatter and expectancy. First-day covers sell briskly in the log cabin post office set up outside the members' gate. The opening ceremony is timed perfectly and scripted tastefully. The two teams line up with the parade of former Test captains; Bob Parish, Board chairman, makes his speech of welcome, and we are off. The skippers toss, and a sensational day's play begins. By Thursday we are to be conditioned to sensations, and to those who are not necessarily demanding a special match to go along with the off-the-field celebrations, the 225th encounter between the two oldest Test countries develops into an exquisite bonus.

My chair in the Press-box has only three sound legs, but a greater hazard is Ashley Mallett's sports jacket, which compels me to don dark glasses. O'Reilly, Fingleton, Arlott, Bannister are here. Of the rest, none surely could have seen every Test in the hundred years.

Down to the hub of the "Million-Dollar Birthday Party" – the guests' enclosure. This is where Alice's vision seems to be distorted beyond imagination, for EVERYONE – or almost everyone – is here: a unique living pageant of England-Australia cricket: Larwood and Voce, Fender and Ryder, Compton and Washbrook, Tribe and Dooland, Davidson and Simpson, Pellew and Alexander, Edrich and Bedser, Meckiff and Rorke, Darling and O'Brien, Tallon and Brown, Grimmett and Ponsford, Craig and Burge, Harvey and Mackay, Statham and Tattersall, Cowdrey and Graveney, Ames and Bowes, Paynter and Hardstaff, Hassett and Miller, Laker and Lock, Watson and Bailey, Morris and Lindwall, Allen and Brown. Any one of them would be good for a two-hour chat. Bert Sutcliffe, Walter Hadlee, John Reid and Neil Adcock are also here, reminders that the game is played in other countries too.

I go up in the hotel lift with the stricken McCosker and instinctively say to him "How are you?" His jaw is wired [broken by a Willis bouncer]; he cannot talk. I'm sure he knows I meant well.

Sunday, March 13

AUSTRALIA'S DAY, this one. "It'll cost ya!" smiles Bill Ponsford when I ask him to sign my book. Happy reminiscence with Ted a'Beckett. Jack Badcock won't stop smiling. Leo O'Brien, a Bodyline hero, talks of football, horse-breeding, and India. Grahame Thomas, pressed, discusses John Evans, his Cherokee great-grandfather. Wistful "do-you-remembers" with old grade adversaries Philpott, Burke, Taber, and Booth. Larwood still standing: "Every time I sit down someone comes up for my autograph!" During an interval he and Bill Voce are escorted to the middle, where Voce discards his coat and marks out his run. They are cheered today. They weren't in 1932-33.

The latest story to crease everyone up is of the fellow who said: "Didn't you used to be Ernie McCormick, the fast bowler?" "Still am," retorted the unflappable Ern.

Ken Mackay walks past, still imitating Groucho. Unexpected chance to talk with George Hele and George Borwick, the Bodyline umpires. They are completely engrossed by the play today. More and more people are catching the autograph bug – books, prints, bats being signed, the scratching of pens drowned only by the clink of glasses. I meet Peter Allan for the first time since RAAF National Service days in Queensland.

Back in the Press-box, Sydney favourite Geoff Boycott puts in an appearance. Ian Chappell looks more like Starsky than ever. O'Reilly looks bored, Jim Laker reflective, Lawry smiling and elegant in an electric blue blazer. Will this match last out for the Queen's visit on the final day? A limited-overs match seems a certainty.

Monday, March 14
PUBLIC HOLIDAY in Victoria. Plough my way through the crowds assembled for the Moomba Festival parade. Newspaper placard this evening proclaims PIE HITS MOOMBA MICKEY: TWO HELD. Must have been a heavy pie. Some idiot threw a placard at the Queen in Sydney. All this and Walters' fine boundary throwing make it easy to guess at Australia's blue riband activity. Talked cricket and economics with Sir Donald [Bradman] in the pre-lunch sunshine. Later handed Lillee his copy of the *Cricketer* All-Time XI print by Trog. The captain's dressing-room guest, Prime Minister Fraser, took one who had grown up in the Menzies regime unexpectedly.

Back in the main room, an introduction to cricket-lover and ACTU president Bob Hawke – the opposite end of the political spectrum. Back to the 1930s with Tim Wall, Merv Waite and the tiny, frail Clarrie Grimmett. Could find no-one willing to approve of McCosker's return to the crease, valiant though it was.

Tuesday, March 15
REST DAY (for some). I have a book to promote [pictorial history of England v Australia]. Radio phone-in interview at 8am. "Could you lift your voice a little, Dave?" Only with a supreme effort. I tell Australia that her first Test captain, David Gregory, is buried at North Sydney without any kind of memorial. This surely is the year to put things right.

Send off some letters and postcards. Get lost in the park and find myself beside Captain Cook's cottage. All the bookshops seem to be doing steady business with cricket books – as they ought to be. Qantas reception in the evening, and I get to realise how tired the MCC [England] boys are after five months' hard labour.

Wednesday, March 16
BIRTHDAY, and the gladdest of beginnings with breakfast with Sir Don Bradman and the charming Lady Jessie at the Windsor. He had awoken before sunrise and put some ideas on paper: four minutes should be allowed per over, with the umpire (or outside timekeeper?) calling "over" irrespective at the end of that time: restriction on number of leg-side fielders now seen as imperative; and why not permit only one bowler per team to bowl off an unrestricted run-up? My most thought-provoking meal in years.

The barman at the ground can't get over the request by an old England player [Eddie Paynter] for "warm beer". Send a greeting card to Frank Woolley, who couldn't make it to Melbourne; a pal sends one to Herbert Sutcliffe. Time to think of absent heroes.

Today's heroes are Marsh and Randall. The legs are beginning to complain. The smart ones sit themselves down. Frank Misson, with moustache, looks like a squire. Tony Lock looks slightly bored. Keith Miller is the subject this evening of *This Is Your Life*.

Thursday, March 17
WHAT A Test match it's been. Randall is the toast, though Lillee and Marsh did

The principal guest at the Melbourne Centenary Test, HM the Queen. Ray Steele stands behind her, Greg Chappell effects the introductions, with Max Walker extreme right, and Rick McCosker beyond with the bandaged broken jaw. Inset: menu for a gala occasion.

CENTENARY
TEST MATCH

1877-1977

Dinner

Given by the
MELBOURNE CRICKET CLUB
Melbourne Cricket Ground
16th March 1977

pretty well. A hundred years ago today the margin [45 runs] was identical, but this seems to have taken a little while to dawn on the majority. If only every Test match could be played in this spirit and with this amount of hourly excitement and incident.

At last it is confirmed that Lillee will not tour [England]. He gave Randall a bonk on the side of the head as a souvenir. Randall, however, takes the match award. "Hey!" he calls to David Lloyd in the crowded lobby of the Hilton that evening, still wearing cricket clothes and blazer, "fancy me getting hundred-and-seventy!" Was ever a young batsman so chuffed?

The Queen and Prince Philip visit the ground after lunch. Peggy Lindwall thinks he's lovely. "He's the same age as you, Ray," she observes wrily. Randall struts from the arena in a dream, straight towards the royal enclosure. "He's going to be knighted on the spot!" says someone behind me, probably seriously.

The end-of-match formalities are poignant. To counter the growing feelings of let-down I browse through the museum and library. Armstrong's shirt has to be seen to be believed; Stoddart's cap *must* have shrunk.

An interview with Jack Ryder is called off because the grand old man has lost his voice [the eighty-seven-year-old former Australia captain died just over a fortnight later]. The scene in the dressing-rooms is like a Brueghel painting. The international bonhomie is heartwarming to behold. Tonight the touring team is announced, bringing with it the customary elation and sadness.

The last days
BY TAA DC9, a smooth flight to Brisbane, to see relatives. Also a brief call to see Eddie Gilbert, the aboriginal fast-bowling sensation of the 'thirties, hospitalised for years, and in a world of his own. Thence with TAA again down to Sydney to see more long-lost relations, to tread the Sydney Cricket Ground again, with a first sight of the Bradman Stand, and to meet Charles Bannerman's great-grandson. He looks like him. An ideal note on which to end.

Once more aboard the Qantas Jumbo, this time for only one long night in the air. Time for reflection as we cruise over the Simpson Desert, with its odd bare-poplar-tree patterns of sand-drifts; over Alice Springs. A tired smile and a nod to the hardy Freddie Brown and Bob Wyatt, and mutual lamentations with Trevor Bailey. All I have now is a stack of cuttings: MATCH OF THE CENTURY; POMS' PACE TOO HOT; RICK KO'D; ENGLAND BLITZED!; HAIL HOOKES; IT'S IN THE BAG; RANDALL REIGNS.

The movie begins, the earphones are inserted, dusk settles, and Australia recedes as we speed into the next hundred years.

The Cricketer, May 1977

There was something else to celebrate in that special year of 1977: the centenary of the birth of Australia's sublime batsman of the Golden Age, Victor Trumper. All the author's powers of imagination went into this "interview":

Talking with Trumper

November 2 marks the centenary of the birth of Victor Trumper, the Australian batting genius, who died in 1915 at the age of thirty-seven. This commemorative "conversation" comes from David Frith:

TO THIS day the tributes to you and your batsmanship continue to pour forth, even though there are very few people left alive who watched you play and we have only a few frames of jerky cine-film taken, I think, in 1905. This lasting affection must be some comfort to you in your ethereal state?

Yes, I have to admit that it's nice, though I'm not sure it's really deserved. As for those moving pictures, we were just having a lark when they were taken. They didn't come out very well, did they? Not like some of the photographs taken by George Beldam, though that one of me jumping out to drive is a bit overused, don't you think?

It certainly hangs in numerous pavilions and homes, even today; but it is the most thrilling of cricket pictures. As for your "immortality", there can be no doubt that it is deserved. Fellows who played with you and against you and lived many years longer, men like S.F.Barnes and Wilfred Rhodes and Frank Woolley, have testified that you had four or five strokes for any one ball, and that you had an air of being able to bat just as long as you wished, even if sometimes you threw your wicket away when others would have batted on.

I never saw much point in making runs for the sake of it. There were other chaps who wanted a knock, though there were times when you had to get your nose down.

Like at Hove in 1899, when you hit 300 not out?

We were chasing over 400 against Sussex, if I remember right, and I was in for around six hours. I was only twenty-one then, and didn't tire all that easily. I never felt quite the same after an attack of scarlet fever. I was only on reduced pay - £200 – at the start of that tour, but when I made a few runs I was put on a full share of the profits – about £900. It was very good of them. They didn't really have to do it.

Your performances on the next tour of England, in 1902, are still often recalled – 2570 runs, with 11 centuries, the highest only 128 and one of them before lunch on the opening day of the Old Trafford Test match. All that in a wet summer.

Yes, well, figures aren't very interesting. I doubt I would have got that score at Manchester if Bill Lockwood had been able to bowl before lunch. The ground was too wet for him to get a foothold and Archie MacLaren kept him back for a time. I suppose if I had to think of a knock that gave me most satisfaction it was in the Sydney Test of 1903 – you know, when "Tip" Foster made that wonderful 287 for England. We were nearly 300 behind on first innings and I managed a few. Len Braund bowled leg theory, so I had to move back and cut him, and I had a grand duel with Wilfred in that match. His flight and length were very good and it was hard to attack him. I simply had to defend sometimes.

You managed 112 between tea and the close of play, and finished with 185 not out.

Well, I was lucky.

Your first century in big cricket was 292 not out against Tasmania, and this was the highest first century until someone beat it quite recently in a match in Pakistan.

Where's that – in the Pacific, isn't it?

Sorry. It's easy to forget that so much has changed. I suppose the thought of West Indies, India and New Zealand playing Test cricket, and South Africa not playing, must surprise you?

I'm sorry to hear about South Africa. What happened?

It's political.

They seemed a good enough bunch of chaps when we used to play against them.

Didn't you once open the bowling against them in a Test match?

Yes, I liked bowling fast – or fastish. I remember getting poor Louis Tancred and

Buck Llewellyn out at Johannesburg when they were both in the nineties. Jimmy Sinclair was a marvellous bat, a powerful striker. And when the South Africans came out in 1910 Aubrey Faulkner taught us a thing or two about batting.

I can't believe you had much to learn. They're still talking about your innings in the Adelaide Test of that series, described as "faultless" and "incomparable" – 214 not out at almost a run a minute.

Another lucky day.

Oh, Vic! Anyway, what went wrong in 1912, when you and five others refused to tour England after an upset with the Board of Control? The Board is having considerable difficulties today, but that confrontation must have been pretty unpleasant?

If you'll excuse me, I won't talk about that. It was unpleasant. It would have been nice to have gone to England again. I really enjoyed my four tours. The wickets were often quite different and made batting more interesting than on some of the pitches we had in Australia. I don't suppose things have changed much?

You'd be amazed. Where do I begin? Pitches are covered much of the time; big matches are not only broadcast around the world by radio but visually by means of television; something like thirty major books about cricket are published each year; teams fly between England and Australia in a day and a half; some Test players' earnings run into five figures; bats have gaudy manufacturers' motifs all over them; restricted-overs cricket is widespread; leg-spin is almost dead; we usually get well under a hundred overs in a day's Test play . . . .

Stop, please! Goodness, does anyone get any enjoyment out of cricket? What about club cricket?

That's taken a lot more seriously. Sledging – verbal abuse of the batsman – is not unknown . . . . Are you still there?

Yes, I am.

Have I shocked you?

I suppose so. But I feel more sorry than anything else. We really did have fun, whether we were playing grade, Sheffield Shield, or Test cricket. We played because we loved the game, and it was a joy to be out in the warm sun, pitting our skill against the opposition.

But think of the realities of life: a man has to earn a living and that can't be done on peasant wages.

I was lucky, because through cricket my name became known and I was able to get into business.

But it wasn't very successful, from what I've heard. You kept giving stuff away!

When a customer left his bat out in the rain you'd replace it for him free of charge. And what about the boy whose eyes settled on your bat after you'd scored a Test century with it? You gave it to him cut-price because it had been used!

What else could I have done?

You make me feel ashamed even to think of an alternative.

I always thought it was a privilege to be able to spend so much time travelling and playing the game, meeting people like King Edward and Doctor Grace, and seeing places I would never have seen otherwise.

To return to some of your great deeds – you may well look down at your toes! – how did it feel making six centuries and two eighties in your eight innings for Paddington one season?

Wonderful . . . and tiring! But I didn't do too well against Mr Stoddart's team. Five and a duck, I think.

Maybe, but your friend Monty Noble has recorded that your catch to dismiss Hayward was perhaps the most sensational and spectacular ever seen in the outfield – a top-speed dash, a baseball dive, and a somersault! Why do you smile?

It's just that I thought I had no hope of catching it. I just flung myself. You've got to try all you're worth, haven't you?

You must have been trying when you hit 293 in 190 minutes in New Zealand just before the Great War?

I was dropped a couple of times. But, yes, it was one of my better efforts – and just about my last big score. I enjoyed New Zealand. Jack Crawford and I put on almost 300 in just over an hour at Temuka. When the ball's there to hit, you hit it, even if it's the first of the day. Isn't that still true? Even the best bowlers need to be hit off their length. That's what a batsman has to try to do. And if your partner isn't having much luck you should try to take the bowling on on his behalf. You wouldn't be doing the proper thing by the team if you didn't do this. Reggie Duff and I batted this way together. Poor Reggie . . . .

Which bowlers did you most enjoy batting against?

The slow bowlers presented a challenge. I liked to get down the pitch to them. It was your best chance against someone like Bosanquet. If you just scratched forward you played into their hands. And it was always a good battle when a field was set purposely to cut off certain shots. That's when a batsman has to really use his wits, playing in other directions.

They say you were master of every stroke, and no field could be set for you.

Oh, I don't know about that . . . .

Of course not. Let's recall your testimonial in 1913, when your eyes filled with tears at the warmth of the reception the Sydney crowd gave you. The match raised £3000, but the Association wouldn't hand it over as a lump sum. They invested it for you and paid out the interest. Why was this?

Well, they seemed to think that I would soon get through the money, with friends borrowing it and suchlike.

I suspect they were right. Didn't you want £60 immediately to lend to a business associate, and didn't you once buy up all of a lad's songsheets as you left the Coliseum Theatre in London one night?

It was cold and very wet. The little chap was shivering. Somebody had to buy his wares. In any case, I didn't expect anyone would notice. There were times when I wished I could have done a disappearing act.

I've heard that you sometimes did. At least one journalist might still to this day be waiting for you for an interview; you said you'd be back in a minute, left the room to get something, and never returned.

I hope it didn't cause any inconvenience.

We've learned about you from others, not from yourself. That's the best way. The writers, your team-mates, opponents. And never a bad word. The streets of Sydney were jampacked with weeping admirers for your funeral . . . . Your picture will stay on our walls, Victor. Your deeds – or more particularly the methods by which you achieved them – will stay in our hearts. Your God-given ability will be cherished in memory and imagination. Your approach to cricket will be held up eternally as an example to those who think only of personal accomplishment. Bless you, and happy birthday, if I may put it that way.

The Cricketer, November 1977

The saintly Trumper flicks the ball away. He died the wrong side of forty.

Halfway through the following summer my career as editor of The Cricketer was summarily terminated. The final editorial serves as a detailed reminder of just how startled we all were at the universal adoption of helmets in response to the excessively nasty fast bowling now sweeping the world. Batsmen henceforth, with rare exceptions, were to perform their duties in near-anonimity:

Here and There

JUST THREE years ago I was in the last stages of researching for a sort of history of fast bowling, a book which recorded quite as much injury, even tragedy, as glory. It became clearer to me than ever that cricket in the 1970s is an appreciably more dangerous game than is generally realised. In 1975 Lillee and Thomson were the principal villains, with Willis about to assume a similar menace. In the seasons since, home and abroad, the physical threat to batsmen has spread like acid. The erosion of batsmen's morale has been carried on by the five West Indians, Roberts, Holding, Daniel, Garner, and Croft. Jaws and noses have been broken, torsoes pounded , with a dozen terrifying near-misses for every hit, and resultant gasps from wicketkeepers, fieldsmen, and onlookers. Casting the mind back, the introduction of batsmen's crash-helmets now seems to have been completely inevitable. Captains have failed. Fast bowlers themselves have been derelict of conscience.

It jars the aesthetic sense; but then so does so much else in today's world, sporting and otherwise. Yet again, cricket reflects its environment, which in many respects has become ugly and violent. Some of the helmets look grotesque, resembling those used by skateboarders or dispatch-riders, and when worn back-to-front, like Sadiq Mohammad's in the first innings of the Edgbaston Test, the sight verges on the ridiculous. The model worn by former Australian wicketkeeper Rod Marsh last winter, jockey-style, in team colours, with transparent visor, is far less incongruous.

Millinery design aside, it is practicability that matters, and while comparisons may be odious, so too are the murderous lifters of the likes of Daniel and Croft. You need only to have faced a rearing spitfire from one of these gentlemen to know how precious life is, how pleasant it is to have an unmutilated head on your shoulders.

There is, of course, always the constructive attitude, as expressed by Mike Brearley in his recent book: "Broken marriages, conflicts of loyalty, the problems of everyday life fall away as one faces up to Thomson." A sublime experience, so long as the cerebral area itself is shielded.

Only the man who used to crack his head against a brick wall for the simple reason that it felt so good when he stopped would have enjoyed facing fast, short-pitched bowling – preferably on a pitch of uneven bounce.

Dennis Amiss has spoken of the vastly increased confidence that the helmet brings – indeed, even a danger of over-confidence. But the oldtimers seem to be almost unanimous in their contempt for protective headgear. Among views aired was that of Australia's champion all-rounder of thirty years ago, Keith Miller, as relayed on radio by Henry Blofeld. "Nugget" apparently said that he would have interpreted a helmet as a challenge for him to put a few dents in. Within the hour Ted Dexter gave an insight into one aspect of the mentality of batsmanship by saying on television that he never consciously *expected* to be hit on the head, and so would not have worn protection. Colin Cowdrey, in the *Daily Telegraph*, deplored helmets, and suggested that the overuse of bouncers was "the act of a bully and demonstrated a shortage of genuine skill".

What are we to conclude? If a batsman feels the need of a helmet, no-one has a moral right to condemn. Where the greatest anxiety abides is in the spread to minor cricket, for spread it almost certainly will, with a resultant increase in fast-bowling madness. This saturation through the ranks was the most pointed evil of Bodyline almost half-a-century ago.

A threatened development that must surely be indefensible: the wearing of helmets by short-leg fieldsmen. Theirs is a voluntary situation. If they are so close to the bat that they feel in need of physical protection, then they are *too near*. They, unlike batsmen, have some choice.

The Cricketer, July 1978

Cricket's John Wayne

LATE IN 1950 I spent much of my time hanging around the enormous marble columns rising from the steps of the entrance to the Hotel Australia, in Sydney. If I had been a few years older I suppose I must have come under the scrutiny of the hotel management, if not the police. My sole motive, of course, was to catch sight of – and perhaps even pass the time of day with – the English cricketers.

They were a fresh-faced lot, most of them, the kind who gave rise, a hundred years earlier, to the term "Pommies", after the similarity between English complexions and pomegranate skin. They looked so young, too, and therefore ineffectual: David Sheppard, in a pork-pie hat, Bob Berry, resembling an underfed Don Estelle, John Dewes, Gilbert Parkhouse, John Warr (another victim of food rationing, it seemed), shy Eric Hollies, shy Doug Wright, diminutive Arthur McIntyre . . . and at last a somewhat more robust figure, heavy of eyebrow, the only Yorkshire player in the team apart from my idol, Hutton (who, not to labour a point, looked none too strong either) – a teenager who had just made a promising century in the opening first-class match at Perth: Brian Close

His subsequent failure on that tour is well-known, as is his career's tendency towards fluctuation. Last year, just before his retirement at the age of forty-six, he used the word "farce" in alluding to the erratic course of his twenty-nine seasons in big cricket. Surely it has been less a tale of farce than of frustration and occasional futility. No tougher cricketer ever lived. That's a fair old epitaph in itself. But that wouldn't have been Closey, would it?

I can only say that few victories have given me as great a delight as England's at The Oval in 1966, when Brian Close was called in as skipper rather as Percy Chapman had been forty years before. Few dismissals, either, have induced a sadness comparable to that when Close was run out for 4 in that match – accident-prone again, and deprived of a substantial contribution towards a famous victory. Never, for that matter, have I felt such pain on behalf of another as when Close, the elderly, was pummelled mercilessly and unnecessarily by the young West Indian "braves" at Manchester in 1976.

Yes – you have to hand it to him: Brian Close repeatedly evoked distinct reaction from spectator, team-mate, and opponent alike. I see him as the John Wayne of cricket. It's as well those marble columns were either side of the steps. If they'd been in his way, the odds are that he would have shifted them – or broken his shoulder trying.

The Twelfth Man (Wombwell Cricket Lovers' Society, 1978)

A NEW ERA
1979-1989

My career as editor of The Cricketer having come to an abrupt end, I was available for whatever writing assignments came within reach. The wilderness period ended just short of a year later when Wisden Cricket Monthly was created. No invitation to write was declined, and even when the magazine was in full sail, invitations were usually accepted, the precarious nature of freelancing – as John Arlott never tired of pointing out – being something like a virus.

Cricket After Dark

TWENTY-FOUR hours later the lights went on. Not just a few bulbs here and there, but 540 of the dazzlers, turning the norturnal Sydney Cricket Ground into a vast and brilliant pool of brightness, and prompting a local architect to monitor the effect half a mile away in south Paddington. "The lights," he said, "are an environmental disaster."

Few of the 44,377 present (plus about 7000 who squeezed their way in when the gates were thrown open) would have cared about the outside world. The frenzy was audible and visible, and sent the World Series Cricket people into raptures. Missing, though, was a takings figure, which lent weight to the belief that many complimentary tickets were in circulation.

I have been used to watching floodlit Rugby League and Soccer and boxing late at night, but cricket after dark seems about as natural as going to church on a Tuesday. And besides, I am surely not alone in feeling too tired to get excited – over sport anyway – at ten or eleven at night. The nausea I felt this evening I put down to fatigue, for the cricket had its moments. If I'm prejudiced at all, perhaps it is in favour of playing cricket in God's sunshine.

WSC Australia won their International Cup match against WSC West Indies, their first limited-overs victory over that particular opposition, and Dennis Lillee was back in business, collecting the match award of $500. There was something very baseball about it – the hard-hats and visors, the constant background roar, the players' voices through the ground microphones, and the glare coming in from all angles. The white ball, while new, was easily seen and therefore seemed to be travelling more slowly, and the glimpses of the black sightscreen made it seem like a photographic negative. The commentators' overkill and the commercials after each over and fall of wicket made it seem more than ever like a telecast of Mets v Red Sox.

Here we were, resisting bed's beckoning, and instead being sold hamburgers, deodorants, cars, hi-fis, tyres, air conditioners, *Playboy* magazines, mortgages, soft drinks, canned fruit, refrigerators, weed-cutters, diamonds, security locks, cassettes, hotel accommodation, and tomorrow night's movie. For those in doubt, animated diagrams showed what a yorker was, and a bouncer, and a good-length ball, with Fred Trueman explaining in the kindest of tones.

Two chaps ran round the perimeter carrying an Australian flag, and were pelted with beer-cans, and when shortly afterwards Ian Chappell was given out caught at the wicket there was a chorus of booing. Few if any police were present. Perhaps there was no room for them. A friend told me that at the end of the game, when hordes ran over the field, a man was seen urinating on the pitch.

David Hookes batted in a hard-hat without face visor, but Ian Redpath wore the lot, and looked like a lanky construction worker striding off for a night's work. Joel Garner, the ball a mere marble in his huge hand, yorked him for 1. After 32 overs the white ball needed servicing by the umpires, but a few minutes later it was all over, and the fireworks burst upon the sky, commemorating a weighty move forward by Kerry Packer's World Series Cricket. Worcester spectators who sat through Ian Davis's four-and-three-quarter-hour innings of 83 during the 1977 tour would have rubbed their eyes at the slender batsman's bold strokeplay here, and Lancashire supporters would have been asking why Colin Croft, the West Indian giant, had not shown such fire while bowling for the county. The stimuli of big prize-money and a large, noisy crowd had much to do with it.

I watched more the following night, when WSC Australia beat the World XI in a match aborted by rain. This time only 20,000 were at the ground, and the following day I could not remember a single detail of the play.

When I turned in at last, bleary-eyed, I was yearning for the smell of mown grass.

The Ashes '79 (Angus & Robertson, 1979)

Cricket had changed drastically – and forever. In the years that followed, the commercial invasion was to spread its tentacles to places we then assumed to be sacrosanct: players' shirts and equipment, every available yard of space around the boundaries and on ground structures, even on sightscreens and boundary ropes. The worst desecration of all was advertisements – lots of them – on the field of play itself, something never stooped to by American sports administrators. The Age of Greed was upon us.

Will You Sign Please Mister?

> *I stopped the old Test cricketer,*
> *His autograph to claim.*
> *So long it was since he'd been asked,*
> *He couldn't spell his name.*

THE DAY I realised I was slightly taller than the Test cricketer signing my book (I think it must have been seventeen-year-old Ian Craig) I felt obliged to give up collecting autographs. Then, ten years later, I started again – why, I'm not sure, except that an inscription, even if it is just the author's name, enhances a book or scorecard, the more so as years pass. The sentimental as well as the real value increases well beyond the rate of inflation. Grace to Gower, Spofforth to Sarfraz – the house is cluttered with them.

It is not the easiest thing to ask a Test or county cricketer to scribble yet again the most familiar word in his consciousness. You know he finds it a chore, you know he wonders what the devil a fully-grown (presumably) adult wants with his signature (I've never resorted to pretending it's for my nephew), unless it should be on a cheque. Esther Rantzen came close when she said: "I don't know why these autograph-collectors don't just forge them. No-one would ever know."

That's what puts you off second-hand autographs – unless they are convincingly authenticated. A pre-war Australian Test player who always got lumbered with the autograph sheets on board ship once reeled off for me a near-perfect Bradman, Oldfield and O'Reilly. Like peas from your garden, those you gather yourself you can trust.

And of course, there is an anecdote behind almost every one. As a lad, I decided to "catch" the 1950-51 MCC team. Len Hutton signed readily, Alec Bedser neatly and strongly, Godfrey Evans somewhat flippantly, and I caught up with Trevor Bailey in Bert Oldfield's sports shop. Now Trevor had just had his right thumb broken by Ray Lindwall, but, plaster or not, he wrote on the page. Quite illegibly. Comparing it with his signature today, I would say there is no difference, though the injury healed a very long time ago.

Back in the hotel lobby, I was in luck. Young Brian Close splattered his name all over the page. John Warr's signature amusingly looked like "John Wan". Cyril Washbrook insisted on using his own fountain pen. Denis Compton, when this determined little pest caught up with him at a speedway meeting, signed across Len Hutton's legs in the photo of the two of them.

Eventually there was only one autograph needed: the captain's, Freddie Brown's. Three times in a week he emerged from between the huge marble columns at the entrance to the Hotel Australia while I lay in wait, and each time his great stature and smoky howitzer of a pipe proved too intimidating. I gave up.

Then a fellow hunter said he had a spare Brown (he didn't explain how he managed two while I was finding it even more difficult to get one than to establish meaningful contact with Pamela down the road) and it was mine for two bob. I produced the coin . . . then slipped it back into my pocket. Truculently I decided I was not going to be beaten by the captain of England! They were saying he had a heart as big as a cabbage. Well, mine was at least the size of a Brussels sprout, and growing beneath the compost of competition.

So it was that I threw myself into his path next time the mighty FRB climbed the steps. It worked. He braked in time, perhaps recalling the inconvenience in 1913 when the suffragette flung herself under the hooves of the Derby runners, and he said something fairly diplomatic in the deepest voice I'd ever heard – and completed the job. I was fulfilled, and could now concentrate on the Australians. And whenever I see Freddie Brown now we exchange greetings that are a totally insignificant incident in his day but which for me trigger piquant memories.

First among the Australian stars was "eith iller" (he added the K and the M with a nice flourish, almost as an afterthought). Then Lindsay Hassett – such a big signature for such a little man. Neil Harvey, Ray Lindwall, Arthur Morris – each written name a splinter of personality. The little blue book was taking on a precious feel.

The next few years brought West Indians and South Africans, as well as a growing awareness that certain cricketers were always away early, while others poured themselves out of the members' bar so late that a boy could be in serious danger of missing the last train home.

Sid Barnes must have mislaid his rubber stamp the day he signed my book, in his own neat hand, and Richie Benaud's name was as legible then as that busy man's is indecipherable today, thousands of repetitions later. After he had failed yet again with the bat, Ken Archer, seeing "Australian opening batsman" printed alongside Morris's signature, said "You'd better write 'Former Australian opener' beside mine!" I even got George Thoms. Remember him? He played Test cricket. Then it was Spot the Oldtimer: Arthur Mailey, Stan McCabe, Duleepsinhji (then High Commissioner for India).

But, as I said, it ended with Ian Craig, and the resumption later on was much more calculating in its nature.

Buying the 1902 Australian team's signatures was like investing in ICI, though the pride of ownership was, I imagine, much richer. The 1936 Indians turned up one Saturday in Portobello Road, on a colourfully decorated sheet of paper which had prompted C.K.Nayudu to write: "Your art is so fine, my best wishes to you in a line" – not as well-measured as his timing with the bat. A Surrey dinner menu displays the signatures of A.P.Herbert alongside A.P.F.Chapman, and Walter Monckton with Jack Hobbs. And hey! There's an F.R.Brown.

If a letter written by David Livingstone recently fetched hundreds of pounds, what is a W.G.Grace letter worth? Or a Jessop? Or a Trumper? How highly valued were they at the time they were written? Certainly nowhere near as much as they are today. And on that principle, letters and signatures have continued to be collected, really for the benefit of future generations.

"Dear Wilkinson, I shall want you tomorrow, we go over by cab, leave my house at 10.15. Can give you a lift if you are here by then. Yours truly, W.G.Grace." What a bother it was for the old man to have to write all these notes to his players. The handwriting gives that away. But what a thrill it was for Wilkinson to receive it. (I'd bet he was at the Grace household on time), and what pleasure the letter has given its owners – or should it be custodians – ever since.

So all this autograph nonsense is really worth the effort, and as if to prove it, some notoriously unsentimental cricketers were carting bats and menus around during the Melbourne Centenary Test, getting them signed until there was barely room for a fly-dropping.

Cricket '79 [Test & County Cricket Board]

Interest in cricket memorabilia grew enormously in the years that followed, some entering the field for love, others as a means of cold-blooded investment. The Cricket Memorabilia Society was formed in 1987, and auction sales and dealerships flourished. The only discernible drawback has been that top cricketers, even though they are now lavishly paid, tend to be suspicious of autograph collectors. They seem to suspect that they make money from the practice, a suspicion justified in some cases. It is still regrettable that most autographs today are barely decipherable – perhaps deliberately so. The moderns would do well to look at some of the elegant signatures of cricketers from previous generations.

In the spring of 1979, after several false starts, I was able to get my own magazine off the ground. Wisden Cricket Monthly was instantly well received, presumably because it was shaped to meet all the expectations of genuine cricket-lovers. The launch coincided with Margaret Thatcher's installation as Britain's first female Prime Minister and also with the "peace" settlement between Packer's World Series Cricket and the established game. The following is an extract from the jubilant founder's first editorial:

Onward and Upward

THE GAME of cricket has left its sick-bed and is taking gentle exercise. By the end of the year it should have regained complete health and attained greater public appeal and financial strength than ever before. The ailment with which it has been afflicted for two years weakened it physically and spiritually, and split its personality. The convalescence will take some time.

The hundreds of thousands of friends and relatives who looked on helplessly while the patient struggled for breath were divided among themselves. Many, indeed, will find it difficult ever to speak to each other again. But, cricket being the essentially friendly, companionable game that it is, the majority of animosities will fast disappear.

What was the one telling medicine? It was the allocation to Channel 9 of Australian Test match exclusive television rights, identified all along as the factor which brought cricket to its knees. When the Australian Cricket Board clung to its traditional arrangement with the Australian Broadcasting Commission in spite of a much higher cash offer from the commercial Channel 9, the die was cast.

Kerry Packer and his associates, having been rejected, harnessed the players' money grievances into a massive enterprise that exploited the public's need for colourful, noisy, glamorous cricket by means of imaginative promotion and – if one can withstand the unrelenting weight of commercials – superb television coverage. Year One was a disaster; Year Two, with much learnt, threw forth glimmers of possibilities. Well may WSC managing director Lynton Taylor have drawn Mr Packer to the telephone midway through a round of golf with Jack Nicklaus to announce that "we've won the war!"

The split has been worldwide. The West Indies Board, with nearly all its players "going commercial", verged on collapse before accepting that some kind of accommodation of World Series was essential. The situation in Pakistan was often thick with intrigue. And in England, of course, open hostilities raged in the High Court and in county committee-rooms as well as on television panel programmes. Reputations were tarnished, some beyond restoration. Cricket continually made the front page – though certainly not because great centuries, hat-tricks or victories were being recorded – for the Revolution was in full swing. As Thomas Paine once said of America, so it could be said of Australia almost 200 years later, that as it "was the only spot in the political world where the principles of universal reformation could begin, so also was it the best in the natural world."

Now the world game is changed. The limitations of the WSC Supertests have been proven and highlighted, for prize-money alone cannot capture the public imagination in the same way as a Test match between nations. On the other hand, floodlit cricket has caught on, the white ball and "transplant" pitches have possibilities, and the scope of multi-camera television coverage has been better exploited.

Test cricket in these stormy months has been weakened by the mainly involuntary exodus of a host of star players; but by way of counter-action a lot of sponsorship money has come into Test cricket. This has been the chief gain. And this is where cricket pauses for a deep breath before entering the 1980s. The game now looks to the working committee to protect its interests. There must be no sell-out. This is a golden opportunity to blend the best of both species.

Wisden Cricket Monthly, Volume 1 Number 1, June 1979

Soon there was another controversy, though minuscule in comparison to the Packer storm. The shocked editorial closed with an almost psychic prediction which two of the Chappell brothers were to fulfil within two years in a scandalous finish to Australia's one-day international against New Zealand at Melbourne:

Rash Rose

PERHAPS IT was inevitable. Perhaps it even *needed* to happen. A team has gone for the money with a blunt singlemindedness that left spectators shocked and horrified and the cricket world at large outraged and disgusted. On Thursday, May 24, Somerset's captain, Brian Rose, declared his side's innings closed after one over (one run – a no-ball – without loss) in the Benson & Hedges Cup match against Worcestershire at Worcester. The home side then proceeded to score two runs off ten balls to win by ten wickets. Somerset's calculation was that, although the match was lost, their favourable wicket-taking rate throughout the zonal matches was preserved and would see them through to the quarter-finals in the event of a three-way tie on points with Worcestershire and Glamorgan in Group A. As it happened, Glamorgan's match against Minor Counties South at Watford was ruined by the weather, leaving Somerset and Worcestershire to go through with nine points each. Meanwhile, at Worcester, after the 18-minute fiasco, gate-money was refunded to the angry and disillusioned spectators and the Somerset players made a hasty exit!

But the matter was not going to be left there. After an emergency meeting of Somerset officials the following day, when Rose was exonerated, an emergency meeting of the TCCB Disciplinary Committee was set down for June 1. The chairman happened to be Ossie Wheatley, who is also chairman of the aggrieved Glamorgan. The views of the controlling body were soon made known, however, and in decisive fashion. By a majority of 17-1 (Derbyshire's the sole vote against) Essex's motion, seconded by Lancashire, to expel Somerset from this year's B&H competition and to allow Glamorgan into the quarter-finals was carried.

"CYNICISM" IS a word often used during debates on modern sport. I have been waiting, with trepidation, for the moment when, with six runs needed off the final ball and a lot of money at stake, the bowler informs the umpire of a change of action and rolls the ball along the ground. Maybe this dreadful vision will now vanish. The "Rose Affair" has sent shock-waves through the game, possibly restoring sanity.

Wisden Cricket Monthly, July 1979

That last conjecture was to prove ill-founded. Cricketers found more and more ways to bend the Laws and the spirit of the game as the years passed. I never subsequently thought to ask Greg or Trevor Chappell, perpetrators of the underhand outrage at Melbourne on February 1, 1982, whether they had read that editorial.

Thommo

I FIRST laid eyes on Jeffrey Robert Thomson at a reception to the 1975 Australian touring team at Australia House, London. There he was, in the corner of the room, tall and clean-cut, wearing a caramel-coloured suit, gazing towards the chandeliers, sucking his teeth, obviously as bored as a rock'n'roller at a string quartet recital. The dark-suited gentlemen gathered around him put their mainly banal questions, and sometimes got a "Yeah" by way of response. I think it was his mate and comrade-in-homicide, Dennis Lillee, who rescued him, and he was more at home with his mates. They formed a kind of pack, a protective formation, tribal, defiant, very self-satisfied.

He has seen a fair bit of the world since then, but has changed little. Less hesitant in a gathering, certainly, and not the complete reprobate. Certain responsibilities have come his way, some to stay, others short-lived. In the mid-seventies he was busy not only mowing down Poms but mowing down females as well. Melbourne *Truth* in February 1975 rated him cricket's Alvin Purple, quoting him as saying: "When we go on tour we usually have a few beers at night and I often get hold of a

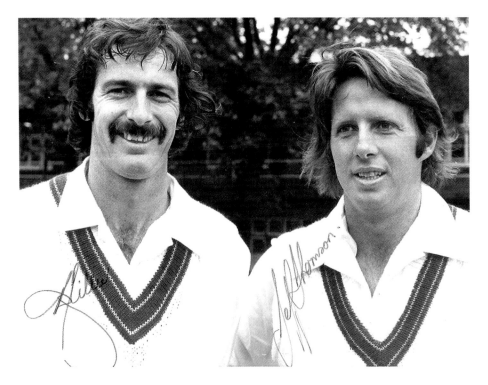

The terror twins, Dennis Lillee (left) and Jeff Thomson.

bird or two. I choose the good-looking ones." The only single man in the Australian side at that time, he was able to claim: "I've taken out some real dolls, like beach beauties and models. They're the best."

Now all that has changed. He married one of those pretty models, Cheryl Wilson, on December 18, 1976, at Holy Trinity Church, Valley, Brisbane. He couldn't recall the church, but said it was opposite Valley Police Station. The great fast bowler of earlier days, Ray Lindwall, now a Brisbane florist, supplied some of the flowers.

Earlier that same year Thommo was being put across as the playboy of the cricket world. Whichever ghost-writer of his it was saw fit to have him saying: "I don't try to be Joe Blow the superstud – it just happens. But I don't let it get the better of me and reach the stage where my bowling is affected. No sir, everything in order."

His name was once linked with the daughter of a prominent Australian politician, which tensed him up somewhat when he found out. And in England he was once the target not only for countless approaches by girls, but by a lady journalist who concealed her profession and intentions if little else. The team closed ranks, pooling their intelligence to prevent such infiltration.

Still they came, "all shapes and sizes with just one thing in common – they wanted my body". He was engaged twice and in 1976 he was expecting an English lass to join him in Australia. Of all things, she had been studying Law at Oxford.

Then there was the homesickness on that first tour. Articles under his name appeared during the tour of England in 1975, and brought a risk of his being sent home. Fred Bennett, the manager, had to spell it out for him. Ian Chappell, toughest and most forthright of captains, threatened that if Thommo was told to pack his bags and go home, he would do so too. It died the death. As, eventually, did the homesickness.

His attitude to sport is honest. He wants to be best and to win. He likes to laugh. He doesn't believe in backbiting – though when stung he can be unforgiving. He is even slightly old-fashioned in some of his attitudes and some of his expressions. This springs from being a home-loving boy with uncomplicated, caring, loving parents and three elder brothers and one younger. He is not ambitious, except to escape life's economic pressures. He loves the sea and the open land, and can admire a cloud formation with schoolboy wonder. But above all, he has brought to the game of cricket a most glorious bowling action that, fortunately for generations to come, has been captured over and over on film and videotape. If only we could sit back and savour now Tibby Cotter and Tom Richardson in action, hurling them down at MacLaren and Trumper at the turn of the century.

Thommo: Jeff Thomson, the World's Fastest Bowler (Angus & Robertson, 1980)

The centenary of the birth of Herbert Strudwick came in January 1980, and it was a pleasure to honour his sixty years of service to Surrey as well as his friendly nature:

Struddy's Century

THERE SEEMED to be every probability that Herbert Strudwick would become the first Test cricketer to reach 100 years of age. Admittedly, down the coast near Bournemouth was Wilfred Rhodes, then ninety-two. But Wilfred, seemingly content in his darkness, was frail – so obviously old in frame and rasping voice. "Struddy", though ninety, had a boyishness about him and an alertness that perhaps is inborn with Test wicketkeepers. Bert Oldfield was as animated as a sparrow even in his seventies.

Then, one evening in 1970, news came through that Struddy had died. Anyone who had spent anything from an hour to a lifetime with him knew he had lost a friend, a true little gentleman.

He was not a "gentleman" in the sense that he was unpaid, of course. He was a professional, albeit one who always enjoyed playing. You would need to enjoy it if the pay was £1 per week, the terms he accepted when he left his father's firm to join Surrey in 1898. Then began sixty years of memory-collecting, starting with the recollections of injuries caused by leg-spinner Len Braund's fast ball and the exhilaration of keeping to Tom Richardson (past his best but still able to slide a fast ball from outside off stump down towards leg slip).

There were three other wicketkeepers on the Oval staff around that time, which persuaded Herbert Strudwick to weather injuries silently, lest he be replaced only to find his position gone forever. The early days were a battle all right, with people like Tom Hayward snubbing him at every opportunity and hardly anybody thinking personal introductions were worthwhile. But within a few seasons the diminutive chap from Mitcham was earning himself a deep if unobtrusive popularity among team-mates and opponents, and friendships were formed for life, none stronger than with Jack Hobbs, three years Struddy's junior. Half-a-century later, in retirement, and both living near Brighton, they were to enjoy each other's company on the golf-course, away from the heat and clamour of their cricketing years.

I used to visit Struddy at Shoreham often during the 1960s. Out would come the photo albums, on would go the kettle, and every cricket name tossed onto the fireside table evoked a cluster of reminiscences. He went with P.F.Warner's MCC team to Australia in 1903-04, deputy to Dick Lilley, and though he did not play in a Test match, he did take *three* catches as substitute fielder in Australia's first innings of the second Test, at Melbourne. He was still capable of a genuine wince as he recalled standing at silly point to the mighty Trumper.

And on the voyage he indulged in some mischief by banging on the cabin window beyond which relaxed Plum Warner and his fiancée. A startled MCC captain flung back the curtain but never did discover the perpetrator of the little jest.

A thrill during that Australian tour, the first of four, was meeting the great Australian 'keeper Jack Blackham, who gave him words of encouragement. It was eight years before he returned, and then as second choice to "Tiger" Smith, who was favoured after the first Test because of his familiarity with Warwickshire's fast left-arm swing bowler Frank Foster. Not until after the First World War was Struddy to become a familiar figure behind the sticks for England in Australia.

Then he kept in the thankless 1920-21 series (standing down to give Arthur Dolphin a cap in the fourth Test) and in all five Tests in the gruelling 1924-25 series. In those nine Tests he held 28 catches and made four stumpings. The toil led to a rich reward in 1926 when England at last broke through the post-war hardships to win the Ashes at his beloved Oval, a Test match that was destined to be the last of his 28. He was then, amazing to relate, forty-six years of age. The following season was his last with Surrey . . . as a player, that is. He kept the scorebook for a further thirty years, one of his most fatiguing but pleasurable tasks being the recording of Len Hutton's innings of 364 against Australia in 1938.

In first-class cricket he made 1493 dismissals, and those gnarled fingers showed it. John Murray now has that world record, with 1527, and Bob Taylor could climb to the top given two or three more seasons*. Struddy would have been the first to offer congratulations.

He never condemned the modern game: there might have been the occasional factual comment such as that in *Wisden* 1959: "In my time the batsmen found it easier to score faster." In his early days there was often no fine leg, and he willingly did a lot of chasing, remembering with delight how the crowds had cheered the little padded figure as he scuttled after the ball. Neville Cardus, presumably seriously, once described him as one of the best outfielders in the land! Nor did Struddy lose sight of the deterioration of pitches over the years, which, as all players know, controls the quality of the play.

Only with the greatest reluctance would he stand back to fast bowling, but he could not find it in himself to condemn the safety-first methods of post-war years which have been forced as much as anything by the change of direction of the bowling, towards the batsman's pads. But he did keep to some tearaway pacemen and in days of uncovered wickets there were some awkward surfaces about. They only served to stimulate the pro's pride in his work.

And never was Struddy's pride tested more than in South Africa in 1913-14, when S.F.Barnes took 49 wickets in four Tests. His astonishing skill and the matting wickets made batting a nightmare – as was keeping wicket to him. Struddy's 21 wickets in the series included 10 catches and three stumpings off Barnes.

His two tours there produced a fund of memories, not all of them pleasant. He contracted malaria, swallowed half a cockroach, was in a car crash, and also found himself at the reins of a runaway coach and four.

Perhaps this is what makes an old cricketer's later years so bearable – the storehouse of experiences, dramatic to a greater or lesser degree. To think that a dozen years ago it was possible to talk with Barnes and Rhodes and Woolley and Tiger Smith – and Herbert Strudwick. Now they are all gone. I expect to be in Adelaide on January 28, but I shall remember Struddy that day, even if he is not "100 *not out*".

* He did. The popular Taylor finished with a colossal 1649, a mark unlikely ever to be overtaken.

Wisden Cricket Monthly, January 1980

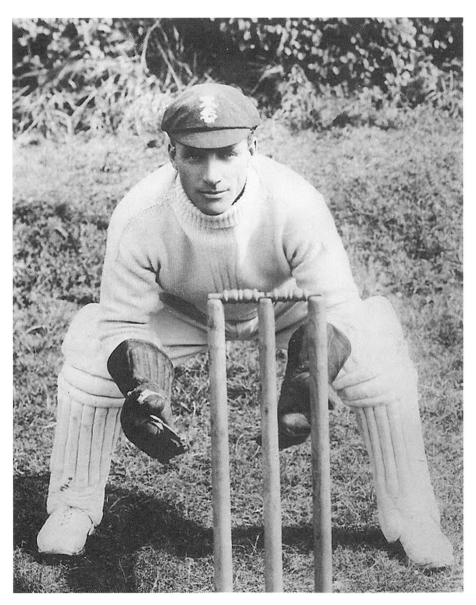

Sweet-natured Struddy: standing up at the stumps to all but the very fastest bowling.

As the 1980s unfolded it began to seem that cricket would always be burdened by problems, most of them avoidable. But the duty of all cricket writers who loved the game was to protest loudly – in the vain hope that those charged with the running of the game would listen:

Trouble at the Studio

THE TROUBLE with the Ian Chappells and Dennis Lillees of this world is that they are prone to misbehaviour on the set, like latterday James Deans. The trouble with the Australian Cricket Board is that, like several of the Hollywood producers, they are prepared to turn if not a blind then a myopic eye. Anything so long as the show goes on.

Chappell's second misdemeanour (the first cost him a three-week suspension for swearing at an umpire) brought him only a suspended six-week "sentence" and a reprimand. Lillee's "tin bat" fiasco prompted a similar reaction from the Board. Both, it seems, are vital to the success – box-office and otherwise – of the complex 1979-80 international season. It matters little – if one is to interpret the Board's attitude literally – that an umpire has been challenged by a player (in Rugby League, where the referee is still respected, the player would have had an "early bath") or that play in a Test match has been interrupted for over ten minutes because a player, with Christmas approaching, wished to promote a new product. Lillee may have had his point: the Laws as they stood did not forbid a non-timber bat, though if his aluminium weapon was damaging the ball, the umpires were right to intervene after Mike Brearley's objection. But, being a highly-strung gentleman, Lillee reacted somewhat dramatically.

Some viewers and spectators were incensed. They would rather have been watching some cricket, not a pantomime. Others enjoyed it: it was different, something to talk about, tell their children about. And that was where the greatest danger lay. Those of us who are convinced of the maturity of our make-up have fixed opinions, can define our right and our wrong, and fancy that we have established our own moral codes. Not so the youngsters. Any boy looking at the Lillee spectacle must have thought it was all an acceptable part of the showbiz into which cricket is being transformed. And when that boy learned a fortnight later that the Australian fast bowler got off with just a wagging of adminstration's forefinger, he must have felt that truly we do live in a "free world".

In an age when prison sentences have become more lenient and do-gooders abound, counter-reaction has come in the shape of finance. Footballers have at last been "tamed" by the threat of severe cash penalties for on-field transgressions. Perhaps the Australian Cricket Board should have shown the way here.

Instead, the studio stars have had their tantrums, the producer has bitten through his cigar, but the show goes on. The fast bowling and batting of those spared will have to be of a very high quality to justify the reprieves. Though early attempts have already been made to win them, the Oscars have yet to be awarded.

ENGLAND-AUSTRALIA Test matches have been, for so very many of us, the *crème de la crème* of cricket, the emotional high point that used to come every fourth summer, with nocturnal radio narrative from afar between whiles. The advent of exciting new names and the return of old favourites revived that familiar feeling just when impatience was getting the better of us. Frequently was uttered the complaint that the Grand Combat should be staged more often than was traditionally the case.

The five-year gap between the 1948 and 1953 series and the 1956 and 1961 series seemed interminable.

Then, in the 1970s, the frequency was increased. From 25 England v Australia Tests in the 1950s and again in the 1960s, we have had 34 in the 1970s (excluding the two this winter in the New Year). The three six-match series in Australia, plus the Centenary Test, have contributed to this increase, and in Australia, because of the introduction of Perth as a Test venue and the reluctance to abandon the traditional sharing of three Tests between Melbourne and Sydney, the six-Test schedule is unlikely to alter.

Now we have the decision to stage six England-Australia Tests in England for the first time in 1981. The Anglo-Aussies should be in their seventh Heaven.

But there are serious misgivings, for the golden goose is at risk – in danger of passing out with exhaustion from multiple birth. The golden egg is tempting; domestic first-class cricket is financially anaemic; the money comes in for limited-overs cricket and Test cricket involving England, Australia and West Indies. That is why the one-day game has proliferated, and that is why the temptation to protect Test cricket by widening the projection of it has been accepted as a counter-reaction.

The risk is there for all to see. While quality can hardly be controlled, quantity has been the prime consideration. Consider how the "box office" West Indians have been heavily scheduled almost to the point of exhaustion. Consider how the Indians have been sent into the field over twice as often in modern times as before. Consider what a Test match means now: it is a common event, lacking the special freshness of the annual Wimbledon tennis tournament or a Wembley football cup final.

An obvious danger is that an ill-matched series will drain of interest long before the sixth match. Many of us in Australia last winter wondered what point there was in being in Sydney as the sixth Test got under way. Even the finances of that match were slim justification.

Shaw (George Bernard, not Alfred) put his finger on it when he wrote, "It's just as unpleasant to get more than you bargain for than to get less." Test cricket must not only be protected against gimmickry; it must be saved from over-indulgence.

Wisden Cricket Monthly, February 1980

So much for wishing, warning and hoping. The greed factor simply ballooned with each passing year, and as more countries were elevated to Test status, the calendar became ludicrously cluttered. With the additional limited-overs tournaments dreamed up by the money men, with Twenty/20 cricket adding to the cash frenzy, the blissful days of leisurely Test tours became a remote memory.

But there continued to be much fun and interest around the cricket world, not least when we brought together a Wisden readers group for a tour of Australia – a journey that came close to being the last for all of us:

Wisden on Tour

WE WERE off to the cricket – not a drive up the A3 or ten stops down the railway line, but 12,000 miles by air, through half-a-dozen countries and two nights, from frost to heat, English darkness to Australian light. The *Wisden* party came from all parts to Heathrow. Only Bob Berry of Lancashire and England failed to show. Small our group may have been, but it was compatibility that mattered.

There was an unreality about it so early on a midwinter morning. Amsterdam brought no relief. It was foggy, grey, uninviting. All of Europe was; and by Athens dusk had descended. While we watched *The Champ* on the screen, Frank Keating of *The Guardian*, having borrowed D.H.Lawrence's *Kangaroo*, duly became that novel's latest victim and sank into a blissful, much-needed sleep.

Seconds before touching down at night in a vicious storm over Bali the pilot suddenly found himself in total darkness as lightning fused all the lights of the airport, including those marking the runway. He throttled and just cleared the short runway. Two further approaches, and we made it, the necessary reversal of power blowing a valve in the port engine. We gave the aircrew a spontaneous round of applause for their perseverance and skill before drying the palms of our hands. The nervous jokes turned to nervous laughter; the *Wisden* group skipped plans to harmonise in *Abide with Me*; and in the transit lounge Keating's gin concoction was unusually popular.*

Dawn light brought shadowy visions of Central Australia, and breakfast smells preceded sunlit Sydney. But the news for English travellers was mournful: Greg Chappell had steered Australia to victory in the second Test and the Ashes were lost – or so claimed Chappell and some of the newspapers.**

We paid our respects to the touring team at their hotel. Bob Willis was relaxed by the pool; Graham Gooch nodded in the rising heat; Ian Botham appeared to be trying to drown his two toddlers; David Gower enquired if he was still on the *WCM* Editorial Board after sending nothing for publication last month.

After the one-day wash-out, the happy band headed for Sydney: 450 miles in sixty minutes – "Just like a bus ride," proclaimed one of us, nerve restored. Torrential rain threatened the match, yet it started promptly and our tourists got their moneysworth with a thrilling English victory. For those new to floodlit cricket the impact was favourable, though nobody at the SCG that evening could have relished the blaring pop music in the interval. Sign language was useful. John Paul Young, next time round, was more acceptable. Lasting images are of the army of seagulls which actually moved in with the bowler, and perhaps the final sight of Jeff Thomson in action.***

England were outclassed in the second final (odd expression, that), poor Goochie again being denied as he tried to amuse everyone at the end with his bowling impressions. Greenidge did nothing to slip from the highest esteem.

By now the message was clear. The West Indians were the Australian cricket-followers' pets. They had regained their charisma and winning ways of two years earlier when under World Series colours. It mattered little that they beat Australia. There was only one team Australia had to beat *at all costs*, and that was England. Mike Brearley was the villain, despised for all manner of real and imagined defects. He'd had the match regulations changed to suit his side, he wasn't Test class, he'd expressed his distaste for Australian spectators. The greater pity of it was that the rest of the team automatically felt the unreasonable hostility – harmless Gooch, cheery Bairstow, inoffensive Willey and all. Most of the booing, of course, was schoolboyish – even if the instruments of the noise were mainly sixteen stone – the mindlessness of a mob. But some of it was passionately sincere and concentrated, fired by resentment and revenge.

Adelaide is just the place to visit when things are getting on top of you: all was cleanliness, space, light and innocence. There was also wild anticipation before the Test match – to be won by Clive Lloyd and his unstoppables, a punishing postscript to the Australia Day celebrations.

The *WCM* group continued to "do their own thing". The Barossa Valley, Henley

Beach, the Torrens, the Art Gallery, the shops all beckoned. For Frith and wife the supreme pleasure was an evening with the Bradmans. Sir Don and his charming Jessie, in the home they have dwelt in through triumph and setback for close to half-a-century, are wonderful hosts. So much was packed into the hours either side of dinner – a journey through scrapbooks and cricket talk ranging into a hundred areas. In the billiard room was a row of brown bats which had written chapters of history: 452 not out, 340 not out, 334, and the first of DGB's 29 Test hundreds. Was this really the small, smiling god of the 1930s, the most familiar of Australian sporting faces? It was – and it was also one in the morning, so Sir Don drove us back to the hotel, and there was a consequent loss of reality about the next day's play in the Test match.

Now back to Melbourne, where our tour started: again the boisterous cauldron of the MCG, the precious last hours of genuine sun-warmth before the flight to the Northern Hemisphere, attention split between on-field events like Gooch's emotional execution at 99, the magnificence of Lillee, and the restoration of Ian Chappell, and the wry press-box wisdom of Bill O'Reilly and Jack Fingleton; the gentle courtesy too of Ray Robinson, whimsical and conscientious as ever.

Goodbye to the punch-drunk world of Australian cricket with its top-heavy programme; goodbye to the innocence and abandon of Australian life. *Wisden's* first venture into travel had been a sweet success – worth all the pain of the sight of cold, grey, damp London as Qantas gently put us down.

* After the emergency landing and after the cheering and clapping had subsided, Keating's fellow passenger, an elderly Yorkshireman, turned to him and solemnly asked if he thought Boycott would stay with the county club, an astonishing piece of *sang froid*.
** The English authorities had asserted that since the 1979-80 series had been hastily arranged following the settlement between the establishment and World Series, and since there were to be only three Tests, the Ashes would not be at stake. This claim was rubbished by most cricket fans in both countries.
*** Unduly pessimistic: Thommo was around for several years afterwards.

Wisden Cricket Monthly, March 1980

Clarrie Grimmett – Slowie Supreme

IN THE corner shop near our home in a suburb of Sydney there hung a poster. It mesmerised me. Mum sent me weekly for sugar or potatoes or something else that in the early 1950s used to be weighed from bulk bins and did not come pre-wrapped in plastic. There on the wall, curling at the corners, was the poster – or it may have been a calendar – the multiple photographs of a wizened little man pointing his wrist towards the camera, holding a cricket ball this way and that, always with a sly grin, always with his large cap pressed down over his creased-up eyes. He was Clarrie Grimmett, long abandoned by the first-class game but still, by the suggestion of craft and mystique, capable of sending a youngster running back from the shop to grab a tennis ball and send it spinning haphazardly all over the empty, dusty street.

Grimmett's influence on the thousands who watched him and later read about him was profound and secure for all time, especially in days of spin drought. Now, slow wrist bowlers are a threatened species. Then, Grimmett was one of many – but unmatched in skill and temperament. He became, quite simply, a legend, and unlike Arthur Mailey, who spun with gay abandon, he would have prospered today, given that selectors and captains did the right thing by him. He was wonderfully accurate because he was endowed with that special physical co-ordination without which not even endless practice can turn into international class. It so happened that he did also practise endlessly.

Bowling to a marked area in his backyard, with a fox terrier to fetch the ball (and who apparently could also count to six), he *made* himself as accurate as a machine, and he mastered the variations of spin bowling, never believing that he knew it all. After the standard leg-break, top-spinner and googly there came the "flipper" – which took several years to perfect, and which, when batsmen tried to discern by the snap of his fingers, he smokescreened by snapping the fingers of his left hand as he released a leg-break – and beyond that, well on in years, further experimentation: truly the Barnes Wallis of the cricket world.

He was as representative of Australia and her cricket as was Chips Rafferty of the men of the bush. Yet Grimmett was born in New Zealand. He spun his way into the world on Christmas Day 1891 (confessing to me in a letter in 1972 that it was a year earlier than shown in cricket records). Practising assiduously at the Basin Reserve, he first attracted attention at fifteen when he took 6 for 5 and 8 for 1 for Wellington Schools. He was playing Plunket Shield at seventeen. He was named as emergency for Reese's side which toured Australia in 1913-14, but no SOS came. So he decided to try his luck alone, and crossed the Tasman the year the Kaiser's War broke out. There followed three happy years of club cricket in Sydney.

During this period he was once stopped in his tracks by M.A.Noble, his captain. "D'you think you're the only one playing in this game?" said the great man. Clarrie was taken aback. He asked how he had offended. "Don't you know there is a bowler on at the other end?" pursued Noble. "Yes," said Clarrie, "but what's that to do with me?" He was told that the fast bowler at the other end hardly had time to put his sweater on before he had to take it off again. The little chap was taking only 1½ minutes to bowl a six-ball over. He was instructed henceforth to wait down the pitch and to walk back more slowly to his mark. How proud Noble would be today to see the doctrine so widely accepted.

Grimmett, a signwriter by trade, followed the signposts to Melbourne next, where former Test bowler J.V.Saunders gave him sound guidance. Soon he managed to find a place in the Sheffield Shield side. But the glow of his future shone from Adelaide, even though he finished with an 8 for 81 for Victoria. In February 1925, at thirty-three, he won the first of his 37 Test caps. In that Sydney Test his figures were 5 for 45 and 6 for 37, his victims including Hobbs, Sandham, Woolley, Hendren, Hearne, Whysall and Kilner. Woolley, with a crowd of 40,000 looking on, was his first Test wicket, bowled by a wrong'un.

Eleven years later at Durban, van der Merwe was his 216th and last, in a Test in which he took 13 wickets. He was a very unlucky man not to have been given further international appearances.

As it was, he averaged exactly six wickets per Test (he didn't bowl in the Melbourne Test against South Africa in February 1932), with a striking rate of a wicket every 67 balls and an average cost of a mere 2.16 runs per six-ball over. There were some great batsmen around in those days, and some heartbreaking (for bowlers) pitches. Grimmett's rewards were earned by canniness and hard work. Often enough he got Hammond and Bradman out, and never did he bowl mechanically. The straight or barely-breaking ball was a main weapon, gaining him a high proportion of lbws. When the wicket was unresponsive he roundarmed to a teasing length, often at the leg stump; he could use looping, swerving flight quite as cleverly as "Tich" Freeman, dropping the ball two feet short of the batsman's expectation; he closely

Clarrie Grimmett, first to 200 Test wickets and cut off in his prime when forty-five.

analysed the opposition man by man, as if he were a demolition contractor, though their downfall he executed by guile, not violence.

His 29 wickets in England in the 1930 series were a record, and it is accepted that his bowling was at least as important to Australia as was Bradman's phenomenal batting (he took 144 wickets at 16.85 on the tour). In each of the next two home series – against West Indies and South Africa – he gathered 33 wickets. Highly effective in England again in 1934, he took 25 more (O'Reilly 28), and in 1935-36 he set a record for Australia which still stands of 44 wickets against South Africa. He crowned his career with his 200th Test wicket in that sensational rubber, the first bowler to do so, but at forty-four he was considered by some to be too old for further service. He himself had always been conscious of his weight of years; indeed, he and his cap were almost inseparable, lest his baldness be taken too seriously (shades of Arthur Shrewsbury).

He was aggrieved at being shelved, and the premature breaking-up of the destructive spin partnership of Grimmett and O'Reilly almost certainly weakened Australia in the few seasons remaining before the war. But still there was Sheffield Shield cricket, and in 1939-40 Clarrie showed 'em with 73 first-class wickets, lifting his Shield total to a record 513. So he was still very functional at forty-eight.

He was also very affable almost forty years later, when, at the Centenary Test in Melbourne, where he made one of his last public appearances, moving very slowly, bent over his walking-stick, the fragile old hero remembered his 10 for 37 against Yorkshire in 1930, still one of only three all-tens by Australians in England (the others were spinners too: Bill Howell and Arthur Mailcy). Hallowed still in his memory was the strokeplay of Stan McCabe.

He thought deeply about the game all his life, and wrote one of the finest of coaching manuals in *Getting Wickets*, which should be reissued and distributed to every school and club in these monotonous times of pace, pace and more pace. Towards the end Clarrie Grimmett was touched by despair at the dearth of spin bowling. Ever ready to pass on advice, he hated to see the art at which he had been a master gradually fading to obscurity. In 1930 he met B.J.T.Bosanquet, who brought the googly to prominence and acceptability. "Am I responsible for you?" the inventor said kindly to his Antipodean successor. The dynasty of wrist-spin seems to have lasted no more than three-quarters of a century.

He had more than the average share of nicknames, marks of respect and affection: "Scarlet", "Grum", "The Gnome", "The Fox". He was the "miser" against Mailey's "millionaire", but there was nothing mean about Grimmett, except that he bowled a strict length, and was only once in his life called for a no-ball.

The corner shop's closed now, the poster disappeared years ago, and Grimmett is no more. His old team-mates Bradman, Pellew, O'Reilly, Darling and Fingleton were at his funeral. No moderns. Luckily I've got one of those pre-war flicker books, and I can see The Fox bowl his googly – six times in 1½ minutes if the timing is right. Might take it to the Test matches this summer and flick it through as the fast bowlers tramp back to their marks.

Sufficient to say that cricket owes a mighty debt to the schoolmaster in New Zealand who forbade the infant Grimmett to bowl fast and instead insisted that he develop his spinners.

Wisden Cricket Monthly, July 1980

It was to be some years before a noisy blond from Melbourne – Shane Warne – emerged to become leg-spin's salvation and inspiration.

Three years on from the monumental Test centenary celebrations in Melbourne, it was England's turn. The Oval, where the 1880 Test had been played, was not thought fit for the celebratory Test match one hundred years later. With many functions accompanying the event, Lord's staged what turned out to be a somewhat blighted Test match:

The Ha'porth of Tar

THE PARTY'S over, and, to be honest, it didn't go all that well. Comparisons between the 1980 Centenary Test match and the 1977 celebrations in Melbourne are not likely to prove constructive, but remain inevitable. Much effort was put into both undertakings. But the weather was bad this time, and the ranks of distinguished guests were depleted by illness. It was probably all part of the retribution from "above" for the appropriation by Lord's of an Oval occasion!

The determination to enjoy cricket's great birthday party was evident from the start, but rudely strained on the Saturday when play was delayed until 3.45pm on a warm, sunny afternoon and excesses in the Lord's members' area brought shame upon the time-honoured Marylebone Cricket Club. The umpires and captains were jostled as frustration got the better of an unrestrained minority, collapsing any concept that violence lurks only in the "outer".

Patience was stretched to breaking point as one ground inspection followed another, and anger festered at the realisations that the square had not been adequately covered and the umpires [Dickie Bird and David Constant] were prepared only to play utterly safe and cautious on the matter of footholds. Further, the captains [Ian Botham and Greg Chappell] were not pressing for a resumption, though certain officers of the TCCB were applying behind-the-scenes pressure. It looked like throwing up a repetition of the 1879 fracas at Sydney, when Lord Harris was among those to be assaulted by a mob in foment. This was not quite the event any of us sought to celebrate.

The root problem was a lack of protection at the lower end of the square, where two club finals had recently been staged. This was the ha'porth of tar for whose lack the ship went down. The responsibility will lie heavily upon the souls of those whose oversight or negligence it was. If there be one small saving aspect it is that, with the eyes of the world upon this would-be extravaganza, the vexed question of ground protection came to a head as never before. If it leads to more inspired care and recovery of our constantly-saturated cricket grounds it will almost have been worthwhile.

OFF THE field, there was much to enthrall. At the Lord's Taverners dinner John Warr, in the course of a witty address, lamented that his only Test victim, Ian Johnson, hadn't come over! Bill O'Reilly, who had worked tensely for hours on his reply, asked for forgiveness that it was he and not Sir Donald Bradman ("the best cricketer ever to set foot on a cricket ground") who was speaking for the Australian guests.

"The Tiger" claimed that Old Father Time on the Grandstand at Lord's caught sight of him and said, as he sharpened his scythe, "Hello, you're back again son. What have you got to say?" Bill grumbled about the 1937 change in the lbw law: "No-one asked us bowlers. I've always resented it." "So have I," said Father Time, "and we must get back to the old law." "Give me enough time," begged Bill, "and we shall!"

Special toasts were drunk to The Don and to Harold Larwood, who was laid low by the ubiquitous virus for much of the week, O'Reilly stating with a grin: "Lol belongs to *us*, no matter what you Englishmen think. You've got no hope of ever getting him back."

The Anglo-Australian spirit burned bright again at the TCCB dinner, when Bob Parish presented, on behalf of the Australian Cricket Board, a silver figure of a kangaroo backed by a silver tray engraved with the signatures of 101 guests. Colin Cowdrey in turn spoke of the bond of friendship begun in Melbourne three years earlier. "It is here with us today. We need each other."

AT LORD'S, the Q Stand enclosure was a hive of activity as players from several generations – those game enough to wear their badges – signed books and bats galore. It was a classic game of identification as well as recollection. Larwood and Lindwall, greatest of fast bowlers, missed most of it through illness, but Bill Ponsford sat quietly with his son throughout, his memory stretching back further than half-a-century. Bill Brown, who carried his bat for a double-century in a Lord's Test, sat almost unnoticed, as did Ted a'Beckett of the 1930 touring side and Len Darling, Jack Badcock and Arthur Chipperfield, 1934. Bob Massie took it all in quietly, eight years after sensationally taking 16 wickets at Lord's in his Test debut. Arthur Morris looked hardly a day older than when he opened in 1948. Jack Fingleton hid under a cloth cap, Alan Davidson under a head of grey hair, still fighting the virus.

If one man typified the fierce resolution to enjoy the Centenary – he might almost have been trying *too* hard, self defeatingly – it was Dennis Lillee, who seemed burdened by the knowledge that he was unlikely to see the Bicentenary. He even refuted the possibility that he would be at the 150th anniversary celebrations, when, at eighty-one, he would still be younger than this year's senior visitor, "Stork" Hendry (eighty-five).

England's oldest were Andrew Sandham (ninety) and Percy Fender (eighty-eight). And others seldom seen made appearances: Hollies, Wright, Dollery, Dewes, "Nobby" Clark, Hardstaff, Prideaux, Cranston, Loader, Watson, Tattersall, the king-sized Lock – all entrenched in the annals of England-Australia. Unique it was; stunning, too, in the nostalgic power of it all, the great figures reminding us not only of their achievements but of days when we ourselves were younger. On top of all was John Arlott's hard-to-bear farewell.

Pity about the Saturday fiasco.

Wisden Cricket Monthly, October 1980

Soon it was time to go in to bat on behalf of Sir Donald Bradman, who had been the target of some particularly unpleasant remarks in the fashionable English newspaper columns, smears to which he would never personally respond:

Fleet Street Below the Belt

AUGUST 27 was the seventy-second birthday of Sir Donald Bradman, the greatest rungetter in cricket history. It was also the day on which one of Fleet Street's most colourful and polished sportswriters chose to discredit him – through the expressed opinions of nameless contemporaries – in a rather tasteless rebuke for his absence from the Test Centenary gathering in London. "His contemporaries shake their heads," wrote Ian Wooldridge in the *Daily Mail*, "implying that The Don . . . is averse to sharing anything, limelight not excluded."

Then came an analogy with "Patton's lust for glory", and a "re-enactment" of Keith Miller's "deliberate" duck at Southend in 1948, when the Australians made 721 runs in a day against Essex.

On the facing page of this issue will be seen a list of seventy-seven players missing from the Test Centenary photograph. Among them were fourteen who were unable or unwilling to travel from Australia and fourteen Englishmen who were also absent from the celebrations from start to finish. But Bradman was singled out for criticism, as he has been for half-a-century for such misdemeanours as receiving presents from admirers that he did not put into a players' pool, for travelling separately at times, and for keeping his own company. A big and not very attractive club could be formed by disgruntled journalists who have sought and been refused an interview. For many of them, notwithstanding their apparently A1 powers of imagination, it has clearly been impossible to visualise what it must be like to be the most sought-after.

Perhaps an explanation is in order. Sir Donald Bradman has approached the autumn of his life with the same degree of meticulous organisation he has shown as boy, batsman, captain and businessman. He has gently wound down his affairs. He has been troubled by physical ailments, some merely irritating, like the knee which hampers his golf, some of acute concern, such as diverticulitis. The health of his son and daughter has been a constant source of anxiety. But even above and beyond that has been the ill-health of his wife, Jessie, who has miraculously survived open-heart surgery and periodic relapses in recent years.

Few couples have been as devoted as this during their forty-eight years of marriage. Earlier this year Lady Bradman was eager to journey to England with her husband for the Centenary celebrations. The trip could only have been conducted in conditions of near-total privacy, and there would have been mutual anxiety throughout, whether together or separated. The prospect militated decisively against the venture. That is why there was no Bradman at Lord's. It had nothing to do with glory. He has had his share of that. He has frequently been slated for shunning it.

As for Miller's personal protest at Southend, Bradman could hardly have ordered him to put down his playing cards and go to the wicket, for he himself was batting at the time, entertaining the 15,000 crowd hugely with an innings of 187 in just over two hours – his only innings against Essex in four tours of England. Miller, who would hardly have been playing cards in the dressing-room if his captain had been present, lost his off stump to a ball from Trevor Bailey which Robertson-Glasgow described as "a very good ball". Moreover, he needed some runs, having made only 36 in two weeks.

No appetite for the slaughter? There can be nobody who knows anything about Keith Miller who doesn't admire him enormously as cricketer and man. But when the fancy took him he could kill bowlers with the best of them. Only a fortnight earlier he had mauled Leicestershire with 202 not out. On the next tour of England he scored 220 not out against Worcestershire and 262 not out off the mighty Combined Services. And in the famous 1948 Essex match he did his bit in dismembering the county with 3 for 14 at the start of their first innings. The match was over by the second evening.

It has been said often before; we say it again: Don Bradman scored far too many runs for the comfort of some.

Michael Parkinson had his two penn'orth in the *Sunday Times* a week or so before the Centenary Test, again relying with avid receptiveness on the distorted memories of others. This time the inference was that Bradman cheated at Leeds in 1930, when he made 334. Duckworth is supposed to have caught him off a Larwood bouncer at the start of the innings. "You could hear the snick all over the ground." There was a debatable not-out decision for Kippax. But not Bradman. He was missed only once, at 273, a difficult chance to Duckworth. If he did snick a catch before he had scored, Percy Fender (no great fan of his) didn't hear it. Nor did Plum Warner. Nor did Geoffrey Tebbutt. Nor did anyone else who was there. So why, one asks? Why cultivate the slander?

The venerable hero lives on quietly in Adelaide. Word of these smears doubtless gets back to him. Is this English sportsmanship (to echo a 1933 Australian Board of Control cable)? Get off his back, Fleet Street.

Wisden Cricket Monthly, November 1980

The Search for Cricket Films

IT WAS as if I'd slipped into a cosy armchair in the cricketers' Heaven. There they all were – "to the life". The 1905 Australians, led by Joe Darling, came striding down the steps towards me: Syd Gregory, Frank Laver, Warwick Armstrong, "Tibby" Cotter, Jim Kelly, Bert Hopkins, Clem Hill, Monty Noble, Reg Duff, and, after dallying in conversation, Charlie McLeod. Next, they were going through a routine for the benefit of the hand-cranked cine-camera, Armstrong and Trumper looking unexpectedly awkward as they messed up a pull and a cut.

A few minutes later I was watching the cream of English cricket of the Golden Age parading in a column of two ranks at W.G.Grace's Jubilee Match, Gentlemen v Players, Lord's, 1898, on his fiftieth birthday. My eyes told me but my intellect could barely accept it: there they were – Shrewsbury and WG, Stoddart and William

Gunn, Lilley and Sammy Woods, Abel and Wynyard, Tunnicliffe and F.S.Jackson, J.T.Hearne and MacGregor, Storer and Dixon, Lockwood and MacLaren, Brockwell and Townsend, Haigh, Alec Hearne, J.R.Mason, Wilfred Rhodes, and the mighty Kortright. The written word, even the still photograph, shrank into relative triviality. Here was *motion*, indescribably precious film footage saved for all time by the National Film Archive*.

The most pleasant surprise as Wisden Film Search got under way was the gradual realisation that there really are vast quantities of cricket film, in good condition, reflecting – often quite vividly – all the great personalities of the past eighty-five years, and, having survived the ravages of decades, now safe in perpetuity thanks to the restoration and preservation skills of the NFA. That so little archive film is seen on television has much to do with prohibitive fees applied by copyright-holders, as well as a shortage of awareness among researchers as to the riches held by the NFA.

The most exciting discovery of recent years has been the collection of 16mm film shot during the 1930s at Trent Bridge by a member, a Mr Stevens. Some time after his death the cans of film were discovered in the attic, and the family consulted officials of Nottinghamshire County Cricket Club. Soon the reels were being shown to wide-eyed audiences all around the country by the untiring Frank Woodhead. Wisely, the advice of the NFA was then sought, and a fresh master negative was made at no cost to the owner and without threat to the copyright.

Moving pictures were first offered to a semi-credulous mankind in the mid-1890s. The earliest sports film was probably of the Corbett-Courtney fight in New Jersey. Those who have been complaining recently that cricket is being tailored to suit television might care to ponder on this event in September 1894, for it was staged in Thomas Edison's 15ft wide "Black Maria", which was rotated slightly between rounds so as to retain the shafts of sunlight: and the rounds lasted 1 ½ minutes, the maximum time before fresh film had to be loaded.

In 1896 came the first major horse-race film: the Melbourne Cup, shot – to the chagrin of the Aussie turf fraternity – by a Frenchman, Lumiere cameraman Maurice Sestier. Then sports film took a giant step forward in Carson City, Nevada in 1897 when "Gentleman Jim" Corbett lost his world heavyweight title to Bob Fitzsimmons in an open-air fight. This "Battle of the Century" (oh, for some film of the 1897-98 Australia v England Tests!) was filmed from start to finish, running to the astonishing length of 11,000 feet and taking $750,000 at the nickelodeons.

Now the laments may cease, for in 1898 was shot possibly cricket's single most cherished sequence – cherished not merely because it is the earliest known**, nor because it includes the only moving images of my biographical hero Drewy Stoddart, but because it gives a clear, leisurely, mobile impression of a score of time-honoured cricket names.

The first actual cricket action comes in the now-famous W.G.Grace net sequence, seen fairly often now in television features. I was surprised to discover, though, that there is appreciably more of WG in the original than just the two jerky strokes usually to be seen. He stoops to collect a ball from the rear netting; drives; drives again; punches off the back foot; and plays defensively three times, turning once to make a lost-forever remark to the spectators.

Dry-mouthed with wonder, there is no time for the viewer to recover before Ranjitsinhji, clad in blazer and flannels, plays two easy and casual strokes towards the camera, which was set up in the short cover area. All this was preceded by Ranji, in sun-hat, and fellow players approaching the lens, followed down the pavilion steps by a batsman unidentified in the catalogue. It is Lord Hawke.

Chronologically, the next major material is that taken of the Australians in 1905. Mention has already been made of the players' descent down the steps and the staged batsmanship of some of them. Additionally there is a captivating sequence of them sorting themselves out for a group photograph. Utterly mesmerised by now, I ran this back and forth several times, seeing something new each time. Bill Howell,

Frith and film: delights way beyond the capacity of the printed word. Inset: the earliest known cricket film: Ranjitsinhji plays a few strokes at Sydney after his 175 in December 1897.

standing in the back row, balances a ball on the capped head of Victor Trumper. As the rest adjust their clothing, Frank Laver delivers a vigorous V-sign to Armstrong and they both laugh loudly (I *know* the film is silent!) as the camera shutter closes on them forever. My Queensland friend Pat Mullins has found reference to a film of the fourth Test, at Melbourne, of the 1911-12 series. Hope for its re-discovery will live on.

Next came the sighting of *The Life of Jack Hobbs*, made in 1925. It is silent of course (talkies came about the same time as Don Bradman, in 1928-29), and the captions convey a flavour of the simplicity and innocence of the times: "If you were to ask Jack Hobbs the reason for his consistency and success, he would answer 'Mrs Hobbs'." This quarter-hour film begins with the letter of agreement whereby Hobbs placed the rights to film his quest for WG's record solely in the hands of New Era Films Ltd. The close-ups of our hero are sharp and clear, as they are of Andy Sandham and old Tom Hayward. Hobbs demonstrates some strokes, not all of them the acme of poise, and a telling glimpse of him buckling on his pads conjures a distinct impression of the dimness of the professionals' low-level locker-room.

Hobbs and Sutcliffe walking out to bat at Adelaide; Hobbs outside his Fleet Street shop; reading a scrapbook; filling his pipe. And then – the big moment: out he comes with Sandham at Taunton: there's his fifty, 91 at the end of the day. Back again on the Monday, this time escorted by Jardine. And soon the record is his. We are even shown the insurance policy covering his historic bat for £200.

Gradually, with the guidance of NFA deputy curator (and cricket buff) Clyde Jeavons and his team, we worked our way through the cricket lists: Woolley's farewell at Folkestone in 1938 (Gaumont); Hobbs (smoking again!) besieged by autograph-hunters at a charity match where among players glimpsed are Amar Singh and the twenty-year-old Bedser twins; night cricket played by Australian clubs pre-war; a 1945 "Victory Test" at Lord's (British News), the dashing Keith Miller reaching his hundred with a single off George Pope; *Cavalcade of Australia* (1952) with its thrilling glimpses of Jack Gregory and Arthur Mailey bowling, and white-haired veterans Garrett and Blackham in conversation with Armstrong; Larwood almost braining Leo O'Brien and crunching Woodfull's ribs (Pathe Scrapbook); Ivan Barrow reaching the first century registered for West Indies in Test cricket, and Headley soon emulating him, Manchester 1933 (British Movietone); Bradman hitting Mankad for a rare six, and placing Kishenchand for a single to bring up his 100th century.

The miles of magic were beginning to tot up. Tiring work, but gratifying as it became apparent that cricket does have a rich film heritage after all.

* Later becoming the National Film and Television Archive.
** An earlier gem later came to light: Ranjitsinhji playing some strokes at the nets at Sydney following his 175 in the Test match there in December 1897.

Wisden Cricket Monthly, March 1981

The crusade to find, log and show cricket film continues, with many further fascinating discoveries having been made. The annual showings at London's National Film Theatre have been running for almost thirty years, to appreciative audiences. But the dream of compiling a twenty-hour history of cricket using private and commercial footage from 1897 onwards remains unfulfilled.

George Headley: an Old Master

"NO," SAYS George Headley, "I don't want to do that. I had a little heart trouble a while back. I don't want to do that." So I put the tape-recorder under the seat and, while the Bridgetown Test match proceeds along its inevitable course, we carry on talking. This reduces the number of direct quotes but widens the scope for discussion as the slight figure in patterned shirt and dark trousers sits, barely recognised, in the members' stand, picking off reminiscences like short singles and reacting to the action below us in a deep, craggy rumble. "Oh, no!" he exclaims when Peter Willey is adjudged lbw. "That spoils my day."

His heart missed a beat, he says, when he was called on the public-address system. But the call was not concerning his mother, who is ninety-five, lives in New York, and has recently undergone surgery.

He was born in Panama on May 30, 1909, of West Indian parents. He became known during the 1930s as the Black Bradman, though not necessarily within the Caribbean territories, where Don Bradman was often thought of as the White Headley.

He is no hardliner on the issue of race, and he has no wish to be quoted on any matters of controversy. But he expresses regret, from a cricketer's point of view, that the great South Africans of the 1970s were not seen in Test cricket. Here speaks a man who proudly wrote "African" on his immigration form before the 1930-31 West Indies team entered Australia. One of the other players – he won't say who, though the edge of contempt in his voice is sharp – put "European" even though he was a half-breed.

He enjoys thinking back to that tour, his first, even though the first four Tests were lost catastrophically. "Chappie" Dwyer, he says, not M.A.Noble, was responsible for getting a faster wicket at Sydney, where the sweet first victory was secured – Headley making his second century of the series. He recalls how often the old-time Australian Test players bowled at the touring team in the nets – "sussing them out" for Woodfull. He remembers, too, trying to play Grimmett's crafty spin by moving down the pitch: "I was stumped!" he says, gripping my arm and shaking with laughter, his blue eyes disappearing beneath dark brown curtains. Nonetheless, Grimmett regarded him, according to C.L.R.James, as the best on-side player he met.

Clear in George's memory is how the Queensland aborigine fast bowler Eddie Gilbert skipped down the pitch and shook Learie Constantine's hand after being hit for six for the first time ever. And he seemed particularly fond of Stan McCabe and Archie Jackson. His tastes today centre upon Dennis Lillee, for whom he has unbounded admiration.

Headley needed protection after the commemorative photo session of the veteran Test players during an interval in the Bridgetown Test. Dozens mobbed him as identification spread, wanting to be photographed with him. Hundreds sought his autograph. In the eyes of many senior cricket-watchers he is still the greatest of West Indies batsmen. He carried a heavier batting burden than any of his successors, with a fast attack to back him up which, if often fairly spectacular, contained only half the ferocity of Clive Lloyd's squad.

He believed in attack, this diminutive genius, and, like Len Hutton from another context, deserved the freedom which stronger batting support would have permitted. Twenty-one of his 22 Test matches were against England or Australia, and he made eight centuries against England and two against Australia in his 40 innings: a staggering ratio of one in four. Twice he made two centuries in a Test against England, and his two double-centuries came off English bowling. His Test average of 60.83 is higher than those of Sobers, Kanhai, the three Ws, Lloyd and Greenidge, and decimal points away from that of Viv Richards.

Now, his career seen out in English league cricket and a couple of Test caps earned by his son Ron*, George Headley takes life easy, quietly proud of his record and of being, in 1948, the first black man to captain West Indies ("It wasn't altogether a popular appointment").

It delighted all at Kensington Oval that he had taken the trouble to travel down from Jamaica for the Test, and to see him in concentrated discussion with former players such as Andy Ganteaume, Derek Sealy, Everton Weekes, Teddy Hoad and Jim Laker conjured swimming, sunlit visions of former times.

The shoulders are thin but squarely-hung, the hair ash-grey, the eyes dreamy yet alert. The whole countenance seems compounded of wisdom and cool practicality – a practicality which surfaces after such questions as would he have worn a helmet if playing today? "I might," he drawls, "I might."

At lunch he warned me about the pepper sauce, and chuckled when I ventured and had my lips badly stung. To every wellwisher he attempted to rise, grateful for their cordiality. He signed postcards, booklets and napkins. There was so much else I thought of too late to ask: how would he have scored runs off this four-prong pace attack – his answer would undoubtedly have been cautious – and did he truly lack a night's sleep before a Test innings – not through apprehension but through long analytical anticipation – and were his morning bowel motions as described by C.L.R.James in *Beyond a Boundary*?

We parted not at his bidding, and I watched the afternoon play with a certain distraction.

* With, a few years later, fifteen England caps won by his grandson Dean.

Wisden Cricket Monthly, May 1981

A memorable meal with George Headley, who was constantly interrupted.

A player who would stamp an immortal mark on a famous Test match in the year of his benefit was Bob Willis. With the 8 for 43 Headingley performance only weeks ahead of him he released his benefit booklet, which included the following contribution from his persevering editor:

It's Only Once a Month

MR ROBERT WILLIS is one of those chaps who deliberate long and hard before committing themselves. I know this because when I put to him the question "Would you like to be part of a new magazine I plan to produce?" – this was in Brisbane in December 1978 – I got my answer in Sydney two months later.

Typically, once he'd made up his mind he attacked his responsibility wholeheartedly. If he has yet been late with his monthly article, I can't recall. (We hapless editors have a habit of erasing such traumas from our cluttered minds anyway.) He writes as he bowls – with plenty of shoulder. Sometimes he slips in a bouncer, causing alarm to target and umpire. Sometimes his wife has to help with his "run-up" and his followthrough. Always he is to the point, disciplined in length and ON TIME.

If this matter of punctuality seems to be unduly stressed, it is only because erring contributors make an editor's lot even more uncomfortable than it need be. (This slight offering, by the way, is being sent a week early. Now I have a headache of a different kind – my halo's hurting my temples!)

The least appealing thing about a monthly magazine is that it comes every four weeks. The rare five-week month evokes cooees of delight. The big effort that goes into planning, assembly and completion would appear, in graph form, as a steadily rising curve, with lots of little red stars at the climax to represent the editor's peak blood pressure as well as the furious industry at the printer's plant.

So much for the big effort: but is a mile-runner, having breasted the tape, usually asked to prepare immediately for another four circuits?

Everything is tolerable if things go well during the month; if overseas articles come by airmail jet and not Piper Comanche; if David Gower's piece isn't sent back by the censors; if the distinguished Guest Columnist is as good as his word in respect of deadline; and if the living stay that way and don't create a sudden mad panic on the obituary page.

But things seldom *all* go well at once, and I've often explained to friends who are sweet enough to enquire as if they really cared, that it sometimes feels like one of those circus acts, where the fella spins a load of plates on bamboo rods and has to keep dashing from one end of the stage to the other to keep them all spinning. Any fast bowler who has lost his run-up and his rhythm would know the feeling.

You need support from your management, support from your printers, support from your distributor, and of course support from your readers. With all this support you can end up feeling like the fat lady in the aforementioned circus.

It's all right for the newspaper chaps. If a story goes wrong one day they can correct it, update it, deny it the next. A monthly is altogether more unwieldy. You sometimes feel a story coming on, but go to press you must. When it appears in the subsequent issue it is history. It takes time to print and distribute a magazine.

It takes time to interpret some people's handwriting. When our annual profits are into six figures we'll start handing out typewriters to the uninitiated (Bob's OK). Until then, Mike Brearley's "exotic" can flaming well be printed as "erotic", and Tony Pawson can be allowed to take a "second glass" instead of a "second class" at

Oxford.

Readers' letters can be fascinating. The more intense go on for pages, putting all cricket's wrongs to right. It might perhaps be possible to predict the contents from the postmark: "Disgusted of Tunbridge Wells" hates Packer, objects to overseas players in county cricket, wants the Gentlemen v Players fixture restored, and thinks Colin Cowdrey should still be leading England. Susie of Market Harborough is interested in photos, autographs and David Gower's features. Mr Soggins of London E11 thinks we should have more articles about great Essex players between 1926 and 1932. Arnold Trudgewater from East Yorkshire protests at the Test selectors' southern bias. Sanjhi Patel from Slough wants a free trial copy of the magazine. Major Ransydd-Breth from Nairobi asks for more articles by Plum Warner. Wouldn't *you* find breakfast somewhat indigestible in the face of that lot?

Small wonder, then, that a fantasy came to me recently. When Bob Willis has finished the demanding grind of his benefit year, when he has gone on to take his 310th Test wicket, when he has burned his boots and raffled his bat, perhaps he'd like to come down here and take over. I promise, Bob, I'll have my monthly articles with you in good time.

Bob Willis Benefit Year 1981

The Headingley "Miracle"

AT TWENTY-past-two on Tuesday, July 21 at Headingley Cricket Ground the greatest reversal ever seen in a Test match was completed. Hours after Bob Willis had rocketed a yorker through Ray Bright's defence to snatch an 18-run victory for England, the enormity of the turnaround had still not soaked in fully.

The point at which the resident bookmakers were offering 500-1 against England in this third Test match was around three o'clock on the fourth day, when England were 135 for 7 in the follow-on and still 92 in arrears. Hotel bookings for that night were being cancelled, and the English depression had deepened to somewhere between the levels of valium and alcoholism. Even when the laughing Botham continued picking off fours with gorilla power and surveyor's precision, the imminent prospect of being two down with three to play produced English exasperation in equal dollops to Australia's incredulous satisfaction. If only we had all realised what lay in store.

The match had embodied numerous landmarks and frustrations in its first 3½ days. On the opening day John Dyson, the handsome schoolteacher from Sydney, made his first Test century in his 22nd innings, but Gower and Botham both dropped Chappell, and rain stole three-quarters of an hour nett. On the second day, the same amount of time was lost, but the extra hour was played through, and England's wicketkeeper, Bob Taylor, marked his 40th birthday with two catches, while Botham claimed five wickets in an innings for the 15th time – and the first time since the Test before he was made captain. The dropped catch this day besmirched poor Gooch's name, Kim Hughes adding a further 24.

The third day, Lillee's 32nd birthday, saw his pal Rod Marsh equal and then pass Alan Knott's Test record of 263 wicketkeeping dismissals, Marsh playing in his 71st Test against Knott's 93. Lillee took five wickets on his birthday, one of them at the end when England followed on, Gooch going for the second time that day in the space of four scoreless balls. The frustration and disappointment felt this Saturday around the ground – and up and down the country – were exacerbated by the latest umpiring disaster: a minute or two after six o'clock the ground was bathed in bright sunshine; yet Messrs Evans (in his first Test) and Meyer had decided that conditions were not suitable at 6pm and had ordered the covers on. A little discretion here would have worked wonders. But it was played by the book, and some of the spectators not only chucked cushions but vowed never to return.

Monday, the fourth day, saw English wickets tumble with montonous regularity, while criticism of the occasionally spiteful pitch became widespread. (Even Australia's cricket manager, Peter Philpott, described it as a "disgrace" for a Test match). The milestone this day was Lillee's 142nd England wicket, taking him past Hugh Trumble's Ashes record. After 3pm, however, all the incident and memorabilia which had gone before slipped to the back of the mind as the astonishing England fightback came to pass.

HUGHES successfully called "heads" for the third time in the series, but for the first time chose to bat. Selection of spinner Bright may have committed him to do so, with fine cracks already in the pitch; but England's omission of Emburey meant that Australia were committed to facing a four-prong pace attack. The ball moved around, but 55 runs were made by the 18th over, when Wood fell to Botham's third ball just before rain interfered. The afternoon brought with it a grim struggle, Dyson batting like a Woodfull, Trevor Chappell, spared at 3 and 7, clinging on for all his pedigree was worth. He lasted until the 63rd over, and at half-past-six Dyson ran Willis down to third man to reach his hard-fought century. Dilley returned to bowl Dyson first ball, and nightwatchman Bright joined his captain to see it through to 203 for 3 at the close.

The new ball was taken early on the second day, and Dilley, after hitting Bright resoundingly on the box, yorked him, gesturing to the crowd in the outer who had been shouting their opinion of his often wayward direction. Meanwhile, Willis was bowling some fiery but fruitless overs, once beating Hughes three times after jerking his cap off with a snorter of a short ball. This the crowd loved. Hughes, as ever, was looking for runs and striking with gusto. After the luncheon rain hold-up he reached his fifty with a vindictive-looking cover-drive, and by tea he was 81, with Yallop a measured 34, and Australia well on the way to shutting England out.

Botham was now embarked on a long, productive spell. Leave it with me, he told his skipper, and I'll get you five wickets. Hughes was the first, spooning back an attempted leg-side shot. An in-curver trapped Border. The old Botham luck accounted for Yallop, who played at a widish ball and didn't miss. Taylor took the edge. Lawson was bounced out, and Marsh was bowled heaving ambitiously. The declaration came at 401 for 9, and England had a nasty eight minutes to see out.

If the follow-on could be avoided a draw seemed assured. But in 17 overs England slipped to 42 for 3, Alderman having Gooch lbw as he tried to play his first ball to leg, Brearley caught behind after some determined resistance, and Boycott being bowled by a ball from Lawson which defied analysis. It pitched on or just outside off stump, passed outside his left pad, and took the leg stump around halfway up. As the rangy fast bowler buzzed a ball past Gower's head, England's task seemed no easier than that of the policemen who had been trying to restore order to the riot-torn streets of Liverpool and London.

Sometimes Gower would stroke a boundary, standing stock still in the knowledge that the ball could never be intercepted. Gatting too pounced on the half-volley when it made one of its rare appearances. But when Lawson hit Gower in the ribs, it obviously hurt. Dyson dropped him at slip after lunch, but Lawson had him next ball, an impossible lifter which Marsh took high above his head. Soon Gatting was gone; then Willey, hopping as the yorker screamed through. Taylor saw 27 runs added before he got off the mark. Soon he too was out, and England were down to Dilley.

Botham's 50 came in 75 minutes, to noisy acclaim, before Marsh broke the record with a mobile catch. Then Old went; then Dilley; and England were back in again. Gooch edged low to Alderman, and Sunday prayers in many a village church must have turned towards the invocation of rain.

Even then, England, if not 500-1 against, must have been very long odds, only the weather seeming to be their champion. Brearley went the same way as Gooch, and Gower, nine overs finding his first run, touched a seamer heading for first slip. The demoralisation when Gatting was lbw again to a low ball was increased just before lunch when a lifter from Lillee sent Boycott's head back and his helmet toppling to earth. Willey, with his woodchopper's forearms, and Boycott, a seething mass of concentration, held firm for 19 overs, picking up twos and the odd boundary. Willey punched the ball with awesome strength, and sometimes uppercut to third man; but this stroke was his undoing. Hughes placed a man there, and the catch was held, giving Lillee his Ashes record.

Botham, with nothing to lose, hit hard. But soon Boycott, 46 in 215 minutes, was gone, lbw well forward, and Taylor could not cope with a lifter. Thus the bottom of the graph was reached.

In the next 18 overs, either side of tea, Botham and Dilley put a gloss on matters with a booming stand of 117 – seven short of the record – in 80 riotous minutes. Botham was missed at 32, a hard left-hand chance to Bright at gully, and there were two big shouts against Dilley for catches behind. There was no other interruption to the batting assault, and the tiring Alderman found himself taken for 16 off an over. The ignominy of an innings defeat was erased, and now even mis-hits were going to the boundary, a sure sign that whoever manipulates the luck of this cruel game had decided it was England's turn.

Dilley reached his first Test half-century with a cover-drive off Lillee which could never have been bettered by Pollock, and excitement rose a further decibel as Dilley smacked the ball to leg and ran four with the help of a desperate overthrow.

When Dilley was bowled as he aimed violently at Alderman, there was still a chance the match would be wrapped up that evening. But Botham went down the track and hoisted Alderman for six, then drove him disdainfully for four. A Hammond-like cover-drive off Lawson took the deposed captain to 99, and then a thick edge brought up his seventh Test century, his second against Australia. As a prolonged standing ovation brought a dewiness to the eyes of the sentimental, the scorers calculated that Botham had sprinted from 39 to 103 with a six, 14 fours and just two singles. His second fifty had taken a mere 40 minutes, and his century had come in 157 minutes off only 87 balls. If the captaincy had not affected his play, it was the mightiest of coincidences.

When Bright came on in place of the weary Alderman, it was the first bit of spin for Australia in the 129th over of the match. He set no real problems. A blind hook at Lawson almost cost Botham his wicket at 109, but Marsh, leaping, could not hold a most difficult catch. By the time Old was out in the 81st over, England were 319 for 9, 92 ahead, the precious stand having realised 67, the 184 runs added since the fall of the seventh wicket having come in 31 overs. The crowd was now in a frenzy, the Australians reduced to waiting for something favourable to happen.

Willis stayed with Botham through the remaining minutes, during which Lawson was still able to whistle down some nasty short deliveries – and two accidental beamers. Botham passed his highest Test score, and completed the astonishing sum of 106 out of 175 runs in the two-hour session, raising England to 351 for 9, a lead of 124.

Still the match was to be Australia's. Unless the British blitzkrieg had disguised the fact, the pitch now offered less to bowlers, and it would take another 50 or more runs to stretch Australia on the last day.

Speculation was confused, nonetheless, as the final act began, the field sunlit. Botham drove the new ball to add four to his overnight 145, and Willis took a single. That was to be the extent of it. Alderman took his sixth wicket, ninth of the match, as at Trent Bridge, and Australia's target was set: 130. After two balls it was 122, Wood helping himself off Botham. Four quick singles off Dilley put Australia in good heart . . . until Botham had Wood caught behind. Even then, panic was a mile away. Dyson was cool, Chappell grim. Old came on, then Willis, uphill and into the breeze, no-balling with galling regularity. Willey was tried. Willis switched to the Kirkstall Lane end. This was the decisive move.

Like a man possessed – and a 21-year-old at that – Willis came belting down the hill, hair streaming, knees pumping. A horrible ball jumped at Chappell and lobbed from his bat through to Taylor. Four overs later Hughes, having just had his hand sprayed after a bruising by Willis, nicked to third slip, where Botham swooped to secure a fine two-handed catch. Yallop, with lunch seconds away, was welcomed by a fast bouncer, and could only jab at his third ball for Gatting, perfectly balanced at close short leg, to plunge and hold the catch. Suddenly Australia were 58 for 4 – 72 still needed – and Willis had plundered three wickets for none in 11 balls.

The interval comprised forty minutes of simian chatter. The game's turnabout had an unreality about it. It was if the Englishmen had only been fooling for the past few days; the rampant Australians now seemed helpless.

Old struck a vital blow by bowling Border through the gap, and when Dyson surprisingly got out, hooking at Willis, Taylor had equalled John Murray's first-class record of 1270 catches, something which would normally have had headlines of its own. Six down for 68. Now seven for 74 as Marsh hooked what looked to be a six until Dilley positioned himself four feet in from the rope and let the ball sink into his large hands, below his chin. Willis's speed was too much for Lawson, who could only flick to Taylor, who now moved ahead of Murray. Eight down for 75, and all over bar the shouting. Soon it would be all shouting over the bar.

Yet the next four overs saw 35 runs hit by the predatory Lillee and Bright – pulls, uppercuts, sweep/drives. Englishmen knew it was too good to be true after all. No heart attacks were reported, and it was too sunny for anyone to have had an umbrella, the handle to be chewed through. This, though, was exactly the excruciating tension our forefathers knew at The Oval ninety-nine years ago, when The Ashes were created out of a shock seven-run result.

Lillee popped Willis up towards mid-on. Gatting temporarily lost his footing, recovered, ran in, and threw himself forward for Queen and country. He held it at turf level. Australia were 110 for 9.

If all this was agony, it was nothing against Botham's next over. Twice Alderman edged to Old at third slip, low, awkward chances. Both went down. So *that* was it? The English escapees to be recaptured at the very outer limits of the prison camp? Such vain expectation of an impossible win.

In stormed Willis again. One journalist remarked that if this is what effect his writing Willis off had had, he would do it more often. The Australian end of the press-box was quiet, thoughtful.

A desperate muddle almost cut short the exasperating (for Australia) Botham-Dilley stand of 117 for the eighth wicket which put England slightly ahead. The eventual challenge to Australia of a mere 130 proved beyond them once Willis became fired up. (PA Photos)

The yorker with which Willis finished it all will be set apart in history, like Saunders' delivery which gained a three-run victory for Australia at Old Trafford in 1902, or Peel's which produced a caught-and-bowled from the injured Blackham at Sydney in 1894, when Stoddart's England team won the only previous Test after having had to follow on.

Eight for 43, Willis's best Test figures, were the best for England in a Headingley Test, bettering "Charlie" Blythe's 8 for 59 against South Africa in 1907: but the match award went to Ian Botham for a little matter of 199 runs, seven wickets and two catches. Only Jack Gregory had previously recorded a century and five or more wickets in an innings in an Ashes Test.

It was England's first victory since that at Bombay, 13 Tests ago. It was the first ever tasted by Willey, Gatting and Dilley. It was the first Test to be reflected on Headingley's new electronic scoreboard. (India will not regret the passing of the old: it once showed them four down for none). Only a few sour words directed indiscriminately at the Press by England's captain and bowling hero dampened the euphoria.

While everyone drew fresh breath, groundsman Keith Boyce dug up a piece of the pitch to send to the Soil Research Centre for analysis. A portion should have been consigned to the Department of Information as a symbol and reminder of the fighting spirit which not only won a famous Test match but can win much larger social and economic battles.

Wisden Cricket Monthly, September 1981

Whether an inspired prediction, prescience or flukey guesswork, the following was written as Botham began his famous innings, half played with eyes shut, it seemed, and a broad grin. As I was writing the report for an Indian newspaper it needed to be filed at the tea interval on the fourth day, just as the fun started:

NOW CAME Botham, ever the favourite, to a rousing welcome. All that was required of him this time was a speedy 150. As if he knew it, he launched into Alderman . . . .

Deccan Herald, July 21, 1981

A popular cricketer had a benefit in 1982. It was a pleasure to contribute to the booklet:

Bairstow the Ebullient

THE 1978-79 England tour of Australia produced a weighty store of memories, many of them from the final month, when Roger Tolchard's injury resulted in a reinforcement joining the team: David Leslie Bairstow. One couldn't help noticing him from the very start.

During the match against Tasmania at Hobart, he was called upon to substitute in the field. Wicketkeepers don't usually get a lot of practice at throwing in from third man. Consequently, when a ball was run down into that area, "Bluey" bent, gathered, and hurled. The batsman made it safely to his crease. The danger zone was fifteen yards to his right, where the umpire at square leg copped an admittedly fast throw smack on his fleshy thigh. "Bluey" didn't blush – or did he? His face was florid already from the heat and the exertion.

We noticed him again on the second day, when he came up into the pavilion for lunch. He looked like your typical British heavyweight hope – an already chronically battered nose badly chipped and eyes swivelling. From under the white towel draped over his flaming hair, he announced that he had crashed to the stone floor of the dressing-room while doing stretching exercises and that he had double vision.

He then proceeded to pass comment in rich Yorkshire tones on everyone in that crowded room. When a waitress bent over low to serve us, he claimed he had treble vision, and none of us could tell if he had, or was fooling himself, or was fooling us.

Later, in Adelaide, on the rest day of the Test match, we were all taken to Yalumba in the Barossa Valley, where the swimming pool, tennis courts and limitless wine bars were made available till dusk. Someone tossed lemons from the far end of the pool and several of us dived in, trying to catch one-handed. It worked well, until Mr Bairstow came to join in. He decided to jump from the opposite side, his great noble head representing a battering-ram threat to all craniums coming from our side.

Suddenly, even allowing for the fact that each man good and true would have consumed well over a bottle of best white, the eye was not on the ball (lemon). Like a lot of timid slipsmen, we allowed him right of way. He loved it. Having recovered from his Tasmanian tribulations, he now gave full wind to his great rasping chuckle. It echoed throughout the rest of the tour.

He still had one further unique performance in store. On the Qantas Jumbo flight back to England, he managed to cut himself while using an electric razor! Poor manager Ken Barrington. He was so keen that his boys should all look smart at Heathrow. And there was "Bluey" with blood on his collar.

Few were gladder than I when he won his first Test cap a few months later. Or when he and Graham Stevenson pulled off a thrilling victory in a night match against Australia at Sydney the following winter. His merry attitude is vital to the game, and warrants a generous response to his benefit fund.

David Bairstow Benefit Year 1982

Sixteen years later came the tragedy of David Bairstow's suicide. And ten years after that it was delightful to see his son Jonathan making his way in the first-class game with Yorkshire, his father's beloved club.

David Bairstow (right) with that slightly bewildered look. The author is to the left, with Ray Illingworth centre.

A momentous occasion was the introduction of an eighth Test-playing entity with the elevation of Sri Lanka, the island of serendipity:

Sri Lanka Odyssey

COLOMBO HAS become faster, noisier, more commercial, since 1977, according to those who toured with Tony Greig's team. I was in no position to judge. My last visit had been in 1949, when all a boy knew about Test cricket was that it would never be the same again now that Don Bradman had retired. Ceylon, as it was then universally known, had about as much chance as the Isle of Wight of playing Test cricket. Now, the Air Lanka Tristar having disgorged its stiff-legged passengers into the steamy airport lounge, the mission was to see cricket's newest Test side substantiate its supporters' wisdom and judgment.

Ranjit Fernando, Sri Lanka's former wicketkeeper-batsman and now Cricket Board member, explained during the long drive into town that cricket was still essentially a Colombo game, which made it difficult to set up a national first-class competition. Club matches, however, are played over three consecutive days, and with interest in schools cricket at such a high level that few would credit, standards would be maintained, even improved. This was about to be shown in the Test match, as it had been in the thrilling one-day matches.

My journalist and broadcaster friends seemed travel- and battle-weary when I met up with them by the pool at the Intercontinental. Some were almost as pale as if they had spent the winter in snowy England. All were keen to tell of the hardships of Indian travel and accommodation. One poor chap still carried toilet rolls with him everywhere.

The players all seemed relaxed enough at the Tamil Cricket Union reception at the P.Saravanamuttu Stadium. There was the usual hunger for football scores and other news, and an undisguised relief that one more week would see them winging back to their homeland. During the drive back in the team bus, I seemed to be the only one listening to Graham Dilley's "Windsor Davies" commentary, "lovely boy" and all. It had, it seems, been going on for three months.

The Board dinner at the Holiday Inn was a memorable event, from the fine menu to the apposite speeches – even if there was an outbreak of giggling on my table. Charles Palmer warned against the "snakepit of commercialism", and Board president, the Hon. Gamini Dissanayake*, who also happens to be Minister of Lands, uttered a masterpiece of celebratory prose laced with both a sense of welcome and a combative defiance. Gifts were handed out, and the spirit of conviviality brought back memories of the Melbourne Centenary show of 1977.

Back at the hotel, the evening was almost spoilt by a territorial dispute at the bar with one of the hordes of German tourists, but the girthsome adversary was still a few pounds lighter than "my friend" Ian Botham, and an international incident was averted by clever use of the eyes.

On the rest day, David Gower and I went up to Negombo to share a glass or two with the Wisden holidaymakers. The sea water was swimmable up there, and while our hero, 79 not out in the Test, took a siesta, I bobbed up and down in the warmest water I'd known before resisting the exquisite but pricey carved ivory Buddhas in the bazaars. That evening, the *WCM* tourists showed their pleasure by presenting Fred and Colleen Rumsey, tour organisers, with a miniature bejewelled elephant. Fred for once was speechless. The driver, on the way back to town, still couldn't believe that Sri Lanka might win the Test match.

Someone said that Sri Lanka today is like some of the West Indian islands twenty years ago. Certainly the folk readily smile a handsome almost curious greeting to the foreigner, even in the shanty areas. As the Press bus made its way to and from the Test ground each day, it was refreshing to lean out and exchange waves with the populace, most of whom, admittedly, had something to sell. The numerous lame beggars stirred the conscience.

At Ranjit Fernando's "at home" several Board representatives were genuinely concerned to know that facilities at the ground had been satisfactory. Cricket is now bounding ahead in Sri Lanka, with the setting up of the Cricket Foundation, supported by hundreds of business organisations, and one got a strong impression that the game is in the right hands. It was with some shame that I recalled feelings of scepticism over the years whenever Sri Lanka's Test admission was raised. Their cause can now be seen as deserving and justified.

Another light moment came under a street-lamp, around midnight, when I had an unlikely confrontation with one of my heroes, Chandrasekhar, host Fernando patiently providing a bat and tennis ball. Chandra bowls only off-breaks now, and as the pink ball swerved out of the shadows, I wondered if the dinner-jacketed Mailey and Cardus could have had such fun with their orange on the Piccadilly pavement all those years ago. As in the Test match, we soon had to stop when there was trouble with the ball.

The week went quickly. The souvenir stall was attacked wholeheartedly: tankards, ties, plates, wall tiles, cassettes, first-day covers, "I was there" caps, matchboxes, S.S.Perera's mightily informative brochure, the precious medallion. Then there was the vital autograph quest, and the verification of spellings. The chats with old captains Tennekoon and Tissera. A radio spot. A bit more restorative suntanning. Purchase of Ceylon tea. Grade cricket reminiscence with Goonesena. Gathering up of newspapers. Final dip in the pool, mercifully with no swim challenges from the Press. Then strapping on the safety-belt – and Don Mosey's: he was sleeping already – as Air Lanka set out on the marathon return flight. Willis told a rabbi that we had a rabbi of our own, and when the holy man discovered our "rabbi" to be none other than Frank Keating, the joke backfired, for one turned out to be the favourite sportswriter of the other.

Willis was strapped into his seat and told to write his *WCM* article. Gower was asked to try out a game of Armchair Cricket. Lever celebrated his birthday with cake – generously distributed – at 35,000 feet. Geoff Cook's toddler was amazingly well behaved. As usual, Tavare's silence helped balance out Botham's noise.

They managed to lose thirty of our suitcases, but body and soul were safely delivered into the inhospitable greyness of England's late winter. We were almost stranded in the snow and ice of Zurich, where a few handfuls of retaliatory snow were hurled by players at journalists; and Willis, Gower and Frith had the briefest and most meaningless of Editorial Board meetings, just to say we had had "a Board meeting in Zurich" – sounded grand.

Then it was all shut off behind us. A tour had ended. Another summer beckoned. Sri Lanka, bless them, had been safely launched, and Keith Fletcher had at last registered the Test win he had craved. It might not be so easy next time.

* Assassinated by Tamil terrorists at an election rally in Colombo in October 1994, the explosion also killing about fifty others. He had hoped to lead his opposition party to victory in the forthcoming election.

Wisden Cricket Monthly, April 1982

Sure enough, Sri Lanka grew in strength to the point where Test matches – and a World Cup – were won in the years ahead, to enormous national delight.

There was much to excite during the 1982-83 Australia v England summer:

Australia Revisited

THREE WEEKS of the five gone, and being back in Australia is like never having been away. Family gain preference over the Melbourne Test, which consequently is watched from a sticky armchair in scorching Queensland, the first two sessions each day on Channel 9, the third on ABC TV. The cost is having to listen to a fellow named Morphett, whose appearance and insight suit him better for something like *Blankety Blank*. Still, we form our own opinions when watching cricket, don't we? Who needs commentators?

The ABC's camerawork and commentary *are* dreary by comparison, but that dreaded, merciless stream of commercials has to be dodged. Sure, they pay for the cricket transmission, and few of the locals seem to resent them. But don't let it happen, Britain. *Cricketus interruptus* is not conducive to good health.

Norman Cowans, encouraged throughout by Bob Taylor, was belatedly let off the leash in the Melbourne Test, giving England some much-needed lift. He has elements of Wes Hall about his run-up and Wayne Daniel about his powerful thighs, and he takes some explaining to many Australians who fail to appreciate the multiracial nature of British society.

Australia's suburban society goes on its materialistic way, if miserable at the economic recession. Favourite towns along the New England Highway remain little affected by the 1980s, though the drought has taken vicious toll. The land is a graveyard for dead trees, white and gaunt. The urge to find old Test captain H.J.H.Scott's grave in Scone* is overruled by the family. Then, further up, at Tamworth, an enquiry after Johnny Gleeson finds him, according to the petrol pump attendant, playing bowls these days and "givin' 'em heaps" (achieving remarkable success). The former mystery spinner now writes a sports column – in which he also gives 'em heaps.

We began in Adelaide, where a cool and blustery introduction eased matters for the first-time tourists, who loved the spacious city and the elegant cricket ground. Understandably. The mound at Adelaide Oval was awash with beery good humour. Passing girls were accorded howls of acclaim and awarded from ten points down to "old bag" or "ET's sister". Our womenfolk stayed in the stand, taking no risks with the baretopped judges or the laserlike sun. In a match made memorable by beautiful hundreds by Greg Chappell and Gower, not the least fascinating statistic was that sponsors Benson & Hedges gave away over 40,000 cigarettes during the match.

On Wyndie Hill-Smith's open day at Yalumba in the Barossa Valley, where the photographers were all after Botham's belly, a picture of Lillee partaking of wine direct from the bottle might have set Mr Arlott's brow afurrow. Friendship renewed under the leafy trees with Sir Donald and the decorous Lady Jessie crowned a rare day of pure relaxation. The Don's kookaburra, creased-eyed grin shone out splendidly from beneath a Greg Chappell wide-brimmed sun-hat. The right wrist has recovered now, and he can play golf and the piano once more.

There was an evening of fellowship with the Adelaide Cricket Society, where the witty Dick French and the dry Mel Johnson showed that Test umpires are human**. I liked French's story demonstrating the tension of Test cricket. He once went into the Australians' room to tell the batsmen that play was starting. Graeme Wood was "perking up" into one basin and Rick Darling was perking up into another. So Dick went back to his fellow ump . . . and found *him* perking up.

The penalty for being a relatively impartial observer of Ashes Tests – for a compassionate chap, I plead – is that the sympathies consistently pour out to the underdogs. What agonies I shared with the 1981 Australians (while delighting with the multitude in Botham's exploits). Now, after compensatory vengeance victories at Brisbane and Adelaide, they have to do without my support. I have a fair idea how a father felt with sons in both the Union and Confederate armies.

Watching the Melbourne Test, I could scarcely recall ever wishing so fervently for an England win – not just for the sake of friends in the team or the *WCM* tourists but for the sake of the series itself. The feeling is also a long-held expression of aversion towards the loud-mouthed public gloating that invariably accompanies success.

England's chances took a dive on the crucial third day at Melbourne when David Gower fell victim to a poor decision, given out caught behind when his hook shot was a long way from the ball. Mr Whitehead wears glasses, so presumably his eyesight is better than many. Except for that particular delivery, which seemed potentially so fateful.

There seems to be a thrilling finish in prospect for this enthralling match***, and I'll be watching it down on the Gold Coast, trying out the surf during the lunch break. I've done my share of listening from my early-morning winter bed.

If England win it will not exactly shatter the Australian Dream; but it will swell the gate at Sydney. By then we'll be on the sad last lap. There are many new Australian cricket books to gather in and old friends to greet. Another pleasant cluster of images goes into the memory bank, among them the unexpected sight of Hoggy and Thommo bowling for Australia again. Thommo is due to become a father in April. That and his precious garden will complete the scene for him, and help him forget all those English playings and missings. And heaven help the dandelions on his lawn. As they poke their heads up I can see my favourite fast bowler givin' 'em heaps.

* It was located on a later trip.
** Just how human was disturbingly revealed in the upcoming Sydney Test match.
*** And how: England winners by three runs.

Wisden Cricket Monthly, February 1983

A month later came a fateful editorial. For the first time in print anywhere the suggestion was raised that the game would be better for television replay assistance for the umpires, putting an end to the steady deadly trickle of poor decisions. It would have been depressing to have known then that a quarter-century later the authorities were still pussyfooting over this issue:

Help the Umpire

OPENING OVER of the Test match to decide the Ashes series. Batsman [Wessels] plays to midwicket, runs. Bowler [Willis] makes ground, gathers ball, hurls at stumps, bails fly. Batsman [Dyson], well out of his ground, is given "not out". "Six inches either way," says umpire [Johnson] later, having given batsman benefit of what, seemingly to the umpire alone, was doubt. Reprieved batsman [Dyson] is dismissed five hours later for 79, and his team, Australia, eventually buoyed up by a first-innings advantage of 77, go safely through for a draw and thus retain the Ashes.

Justice is the theme. What pleasure can there be in sport when controllable conduct factors are wildly awry? All through the 1982-83 Test series there had been dissatisfaction at the standard of umpiring. For a time the pain and fury were absorbed in the beliefs that the misjudgments were evening themselves out between the two sides and that there was still time for either side to seize the initiative in the five-match contest.

That Australia were the better team was plainly obvious by the end. Yet their victory lacked the gloss to which it was entitled. Incompetent umpiring was a constant distraction, a menace to the confidence of batsmen, a source of distress to bowlers (though they picked up the odd surprise), and a crushing disappointment to spectators who expected the only mistakes on the field to be made by the players.

The errors of judgment made by cricketers are the very essence of the sport, which depends for its charm as much upon uncertainty as anything else. Alas, in several countries the standards are cause for despair.

Not so long ago it took a newspaper photograph (e.g. the Stackpole run-out, Brisbane, 1970) to establish that an umpire had blundered. Now, with the spread of "the umpire's curse" – the television action replay – which began as an aid to ice hockey viewers who had no hope of following the speeding puck, major cricket matches are transformed into matters of close optical analysis.

Why were TV sets introduced into press-boxes? So that journalists would not be at a disadvantage against the home viewer who sees everything played back. So dominant has the "box" become that some writers and many a spectator at the bar will rely upon the roar of the crowd to trigger his attention to the TV screen, allowing him to get on with other things during the quiet periods of play. Countless journalists' reports have been rendered more accurate by access to the TV playback.

This leaves only the umpires without access to the truth as revealed by the close optical analysis. Hang "human fallibility", with its supposed beauty. When it ruins an Ashes-deciding Test match, having already spoilt the series, it has to go.

The introduction of electronic assistance will have to be carried out discreetly. Two-way contact will be necessary between the umpires in the field and the assistant at the TV monitor, and the exchange will be as confidential as a whisper through an earpiece. The gain will be that major matches will be conducted, in umpiring terms, on lines of almost unchallengeably fair scrutiny. Leg-befores, stumpings, run-outs, caught-behinds are all accessible from different camera angles: would umpire Rex Whitehead have given Gower out at Melbourne if he had seen the incident from the rear?

Gower took his bad luck like a big man, but one of the less attractive sides of cricket is the dissent shown by some players. This should virtually be exterminated by the reliance on instant film evidence. However did losing punters tolerate split decisions before the installation of the photo-finish technique?

Umpires' pride will initially be dented. That is inevitable. Australian umpire Dick French has protested that video evidence is inadmissible in court, while Mel Johnson has rejected any thought of standing out in the burning sun while someone else makes decisions for him up in the shade of a viewing-room. Were it not for the succession of poor decisions that swung the umpires onto the front page, one might sympathise. Were it not for the worldwide and incandescent controversy concerning umpires' performances at Test level, one might leave the matter be. Were it not for the fact that millions see a batsman out and only the umpire sees him "in", human fallibility could continue on its merry way.

Umpire Robin Bailhache, for whom it all became too much during the '82-83 series, retired in face of the criticism heaped upon him. He later had the good grace to admit that he had been wrong in giving Hookes out in the Brisbane Test. And a further comment of his, as reported in the *Sydney Morning Herald*, deserves digesting: "There are so many times during a day that an umpire doesn't really have a clue what's happening."

Wisden Cricket Monthly, March 1983

Any idea of errors "evening themselves out" became the more preposterous the longer one considered it. And even this pioneering essay recognised that the official upstairs examining the replays should not be from the umpiring ranks, for they are usually too concerned with avoiding what they perceive as embarrassment for a fellow ump in the field who got it wrong with the naked eye. Pride problematically intruded. As the International Cricket Council moved snail-like towards adopting the obvious solution to the problem of highly visible human fallibility, the concept of referrals by the players themselves gained popularity. Anything that put an end to the damaging succession of obvious (to us) umpiring blunders was welcome. But why, oh why, did it have to take so long?

Meanwhile, the South African question raged on. Here is but one assessment from the many aired over these frustrating years:

Passions and Hypocrisies

THE OLD argument is given blazing new emphasis: will or will not the punishment of South Africa by means of sporting isolation cause a dismantling of apartheid? Or, conversely, will tours such as the unauthorised West Indian venture prompt a tightening in the Afrikaner stranglehold, so that ultimate black and coloured liberation must come eventually only through the extreme course which hardly bears thinking about?

It could be that the rampant hypocrisy of the matter is blinding fair-minded people to the deeper truth. Certainly the simple-minded (but *not* cretinous) man in the street who cares about civil liberty will have been left in no doubt about the deplorable plight of the underprivileged non-whites in South Africa. As to the practical matter of how to improve their situation, Lawrence Rowe, maker of a Test treble-century, a proud Christian, says: "I pray we can do some good by giving the whites here a different perspective on black people."

But former Jamaican colleague Michael Holding sees the "rebels" as "worse than slaves". Clive Lloyd, who, it must be admitted, would have few financial anxieties, says that money "is not all in life".

To most government treasuries it is. How else can it be explained that Australia sold $146-million-worth of goods and services to South Africa in 1981-82, importing $90-million-worth? The opposition Labor party have promised to bring in trade sanctions against South Africa if elected in the forthcoming poll. Then, any ban on cricketers – so long as it goes along with a ban on all sportsmen and entertainers – would make sense.

Rowe pointed out past inconsistencies by the Jamaican government: when most black nations boycotted the 1976 Olympic Games, Jamaica took part. "Why?" he said. "Because they knew that Don Quarrie would win the 200-metres gold medal. Singer Jimmy Cliff comes to South Africa, yet still wins top showbiz awards back home in Jamaica."

Australian Liberal MP Ray Groom has asked why good law-abiding citizens and sportsmen are kept out while people like Dr David Bellamy are not. The British environmentalist, who was arrested after a protest sit-in at the proposed Franklin dam in Tasmania, had "the expressed intention of breaking the law".

Double standards proliferate. At least it can be said of the West Indies territories that they are not guilty of hypocrisy in that they do not trade with South Africa. Australia does. So does Britain. And Sri Lanka sells tea there.

For the time being, passions all round might cool if the words of David Miller in *The Times* are studied: "The sort of five-figure sums being paid by South African business to bribe, irony of ironies, a team of West Indians to return to their continent of origin is a mark not of success but of failure."

Wisden Cricket Monthly, March 1983

More Australia Revisited

IT WAS probably the worst piece of television planning in cricket history. Border and Thomson had added 70 for the last wicket, and needed only four more runs to complete the most amazing of all victories. It was the end of an over, and, advertising revenue being the demi-god, on came a commercial for steel spanners. We'd seen it probably a couple of dozen times during the four days of transmission of this Melbourne Test match, and had already vowed never to buy the damned things. Now, though, there had been a quick changeover between overs, and before the commercial had run its self-defeating course, the match was ended. Onto the screen came pictures of a leaping Botham, a frenzied Geoff Miller. It was the only ball missed "live" throughout the entire match.

Eventually they showed the fateful delivery: Thommo's edge, Tavare's clever overhead pass, Miller's plunging catch. Then, even though it spelt three-run defeat for Australia, they showed it again . . . and again . . . and again. But nothing could make good the deprivation of instantaneous joy. I was certainly not going to waste mother-in-law's money by phoning Channel 9 in protest: probably wouldn't have got through, as the switchboard was jammed for ages. Nor, had a wheel on the car come loose as we headed down the Pacific Highway next day, would I have sought one of those wretched spanners. I was still in a mood to have used my teeth.

Sydney, city of my youth, tall and vibrant at the heart, sleepy and sprawling in the suburbs, and putrid with the odours of vice and over-celebration in Kings Cross. Jim Laker and poor, doomed David Kenning [BBC TV cricket producer, who died shortly afterwards] stood in the hotel foyer when the bedraggled Friths limped in. Then a beautiful bonus: from our 12th-floor room at the New Crest, views of old cricketing haunts: Rushcutters Bay Oval and Trumper Park.

A taxi to the Sydney Cricket Ground deprived me of the absorbing stroll through Darlinghurst, but returning to the SCG always – *always* – mists the eyes, no matter what changes have been wrought. The new Brewongle Stand – why didn't they name it the Trumper Stand? – is a beauty, but the best news was that, even if the days of the famous old scoreboard on the Hill are numbered, the "showboat" pavilion will be protected from the "visionaries" who specialise in knocking things down and replacing them with modern eyesores.

The company was good in the press-box. Bill O'Reilly – once we'd got the Irish question and the Falklands out the way – was the usual warm fund of anecdote and observation, no armchair stay-at-home at seventy-seven. And Jack Pollard, "high" on the publication of his magnificent new book, took welcome credit for advising a young, aspiring cricket writer to try England all those years ago. Keith Miller, though he, like the "Tiger", wins no plaudits from modern Test cricketers, was effervescent, belying his sixty-three years. Our heroes don't grow old, so long as you can blind yourself to their ageing exteriors.

I took an old friend along on the fourth day. Fifty-three years ago he had sat by the fence at the foot of the Hill and watched Bradman complete his 452 not out. He remembered a Queensland fielder saying how glad he was that The Don kept hitting fours: spared his feet. I had random memory glimpses of my own: David Sheppard, square-shouldered at deep square leg in 1951; Cowdrey on the boundary in 1955, with grubby, crumpled flannels; Trueman in 1959, saying, as I snapped him, "It won't come out, son." Miller making a noble Test century; Worrell cutting still the most elegant figure I've ever seen on a cricket field; Craig, a tiny boy, making a double-century against the South Africans; Lindwall flattening Tyson; red-faced Graveney cruising to his only Australian century; Hutton bowling Benaud; Barrington battling; gallant little Harvey.

Now all that really mattered, an Ashes-deciding Test match, slowly writing itself into the good book.

Bumped into Norman Cowans in Macleay Street that evening; suggested an early night since a few runs were needed from his bat tomorrow (England still needed 452 to win); got a wonderful grin in return. He gets bigger every time you see him.

The Ashes were lost by then, of course. No side was going to get that many in a day, even if the pitch was benign enough to call to mind fast bowler Ian Callen's reaction to the wicket at Melbourne earlier in the season. The one-time Northumberland player had bent down and sounded out both ends of the pitch with a doctor's stethoscope, searching for signs of life.

Dr Richard Cashman, who has contributed much by his studies of sporting crowds and their behaviour, achieved the ultimate in subject research by copping a loaded beer-can between the eyes. He crawled back into the press-box and told us how he had been interviewing a British migrant on the Hill. The Pom had been waving his flag and challenging the locals to let him have it. "Coom on, chook it at me!" he bellowed. They did. But their aim was wild. The sticking-plaster on Richard's forehead was viewed by the more compassionate as a badge of courage, by the rest as a mark of lunacy. You don't go on the Hill these days unless you have to.

Some faces will never be seen at the SCG again – Ray Robinson and Jack Fingleton – and the draw of the old spiritual home is lessened for it. A few days later I was sitting, jet-lagged, in my own living-room, watching it on the box, with only cuttings, a few photos and a fading suntan left.

Still, as many English folk have comforted themselves in years gone by, the Ashes are still to be seen at Lord's – even though Mungo MacCallum, of the Ned Kelly beard, is claiming in a Sydney paper that they should now rightly be shipped to Australia. Refuting MCC's claim that the urn is now "rather old and fragile", MacCallum wrote: "The same could be said of most of the MCC administrators, but they still manage to travel when it suits them." He feels that the urn could safely be transported – "and I am sure we could persuade the members of the Australian side not to play football with it when it arrives".

Wisden Cricket Monthly, March 1983

Book reviews were undertaken with a sense of responsibility. It may not have been in the world of cricket alone that publishers dished out shoddy productions, their eyes being solely on quick profits, but this reviewer faced up to the need to condemn books which fell short of reasonable expectation. There was a price to be paid, of course, with stinging letters from authors and proofreaders who felt they had been unfairly treated: but they hadn't been. If I set punishing standards for myself then I felt entitled to judge other books in the same way. The following review of a book by R.S.Whitington which purported to be a history of Australian cricket was one of the more provocative:

Perplexingly Slipshod

THERE HAVE been some perplexing cricket publications in recent years, but few to match, in that context, Dick Whitington's "history", which first came out in 1972. The revised edition, for all the injection of fresh and interesting illustration, is at least as slipshod as the first. The frontispiece is claimed to be cricket's earliest print, "possibly 16th Century". This predates it by around 200 years. The entertaining foreword by Lindsay Hassett in the 1972 edition has been omitted. Then the heading Acknowledgements is mis-spelt. Then, right in the middle of the section on the 1860s, comes a glorious colour photo of Greg Chappell batting "against Pakistan" – with Kallicharran at square leg! Turn on four pages , and there is *that* picture again: the 1859 English team to North America captioned as the 1861-62 team to Australia. And they had it right in the earlier edition! A picture of Syd Gregory is captioned as C.T.B.Turner; Barnes as McCabe; Hamence as McCool. Action shots of Miller and Morris are reversed, and Godfrey Evans is knighted! Pictorial gems include WG taking off for a run against Victoria in 1891, and studio personnel during a pre-war synthetic wireless commentary – in which Ray Robinson, Jack Ryder and Keith Rigg ought to have been identified. Thus, the book, which is more specifically a reflection of Australia v England, has to be taken with a pinch of sodium chloride. A great pity.

Wisden Cricket Monthly, April 1983

A heated letter from the author spelt the end of a good friendship, to my great regret.

The benefit season of three cricketers greatly admired presented the chance to write heartfelt tributes:

One of the Batsmen of the Age

WE ALL have favourite batsmen. One of mine is, pronouncedly, Gordon Greenidge of Hampshire and West Indies. He almost played for England, and that would have ensured that some of us would have seen gratifyingly more of him over the years. But perhaps it was as well that he was awarded the maroon Caribbean cap before Alec Bedser could make an England player of him. His inventiveness and dash are West Indian qualities. He would always have seemed a "ring-in" among England Test batsmen.

Gordon came to England at a tender enough age, but the origins are always going to be evident, creating a kind of twin identity. A long county residence and allegiance persuade the heart that Hampshire is the natural habitat; yet, when he joins the West

Indians for a Test tour, I've noticed the Barbados accent thickens. He is in the line of Headley, Weekes and Worrell, and therefore a rare breed.

Unlike Headley, he has not had to carry the West Indies batting almost single-handed. They say that Greenidge and Viv Richards cannot bat together with "tunnel vision". Each needs to prove something in the company of the other, rather as Kim Hughes and Greg Chappell indulge in a personal batting rivalry based on pride. Probably there has been no greater batsman in modern times than Richards, but I've always preferred to watch Gordon Greenidge.

I find it difficult to make myself understood on this point. People travel miles and cancel important appointments to watch Somerset's Antiguan at work. Yet the daring, the fluidity and the crisp strokeplay of the Hampshire Barbadian are, for me, the most enchanting of spectacles.

Many regard him as the ideal player in limited-overs cricket, pointing to the astonishing record he once held of record scores in the Gillette, Benson & Hedges and John Player competitions. But his most outstanding achievement was a pair of centuries against England in the Manchester Test match of 1976. He saved his side with 134 in the first innings, when they saw their first four king-sized wickets lost for 26; and made 101 in the second innings to make West Indies secure. There was a profound emotional satisfaction in the performance, for he had recently returned from a disastrous tour of Australia, one in which he reached rock bottom with a "pair" at Brisbane and the cold shoulder from his captain in his hour of desperation. The flashing Greenidge smile was noticeably absent, just as it had been the previous winter, when back injury rendered him a passenger in Pakistan. He looked like an old man in the nets as he struggled to regain touch.

By his own admission, he used to be cocky – a common failing among those who have risen from obscure backgrounds and overcome adversity. The hardships of 1975-76 gave him a sense of balance.

His balance at the crease, of course, has hardly ever been in question – not even when he smashed an unbeaten 273 for Derrick Robins' XI against the Pakistanis at Eastbourne in 1974. The thirteen sixes he hit in that innings were repeated in the Championship match against Sussex at Southampton the following season. The main difference was that the Eastbourne effort left him with only meagre recollections, since an overnight hangover had affected his retentive powers, if not his vision. Anyone watching those innings – and many dozens besides – would have known he was seeing one of the batsmen of the age.

He may never shrug off a blend of super-confidence pursuant upon success and a constitutional apprehension when facing the unknown. This is what makes him a peculiarly human cricketer, and therefore more interesting than those who come across as "run machines". This is what separated Ian Chappell from his cool, dignified brother Greg.

Since the day in August 1970 when Gordon Greenidge was first called up by Hampshire, he has had to endure the worrying periods of lost form familiar to all cricketers, plus the incidence of colour prejudice and dressing-room disharmony known by only the few. He has wrestled with crises of attitude, injury and mood.

On those many mornings or afternoons when he has prospered, bowlers have looked alternatively at the Heavens and their boots. And spectators have glowed with shared privilege and pleasure. Long, long may it continue.

Hampshire Handbook 1983

Zaheer Abbas: Sporting Impartiality

ZAHEER. I can now bring myself to write that with two "e"s. But the prolific Gloucestershire and Pakistan batsman once bowled me a googly.

Soon after that amazing innings of 274 against England at Edgbaston in 1971, Zaheer played for a World XI in Australia. It was during that tour that, having checked newcomer Dennis Lillee's bio-data (and announcing to the startled fast bowler that he shared W.G.Grace's birthday), I questioned Zed on the spelling of his name. "Zahir", he told me.

For years I corrected people who spelt it "Zaheer". But something seemed amiss. By 1978 I seemed the only person in the world to be using "Zahir". Even my printer was querying it.

I checked with him again. "Zaheer", he told me, his expression intimating that I really ought to have known better.

Perhaps he did us both a disservice. Whenever I've watched him bat, there has probably been a persistent background distraction over this cussed spelling. I'm sure men watching Wally Hammond didn't have to cope with this.

Anyway, he's known as "Zed" now. Or is it just "Z"?

I must just say that as a cricketer he rose even higher in my estimation last summer when my wife sat with his – Najma – and I saw Najma applaud some boundary strokes by *England* batsmen. One assumes she was trained as a cricket-watcher by her husband, and that he taught her to appreciate good cricket no matter who was displaying it. That's the sort of sporting impartiality that goes down well with many of us.

I only wish I could assure Zed that I'd applauded all his numerous boundaries, but of course that sort of thing is forbidden in the press-box. It is a temple of impartiality. But he ought to know that we applaud his classical, graceful batsmanship in our hearts.

Zaheer Abbas Benefit Year 1983

Randall: a Treasure

IT'S EASIER to get emotional about emotional cricketers. Some great batsmen have been somehow less than human. You haven't been able to laugh with them or at them, or cry for them. The shared pleasure is always greater when the batsman making those vital runs is so obviously one of us – a guy-next-door type.

I've been lucky enough to see all four of Derek Randall's Test hundreds. The first, in the Centenary Test at Melbourne, began with a few laughs. Dennis Lillee had never been confronted by a creature quite like this before, and wasn't certain how to treat it. The doffing of the cap, the backward roll to escape a bouncer – then the flashing cover-drive. What was the man playing at?

There's a clue here to the central enigma of "Arkle". He has the widest shoulders, the danglingest arms, the most tragic of eyes, the most ready of grins. He darts around in the field like a Constantine, and utters sometimes unintelligible things. Never still, never quiet. Compassionate. Quizzical. Jittery in such a way that it is anything but relaxing to watch him.

So, from all this, how can you accept him as a world-class batsman? Quite easily, really – if you can penetrate this extraordinary surround of near-madness. See that hook, that cover-drive. See the disciplined defence. See the counter-attack, the mark of a challenging man, stung at the thought that the bowler was about to put one over him.

That cover-drive in particular is one of the most impressive strokes I've seen in a lifetime. Across goes the left shoe, down comes the bat in a decisive sweep, and those laughing eyes peer after the punished ball as it whirls to the boundary. No need to move. Randall's picked the half-volley, and that's the end of the matter. Lacking in confidence? Anyone who feels that after a shot like this – or perhaps the belting hook off Lillee – can't have the whole story.

He can don a grim cloak. Mike Brearley helped him put it on at Sydney during the 1978-79 series. England were up against it, and Derek Randall proceeded to bat for ten hours for 150. Such self-denial in a stroke-player was to be marvelled at, yet it proved again that the young man had something special. He just needed to be a bit more serious, on and off the field, to convince some people. God forbid!

He made his first home Test century at Lord's in 1982 against India, and won further legions of admirers who had only read about his service to his country on foreign fields. Then in the third Test he scored 95. The day before the Test team was to be announced for the next contest, believing somehow that I had private access to the England captain's thoughts, he enquired: "Am I in for Edgbaston?" He had to be fooling! Or was he? Probably even he didn't know.

He saved England in that Edgbaston Test. Without his hundred, made uninhibitedly from the alien opening berth, England would have suffered their first defeat by Pakistan in twenty-eight years. I suppose if I'd bumped into him later that week he would have asked, with a quavering frown, if he was in for the next Test at Lord's.

I had to write about him straight after that Melbourne Centenary hundred. Cooped up in that little hotel room, without reference books, I could only keep thinking of George Gunn, an earlier Nottingham genius who also happened to score a Test debut century, and who abided by his own set of rules, one of which was to run out to fast bowlers. He is even said to have blown raspberries at the West Indians after playing bouncers down from in front of his face. And he was fifty years of age!

Now we're not expecting "Arkle" to be so irreverent. But if he chooses, and is able to go on till he is fifty, nobody I know will object; for his enthusiasm, his skill and, most of all, his unpredictability are treasured assets in a game which needs all the character and individualism it can find.

The Derek Randall Testimonial Year Souvenir Brochure 1983

Midsummer 1983 brought a memorable World Cup final at Lord's:

India's Crown

"NO HOPE!" That would have been the average cricket-watcher's verdict on India's chances in the 1983 World Cup as the teams flew in. Even when they beat West Indies, the 1975 and 1979 champions, in the opening match, few considered India likely to reach the final. Even when they beat an out-of-sorts Australia, they were given little chance in the semi-final against England. They kept chipping away. They seemed to be but mice before the mighty West Indies panther, now fully awake and licking its lips.

There was a resonant groan around Lord's when it was announced that West Indies had put India in to bat. So lop-sided did it seem later, when India were all out for 183, that Ladbroke's were offering 100-1 on them.

Derek Randall (left) conjures up another of his mad witticisms soon after returning from the 1978-79 tour of Australia, with a less forthcoming Ian Botham to the right of the author.

Six hours later the jam-packed ground floor of the Westmoreland Hotel was vibrating to the throb of a *bhangra*, a tribal dance of the Punjab and Haryana, and India's jubilant young captain was at the centre of it, eyes flashing, arms high, gyrating to the drums and handclaps and shouts like a cricketing Omar Sharif.

No batsman reached 40. No bowler took more than three wickets. Twenty wickets fell – and not one to a run-out. Tales of the unexpected. Roberts struck first, completing Gavaskar's wretched series and taking his first wicket in three World Cup finals. The early loss was soon forgotten as Srikkanth, Test cricket's village batsman, hooked Roberts for four and six into the Warner Stand before dropping on his right knee and scything a half-volley to the Tavern boundary. He then began to play and miss against Marshall, who is conceivably the fastest bowler he has ever seen – or not seen.

A recovery was under way, Srikkanth having hit some more boundaries (and run a second run backwards all the way – something rarely seen at Lord's), when he played across a straight ball, and India were 59 for 2 after 19 overs. We had just witnessed the biggest stand of the match.

Gomes came on and a tantalising situation presented itself: the chance to hit some runs hinged to the risk of getting out to powderpuff bowling. The blue-eyed Trinidadian with the bouffant hair bowled to a leg field, and with Holding settled into a tight line the rate was wilting at 72 off 26 overs. Then Amarnath lashed Gomes through the covers, Yashpal pulled Holding for four, and Amarnath hit Gomes for four more.

By halfway India were 90: but Amarnath, almost rooted to the spot, was bowled by Holding off his short run. Next over, Yashpal slashed Gomes to point; and immediately after lunch, taken at 100 for 4 (32 overs), Kapil Dev heaved Gomes for two boundaries before holing out at long-on. Kirti Azad was caught off a hook; Patil swung a six over square leg; Binny was caught at short midwicket; Madan Lal helped himself to six off Gomes; Patil messed up a pull and was caught; Madan Lal had his bails trimmed as soon as Marshall returned. All that in 11 overs while 50 runs were added. It seemed everyone wanted to get home early.

Nine down now, India tagged on a further 22 runs in 10 overs, Kirmani and Sandhu making what few considered would be vital runs. Marshall hit Sandhu's helmet, perched on his red patka; but the No.11 remained calm. The total was raised to 183 by the time Holding bowled Kirmani, India having failed to avail themselves of 5.2 overs. It was 3.16pm.

It was generally agreed later, not least among the West Indies players, that a target of 184 generated a casual, even cocky, approach. "We'd have made 270 if that had been the target," said Greenidge. "We got carried away with this 184," said captain Clive Lloyd. "It was an amateurish performance."

The debacle began in the fourth over, when Greenidge raised his bat to an off-side ball from Sandhu which nipped back and took the off stump. Viv Richards was soon menacingly into his stride, taking fours off Kapil Dev and beating Madan Lal to the long-on, cover and point boundary in four balls. It was as if he knew he was expected to put on a show.

Again, a lofted shot in front of the wicket proved fatal, Haynes hitting to cover. West Indian tension increased further when Lloyd began to limp agonisingly. He was allowed a runner.

Before Lloyd's brief innings ended there were two other profoundly important casualties. Richards pulled Madan Lal high towards the Grandstand and Kapil Dev took off in pursuit. He covered thirty yards before holding the catch lovingly. Over-confidence had killed the warrior king.

Binny tied up Gomes with a leg field; in the 18th over the left-hander fished outside off and was held at slip by Gavaskar. All hope seemed lost when Lloyd lunged painfully and hit Binny to Kapil Dev at mid-off: 66 for 5, and the old ground awash with excitement.

Down by the Tavern two bloodstained policemen carted off a Rasta who had departed from the peaceful stance, while a policewoman lost her cap, her smooth hairdo, but not her composure. Lord's was seeing, for the first time, West Indies in real adversity. The score at tea was 76 for 5 after 25 overs, with Amarnath just introduced into the attack. "We were waiting to get after 'Jimmy' Amarnath," said Lloyd later.

The explosion never came. With the sun now filtering through an oystery sky, Bacchus slashed wildly at Sandhu's third ball and steered it into Kirmani's gloves: 76 for 6.

It was now up to Dujon and Marshall to retrieve an unimaginable plight. Cautiously, apart from a Dujon six over square leg off Sandhu, they restored some calm, running daringly, refraining from the mighty swipe. It seemed time for an all-out assault, to throw India back on their heels. But no. The bat was placed steadily in line: two or three runs an over was the requirement, and that was all that was sought.

Then, in the 42nd over, with 65 still needed, more disaster befell West Indies. Dujon tried to withdraw his bat from Amarnath's good-length curler and played on. If ever it was time for West Indies to play the West Indies way it was now. There was no Collis King to drag them out of the crisis; but Garner or Roberts might have been sent in with licence to kill.

In Amarnath's next over Marshall went out to him and ended up poking at the ball as it veered away. Gavaskar held another catch safely, and the Indians' excitement could be felt. The subdued Roberts went, adjudged lbw to Kapil, next over, and that made it 126 for 9. And for the remaining seven overs we knew we were about to see one of the biggest upsets in international cricket history. The duration of the tenth-wicket survival added a tang to the anticipation.

Amarnath rolled and bobbed in, like an elderly bank clerk out jogging; Holding swung at a ball just short of a length, and umpire Dickie Bird answered the appeal with a raised finger which, in effect, granted countless millions of Indians a joyous if short-lived reprieve from the miseries of poverty and deprivation. Holding stood dumbfounded, and was soon to be trampled by near-hysterical fans as they flooded across the ground. (He missed his scheduled Derbyshire debut four days later, his ankle still sore and swollen.)

West Indies had been bowled out, on a pitch described as "near perfect" by their captain, for 140, to lose by 43 runs. "If only West Indies had batted like this in the 1979 final," said Mike Brearley before awarding Amarnath the Man of the Match prize.

Meanwhile the champagne corks were popping in the Indian dressing-room, every member of the team suddenly £1150 better off, courtesy of an ecstatic Indian Cricket Board. The party was to go on for hours. All that remains is for Sir Richard Attenborough to make a movie of it all.

Wisden Cricket Monthly, August 1983

An amusing postscript to India's shock success in this World Cup final was an impassioned letter from an Indian fan in reaction to goading remarks I had made in the competition preview. The essence of those comments was that if India didn't improve on their shameful past performances in World Cup cricket then they might as well withdraw from them in future. I therefore felt marginally responsible for their 1983 success. But my correspondent now suggested that if I were a true sportsman then I should eat my words. This I happily did, helping the pulp and printer's ink down with some pretty good red wine.

How an Indian artist saw the eating of the editor's words.

Umpire Bird

THE MAN from Barnsley, with the tragi-comic face, is that rarity among umpires: he keeps the game going with a pleasant good humour while at the same time maintaining a universal reputation for high efficiency. There was a time when he seemed a bit of an exhibitionist. I recall nine or ten years ago, in a Test match at Lord's, that he hared down the pitch to pick up a speck of something, perhaps a tiny leaf, when we all thought that if the batsman hadn't noticed it or bothered about it, then it really must be inoffensive. In that same match he added to his reputation for athleticism by covering about fifteen yards backwards as a run-out threatened. The problem this time was that he backed straight into little Kallicharran as he bent to field the ball at mid-on.

Dickie's keen all right; and thank God for that. Even more should we be grateful for his readiness to smile. On many occasions his wry grin and verbal aside have taken the heat out of a potentially explosive situation out there in the middle. He would have made a marvellous schoolteacher, firm but never over-serious.

Of course, he worries. It is a source of amusement – and perhaps not just inside the game – that H.D.Bird views the task of deciding whether play should proceed in drizzle or dubious light with the same gravity that Chamberlain applied to the German threat. We love his little twitches when the sky darkens.

But like all things cricketing, Dickie is best in the blazing sunlight. White cap Persil-white, that craggy countenance relaxed, a gentle refusal to the hysterical appeal, a perpetual aura of *enjoyment*.

He found it hard to enjoy the game when Dennis Lillee first switched to his shortened run-up midway through an over. This caught Dickie on the hop, and seemed to shake him. Thereafter, for every ball Lillee bowled, even off his long, long run-up, our umpire kept sneaking untrusting looks over his shoulder. This is the mark of the cricketer's best friend: an umpire ever-alert, quietly and good-naturedly in control.

The Twelfth Man (Wombwell Cricket Lovers' Society, 1983)

Soon New Zealand made sweet history in the Test against England at Headingley, a contest containing many oddities:

New Zealand Make History

OUT OF this summer of cricket sensations came New Zealand's historic maiden victory on English soil. It was a well-deserved victory, and if the excitement surrounding it did not measure up to the fervour at Lord's in June when India won the World Cup, the satisfaction for New Zealanders and many other sports-lovers was, if possible, more sublime, for New Zealand had to wait fifty-two years for this triumph.

There had been times in the series played here ten years ago when that elusive first victory had seemed there for the taking, notably at Lord's, where Keith Fletcher made a lengthy century and poor, doomed Ken Wadsworth missed two chances behind the stumps in the crisis hours. In the previous match, at Trent Bridge, New Zealand had failed by only 39 runs to make the 479 required of them.

On their next tour of England, in 1978, they lost all three Tests, but by then they had at least recorded their first win over England in their own country, at Wellington, where, it was predictably stated, England met their Waterloo.

Humiliations have been fairly numerous. To their "credit" remains the lowest score in Test history, their 26 against England at Auckland in 1955. In 1958 they were five times dismissed for under 100 in five Tests.

This famous 1983 victory was not achieved easily. Bob Willis bowled with fury on the fourth day, when New Zealand were set a mere 101 to win. He steamed in from the same end as when he took his 8 for 43 against Australia two years ago, and captured five New Zealand wickets by the time they had moved to 83. But he was tiring, and there had been only moderate support from the other end. Graham Dilley had a bruised heel, and was bowling only because an injection had eased the pain. Norman Cowans, who sent down some fiery overs, could not make much impression towards the end.

But most significantly, Ian Botham, now seen as yesterday's hero, was not even called upon to bowl until New Zealand were two runs from victory. Willis has finally, noticeably and probably indefinitely lost faith in him.

The Headingley pitch came in for much adverse criticism. It was watered heavily before the match to ensure that the drying and cracking would not occur too early, for when this pitch cracks it results in inconsistency in levels. The seamers loved it from start to finish. All 20 England wickets fell to the medium-pacers, and, astonishing to relate, Richard Hadlee, who for so long had been billed as a one-man Test team, took not one solitary wicket.

He did make vital runs in the first innings, when New Zealand stretched ahead of England by 152 runs. They knew they needed a long lead, for if England had gone on to a large second-innings total, as at The Oval, there could have been trouble for the Kiwis on the fifth day.

England fell apart second time round, the dependable genius of David Gower excepted. The sixth wicket had fallen before the arrears were wiped off, and New Zealand's prize loomed large in vision as the rest day arrived with England leading by two runs with four wickets in hand, one of them Gower, 54 not out. It needed for him to play the innings of his life. And he almost produced it. With 99 to his name, he had to forsake several singles as he retained the strike against a far-flung field. But Cowans stayed with him somehow, and New Zealand's target just made three figures.

By now all reasonable thoughts of Headingley '81 – rated by many as the greatest Test match of all time – had disappeared. That is, until Willis set about his barnstorming. Geoff Howarth took control for a while, keeping the runs coming, an essential factor. But Willis forced errors from him and from Wright, and not only did millions of television-watchers and radio-listeners in Britain stay tuned, but countless excited folk watched specially-laid-on direct television to New Zealand through these historic hours at $US12,000 per hour. Almost certainly a public collection would have reimbursed the New Zealand TV service most eagerly, with a few dollars left over.

When the match is recalled decades from now the names which will ring out will include Lance Cairns, the quiet strongman from Te Puke, whose return to form could never have come at a more apt time: his 7 for 74 which destroyed England's first innings won him the match award. The left-hand openers Wright and Edgar, the latter with a bad hip injury, made 93 and 84 to establish New Zealand's reply. Then Hadlee came to make a sensible 75. In the second innings it was Ewen Chatfield's turn to strike a few blows for his country.

Like England's Mike Hendrick, Chatfield, the man who nearly died eight years ago when struck on the head by a bouncer, has often bowled well without tangible result. Now, skilfully used by Howarth, he broke the back of England's attempted resistance, taking five wickets for the first time in a Test. That most useful of cricketers, Jeremy Coney, chipped in with the wickets of the dangerous Lamb and the frustrated Botham, and Cairns took his match tally to 10. Not to be overlooked was the faultless performance by Ian Smith, who replaced Warren Lees behind the stumps. He held seven catches.

And ringing out loudest should be the name of Geoffrey Howarth, who coolly controlled his team of club cricketers and outplayed England's professionals (one hesitates to refer to them nowadays as mighty) in every department of the game.

There were not many New Zealanders present at Headingley to witness their country's finest hour, but they waved their flags and the cheers rang out and hands were shaken vigorously. It is now twelve years since India won their first Test on English soil, and the jubilation among the thousands of supporters that afternoon is still vividly recalled.

The Times of India, August 7, 1983

By the Pearly Gates

THERE WAS the usual gathering around the Pearly Gates as Christmas approached. It was almost as congested as the forecourt at Lord's, by the Grace Gates, on the opening day of a Test match.

"What d'ye make of it then, Wilfred? What awaits them now that Orwell's 1984 is upon 'em?" piped WG.

The Yorkshireman shook his head slowly. He'd been worried for some time about the loss of popularity of slow bowling. And now, to add to his anxieties, his old county was torn apart by the Boycott dispute.

"I doan't rightly know," he whispered; and then lurched into a treatise on flight, the use of the feet, and the positioning of the left elbow. An unmeasured time afterwards, he confided huskily to the Old Man that he thought it was about time players' onfield behaviour improved. With his eternal interest in cricket, he'd watched more around the Universe, from his privileged station, than any of the other spirits, most of whom spent aeons in places where their busy cricketing lives had prevented them from going. But Wilfred had seen it all: the umpire-bumping, the stump-kicking, the abuse, the bouncer blitzes, the growth of the limited-overs game.

"Well, Wilfred," squeaked WG, as one who should know, "it wasn't much different in our day, was it? Old Jones tried to knock me head off. And an umpire's a fool if he lets you take him too far."

"You shouldn't take him that far," muttered the handsome young Australian leaning shyly against the pearly pillar.

"Ever the angel, Victor. Ever the angel."

"Not really, Doctor. I just don't reckon it's on. Why should . . . "

"I quite agree." The interjector was smiling, as ever. "There's nothing to be gained by being nasty."

"You'll never change, Jack," WG groaned. "How you ever made – what was it? – a hundred and ninety-seven centuries without a trace of what these moderns call the killer instinct I'll never know."

"One thing I would say," said Victor. "They were wrong to cover the pitches. The game doesn't seem as chancy nowadays."

"Finance, old chap, finance," offered a sleek fellow who was stroking the crease of his shirtsleeve.

"You should know, Herbert," said Jack with a wry grin.

"What you were saying about the bouncers," cut in a small, square-shouldered man, jaw jutting, cap peak hard on the bridge of his nose. "They should belt 'em back over their heads."

"I agree with Charlie Mac," said a tall, dark-haired figure, hands casually in pockets. "Gregory and McDonald would have run all over us if we hadn't hit back."

"They *were* all over you!" growled a mountain of a man drifting towards them through the eternal mist. "Maybe not you, Frank, but the rest of the Pommies didn't put up much of a show!"

"Steady, Warwick," cautioned WG. He pulled lightly at his beard. "We're at peace now." He chuckled wickedly. "The old game has changed, and none of us think it's for the better. But we've got to admit that it's very popular still. And for that we should be glad."

Wilfred wanted to debate the weakness of the lbw law, and the bubbly little monkey-faced Patsy was still asking why his old county had three West Indians doing the fast bowling. Another diminutive figure hesitantly reminded the group that 1984 had reminded him that a short while ago, in 1884, he had twice scored a century against the Australians at Lord's. "If I remember rightly, WG, you were kind enough to write that you would not readily forget the unceremonious way in which I treated the Australian bowling."

"And my editor referred to your Test hundred as remarkable and magnificent, Allan," chipped in John Wisden.

"Well, now it's 1984," said WG thoughtfully, "and I must say I envy those chaps all the money they make."

Several of the others looked at him sceptically, sidelong.

"But we do wish them well, don't we, chaps?"

"Aye, especially them in Yorkshire," whispered Wilfred sadly.

Happy New Year, readers.

Wisden Cricket Monthly, January 1984

FOR THE benefit of those who are uncertain: Wilfred (Rhodes); W.G.(Grace); Ernie (Jones); Victor (Trumper); Jack (Hobbs); Herbert (Sutcliffe); Charlie (Macartney); Frank (Woolley); Warwick (Armstrong); Patsy (Hendren); Allan ([A.G.] Steel).

In February 1984 there was a sensational Test match between New Zealand and England at Christchurch:

Carnage on a Cracked Crust

IT WAS all over in only twelve hours of play, but if it left people wondering how the fully professional England XI could have let themselves be so completely overrun by the mostly part-time New Zealanders, the explanation was hardly shrouded in mystery.

New Zealand's cricket authorities decided against switching the match to Napier, and thus condemned the batsmen (of both sides, of course) to the trials and torments of a highly suspect pitch, cracked, shifting and uncertain of bounce. One New Zealand batsman, questioned whether the match might be over in only four days, predicted, with a grimace, "More like three!" The macabre observation proved over-safe. It was New Zealand's quickest and largest Test victory and England's worst humiliation this century: not since 1894-95 had they failed to reach 100 in either completed innings. It had New Zealand roaring in joyous semi-belief. And it sparked an aggrieved murmur from the England camp which claimed, inherently, that Test match cricket was too precious a commodity to be spoilt by sub-standard pitches. It was all right in the 1880s, perhaps, when the majority of the low-scoring and best-bowling figures were recorded; but in the 1980s – also with an anxious eye on gate takings – batsmen, it seems, can show their worth only on perfect batting surfaces. Tyldesley, Trumper, Hobbs and Hutton, who all made so many of their runs on wet or broken pitches, are merely over-rated museum pieces to so many of the moderns.

In fact, batting at Lancaster Park was a precarious but not hopeless pursuit, and it was simple to imagine a Barrington or a Boycott selling his wicket very dearly. If New Zealand had bowled as loosely as England had done on the opening day, England must have come close to equally the home side's 307. But the ball's impact marks on the pitch covered a wide-ranging area when England's bowlers had finished, in contrast to the concentrated off-stump "line" of Hadlee and Chatfield. Confident, athletic catching in the Kiwi slips crescent secured their grip on matters, and it was soon plainly obvious that for Willis's hapless batsmen there was no place to hide.

Before a crowd of under 5000, Willis got plenty of bounce on the opening morning; but a New Zealand lunch score of 87 for 4 might have been – should have been – a lot worse. Botham began one of his disappointing matches with some wides and a dropped catch before having Martin Crowe, the new Somerset signing, caught at slip on the stroke of lunch. Tony Pigott, twenty-five, of Sussex and Wellington, called up in the emergency of injury to Dilley and Foster, and thus forced to postpone his wedding, took Edgar's wicket with his seventh ball in Test cricket – supporting early his 1983 unguarded claim that he deserved a Test cap – and Cowans, high in pace and acceptable in direction, struck twice and then followed up with Jeff Crowe's wicket to put New Zealand shakily on 137 for 5.

The match then swung, Hadlee and Coney playing strong strokes off weak bowling. Only one wicket fell in the second session, and Hadlee was launched on a fearless Botham-type assault full of lofted drives and other spectacular carves and cuts, having got the taste for it early with four boundary hits in one of Botham's wilder overs. Having crashed nine fours off six overs from a tiring Pigott, who actually had a fieldsman at long-off, Hadlee raced to 99, missed a short leg-side offering, and then perished by flicking Willis to Taylor. He had batted only 111 minutes and faced 81 balls, 18 of which he converted to boundaries. Only John Beck (1953-54) had previously scored 99 for New Zealand.

With Willis and Botham operating off shortened run-ups, England managed to capture the last four wickets in eight overs, but New Zealand had still scored at over four runs an over as they fed off undisciplined bowling and exonerated the groundsman thus far. There was no suspicion that England would do less than get within sight of their opponents' 307.

Even when Howarth called up Boock for the final over of the day, and the left-armer took Fowler's wicket with his first Test ball in four years, England's depth of batting seemed adequate in prospect. Twenty-four hours and a few millimetres of rain later, all was just about lost. Play on the second day started at 4.30pm, and in ninety minutes England were reduced on that cracked and spongy wicket to 53 for 7. Botham was straining for the initiative when he picked up a leg-stump ball from Cairns and landed it in the hands of deep square leg. The rest fell to rising and/or deviating deliveries. Straight-through balls were almost as rare as heat-stroke in that shivering oval.

The follow-on, England's death sentence, was not avoided. The last three wickets added 29, and with a mammoth deficit of 225 – the penalty for misdirected English bowling and disheartened batting – the second cortege moved off soon after lunch on the third day. Hadlee bowled some giant leg-cutters, as did Cairns between boomerang inswingers, and Boock spun widely, with England's most sickening moments coming when the fourth, fifth and sixth wickets fell between 31 and 33, Botham smartly caught at forward short leg first ball from an unduly firm stroke. Lamb, playing well out from his body, saw Coney hold a glorious left-hand diving catch, one of several memorable slips efforts by New Zealand, but Taylor hung on resolutely for 19 overs until run out after a handsome drive straight to cover. Randall, like Gower, was caught high at gully, further dismissals attributable partly to the oddities of the pitch and partly to human limitations. Seldom can England have been made to look so helpless by a team of apparently similar strength.

New Zealanders were impatient at suggestions that the pitch was to blame. Their Richard Hadlee, Man of the Match, had hit 99 on it, after all. He also took eight wickets, and at times looked unplayable. When a hangdog Old English sheepdog loped onto the field to hold up play in this memorable uneven contest, it was more than a little symbolic.

Wisden Cricket Monthly, April 1984

This was the first Test in the 20th Century in which England failed in both innings to reach 100. England's first-ever defeat by an innings margin against New Zealand led to volcanic repercussions, with charges of serious off-field misbehaviour being levelled at some of the touring players, and writs flying around.

It was always a pleasure to write something – no fee, of course – for a favourite cricketer's benefit booklet:

Graham Barlow: the Lively One

NICE SET of initials: GB. Patriotic. Other cricketers have the same set, but I can't think of one of them who is as lively a customer as Graham Derek Barlow of Middlesex, England . . . and the Wisden All-Stars.

That latter representative honour befell him when he came with us to Barbados last year – and was our only batsman to make a half-century. Even then, he got the rough end of the umpire's forefinger. Smiles and a rueful wagging of the head. Next match, run out because he forgot he wasn't batting with the Olympic sprinter Wilfred Slack. A quick flush of the cheeks, gnash of the teeth, stroll around the boundary, then he was all right. Came the third match, and Milton Small whipped one down the leg side and had Graham "caught" off his thigh-pad. A cheery, cheeky, cockney quip, and that was that.

A nice temperament, and admirable patience. But you had to watch him carefully poolside. Never turn your back, especially when fully-clothed. Charm, too. We'd no sooner sat down for our first meal with him and his lovely wife than he leaned across confidentially and asked, "Now, when did you two meet?" Unused to that kind of questioning after a tranquil quarter of a century, we racked our memories and gave a suitable reply.

But still don't turn your back poolside.

His fielding is world-class. We saw that on the uneven outfields of Barbados. And it took me back to the Centenary Test match at the MCG in 1977, when GB took the field as twelfth man. Australians love lithe fielding – and especially long flat throws – probably more than any other aspect of cricket. Graham gave it to them.

Some players you see only intermittently over the years when they aren't England regulars. First sight of GB was when he was but a lad, receiving an award at the Cricket Society. Eight years later he was hitting 80 not out against West Indies in his first one-day international, which innings got him on the winter tour. In '77 came that memorable run-out against Australia in another one-dayer, when he was dreaming on his way back to the bowler's end, and Rod Marsh chucked him out. That is remembered when his match-winning top-score 42 is more readily forgotten.

There's a lot of luck moving around in cricket, as we all acknowledge. With a little more of it, Graham might have won more England caps. It is still not too late. In the winter, England tour India. With a 1984 summer comparable to his wonderful 1983 summer, GB could go back under the "every eight years" principle. They may well need fellows on that trip who can laugh almost non-stop. Watch your back at the pool-side though.

Graham Barlow Benefit '84

There were to be no further Test caps for G.D.Barlow. Back injury hastened his retirement and he sought a life in coaching in South Africa.

Some have a particular hero, others have several. I persuaded the compiler of an anthology in 1984 to allow me to indulge myself with two of the species:

Cricket Heroes: Lindwall and Harvey

IT TOOK a lot of sorting out over the years before I knew who were my durable cricket heroes, for there had been much competition for my eager admiration and affection, from teenage years onward. Many nights, as I lay waiting for sleep to come, the "film" I ran through my mind showed Denis Compton and myself taking the score from 20 for 3 to well over 300. Only marginally was the best of the strokeplay my partner's. Then Len Hutton's delicate poise – quite apart from his average of 88 in the 1950-51 Tests – persuaded me to assume his personality and straight bat in the marathon international contests on the strip of coarse lawn at the front of the house. Alec Bedser's skill and mighty stamina impressed deeply; but he was too hefty a man to mimic successfully. Then came Arthur Morris – principally because I was attending his old school in Sydney, but also because he was patently such a *nice* man. Keith Miller was too awesome, larger than real life, beyond emulation. It was only years later that the understanding dawned that here was the ultimate in sporting gladiators, nonchalant, bold and chivalrous. Probably the only bloke in Sydney who was apeing Miller in full seriousness at that time was young Richie Benaud.

Two Australian cricketers of that time, though, were idolised by many thousands. It was a pity that the idolatry had to be on a shared basis. But it was firmly founded, and for me, I have since discovered, perpetual in its nature. I have seen them both recently, playing fun-nostalgia cricket when comfortably old enough to be grandfathers. The sight of them out there in the middle tended to choke me, for those two no-longer-slim figures stood for the iniquities of Time, which slunk away with their youth, my youth, and conceivably your youth.

Ray Lindwall was the pride of our alley. That he was the world's greatest fast bowler and represented New South Wales and Australia seemed only slightly more important than the fact that he played for St George, our district club. Bradman and O'Reilly had played for St George before the war, and now we had Lindwall and Morris, with one of my under-16 team-mates, Norm O'Neill, already also showing signs of genius.

Many things about Ray Lindwall appealed to me: his easy-going manner; no trace of swank. Nor was he actually a physically intimidating giant. Most of all, there was his bowling action, the cruising, shoulder-rolling, menacing run and precision delivery, billowing trouser-legs spread wide, trigger right arm sweeping through low in a blur, leaving him with hair aflop, sleeve hanging loose. Carefully I practised that action, every developing movement mapped out like a ballet sequence. Many years later, when I was still trying to pitch leg and take the off stump, remarks about the low arm were meant to disparage. Yet what my friends failed to realise was that the "low arm" was the very link that gratified. However futile the rest of my efforts to emulate Lindwall, the roundarm sling was the mark of the freemasonry – even if it had only a one-way flow.

Only the weakest boys refrain from approaching their heroes. I moved in closer, evening by evening, at the back of the Sydney Cricket Ground pavilion. Autographs bred short conversations . . . and then a request for a lift home with him, delivered so softly as to be a whimper he did not comprehend. But one night the question was audible, and the reply came: "Sure!"

The journey to the match had begun as usual after school: an uphill walk from Central Station started under a mushroom cloud of alcoholic fume from the brewery, wound past the loading bays of the *Daily Mirror*, where I was soon to start my working life, and where the smell of newsprint clamped my very soul, then through the old terraced streets of Surry Hills. At last the view flattened out across the expanse of Moore Park, and there were the cream and green stands of the SCG on the horizon. The pace quickened. Just short of the turnstiles it was possible to get a glimpse of the scoreboard on the Hill. It was always a better sight when the yellow arrow marker indicated that Lindwall was in action. There was I, shuffling, part-mesmerised, through the shadows beneath the old Brewongle Stand; and there he was, out in the dazzling sunlight, face pink, hair ruffled, and cheeks taut from effort.

It was best to sit up in the Sheridan Stand, to watch the glistening red ball burn a path away through space, swerving to the left and leaving the mug batsman fanning at nothing; or ducking to the right and clacking against the stumps, usually removing one of them for a thrill equalled in all sport only by Randolph Turpin's knockout left hook. Lindwall's bumper, used, on the whole, sparingly, caused a rippling murmur, broken by a few exclamations from the Hill. And all this was even more dramatic when he bowled from the Paddington end – in effect at me. Effort given, he would struggle into his sweater, often losing half his shirt collar; then the loose cap was flicked on at an undisciplined angle, and he would shuffle off to his position in the gully.

A few hours later, showered and with the lost body fluid well and truly replaced, Ray Lindwall, in sports jacket and suede shoes, emerged from the rear of the pavilion, crossed the lawn, and found a starry-eyed young chap waiting by his Holden. He was annoyingly modest. He obviously needed to unwind, for he could never be persuaded to explain just how he had got Stollmeyer or Weekes or McGlew out. It was a time to discuss history and geography and biology as we sped round the lip of Botany Bay. It was ludicrous. At first, it was all I could do to speak at all, having taken so much out of myself in engineering the lift. How I used to wish that a gasket would blow, forcing us to stop, and extending the journey time. My classmates wouldn't believe me the first time I had a lift in Lindwall's car. There seems nothing sensational about it now, but in 1952 it was like being invited into Napoleon's carriage or Bing Crosby's limousine.

Carlton was three miles from Hurstville, where Ray had lived since his own boyhood. There he had bowled a tennis ball at a kerosene tin in the roadway in an effort to attract the great Bill O'Reilly as he made his way home from work. Now, while there was still some light, I would grab my tennis ball and do my Lindwall look-

alike, though there was no-one there to watch me, except sometimes my father, who thought I ought to ping the tin every ball, and somehow failed to appreciate the subtleties of the out-swinger – easily achieved with a tennis ball – and the bumper, which had to be retrieved from a grumpy neighbour's garden.

We almost got Ray Lindwall into the house once. As he set me down, Mum waved, called cheerily, and told him the pot of tea was ready to pour. But he leant out of the car window and excused himself – adenoidally, shyly, nicely.

Then came the final car ride, though thank goodness I didn't know it. It was all over. Again, I could only watch from the distant stand and go home by train. He took his 100th wicket against England before my very eyes, and he played on until he was thirty-eight, finishing with a then-record 228 Test wickets for Australia. A lot of Sydneysiders had been disappointed when he married and went to Queensland – not disappointed that he married, of course, but upset that he had "defected". Looking back, I wonder if it was pure coincidence when, a couple of years later, I went to Queensland (enforcedly, admittedly, with the Royal Australian Air Force) and also ended up blissfully married to a Queensland girl. And just to ram home the blind, helpless identification with my hero, allied this time to sweet chance, within the year I had taken 6 for 20 for St George as we got Randwick out for 52. If these figures have no significance, perusal of the Oval Test match score of 1948 will reveal all. Few days have been so cherished.

My other knight in shining armour? He was younger than Lindwall, smaller, and batted left-handed. Neil Harvey always had sunlight gleaming across his cricket. Even to someone as immature as I, he represented youthfulness, audacity and unlikely command – unlikely because of his size. He always looked a boy among men. He was not strident or grossly dominant. Those qualities would not have appealed, anyway, to a youth who himself was unsure about life.

Harvey's dark head was always inclined, as if in partial apology, as he walked

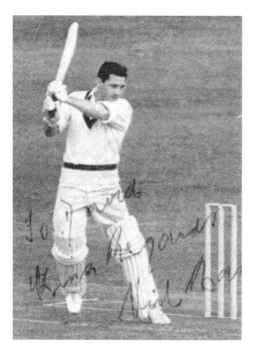

Ray Lindwall (left) and Neil Harvey, two cricketers worthy of adulation and attempts at emulation.

briskly and neatly out through the gateway. He hardly ever wore a cap, that earnest token of shelter; all his accoutrements were white or cream: he was one of the first to adopt white batting gloves, and bats were then devoid of garish flashes and stripes. He always seemed too small to survive, but when he started to move, his genius shone. Those darting little feet took him across the crease or down the pitch, always with a neatness of execution that had the same effect on the spectator as rounding a corner in a gallery and seeing a brilliant canvas or sculpture. Except that Harvey was seldom still. In his batting, flourish and discipline harmonised. After his torrent of Test centuries, particularly against the South Africans, and his brave 92 not out against the fire of Tyson and Statham when the other Australians looked third-raters, news of his pair of noughts in Laker's Test at Manchester in 1956 was dumbfounding. Still, he did captain Australia to victory in the Lord's Test of 1961.

There was one very odd thing about the Harvey-worship. Whenever I heard the clear, glad sound of a Guy Mitchell recording on the radio, I pictured Neil Harvey. Psychologists might have an explanation. Anyway, Guy Harvey – or Neil Mitchell – or whatever his name was – batted and sang me through the carefree summers of my teenage years.

Around 1962 I found I was actually due to play against Neil Harvey in a first-grade match. All the old Cardus-type prayers were revived during the tossing and turning of the night before the match: let Neil make a century, and let's get them all out for 135. No-one ever morally anticipated a Bill Lawry innings in that fashion. Harvey scored only 10, and I could have throttled our off-spinner for bowling him. But at least I had chased a back-cut almost to the fence, and thrown in as they completed a third run. On the second day, Harvey bowled me with a curving full-toss. I didn't want to get out, I swear it.

There was always something "singing" about Harvey's batsmanship, and even when he had to fight, with runs coming slowly, the music was never entirely silenced. He was a prince of sunshine, and looked as alien to the environment when rugged up in sweaters at damp, dark Bradford or drab Kennington Oval as the tanned, short-sleeved Beach Boys when they performed their escapist musical magic in wintry North London. Harvey was summer and eternal youth.

There should be no comparisons. Mozart isn't better than Haydn; nor Dickens than Nabokov. Since Lindwall, there had been Hall and Holding, Procter and Lillee and Thomson and Willis and Kapil Dev. But I can still picture, every bit as clearly, Ray Lindwall going through his loosening exercises at the extremity of his run-up, while the batsman tried to look calm and unaffected even though sometimes it was as if he were tied to a stake, watching his executioner test the bolt action of his rifle. As was said more than once, with vividly good reason, Lindwall moved in to bowl as if on castors.

Lindwall and Harvey were to be seen again playing against Old England at The Oval in 1983. Ray was good for only three overs off a short run. He was, after all, past sixty. The action was the genuine old article, if in slow motion. The arm was no lower than in the old days. Someone remarked that it couldn't have been anyway. He operated from the same end as the lean demon of thirty-five years before, when he took that 6 for 20. Neil Harvey patrolled the covers in a threatening manner which owed much to legend, though there was one memorable pick-up and flat throw. When he batted, Time's ravages were hardly evident. The drive still worked, and the cut which had helped him towards 21 Test centuries was in good functional order. And as the ball blurred its way to the cover boundary, deep inside my head the strains of *Sparrow in the Treetop* jumbled with *My Truly, Truly Fair*.

Cricket Heroes (Queen Anne Press, 1984)

A brief tribute was called for when a good friend was granted a benefit by the Indian Cricket Board. A fanciful little piece penned earlier to accompany a watercolour by John Ward served the purpose:

Bishan Bedi in a Nutshell

THE BRUTALITY and destructive power of the fast bowler are the thunder and lightning of cricket. The guile and patience and imperturbability of the left-arm slow bowler are like a breeze that wafts the unsuspecting over the cliff's edge. The storm will pass; the zephyr persists. No aware batsman could escape a feeling of unease as Bishan Singh Bedi smiles and even applauds after being struck to the boundary, for to have forced the cobra back a yard is not to have captured or controlled it. The Sikh, captain of India and citizen of Delhi and Northampton, has inherited the wizardry of a hundred years of forebears of his art. The soft, substantial figure bobs to the bowling crease, and strong wrist and fingers impart a buzzing gyration to the ball. It spends its flight in anything but a straight line. Its length is faultless. It spins top-like. It may be hit away for runs. It will be returned to the bowler. He can bowl all day if called upon, and so often asserts his will.

Bishan Bedi Benefit 1984

In another summer of incessant West Indian bouncer hostility, some Northern humour was a welcome palliative:

A Little Matter of "Bottle"

EACH EVENING, after the day's play in the Test matches, the sponsors generously bring players, insurance folk and the media together in a marquee known as the "hospitality tent". And here, on at least three occasions during this torrid summer, there has been cause to offer a heartfelt "Well batted" to Graeme Fowler, the Lancashire lad who has kept smiling through the shelling and bombing. "Foxy", the new pride of Accrington, grins his cheeky grin, acknowledges the greeting with a mixture of gratification and shyness, and goes on to say – given the chance – that he owes a lot to David Lloyd, Lancashire and England's other recent Accrington product.

Now this is odd when you consider that Lloyd came back from the 1974-75 tour of Australia with his confidence and technique in ruins, stitch-marks, courtesy of Lillee and Thomson, on his body. But you can't keep a fighter down for long, and as the young colt Fowler travelled to Lancashire's matches in the co-pilot's seat of Lloyd's car he absorbed a philosophy and wisdom which had survived the shellacking of '74-75 without becoming soured by cynicism.

Batting with the veteran brought further enlightenment. "'Bumble' used to speak a mixture of wisdom and humour that bordered on lunacy," recalls Fowler. "The '74-75 tour was a shattering experience for him, and it could have finished him or made him think more about it. He was a great thinker, always analysing and putting it together. He dropped down the order and I came into the Lancashire side as opener. Then when Andy Kennedy went, David and I opened together for a time. He always took first ball. He reckoned you had a good chance of getting a 'buncake' – one you could smack anywhere.

"In this match against Notts the first ball *was* a long-hop. He missed it. He square-cut the next for four, was dropped off the third and fourth balls, and missed the fifth and sixth. At the end of the over he came down the pitch and stated 'You've got to take the chance when it's there!'"

During that period when the Accrington men opened together for their county they agreed the most profitable approach was for Lloyd to take most of the spin bowling and Fowler the high pace.

What other profit came from this somewhat Laurel and Hardy partnership? "Well, when the opening bowlers had been seen off, Lloyd would stress that you shouldn't smash the first-change bowlers or they'd bring back the openers. That would be daft, since you'd already done the hard work in seeing them off. So you picked out a good fielder or two and whacked it to them. Runs but no boundaries. Then you'd look for a bit of concrete terracing or suchlike and hit a boundary in that direction. That scuffed the ball a bit. Later on you'd look for a pile of broken bottles or something! The theory was grand, but got a bit absurd as it progressed."

That, it seems, is what kept spirits up. But, of course, it couldn't have applied against the West Indies attack. Well, could it?

When he was hit on the head in the Old Trafford Test it was the first time for Graeme Fowler. He took the blow on the back of the helmet. His legs didn't "twitch", as stated in one Sunday paper. He was right in line for the balls that followed. Keeping the concentration going is far more important even than keeping the spirits up. The natural perkiness helps, but intense concentration on the job of staying in for England is by far the prime force.

Fowler came into an era of protective helmets. They are as natural to him as leg-guards, and, interestingly, he says he finds a helmet of considerable assistance in fixing vision. The peak and "blinkers" shut off peripheral view. He finds the grille type no use as it gets in the way when he tucks that chin down onto the collarbone as he hops into a defensive crouch across his stumps.

Perky? Yes. Full of guts? Certainly. Lucky? No, says county captain and opposition Test skipper Clive Lloyd: he is far from being the only batsman to have played and missed at fairly frequent intervals during this series.

Fowler rounded off the centenary of Test cricket at Lord's with a century,

A.G.Steel, another Lancastrian, having scored 148 in the first, in 1884. But "Foxy" may have more in common with Eddie Paynter (granted that cricketers detest being compared with past players – even heroes). Both small, left-handed, ready for a laugh, and as well stocked with "bottle" as Steptoe and Son.

And the thing which chuffed Fowler as much as anything as the fourth Test began on his home ground was that, in his fourteenth Test, he made it onto the front row in the team photo. He has probably done enough this summer to sort out some of the doubters and to stay in that front row for a time to come.

Wisden Cricket Monthly, September 1984

From the hundreds of book reviews here is one on Bob Woolmer's interesting Pirate and Rebel?:

Elements of Agony

BOB WOOLMER is one of cricket's "nice guys", and it comes through in an entertaining book which moves fairly urgently, not without humour, but with elements of agony. No more guaranteed of a long tenure in the England side than anyone else, he joined Kerry Packer's World Series unit. Now, with hindsight, he feels a certain regret. It probably cost him the Kent captaincy – perhaps even that of England. The tour of South Africa is another matter. With a long commitment to cricket in that country, he argues vehemently for its reacceptance. He feels that the TCCB were unfair in warning players not to go without being explicit concerning likely penalties. Further, he wonders how a player can offend his county club when he is not even employed by it during the winter months.

For those who cannot remember, Woolmer was a big asset to the England team in the mid-1970s. He made the slowest Ashes Test century at The Oval in 1975 (graphic recollections here of the Australian sledging) and added two more hundreds in 1977 in his next two Tests against the Old Enemy. A gentle person, he shivered as he watched the 1976 West Indies fast attack battering Edrich and Close, and recalls Close coming in and calling for a Scotch as he spat blood into the sink. Touring was not all that appealing to Woolmer the family man, and his nature demanded occasional solitude just when he was supposed to be singing and otherwise disporting himself like an extrovert at silly team parties.

He is good on player-analysis, portraying the fast men of our time, with John Snow winning the accolade as the quickie who knew best how to work a batsman over: he believes he started the modern concept. He can smile now at the kind of jibe dished out by Lancashire's Peter Lever: "You southern bastards have all got round bats!" And among his revelations is the conviction that John Hampshire was played in the Headingley Test of 1975 as a sop to the Yorkshire fans. He is forthcoming, too, on Kent's uncompromising reaction to his joining the SAB tour of South Africa (which returned him £20,000). Then he goes and damages his back last year while – of all activities – washing his trousers. That, plus a probable disenchantment, sees him leaving the game he loves, in his benefit year, with a hardback testimony to remember him by.

Wisden Cricket Monthly, September 1984

Bob Woolmer's life in cricket was far from over. He coached Warwickshire and South Africa with great success before taking up an appointment as Pakistan's coach. Within hours of that team's shock defeat by Ireland in Jamaica during the 2007 World

Cup he was found dead in his hotel room. Murder theories abounded then subsided. The full truth may never be known. What remains unquestionable is that Bob Woolmer was a cricketer of high class and a man widely liked and respected.

A brief and eventful peep at India came later that winter:

Meandering in Madras

REELING FROM inoculations and tablets I'd have bypassed but for the frenzied insistence of friends, I sat for 5½ hours at Heathrow while the aircraft coped with icy runways and delayed schedules – time enough to ring through about Shastri's double-century [world record 113 minutes: Bombay v Baroda] just before the February issue [of *WCM*] went on the presses. By 2pm it was eight hours since I'd set out from home twenty miles away on a chill black morning, and I was fed up. How easy would it be, I wondered, to retrieve my suitcase and go back home? Then the "boarding" signal came. Too late to turn back. Am I'm glad.

The Air India Jumbo lifted above that depressing bank of grey cloud into a bright blue world, and the mystic subcontinent lay only a short night ahead. They actually held the Bombay connection for us for two hours, which saved half a day. But still it was the usual unreal arrival, into the palatial Taj Coromandel Hotel in dusty Madras, just in time for a D.Gower eve-of-Test poolside press conference.

Then, with no time to waste, off to the shops and bazaars, with a young man who had never ventured outside Europe before and who seemed unduly concerned about his health. Now why should Ralph Dellor be so mindful of germs and traffic hazards? Well, it seems he had invested something considerable in what amounted to a full-scale audition with Test Match Special. And Peter Baxter's latest Opportunity Knocks candidate therefore refused point blank to ride in those three-wheeled giant lawnmower-type vehicles they call "autorickshaws". He would not cross any of those lethal streets up, down and across which hundreds of screaming taxis, bikes and trucks careered, horns blaring as if it were a legal requirement. He would not drink the tea served to us when our throats were parched. And he further refused a coffee an hour later when a genteel antiques merchant detected how close to exhaustion we were.

I'm glad to report that Mr Dellor made it to his radio commentary debut, and by the fifth day was venturing into the streets with little inhibition and was even seen taking the occasional drink, though with that ridiculous early bout of self-pampering he deserved to wake up on that first important morning with a green tongue and spots all over his elfin face.

It was one of the most enjoyable Test matches I have ever seen, and if the accompanying account is a trifle over-long, I don't apologise. Test matches come and Test matches go – in ever-increasing numbers – but this one in Madras was something special. The spirit in the England camp was obvious even before the match began, and it was as if the torments of those first tragic weeks of the tour had never been. Perhaps it was this awful background [assassination of Indira Gandhi] which had helped weld the side together – and even brought players and pressmen closer, after several years of strained relations. One or two of the England players at the end were even gracious enough to thank me for turning up as a kind of good-luck charm. What they didn't appreciate was that *we lost the one that mattered*!

I refer to the "Press Test". It seems the English Press XI had won the three matches to date. Now, on the rest day in Madras, the Indian combination inserted a few players of fair quality, like Chandu Borde and Ambar Roy and Bishan Bedi.

Clad in David Gower's sun-hat, Phil Edmonds' shirt, Mike Gatting's trousers (which I'm delighted and surprised to say were slightly too large), Norman Cowans' substantial box, and Paul Downton's favourite shoes, I soon discovered that to late-cut Bedi's arm-ball yorker is not really on, and a few overs later he took his first hat-trick for sixteen years, with John Jameson the distinguished middle victim. We recovered, thanks to a half-century from Andrew Wingfield Digby of Oxford University, Dorset and *The Church Times*; but 140 was not enough, even though Dellor risked bowling without a hat on in the fierce sunlight and knocked a few hobs over.

The evenings were full of surprises or delights. One of them, on the late side, threw up the unlikely sighting at the bar of Engelbert Humperdinck, just in from LA, visiting his native land (without an entry visa) and hoping to consort with the English cricketers and to film them with his new lightweight videocamera. Another evening found Graeme Fowler, 149 not out, resuming his career as a drummer. When the group in the coffee lounge took a break "Foxy" was persuaded to thump out a few rolls in the safety of the half-light on stage. He was great. But his chief concern was that he might get the taste for drumming again and find it once more obsessive.

The gala evening came in the shape of a celebration gathering to honour Dr M.A.M.Ramaswamy, whose achievements on the turf make the Aga Khan's efforts look puny. He had been responsible for 125 Classic winners, which gained him this festive tribute – with nine speeches – as well as an entry into the *Guinness Book of Records*, and ourselves the chance to mix with the sportswriting fraternity of Madras and other parts. The snow and the ice, the miners' strike and the collapsing pound never seemed so far away.

After the excesses of some partisan cricket crowds – the drunkenness of the English, the mindless jangle of the West Indians, the fanatic fervour of the Pakistanis, the verbal violence of the Australians – one of the pleasures of being at the Chepauk was to feel and hear the fair-minded, almost ingenuous delight of the spectators, spoilt only when they gave Gavaskar the raspberry. They cheered the double-centuries of Fowler and Gatting as if they were their own sons. They screamed with ecstasy when a fielder of either side did something spectacular. If there is a case for "neutral" umpires (and the admirable two standing in Madras were a strong argument against) then "neutral" crowds might be an idea too. England would happily play always in front of this eager and innocent gathering.

The welcome at an individual level, too, was unforgettable. One of the most popular things one could have done, it seems, was to eat one's words after India had surprised all by winning the 1983 World Cup. The reminders were constant and beautifully playful. Well, here goes again: if India don't perform creditably in Melbourne . . . [They did, winning the one-day World Championship two months later.]

Suddenly it was time to go. The victory celebrations in Room 705 splashed to a fizzling end. The caravan moved on. My flight to England, so rumour had it, would not terminate at Heathrow. Snow was avalanching down. We'd probably land at Prestwick. There was even fog in Delhi. From midnight there was a ghastly six-hour wait in Bombay's transit lounge. Visions of the nine-day pile of mail and newspapers began to materialise. Struth! This is where I came in.

Wisden Cricket Monthly, March 1985

Having written a book in 1975 on the history of fast bowling it seemed natural to put one together on slow bowling. This came eight years later, with a paperback follow-up. A certain pessimism ran through the book because slow bowling was at a low ebb. But hope had not completely disappeared, and certain speculations were eventually to be justified:

Enigma Variations

WHICH SPIN bowler has had the most profound influence on the game? The traditional answer is Bosanquet, whose "wrong'un" turned the coaching manual inside-out. A facetious answer could be another of Huguenot descent, Benaud, by his important consultancy role during the Packer revolution – which ironically accelerated cricket's headlong dash into an age of media-bred brutality.

Nor, in pursuance of the traditional choice, Bosanquet, is the googly necessarily the last technical innovation, for the "flipper", so much more difficult to bowl, came several decades later, and the Iverson/Gleeson middle-finger delivery after that. What is next? The off-break wrong'un, producing a leg-spinner from a hyper-cocked wrist? A back-spun "hanger" which drops late? The scientists will say that all this – and more – is possible.

Batsmanship can hardly advance in technique. In fact, it has lost some of its features – the delayed late cut, the draw, the "dog stroke". The backhand (reverse) sweep is no new thing. Mushtaq Mohammad, Kim Hughes, Botham are only continuing the line of Lockyer, E.M.Grace, Hornby, O'Brien, Fender, etc. Batting ingenuity has necessarily become directed towards survival against spoiling and persistent short-pitched fast bowling. How much more fascinating it has been to watch a world-class batsman wrestle with the complexities of dealing with an accurate and devious spinner.

Moves are afoot to "rescue" slow bowling. In England, pitches are covered. Long ago, nothing was covered, which meant that after rain the spin bowler had a feast: not only was the wet pitch his to exploit, but there was no competition from the faster bowlers, since they couldn't stand up on the slippery turf. Then came covered run-ups, and the slower bowler – unless he was an Underwood – dropped behind the medium-pacer in the pecking order.

Modern covered pitches, with the added instructions to make them reasonably turnable in the later stages of a match, are intended to bring the slow bowlers back into the picture. Further, the 100-overs limitation on first innings in the County Championship, which again played into the hands of the faster bowlers, was scrapped. Next came the move to extend Championship matches to four days each. If boundaries were extended, no second new balls were permitted, and outfields were made less lush, the spinner would come back into his own. The know-all professional should be reminded that fine spin bowlers like Eric Hollies did not have to wait for the third day of a match before being of any use.

Limit run-ups if necessary – only two bowlers per innings being allowed to cover more than seven yards. Maybe the wicketkeeper should be compelled to stand up at the stumps for all bar the said two bowlers. Perhaps, if things don't work out and future spectators are denied the pleasure of watching a Mailey or a Laker, there will have to be two distinct forms of cricket, just as there are two kinds of rugby. The one-day match can have its excesses of pace bowling and ever-increasing violence. Let the highlights be shown on television late at night, graded X for over-eighteens only. And the three-, four- or five-day match can be played on a scale familiar to the ranks of old, where balance and beauty are paramount. Already it is becoming more than some batsmen can grasp that it is actually possible to feel relief at the return of fast bowlers to the attack.

The Slow Men (Corgi, 1985)

The off-spinner's "other one" did indeed emerge – known as the "doosra" – and the reverse sweep is now commonplace. Fast bowlers' love of bouncers has been curbed at long last by legislation. But pitches remain protected because of the money-men's demands for maximum revenue. This, of course, launches a thousand giggles every time a Test finishes in three days, leaving Lord's empty over a complete weekend, as in 2009. They simply got the scheduling wrong this time.

Some book reviews could be quite felicitous, as this of Alan Ross's Australia '55:

A True Classic

REPRINTS OF what publishers inevitably regard as "classics" are much in vogue. Alan Ross's book on England's 1954-55 tour of Australia lays true claim to the term. It is the best kind of tour book: partly cricket, partly an investigation of the environment and the people. Added to this, for English readers, is that Hutton's tour was dramatically happy for England, after a disastrous start. It was the tour when the brilliant foursome of May, Cowdrey, Tyson and Statham came to flower, and when the old master, Len Hutton, steered his ship to sweet success. Ross's comments on the skipper's manner and personality are revealing and important, and the description of play and of an Australia long since overrun by fresh and not necessarily attractive styles and dictates have considerable impact on one who was but a teenager when it all happened. The narrative brings back visions of a Sydney ground without garish advertising hoardings and floodlight pylons, and makes one recall a thrilling stand-up back cut by Hutton off Lindwall – which amazingly doesn't even get a mention! A book must have something when you recall lines from it thirty years later. Here again is Graveney, "a player of yacht-like character, beautiful in calm seas, yet at the mercy of every change of weather". Here again is the telling assessment of Sydney by night and by day: "Watching in civilised comfort this lovely cooling down of the day I felt one could easily become reconciled to the disadvantages of living on the underside of the world. Today I am not so sure." Cleverly, while writing a good book, Alan Ross was reading a good book. D.H.Lawrence's *Kangaroo* was his choice. It's time I read that again too; but I lent my copy to Frank Keating and never saw it again.

Wisden Cricket Monthly, June 1985

A pleasant assignment was the writing of commentaries to a collection of imaginative paintings by Gerry Wright of cricketers from the Golden Age, the latter years of Queen Victoria and the era of Edward VII. The preface suffices:

Paintings in a Garden

IN THE abrasive age in which we live, where violence and cynicism, atheism and anarchy are such recurring themes as almost to be keystones of everyday life, it is excusable to seek momentary comfort in being wafted away to another age, when manners were gentle, man ruled machine, income tax was 8d (3p) in the £, and a glow of seemingly eternal summer warmed the land.

Not even the most careworn supplicant should subscribe unquestioningly to such an extreme view, of course, for violence there has always been, while medical advances have accelerated, to our emphatic advantage, and the path to affluence is wider and better lit.

In terms of mental equilibrium, though, man would seem to be facing greater hazards today. The Victorians, chin-high in prudery, and the Edwardians, fast being emancipated, had anxieties enough; but they never knew the evil of economic inflation or of the Nuclear Threat. They blessedly had no notion even of world war. Stricter class divisions at least proffered the almost certain guarantee that the rich would stay rich and the poor would probably die prematurely. So what was the point of living in fear of a downward spiral on the one hand or of aspiring to wealth on the other?

The blend of usually well-bred amateurs with from-the-masses professionals worked well in county and Test cricket. The commander-in-chief was always from amateur ranks, carefree, uninhibited in tactical matters. His livelihood was not dependent upon success on the cricket field. He was often trained to lead, and elicited the respect of his men. (The egalitarian Australian system, while not free from the occasional squabble, worked well for them.) Then, the amateurs could afford to play for months at a time, and to sail off during the winter to some outpost of Empire, there to show that it was not only the waves that Britannia ruled. Now, three-quarters of a century on, the complex pressures of making a living, whether real or part-illusory, leave only humble weekend club cricketers free to play purely for fun.

The worship of Mammon has much – no, *everything* – to answer for: the avarice that causes man to devote all his days to material acquisition and the greed that lures nations into war. The First World War exploded under cricket's Golden Age, and much else. It left a world which the late J.B.Priestley averred "could never again be trusted".

There is barely anyone left now who can describe first-hand how Ranji moved and what J.T.Hearne did with the ball and what effect WG's bulky entrance into the field had on the gathering. We can go on reading contemporary accounts and studying photographs and drawings. And we can now also rejoice in the latest time-cheating phenomenon, Gerry Wright's resurrection work with canvas and paintbrush. Immersed in his beloved collection of old books and pictures, he says, with appropriate bashfulness, that he feels like some Grand Creator as he breathes life into old photographs. He gives them colour and vitality, an extra dimension. Not only that: he has brought an authenticity to his mission by consultations with archivists at Lord's and Melbourne, and by studying old pattern-books from the outfitters who manufactured those rainbow blazers nearly a century ago. The extra demands of complex colour-mixing have not affected his natural cheerfulness.

The limited practice of contemplating ancient monochromes, if not past, should at least move over. The new computer process of imposing colour on the old Hollywood movies has a counterpart in cricket. As you look upon the cricketers of old brought back to life, there is a dispensation for letting past your lips the wry verse of E.E.Bowen:

There were wonderful giants of old, you know,
There were wonderful giants of old;
They grew more mightily, all of a row,
Than ever was heard or told;
All of them stood their six-feet-four,
And they threw to a hundred yards or more,
And never were lame or stiff or sore;
And we, compared to the days of yore,
Are cast in a pigmy mould.

Cricket's Golden Summer: Paintings in a Garden by Gerry Wright
(Pavilion, 1985)

Back to the horrors of grotesquely inaccurate projection of cricket's history, in this case perhaps the most sensational of all episodes, the 1932-33 "Bodyline" series, which an Australian production company turned into a laughably inaccurate drama documentary:

Dangerous "Faction"

SHALL WE now pledge ourselves, as from tomorrow, never to mention Bodyline again, to consign it, with death and incest, to the category of unmentionables? Since the realisation in 1982 that the jubilee of that rancorous Ashes series was upon us it has been relived, rewritten and analysed not only to the point of exhaustion but of fantasy too. The Australian TV production must have been seen, at least in part, by over half the population of Great Britain, and became the overriding topic of conversation (following the Brussels football disaster) wherever people gathered. It was such a joke; and it was such compelling viewing.

It would take several pages to list the technical and historical errors, and another to discuss the dubious character-casting, all of which reduced to despair those who saw what a worthy 7½ hours of television it *might* have been. A glance through any book on the 1932-33 series would have revealed to the producers and their so-called technical advisors that on the rare occasions when sweaters were worn, they were not of the village type such as grandma fondly knits. Much more irritating was "Larwood", beginning his run-up with a gay little skip, bowling to a wicketkeeper standing up to the stumps: byes would have top-scored for Australia, and England would have been down to their fifth substitute behind the sticks by the end of the first Test. Amazing, too, how often the Australian batsmen were able to *sweep* Larwood's express deliveries. Some of the crease markings seen were unknown before the war, and the exquisite and renowned Sydney pavilion kept popping into picture even when the setting was Melbourne. Bradman, far from hastening to the crease, taking guard and racing off for his customary opening single, rotated, bat raised, Roman emperor-style, soaking up the acclamation. And when he was out, far from hurrying back to the pavilion, often smiling and often at a canter, glared from bowler to broken stumps and back again. Dramatic licence is one thing, but really . . .

But, to repeat, it was compelling viewing – except for those (Bill O'Reilly among them) who, unable to stand any more after two episodes, punched the off button on the TV. The major purpose of the $A5-million production presumably was to entertain, with the likelihood also that it was meant to stir passions. It can hardly have contributed to Anglo-Australian relations, but perhaps the 1985 Test series will look after that, since it looks like being a total box-office success, steered by two likable and decent skippers in Border and Gower.

Bodyline, subtitled *The Day England Declared War on Australia*, at least put cricket on the screen, and it is going, perhaps, marginally too far to suggest that the game would have been better off had it not done so. It may even have stirred some enthusiasm in those who would otherwise not have taken much interest in the current Tests. But if only the Australian Cricket Board and the TCCB had had the power and the opportunity to insist that the programme carried a warning: "This production can seriously damage your comprehension of the Bodyline series", for future generations, while being entertained by re-runs, could begin to accept it as a documentary. That it *certainly* was not.

Wisden Cricket Monthly, July 1985

I had no inkling then that seventeen years hence I would write a lengthy study of this extraordinary Test conflict to mark the 70th anniversary of the battle. Any thoughts that this might lay the dramatic episode to rest once and for all proved fanciful.

England's cricket pride underwent a welcome restoration in 1985:

The Lessons of '85

THE SKIES scowled and wept more than is usual, but cricket still had the last laugh, for the season of 1985 will go down as one of the most memorable. Not only in the Test series was some thrilling and record-breaking cricket seen, but in the domestic competitions the play was often enthralling and surprising. What were the lessons learnt?

Firstly, should anyone have doubted it, Messrs Gower and Border showed that Test cricket can be fought with a high degree of combativeness and yet with a total absence of malice and pettiness. All of those splendid individual performances are gold-trimmed because of this.

Secondly, the belief that the game can be improved by the introduction of a third umpire watching a television monitor was given further weight, principally by a run-out incident (given in the batsman's favour) in a NatWest semi-final. The argument in favour of the "third eye" is founded firmly upon the fact that millions, including the players in the dressing-room, have seen what has happened, while the most important man, the umpire in the middle, is left to make a snap human judgment. To give them due credit, England's leading umpires are seldom wrong. But when they are, *when a match is being televised*, they can be made to look foolish or incompetent. They have a remedy on hand; all they have to do is call for it.

We learnt also, this year, that crowd control is not such an awesomely difficult matter – at least, on the big occasion, when ground stewarding is strong. When it was fashionable to run madly onto the playing area, people did it with scarcely a second thought. Now, thanks to the concentrated effort of the authorities, it is *not* the done thing, and a person needs to be extremely brave, exhibitionist or drunk to risk running onto the field. Suddenly, a stigma surrounds the practice, and audiences in general deserve the thanks of all in the game for respecting the one responsibility that matters in a paying spectator.

Finally, the England cricketers have shown that there *was* a worthwhile future after all. A year ago, England limped away from the series against West Indies, battered, bruised and forlorn. There followed defeat in the opening Test in India, and the record of the past few years looked so bleak that it was only the rainbow-jacketed optimists who felt that David Gower had a future at all and that England were entitled to consider themselves a power in international cricket.

Now they have won the Ashes back, having beaten an Australian side that some are now saying was there for the beating. (But how many said that when it was 1-1 at the halfway stage?) If Border's men finished up as something of a demoralised rabble, who rendered them so?

The side which sets out for West Indies in the New Year will be strong and confident, especially if the selectors' worthy 1985 form continues shrewdly with the right choice of extra players. They must be tough: first requisite after skill.

It is a time of English pride again, a boom time for cricket in this country. And to that end, we sent a crate of champagne, on behalf of our readers, into the England dressing-room on that overcast but somehow ethereally sunlit September day when the Ashes were retrieved.

Wisden Cricket Monthly, October 1985

Again the frustration at seeing umpiring errors going uncorrected, when the solution was so patently accessible. It is one of the most amazing phenomena in cricket history that so many years were to pass – and so many match- and career-altering bad decisions allowed to stand – before the obvious remedy of replay consultation was at long last adopted.

Political Intrigue

THEY'LL BE grinning in Pretoria, for the rulers of Bangladesh and Zimbabwe, presumably without realising what they are doing, are creating a new form of apartheid themselves. The understanding which is bred through international cricket has been denied to the teeming thousands of cricket-lovers in Bangladesh and Zimbabwe because of political interference which is exceeded in its holy zeal only by its cock-eyedness. The anti-apartheid lobby rubbed their hands in satisfaction at the cancellations and expressed the hope that England's Test tour of West Indies would be the next casualty. None of their spokesmen seemed to explain what good, if any, would come from wrecking cricket tours. The prospect of separate white and black sporting spheres seemed not to have occurred to them; or if it had, then presumably it appealed to their taste.

Any straight-thinking Christian is "anti-apartheid". Any straight-thinking soul of any other religion is "anti-apartheid". The sincerity and earnestness of the "anti-apartheid" movements are not in question. What is in question is the logic of their aim/method/conclusion. And what is also in question is their eager propensity for assaulting the game of cricket, which presents the most defenceless of targets. Like most defenceless targets, its value to the "enemy" is slight by comparison to those that are heavily defended: like, in this case, big business.

The Zimbabwe leg of the "B" tour was a long time dying, perhaps because that government seriously held out hope that English cricket would capitulate to blackmail, perhaps because the national president [Mugabe] clung to his utterance of a year previously, that cricket "civilises people". There is not a reader of this magazine who would disagree with that. In fact the game has such vivid powers to bring men together in brotherhood that it was once considered as potent a factor in expanding and holding together the British Empire as Queen Victoria's gunboats.

Well, places like Dhaka may never again see either British infantrymen or cricketers. The friendship and goodwill which would have sprung from the tour were never to be.

Much of the story has yet to unfold. Will Bangladesh and Zimbabwe hold their places as associate members of the International Cricket Conference? If they are expelled, once more it would be the cricket community alone which absorbs the punishment. Where does the Asian Cricket Conference stand in all this? Is this all part of the Lahore/Karachi aim to centre world cricket power there?

Christopher Booker wrote recently of those who set themselves up as champions of opposition to racism, "thus automatically being invested in a halo of light". Observing that this was a game played by whites as well as blacks, he said: "Once you have managed to establish yourself as on the side of light and right, any kind of bad behaviour is permissible simply because you are engaged in a Holy War . . . In the face of injustice and racism, even if it is only imagined, there emerges a wave of blind hysterical intolerance which sweeps the chance of real justice and real racial harmony further away then ever." These dabblers in inverted racism are, he says, masters of the hatred game.

So say many of us. Meanwhile, the guarded New Year toast is to the cooler, saner thinking of the administrations in Sri Lanka, Jamaica, Trinidad, Barbados, and Antigua. And dare we hope for the utmost of ironies, a final of the ICC Trophy in July at Lord's, in liberal old England, between Zimbabwe and Bangladesh?

Wisden Cricket Monthly, February 1986

These murky world cricket politics still had a fearfully long way to run, and the intrusion ruined many a breakfast in the years ahead. Had one been told that some years hence Zimbabwe and Bangladesh would be manoeuvred to Test status, a soft chair and a stiff drink would have been called for. Zimbabwe, then composed almost entirely of white players, won the 1986 ICC Trophy, beating Holland in the final at Lord's. Bangladesh finished second-last in their group of seven.

Back in the solace of pure cricket history, there followed a delightful chance encounter with an aged gentleman who had once been a schoolboy prodigy:

When Larwood Wore Black Socks

JUST ON sixty-five years ago, a slightly-built pupil from Northampton School went out to bat on the county ground against Essex. The visitors had what might be reasonably termed an ascendancy, for they had scored 604 for 7 and bowled Northamptonshire out for 223. Following on, the home side began to resist, and with Claud Woolley scoring 132, they avoided outright defeat, finishing with 415 for 5. The most captivating performance, though, came from a schoolboy, not yet nineteen, who batted for almost six hours and finished with 154 not out. He was shouldered from the field in Newboltian triumph by his schoolpals, who had circled the boundary to watch in awe. It seemed that a great discovery had been uncovered in the third summer following the First World War.

By chance I recently found that Wilfrid Walter Timms, that promising schoolboy of 1921, lived a couple of miles from me. He is now eighty-three, recovered from two major operations since 1982, and happy to reflect on a cricket career of some achievement and much enjoyment, and several decades of teaching languages at Cambridge, Oundle, Charterhouse and California.

Our meeting led to one of those wonderful afternoons of cricket chat, reaching far, far back and embracing dozens upon dozens of names. It began when his charming wife Evelyn mentioned how she obtained Wilfrid's autograph before she actually met him. She still has it, a "scribble". Very romantic. They married in August 1932.

He did not play against Armstrong's formidable Australian team of 1921, but faced the next team from Australia, the 1926 combination, when Grimmett he found to be "terribly clever". The little wizard had him stumped for 1 and caught-and-bowled for 12. He was pleased to meet Bill Ponsford again at the 1980 Centenary Test match, the only survivor from the 1926 tour apart from "Stork" Hendry.

He might have played for Northants against the 1930 Australians, but A.P.R.Hawtin asked "Do you mind if I play?" "So I let him." Timms missed a good'un: Vallance Jupp (6 for 32) bowled the Australians out for 93 and they followed on, batting their way to eventual safety with centuries from Woodfull and Vic Richardson.

Timms did see Bradman's glorious, unblemished 254 in the Lord's Test that summer. "The way he played Tate and White! I couldn't believe it! I'd been playing these same bowlers . . . "

In 1926 Wilfrid Timms scored hundreds in consecutive matches at Northampton, 128 against Warwickshire, when he and Fanny Walden added 229 for the seventh wicket [then a Northants record], and an unbeaten 112 against Leicestershire, when George Geary beat him with a leg-cutter early in the innings. When next they met, the stumps had been enlarged under the new law, and the off bail was clipped!

Geary was to play a further important part in Timms's life, for he urged Geary's selection as coach at Charterhouse ahead of Frank Woolley, and never had to regret it, for "old George" was a splendid, considerate and shrewd coach. When Timms was a house tutor, the headmaster pointed out the fourteen-year-old Peter May in a junior game one wartime summer. "One shot and I could see his class." Geary went a step further. He told Timms: "The boy's painted in red, white and blue" – which meant he was destined to represent England. Master May was taught cricket and French by Mr Timms.

It was a long way to cast the mind back, to the 1920s, and yet Wilfrid Timms can recall much more about the First World War than the Second. His three brothers served in the First.

But what about the illustrious names of the 1920s? Well, there was Wilfred Rhodes: "I once batted for an hour against him, and felt very proud." Larwood? "Yes, I remember that as a newcomer he played in black socks. Pretty quick off the pitch, but at Trent Bridge he bounced them – but over the off stump. I cut him successfully by stepping back and had about 70 by lunch. But I gather that Juppy said I was a coward for stepping back!"

Amazingly, Wilfrid captained Northants at the age of eighteen, when he was the senior amateur available for the occasional match. He was always a thinker on the game, and even now recalls certain observations, such as detecting Phil Mead's vulnerability around the corner. His captain heeded his advice by going to leg slip himself – and immediately putting a catch from the Hampshire nudger onto the grass. He himself missed a fairly easy catch during his only county match at Lord's, where he found the light "awkward".

He had played at "Headquarters" for The Rest against Lord's Schools and for Public Schools v The Army, but he missed a Blue for Cambridge, Tom Lowry making him twelfth man.

W.W.Timms, county captain at eighteen.

Of his 99 matches for Northants, perhaps the most satisfying was the one at Swansea where the pitch had been coated with manure. Old Bill Reeves, the umpire, seeing the first ball fizz and send a chunk of horse dung flying, turned to W.W.Timms and said, "Anybody who gets a fifty on this deserves the VC!" "I got fifty in each innings," he says, with a twinkle in the eye, "so I got the VC and bar!" Jupp took 15 for 52 in the match.

"I played Jack Hearne well because I was a back-foot player." But of Tich Freeman: "He got me, and do you know, I don't recall a thing. I didn't see it!" Freeman, of course, was "only" a leg-spinner.

He still seemed shocked at something that happened over half-a-century ago. That extraordinary character Leonard Crawley once drove way out into the deep at Lord's, to be caught by Hendren near the line. And the batsman talked the umpire into reprieving him! Such could be the grip wielded by a dominant amateur over a humble ump. The class division has modern echoes. When Timms met Ted "Nobby" Clark at a recent reunion he noticed that the fast bowler couldn't bring himself to address his former amateur colleague and sometime skipper as "Wilfrid". It was always "Mr".

"I used to be a Liberal – until that chap Hain came on the scene."

Wilfrid was born in a house overlooking the Northampton ground. Next door lived Mark Cox, who played for the county (as did two of his sons) and had his jaw broken by Lancashire fast bowler Walter Brearley. Along the street, Bob Haywood lived in digs. All very cosy.

Mr Timms is cosy in retirement. He can see his beloved Charterhouse from his home, and on the landing is a huge photograph of him in the batting stance in 1921, the year of his memorable 154 in only his second county match. He is not sure what happened to the ball off which he stroked those runs. His captain, R.O.Raven, had put a silver ring around it and had it inscribed. The message was tantalising. It read "Do it again".

Wisden Cricket Monthly, February 1986

Wilfrid Timms died later that year.

The batsman of the moment and of the entire period of 1976 to 1991 was Vivian Richards, and considerable thought went into assembling this tribute:

Symbol of West Indian Supremacy

IN THE pre-war Depression years, Don Bradman stood for the powers of endurance of the ordinary bloke. His triumphs brought pride and inspiration to masses of struggling Australians in town and bush. Through The Don they saw that life's difficulties were at least not totally universal. Spasmodically they too tasted success on a giant scale, if only vicariously. "Our Don" took his admirers out of themselves, made their existences less wretched, gave them a kind of hope.

For ten years now Viv Richards has done something similar for the black man. He has not been alone in this. Clive Lloyd gathered together one of the most powerful cricket teams of all time, with wonderful opening batsmen like Gordon Greenidge and Desmond Haynes, himself and Richards and the solid, phlegmatic Gomes to make runs, and Dujon to keep wicket and add artistry to the middle-order batting; and, most significantly, a brigade of ferocious fast bowlers to keep the opposition in an almost permanent state of submission. They came tumbling out of the pavilion, large and loose and eager: Andy Roberts, Michael Holding, Wayne Daniel, Colin Croft, Joel Garner, Malcolm Marshall, Courtney Walsh, with keen youngsters queuing up to replace them. For Viv Richards to stand towering above all these as the symbol of West Indian supremacy emphasises the impact he has had on international cricket since the mid-1970s.

Springing from massive local celebrity in Antigua and polishing his game in county cricket with Somerset, Richards quickly made himself comfortable in Test cricket with an innings of 192 not out against India at Delhi in December 1974. There followed 17 Test innings in which nothing startling took place, and then he recovered his poise with 101 against Australia at Adelaide and 98 in the Melbourne Test which followed. This was the springboard for a most remarkable year in which he established his own utter uniqueness with an unprecedented aggregate of 1710* runs in Test cricket during 1976.

The core of this batting extravaganza was the 1976 series in England, though the preface, West Indies' home series against India, had more than a touch of intimidation about it: he hit 142 in the Barbados Test, 130 in Trinidad, 177 in the third Test, at the same venue, and finished quietly with 64 in the Jamaica bloodbath when five Indians could not bat in the second innings, most of them injured by the speed assault.

Richards thus came to England for his first Test tour with more than just imposing forenames: Isaac Vivian Alexander. He began that 1976 series with innings of 232 and 63 in the Trent Bridge Test, over twice as many as young Bradman had made on that ground in *his* maiden English Test. Richards struck dread into countless hearts, and caused some analysts, in their desperation, to repeat the mistakes made by several almost half-a-century before, when they concluded that Bradman's technique would be found out on English pitches. He played across the line, they said. So did Richards. His pull shot was too risky, being used to punish balls only slightly short of a length. So was Richards's. Bradman showed them with 974 runs in that 1930 series, skipping to a triple-century, two double-centuries and a century in the five Tests. Richards in the 1976 Tests amassed 829 runs. But he played in only four Tests.

I happen to believe that no batsman has ever approached Bradman for skill, concentration and appetite. And however we judge modern batsmen, we must never lose sight of the crucial fact that they are pampered with covered pitches, protective umpires' light-meters and tasty cash inducements. But to reflect on Viv Richards's performances in that 1976 series is to recall his total dominance over Snow and Hendrick and Old and Underwood and Selvey and Pocock and Willis and Ward and Miller and Greig. Especially Greig. The England captain's clumsy remark about West Indians "grovelling" when they are in adversity fired up all of Clive Lloyd's men, but none more passionately than Richards. Never in sport has attempted propaganda backfired as surely as this.

The runs that sparked from Richards's hefty bat that summer came with the rifle-shot crack of the hook, rasping square-cuts as he stepped away to make room, booming drives through the covers, and, in the fashion that brought his trademark, meaty persuasions through the leg side, often to respectable balls pitched on or even outside off stump. His attempt at "art" came in the late cut, when those heavyweight shoulders lined up square to the crease and the mahogany wrists chopped down on the poor unsuspecting ball: it ran away from him as fast as it could go, bruising the advertising hoarding at third man.

Ironically the one field he did not conquer that summer was Lord's. Illness kept him out of that match. But he would be back several times to entertain the St John's Wood folk in the summers to follow. Not that London missed out completely on the Viv Richards brilliance that season, for he signed off at grimy Kennington Oval with what seemed a certain triple-century, being bowled by Greig, of all people, for 291 after batting a shade short of eight hours. In that first Test series in England, his visiting card had dropped onto the table in the vestibule with a force that rocked the entire house.

Since then he has had his quieter moments, always to boom back with a large innings in which bowlers have been not so much taken for runs as flagellated. There have been memorable duels, such as that with Jeff Thomson, bowling probably as fast as man has ever done. Richards's method is never to withdraw discreetly. Between roaring bouncers which singed his hair he flat-batted the blur of a cricket ball straight into the stand beyond square leg.

That noble head surmounts a powerful body which has been compared with Joe Frazier's. Richards might have made a fair fighter, from the flash of those eyes as the combatants exchange glares before the first bell to the evident athleticism, coiled in sinister reserve.

He is a conscious leader of the black people, nursing profound emotions, eternally aware of tortured history, injustice, battered pride. He may be as popular in Somerset

Viv Richards: stamped his mark just with "a piece of wood".

as in Antigua, and one of his most meaningful friendships may be with Ian Botham, but he is a *black man*, as committed as Frank Worrell and Learie Constantine, if not with quite their natural grace and polish. He shrugs off his deeds with the cricket bat. It is just "a piece of wood". With equal modesty, Garry Sobers acknowledged always that he was engaged in nothing more than a sport – to the point where he made a generous declaration against England and lost, bringing down heaps of rancour upon his head. Nor did Sir Garry think politics. His ingenuous visit to Rhodesia cost him dearly in Caribbean eyes. Richards, in contrast, has stated that no amount of money could get him to South Africa. (Sobers did not go for the money.)

So we have here more than a batsman, a quicksilver fieldsman, a teasing bowler, a West Indies captain. Viv Richards is proudly a man of his race, with an unalterable force of opinion which will have been conveyed to team-mates as well as to others in his orbit. Those colourful wristbands, beaming bright red, gold and green, are no mere convenience. When he finishes with cricket he will not finish with life. It could all just be beginning.

At that point what will he have left behind? Almost certainly he will have become the first West Indies player to register 100 centuries. His Test record will be top-shelf. One day in 1985, for Somerset, he slaughtered the Warwickshire bowling and put his name in the distinguished list of triple-centurions. His dominance at Lord's became legend, in Test matches, one-day county finals, and in the World Cup final of 1979. His was the wicket they always needed. When he fell in the 1983 World Cup final, India knew they had it won. And yet more often he seemed to be able to make runs just when he wanted to. His century in his beloved Antigua's maiden Test match in 1981 seemed predestined.

He walks with a swagger; he chews menacingly; he thumps that cricket ball as if it contained all the evils of a millennium of mankind. When he gets settled, the cricket pitch is his domain. Considered literally, there is no such thing as immortality, so Richards will have to leave that domain for good one day. But books and photos and film have a purpose; and if they convey to future generations just how this man's command affected cricket during these past years, they will have served those future generations admirably.

Wisden Cricket Monthly, March 1986

* *Surpassed in 2006 by Pakistan's Mohammad Yousuf.*

A somewhat lighter course is perhaps now in order:

To Dawkes a Plague

ONE OF the great characters of sports-writing, Charles Richard "Dick" Williamson, died in Bradford on February 4, at the age of eighty-five. In his trilby hat, tipped to a jaunty angle, and with his music-hall countenance, he was part of the scene at Headingley every Test match there, his voice crackling across the press-box in repartee or as he announced some obscure finding or launched into a series of sports quiz questions – many of them booby-trapped. Only last summer, during the Australian Test, he produced an ancient, frayed cuttings book in which he had stuck examples of accidentally hilarious cricket-reporting and printers' errors: such as "Verity opened his scoring with a three, all run" and "Davidson neatly pulled Read past point for a four". "Cooper, a well-built 2-year-old, playing in only his second Championship match" triggered mirth down several rows of the press-box, as did "Boycott, an hour for 16, was lbw for 8". And there was "After the match, Jackson was presented with the match ball and Dawkes was given a plague".

Dick will be remembered as much for his profound knowledge of the two sports he loved, cricket and football, and for his ever-present desire to laugh and make others laugh, as for the quality of his writing. He started work with the *Bradford Telegraph & Argus* at the age of fifteen, and upon retirement set up his own agency. He also edited *Yorkshire Sports*, the "pink paper". In May 1985 he escaped injury while reporting the football match which suddenly was transformed into the Bradford City disaster.

Wisden Cricket Monthly, March 1986

It is hard to think of a more controversial figure in post-war cricket than Geoffrey Boycott, but a few kind words were in order when his dedicated efforts came to a close in the winter of 1986-87:

Into the Sunset

"THAT, SIR, is something upon which Time may be depended to remedy," said Pitt the Younger when challenged, for all his brilliance, on the matter of his youth and lack of experience. And Time, taking care of all things, has brought at long last an end to the Boycott era, barring a surprising signing elsewhere. Yorkshire have finished with him as a player, and this time there has been no riot, no club-shattering clamour for his reinstatement. For he is forty-six, and for batsmen of that age there is usually thought to be no future.

But what a past! It is not possible to send Geoffrey Boycott off into the sunset of retirement with an unqualified salute, for his uniquely self-concentrated approach to this team game has caused widespread annoyance and frustration. At the same time, his dedication, application and concentration have been unsurpassed in the history of the game. He would practise until the last weary bowler turned away, and he could never throw his wicket away, no matter what the score, even in a charity match.

The product of all this? Over 48,000 runs in just over 1000 innings, 151 centuries, a record 8114 Test runs for England, with 22 centuries, and a world sharply divided into those who admire him and those who don't. There is no in-between category, unless it be for those who acknowledge his hard-earned skill while deploring his selfishness.

Boycott's first-class career stretches back to 1962, and his Test career to 1964, to be ended, almost predictably, on a sour note, when he again lost his sense of proportion on the 1981-82 tour of India.

While all those runs for Yorkshire brought few victories, because they came too slowly, many of his stands for England in Test matches, the five-day contest, will stay monumentally in the public mind: hundreds and seventies chipped and carved off West Indian pace and bounce, Australian speed and spin, Indian mystic spin, Pakistani pressure. There were times enough when the great British public were glad to see him still at the crease, holding off the enemy while his partners, spared the eccentricity of his running between wickets, were being gunned down at the other.

In truth, he must have been born to be specifically a *Test match* batsman, placing the highest price on his wicket, never helping any bowler to dismiss him, for unconscious complicity remains the greatest factor in the downfall of a batsman. Considering the rate of his runmaking, it is possible that he has batted longer overall than anyone in the history of Test and first-class cricket. That says something.

So farewell, "Sir Geoffrey of the White Rose county". You may lay down your trusty sword, remove your creaking armour, and spend the rest of your days watching old videos in your ivory tower. Unless, of course, you find a way of joining us in the press-box, to tear strips off the faulty techniques of the batsmen of today.

Wisden Cricket Monthly, November 1986

And fortunately that is precisely what he has done, writing and speaking in a refreshingly forthright manner in a world cowering before the sinister onslaught of repression of free speech.

There was something deeply symbolic about the retirement of cricketers of the Boycott generation:

Who Cares?

AN EXPRESSION used in a recent radio sports report stood out. *"With typical British carelessness"* was the key phrase. It was directed at a young woman tennis player, but had vast implications. Everywhere, it sometimes seems, we are surrounded by carelessness – and its equally nauseating cousin, the "couldn't care less" attitude. And since cricket is always inevitably reflective of society, we may well be living through a period when carelessness is proving to be cricket's most costly handicap.

Taking or not taking risks has always been part of sport, as has taking advantage of your opponent's mistakes – or carelessness. Mistakes often stem from inadequacy, but carelessness has much to do with concentration, as well as laziness. Has Britain become lazy, resentful, unable and unwilling to concentrate; and have her cricketers become victims of an unavoidable pattern?

It may be no coincidence that the last of the wartime children, Geoff Boycott, Norman Gifford, Dennis Amiss and Jack Simmons, all at the tailends of careers, were noted for their highly professional approach, and indeed have been accused of being too professional at times. Those old lads may not quite recall the wartime posters which warned that "careless talk costs lives", but they have demonstrably been aware that careless strokes get you out, and sloppy bowling gets hammered, to say nothing of dozy fielding, which accounts for dozens, even hundreds, of runs in almost every match.

So what might we expect of cricketers in this age when no-one seems to care? If it is impossible to get prompt attention in shops and from tradesmen, or to read a newspaper free of misprints, or to drive five miles without encountering idiots hogging the fast lane or edging out of sideroads, or to behold a letter that isn't cursed with the modern misusage of the word "hopefully", then what hope is there for our cricketers? Why should they eradicate sloppiness from their approach when all around them the world that shapes them couldn't care less?

There seems to be much more energy going into the strident claims of racial and sexual minority groups. What sort of game cricket is to become remains inextricably linked to the kind of society now developing. Who, one wonders, late this century or early next, will be England's first green-faced, bisexual, weed-smoking opening batsman?

As a most eminent former twice-times MCC president once advocated: Come on, England, pull your finger out!

Merry Christmas. Drive carefully.

Wisden Cricket Monthly, December 1986

It simply got worse, though (unless we've not been looking carefully enough) England still await their first green-faced, bisexual, weed-smoking opener.

Many a day was spent in auction rooms as major cricket sales took place. This account reflects more frustration than was usual:

The Treasure Trunk

"BUT THERE isn't *room* for any more suitcases and books," said my love plaintively as I left the house, bound for London and the latest Phillips cricket sale. It was a reasonable point. But *she* hadn't seen that trunk of the late Percy Fender's, flung open at the sale preview, with photographs, letters, negatives, original sketches, scrapbooks, menus, invitations, diaries, and a faded, dilapidated Surrey cap bursting from within it. What a heart-rending sight. People were thumbing the precious 1920s negatives and clanking the old framed pictures like so many parsnips on a fruit-and-veg stall. This treasure was desperately in need of a caring owner, who would love and understand it. Preferably me.

So with that and a few other lots circled, I set off, choosing the train this time, just in case the roads became impossibly jammed around Wandsworth or Battersea, the way they so often do. Couldn't afford to be late. "My" lots came up early, within the first three-quarters of an hour.

The 9.21 was due to leave platform five at 9.21. At 9.21 a train pulled in. There was no announcement. I got on. Soon the countryside struck me as unfamiliar. The gentleman opposite informed me that we were bound for Reading, not Waterloo. But there was no need for panic, as there was a fast service from Reading to London. I was still on-side. Then the train stopped: on a long stretch of straight track, for no apparent reason. And ten minutes ticked by. And the guard came through and said that somebody had fallen or jumped under a train. Surely my auction-room rivals would not stoop to such a ploy?

Eventually we rolled back to the nearest station, Blackwater, and eventually three of us located what seemed to be the town's only taxi. We headed for Reading, not as fast as I would have liked. And just as we were getting up speed, we fell in behind a pair of slow-moving Army tanks. It was 10.30. The sale began in faraway London in half-an-hour.

Reading at last. And heavy traffic. No progress. Like Wonderwoman, I leapt from the taxi and ran – puffed – in search of the railway station. Here it was. Then the enquiry, from heaving lungs: the next fast train to Paddington?

He was one of those peaked-capped BR asses who do not enjoy answering questions from members of the public, and who ought to make way for someone out of the ranks of the unemployed who would make a true attempt at *earning* his wages. His reply came as from an answering machine – turned up to high speed. Further enquiries elicited enough morsels of information to suggest that British Rail, this particular morning, did not know where most of its trains were – and cared little. It was time to try to phone Phillips.

The third attempt, from the one phone that was working, established with the Phillips lady that an excited would-be bidder was trapped somewhere in the wilds, but would someone – anyone – take a maximum bid for that Fender trunk? I was left to pray that the message had sunk in. Then a train came along.

Here was the mighty InterCity job, and although it was now time for the sale to start, there was a chance I might make it to Bond Street before Lot 76 came up. We got to Slough, beautiful Slough, waited a long time, and then moved out of the station – in *reverse*. A strangulated voice that had the barest grasp of English communicated something about a "blockage"; in a while the eastwards journey continued. Inside my head I could hear the auctioneer's faraway chant.

Paddington. Twelve noon. The sale an hour old. Myself ten years older. The taxi did its best, but it became absorbed in the jams like a fly in treacle. The driver hadn't done much for my spirits either after I had told him of my agony. He said none of it mattered, because in ten years from now none of us would be here. It was the acid rain, y'know. He'd seen last night's TV programme. I leapt out at Selfridges and ran – puffed – along Oxford Street and up into Blenheim Street, into the saleroom, three hours after stepping fatefully onto that misguided first train.

"Lot 139," intoned the auctioneer, "H.R.W.Hooper, watercolour."

"What happened to Lot 76," I whispered, "the Fender trunk?"

My friend turned back the page. There it was, hammered for £600, just above my maximum. A pal of mine had got it. Ah well.

At least it went to a good home, and at least my other bid was successful, for some of Percy Fender's scrapbooks covering the 1920-21, 1928-29 and 1934 Ashes series. So that was it for another half-year. Home. By train, of course. No alternative. The newspaper accounts of Don Bradman's and Archie Jackson's exploits fifty-eight years ago made comforting reading. The train, needlessly, was on time.

Wisden Cricket Monthly, December 1986

"Goldilocks" Gower was set for a golden summer in 1987 after being granted a benefit. A contribution to the customary booklet was the dutiful thing:

Dave? It's Dave . . . .

"DAVE? It's Dave."
   "Hi, Dave."
   "Next piece, Dave: when d'you want it?"
   "Monday, Dave."
   "Fine."
We don't spend a lot on phone calls, Dave Gower and I. We have that smooth understanding that produces quick singles from gentle taps to mid-on. The postman will duly call on that Monday, and among several items of mail there will be nothing from our esteemed *Wisden Cricket Monthly* correspondent. But, by golly, his offering will be here on Tuesday, the handwriting instantly recognisable for an elegant flow that also pervades his batting, his fielding . . . and his telephone calls.

David is one of the original members of our Editorial Board. In 1978, when the seeds of the idea for a new magazine were sown, I wanted him in the team. He was twenty-one, had just made his Test debut, and was being spoken of as English cricket's "golden boy". There was room for two players on the Board: D.I.Gower, and a chap who probably had a year left in him in the game, R.G.D.Willis. They both became England captains, and brought unexpected additional status to the magazine.

Another presentation for D.I.Gower, whose smooth style at the crease precedes the quantity of runs in public memory.

Our meeting remains one of my fondest memories. We sat in the Tavern at Lord's. He wasn't bothered too seriously by autograph seekers, and I laid out my plans for him to see. He was quietly enthusiastic, and away we went.

About fifty contributions later I find I have quite a journalistic type on my hands: author of books, newspaper columnist, photographer of wildlife (including one or two memorable snaps of Mr Botham). He has gradually come to know that I respect him too much to mess around with false deadlines. With some, you have to knock off six days because they will inevitably and insufferably be half-a-dozen days late. With DG, the 25th means, at worst, the 26th. That's reliability.

I suppose I should have taken a more conventional course by offering a few thoughts on Gower the batsman; or even Gower the captain, though there will be no shortage of technical appraisals in a benefit publication.

All I would say on that count is that the beauty of his batting has been one of modern cricket's outstanding assets, and has given me more pleasure than I can estimate. Since watching my Hutton and my Harvey long ago, I had forgotten what it was like actually to care about a particular batsman's survival at the crease. It seemed that such heartfelt solicitous concern could be felt only by the young. With the years comes a shrug for disappointment. But not, on many occasions, when David Gower has been handling bowlers of all nations with deceptive ease. He and Randall have been the only players of the past quarter-century for whom I have actually prayed, the request being that they at least be spared while others all around them were being gunned down.

And, of course, there is the odd prayer as the postman comes up the driveway around deadline time.

David Gower Benefit Brochure 1987

The most phenomenal auction of all came in the spring of 1987:

Madness, Curiosity and Chaos

INEVITABLY IT was billed as the "Sale of the Double-Century", and inevitably, in view of the enormous pre-publicity the event attracted, the attendance exceeded a thousand – most of them, it seemed, determined to take away at least one item, just to say they got it from the MCC Collection. "You pay for the name," as Mike Selvey wrote in *The Guardian*. But even those who "pay for the name" in clothing don't usually lash out *ten times* the normal High Street prices.

The bidding at Lord's on Monday, April 3, 1987 had to be heard to be believed. A kind of hysteria prevailed. For those of us who stayed from start to finish, through 11½ hours of non-stop auctioneering (incidentally breaking Wettimuny's record for the longest innings at Lord's, 642 minutes – and he had breaks for lunch, tea and sleep!), moods and reactions ebbed and flowed: determination, amazement, scorn, comicality, fatigue. But most of all amazement.

This was not the first auction at Lord's, as was claimed. George Robey conducted one in 1917, when thirty-four lots, mainly bats, raised £100 for war charity. Now, seventy years on, 830 lots fetched £290,474 – plus the buyers' premium of 10 per cent, and VAT on that premium. Robey, "Prime Minister of Mirth", would have split his sides.

There was a serious ethical consideration to all this, beyond even the protest of the Museums Association, who condemned the sale on the basis that the Museum

Authorities' code of practice had been contravened. They claimed that "objects should be offered first to other museums before sale by public auction is considered", and their president stated: "Those people who have given prized objects to the MCC's museum over the years did so because they wanted them preserved. What confidence can people now have that objects conserved or bought with the money MCC hopes to raise will not themselves be sold in a few years' time?" The chairman said: "This is a museum collection, and as such is considered by the public to be held in trust for cricket enthusiasts now and forever. For MCC to sell off its reserve collection in its bicentenary year showed a sad insensitivity to the preservation of the country's cricketing heritage."

Certainly there were those who deplored the "raid" by both Melbourne Cricket Club and a consortium buying for the projected Bradman Museum in NSW. These groups were successful in obtaining such unique treasures as a 1785 linen handkerchief (£7000), an 18th Century oak bat (£5000), and some original works of art.

Some of us were in two minds: it is wonderful to own the first volume of *Scores & Biographies*, inscribed by Fred Lillywhite, who claimed the fourteen volumes as his own work, and annotated poignantly by Arthur Haygarth (who "did the whole entirely and gratuitously"). But such precious particles of history should never, surely, have been allowed to leave Lord's.

The abiding comfort may be that, in exchange for the massive purse, MCC has seen this great volume of "reserve" goods go to a multiplicity of new homes. And no-one who has had to pay such hefty prices is likely to extend anything less than vast loving care to his acquisitions.

How the dealers, on the other hand, could expect to find folk daft enough to pay even more for goods once their margins have been added confounds explanation. Or will yet higher price levels be established relatively painlessly?

So midst an expectant hubbub, we claimed our chairs, loosened our ties, and held on tight. I had a Mars to lift my blood-sugar level later on, and by my side sat Charlie Watts, Rolling Stones drummer and cricket collector, to whom I hoped to be able to offer the occasional helpful hint. He bought well, as it happened, but, acting as his restraint, I damped down his ardour for some signed postcards, 145 of them in three consecutive lots, which reached a dizzying £5200 (all prices quoted are before premium).

After an hour Charlie had got off to a good start by winning a large oil painting of J.T.Hearne. Many hours later, when we loaded it into the car, the lights from the pavilion showed up the splits in the canvas; but it will be a glory when it is restored.

The £1000 mark was topped in the first minutes of the sale, which began with Pictures. Soon an ugly Manuel sketch of W.G.Grace and a handsome one attributed to Harry Furniss each reached £1000, to gasps and stupefied looks. Then came a watercolour surrounding the signatures of the 1926 Australians, estimated at £200-400, but realising £3200: the first sign of rampant madness. Next day I had a call from a former Orient Line steward. He had something similar and was high with hopes. It was difficult to know what to advise him.

Fourteen original sketches of WG by Furniss, which ought to have stayed at Lord's as long as there was such a place, went for £3000, and in the same category were some Felix originals. A "Rip" sketch of WG in carved frame made £2200, and a large oil by Henry St Clair fetched £5500. Immediately following was Eleanor Hughes D'Eath's fine oil of Lewis Cage, after Francis Cotes. A Mr Ondaatje bought this for £10,000, leaving Mick Jagger behind with a lower proxy bid, faraway in

New York. Another shock came in the £1500 paid for an untinted lithograph of Henwood's depiction of Davies, the old Sussex scorer.

Chevallier Tayler chromolithographs reached new heights with a lot of three going for £500, and J.C.Anderson broke records with £460 for his George Griffith and £1100 for a pair, H.H.Stephenson and Tom Hearne. When MCC's genial president, M.C.Cowdrey, made the first of several appearances in the major saleroom, no wonder he was beaming.

Then it was *Vanity Fair's* turn. Lord Harris by "Spy" made £500, Lord Hawke £400. No, these were not originals; just coloured lithographs. Charlie went for a walk.

L.H.Gay's scrapbook for the 1894-95 tour of Australia was hammered for £480 – pretty reasonable really, considering all the memorabilia that went with it, including a list of his dancing partners in Melbourne and an even longer one of the Australian wildlife he shot: enough almost to fill the Ark.

A Stevengraph of WG soared to £480, and a set of six menus featuring stars of the 1890s made £520: caviar and champagne rather than bangers and mash. An undoubtedly singular set of Players "Rip" caricature cigarette cards, signed by all fifty subjects, was acquired for the Bradman Museum for £900, and fourteen cameo buttons featuring the 1897-98 English players who toured Australia, still on the original backing card, a major prize in the sale, almost trebled estimate at £1400.

The Books section began with Lot 361 (*Scores & Biographies* Vols I-XIV: £1000), and already it was gone 4 o'clock. At this rate the sale would end around midnight. What wild bidding might occur as punchdrunk remnants fought over the goods into the twelfth and thirteenth hours of non-stop competition? Maybe some would long since have exhausted their budgets. Maybe some were deliberately holding back. Of the eleven lots which had interested me so far I had managed to buy just one. Many hours from now I planned to have a go at the replica of the Ashes urn, surely the only one ever to go into private hands. Would it have to be an at-all-costs purchase? Should I extend the mortgage on the house for extra funds? Don't worry, son. Look at the madmen all around you. Some are worn out already. Some haven't even bothered bidding. Others keep reaching for their vacuum flasks, clearly buckling at the knees.

On it went, one auctioneer succeeding another. One waved his arms about like Magnus Pyke, though he looked very like the Duke of Gloucester. Another had recently knocked down the Van Gogh *Sunflowers* for £22½ million. What was *he* doing here? The TV cameras whirred; the reporters, wild-eyed, got some quotes and muddled their facts. Oh, for a quiet room and a cool beer.

Someone crazily paid £220 for a damaged photo of Mailey being stumped in a Test match, and then came a grotesque picture *28 feet long*, a panorama of the Sydney Test of December 1894. Bidding had reached £320 when poor old Tony Baer barked "£650!" in an attempt to shatter the opposition. But he missed out to the Bradman Museum, who paid a little matter of £1200. Similar, slightly later and appreciably smaller panoramas went for just under £1000, and then came another of those cameos of idiocy which betokened the very nature of the sale. Somebody paid £38 for a recent out-of-focus photo of an unknown youngster bowling on the Nursery ground. You pay for the name.

Many of the graphic items were of high quality, such as some cabinet cards and carte-de-visite portraits, though it was baffling to behold bidders clamouring over a photo of two urchins which fell eventually for £1100. What those poor lads could have done with just the buyer's premium on that lot!

The pick of an attractive array of belt buckles was one from around 1860, complete with woven belt, which fetched £1300; and then came the personal apparel: Nigel Haig's Middlesex cap (£150), a Yorkshire cap (£160), a battered, faded Butterflies cap (£45), Plum Warner's 1926 MCC touring blazer (£550), Gubby Allen's Eton blazer (£180), a striped blazer said to have been worn by Ranjitsinhji (£230) (Charlie likes dressing up), a 1946 Indian Test blazer, possibly Hazare's (£280), a sweater with Wilfred Rhodes's name stitched to it (£280), and Plum Warner's woollen tennis shorts (£140).

The I Zingari blazer worn by Colin Cowdrey on the May *WCM* front cover went for a mere £160, while the other two items pictured, the IZ pillbox hat and the 18th Century oak bat, made £750 and £5000 respectively. A Duchess of Windsor tiara might not have been out of place on our president's elegant head.

Eleven beautiful silk place-mats bearing coloured illustrations of Golden Age cricketers understandably rose to £550, and commemorative handkerchiefs ranged from Hobbs (£240) and WG (£160-320) to the 1882 Australians (£500), the 1847 All-England XI (£2500), and the 1785 White Conduit delight, which fell to the Bradman Museum for £7000 after some aggressive bidding.

Autographed bats were just as unlikely to go cheaply. One signed by numerous Golden Age players made £1500, and another, signed by England and Australia at Leeds in 1930, made a breathtaking £800. An 1868 bat with North American significance sold for £1000, and yet more interesting bats, one inscribed by Tom Hayward after his 1899 season and one by Bobby Abel from 1896, went for "only" £300 and £550. The Abel bat was particularly fascinating in that the odd little Surrey man, who was branded as weak-hearted against fast bowling, was said, in a note attached by his son, to have scored 231 with this blade against Kortright, the fastest of them all.

Lot 700 came at 8.15pm, by which time we'd been going for almost ten hours. Heads were hot, bottoms were numb. But less than two hours remained. Cricket balls now sold for astounding figures: two from the 1910-11 Australia v South Africa series came back to life at £750, one from the 1867 Gentlemen v Players contest at Lord's, £400, and one hit over the stand at Lord's over 100 years ago by Harvey Fellows, £420. Even a piece of bone, a "cricket bat burnisher", made £85. A huge piece of 1816 Welsh pottery in tribute to James Dean of Sussex sold at £2000. By now people had given up gasping. There was just the occasional tired raising of eyebrows. A cracked Staffordshire mug c1790 went for £1100, a WG Coalport plate £900, a sweet little figure of a 19th Century batsman in a glass case £1300.

Then came the scramble for nine ivory life membership badges, issued by MCC a century ago. No.1 made £300, the rest around £160 each. A gingerbread mould with hallmarked plaque referring to Henry Hall, Billy Beldham's mentor, was secured for Farnham, Surrey by a local syndicate for £400, while fifteen MCC members' voting boxes made of mahogany varied from £450 down to £190, astounding realisations for those whose senses had not by now been dulled completely.

Six pewter beakers engraved after Hayman's Artillery Ground painting were one of the higher-class lots, and sold for £3800 as we entered the 800s. The crowd had thinned. People had gone home to their dinners. Some had raced off to catch the last train. The daylight through the fanlights had long since darkened. A most desirable medallion given to "Dick" Lilley after the 1903-04 MCC tour of Australia sold at £280, and with the last gasp came the Ashes urn replica. I found the strength to raise my bidding paddle on high – and kept it there. The opposition receded at

£150. This Anglo-Australian had won the Ashes! [The trophy was actually a mark of gratitude from Charlie Watts.] A small quantity of adrenalin trickled through the abdomen. Four lots out of thirty-three aimed at had to be regarded as a reasonable result.

President Cowdrey took the rostrum for the last couple of lots, giving this marathon event the perfect send-off. Laughter pealed across the battleground as he prepared to sell the head and skin of a tiger, "shot during the 1933-34 MCC tour of India by C.S.Marriott, the Kent legspin-googly bowler". Two thousand pounds tied up that particular deal.

At 9.55pm it was all over, and semi-stunned survivors formed small clusters and limply exchanged comforting remarks. Why had they done this to us? Squeezing what was patently a two-day event into one day? Was it symptomatic of the modern passion for one-day cricket? Anyway, we couldn't stay there talking all night. Down in the Long Room bar there were goods to be paid for and collected – more Charlie's than mine. That done, I stole off into the night to find the car, down by the Nursery gates. Ghostly figures were staggering through the shadows, paintings and boxes under their arms. They were all right. They had obviously been to the auction. But what if one of the security men stopped me? Here I was, creeping dazedly around Lord's near midnight with "the Ashes" in a crumpled paper bag. What would I say if challenged? Simply, I suppose, that I paid good money for the urn, and that money was currently being totted up by the Arts and Library sub-committee, like so many Peter Sellerses and Terry-Thomases.

I had paid for the name.

Wisden Cricket Monthly, June 1987

Cricket auctions have flourished ever since, though none could quite match that one for scale and publicity. Many of those prices from 1987 might eventually have justified themselves as the ranks of collectors have expanded.

Soon after that memorable auction at Lord's, during a one-day international between England and Pakistan, there came a reminder of grim modern realities:

Cricket Gets a Fright

CRICKET GOT a bit of a fright at Edgbaston on Bank Holiday Monday, May 25. Caught with its box off, it suffered severe if not terminal damage. The unpreparedness was barely excusable, for no prospect seemed more certain, from past evidence, than trouble on the terraces when the hordes of Pakistan "supporters" came not merely to watch cricket but to identify – with a fanatical frenzy and to the embarrassment of Imran and his players – with "their team". Our enquiries have revealed that hundreds of them gained entry without paying, and that a battle plan was actually drawn up among them. It would have been unpleasant and messy enough had there been nobody to oppose them. As it was, a small squad of police officers, some female, stood half-helplessly on patrol, and a not-so-small contingent of men with shaven heads and large boots lurked in anticipation of confrontation with the migrant bands. They were of a kind usually seen on football terraces and not, apparently, all that riveted by the pulsating cricket match being enacted before their very heady eyes. Some were blatantly National Front stormtroopers. One-day cricket was not to blame. It was merely the convenient – very convenient – stage for ugly conflict.

This is no place to discuss the thorny issue of police powers. Cricket's awareness to reality, though, is a cardinal issue. And, the warnings admittedly having been sounded much longer ago than last month, the TCCB are to be complimented for the speed at which they moved and the steps they took. The umpires will not be too enchanted at the decision to continue to allow the crowd onto the field at the end of a match, for they often get trampled underfoot. But the ban on the lethal flag-stakes and banners and the noise-making instruments which are such a nuisance and an incitement to crazy behaviour is just what was needed.

Police video surveillance, too, should be a deterrant, and will also ensure that fewer guilty parties escape into obscurity. As for alcohol control, this should have been introduced as the norm years ago. It will have scarcely any appropriate effect on Muslim spectators, but the "other side" will think harder before entering battle. Crowd segregation remains a complex matter, but the sooner all Test grounds are fully equipped with individual bucket seats the better.

Thus the introduction of high and preferably electrified wire fencing remains only a haunting possibility for the future. But the new measures spell bad luck for so many of the friendly but elderly ground stewards, who now face redundancy as younger, stronger men are recruited. There is no place for Dad's Army in this physical crisis.

The TCCB chief executive admitted that there had been a "touch" of racialism in the unsavoury events at Edgbaston. We would go further and say that it was the fundamental cause, and in view of the tireless credo that cricket reflects life, with racial suspicion and hatred being the curse of our time, what was really so surprising about what happened at Edgbaston?

Wisden Cricket Monthly, July 1987

The reactions to this dreadful day at Edgbaston – and to this editorial – varied from the appalled to the hysterical. Surrey CCC and Warwickshire CCC banned the sale of the magazine at their grounds because of the word "Bloodshed" on the front cover, perhaps unaware that a policewoman saved the life of a Pakistani spectator who had his throat gashed during the nasty goings-on behind the stands. Gradually the authorities revised their approach to maintaining ground security during major events, perhaps inevitably completely overdoing it at times.

WE APOLOGISE to readers who normally buy their copy of *WCM* at The Oval or Edgbaston during the summer. In a melange of righteousness and absurdity these ground authorities decided the cover headline "Bloodshed at Birmingham" on our last edition was not to their taste. MCC had thought likewise for two hours only, then cancelled their "ban" when they realised how ludicrous a posture it would have been. Those who purport to be so genteel are the enemies of cricket, since just such failure to face up to reality saw football sink into a mire of violence. Pretending the horrors at Edgbaston on May 25 did not occur will get none of us anywhere.

Wisden Cricket Monthly, August 1987

There has been no more affable man in cricket than Bob Taylor, who tops the table of first-class wicketkeeping dismissals:

A Chat with "Chat"

YESTERDAY A request came through to pen a few lines on Bob Taylor, the highly skilled former Derbyshire and England wicketkeeper – though I'm not sure about the "former" since he keeps bobbing back into the game: whisked out of the Cornhill clients' lunch to keep wicket again last year, and then guarding the sticks at Scarborough a few weeks later for his captain, iron man Brian Close, while Kiwi Ken Rutherford belted 317.

By one of those small miracles which continue to crop up in cricket, a few hours after getting Jack Sokell's letter, I found myself sitting next to my old pal "Chat" Taylor at a lunch in Cornhill's boardroom. I thought I knew all there was that was worth knowing about him, but he told me a little tale which had me almost weeping into my salmon, even though he chuckled all the way through the telling.

You will remember the scandal over the bets placed for Dennis Lillee and Rod Marsh at Headingley in 1981, when England were so far into a freshly-dug grave that Ladbrokes were suddenly offering 500 to 1 against them? You will recall also how those two Aussie battlers had such difficulty explaining how, in all conscience, they could ever have bet against their own side.

Let me tell you now how that lovely, considerate fellow Bob Taylor was similarly tempted, and how the upshot was rather a different tale. Seeing the sensational odds flashed onto the scoreboard, the little wicketkeeper, grey-haired in his wisdom, decided to have a couple of quids' worth. If successful, he would pick up a thousand quid; though, of course, there was no real likelihood of this particular match being turned round. The best England could hope for was decisive weather interference.

Bob, than whom there has never been a neater or more efficient wicketkeeper, would no more have dreamt of dashing blindly to the betting tent than taking the ball in front of the stumps in attempting a stumping. Instead, he lost time changing into something more presentable than cream flannels and England sweater: out came the blazer and a pair of dark shoes. Then, when time was starting to run out for ambitious punters, our Bob was confronted at the pavilion entrance by a swarm of young autograph-hunters. Players often brush through these swarms as if they were so much overgrown grass. Not Bob. He patiently wrote his name on all sorts of bits of paper as the minutes ticked away.

At last, time for a quick dash to the tent to lay on £2. How could you resist, in a two-horse race? Alas, the one piece of paper Bob Taylor didn't sign that momentous afternoon was a betting slip. He was called urgently back into the England dressing-room: destiny took over; and the next he thought about it was when Australia lost their ninth wicket and then were buried in the grave which earlier had been dug to receive England's limp body. In those closing stages our hero had to fight very hard indeed to blot the thought of the £1000-that-might-have-been from his mind. Moments later the ecstasy of improbable victory swept over him completely . . . well, almost.

So nice guys sometimes miss out because of their consideration for others. Or do they? Is a personal reputation like Mr Taylor's worth a measly thousand quid or more? He always was regarded as the most obliging of England's cricketers on tour. If the PM or Foreign Office is searching for an ambassador to one of the world's trouble spots, like Nicaragua or Tehran or Sydney, need the search go beyond the Gent in the Gloves?

The Twelfth Man (Wombwell Cricket Lovers' Society, 1987)

Another season gone, another review of events:

Leaves and Debris

AS I WAS saying to Richie at the weekend, the 1987 cricket season was probably the wettest and most frustrating since the war. Enough to warp a man's sanity. The Tests were a weather shambles, and even the MCC Bicentenary match was ruined, in the final stages, by the accursed "liquid sunshine". Many folk, it seems, will be looking to the winter as a time to get their suntans and dry out the mildew in their joints, watching England competing in four different countries with three different teams of their own. Out of that little lot should come some sort of combination capable of giving the 1988 West Indians a run for their money. Richie seemed to agree.

No season is entirely without highlights, of course, and the late weeks of the county season brought tension in the Sunday League, a thrilling run by Lancashire to challenge Notts in the Championship, and a gallant NatWest victory by Notts on a memorable Monday afternoon when the great Hadlee actually seemed to be trying to give his wicket away at one point. The Northants fielders were having none of that. Richie seemed amused at the recollection. Was there ever such a sad procession as Geoff Cook and his players trooped along the Lord's balcony to get their losers' medals?

The sadness of autumn sometimes seems close to unbearable. This year, with the deplorable weather being mocked by September sunshine while cricket fields were empty, we need to absorb the loss of favourite old cricketers such as Bill Bowes and Jack Mercer, cut down by age, and the departure from county cricket of such household names as Dennis Amiss, Derek Underwood, Clive Rice, Richard Hadlee, Clive Radley, David Acfield, and probably the colourful Phil Edmonds. Nor shall we see Gavaskar or Imran again. Richie fixed me with his beady eye and seemed to feel the same mild grief.

What compensation is there for such a lacklustre summer? Well, for a start, 1988 hasn't much to beat, and will therefore almost certainly feel a lot more satisfying than 1987. Summers like 1981 and 1985 are hard to follow.

I raked over a few more fallen leaves and gathered more twigs for the bonfire. Richie, my friendly little robin, hopped a few feet nearer. I hadn't seen him for some months. I'd been extremely busy, admittedly, but I suspect he'd been out of the country himself. In which case, did he really miss much?

Wisden Cricket Monthly, October 1987

Turbulence rocked England's 1987-88 tour of Pakistan:

Miscarriages

ARE THEY really that peeved at having been eliminated from the World Cup and beaten three times by England in the one-day internationals? Do they truly harbour that much resentment against the TCCB for their inept refusal to disemploy umpire Constant last summer? Is it so crucial for creed and country that victory should be obtained and defeat avoided on the cricket field that Pakistan has to inflict on Test cricket an umpire as pathetically incompetent as Shakeel Khan and one so overbearing as Shakoor Rana?

Apparently it is. And the scorecards and results of the acrimonious Lahore Test and the even more infamous Faisalabad Test, although enshrined in the annals, have no validity in the minds of true cricket-lovers.

When such a competitive but patently decent person as Chris Broad steps over the line of morality to join his shrieking opponents, the fever must be grave. He was one of *nine* England batsmen – according to England's captain, manager and press observers – wrongly given out in the ironically-named Gaddafi Stadium. His tolerance level in the face of such blatant injustice was the lowest. Capel in particular had a case for dissent, for he was twice robbed and ended with a "pair". How much of this lunacy could such a newcomer ultimately withstand? And the old warrior Mike Gatting cracked at last at Faisalabad under the accumulating weight of dispute and injustice: the latest sacrifice to the monstrous political, racially sensitive and money-hungry thing called modern international cricket. His language might well have been unacceptable, but in fact we were witnessing a player's breakdown after months of strain. Pontificators please bear in mind.

Just as tragic as the nine miscarriages at Lahore (plus the bad stumping decision against Qadir) and the shattering events at Faisalabad was the fact that an astounding exhibition of legspin/googly bowling was obscured by the disgraceful controversies. While the world can happily do without clueless (let us be kind) umpiring, it is in desperate need of repeated doses of the neglected skills of wrist spin such as Abdul Qadir laid on for 73 spellbinding overs. Even if eight of his 13 wickets at Lahore were umpire-assisted, from the number of times he beat the bat he might just as easily have finished with all 20 wickets.

For those who love leg-spin, there was a sense of gratification at seeing the post-war English refusal to acknowledge and encourage it being repaid in the most punishing fashion through this delicate but lethal weapon.

There was no way, short of hypnotism, that Gatting and his men were going to be able to eliminate the uncertainty of the umpiring from their minds as they moved on to the second Test. The Pakistan establishment had them where they wanted them. It may not be without significance that Pakistan cricket is run by military men. Of the cricket team which carries all the nation's fanatical hopes, Miandad is captain; the umpires are the lance-corporals.

The question remains: just as Georgetown as well as Cape Town have seen their last Test matches for some time to come, will anyone want to tour Pakistan again? Will Haseeb Ahsan's dusty kingdom end up extending desperate invitations to all points only for the RSVPs to be "regretful" declines?

International (not "neutral") umpires may be the solution, but surely from the teeming millions of the subcontinent just *two* good ones could be found? If so, they should have stuck to them, not rotate with suspect incompetents. The most urgent need in world cricket – likely, alas, to be unfulfilled – is for Pakistan to put its house in order, and play the game.

Wisden Cricket Monthly, January 1988

The panel of independent umpires was eventually set up, though the quality of umpiring scarcely improved with the political need to utilise umpires from all the major territories. As for poor Pakistan, civil unrest finally rendered it a no-go area twenty years later, when they were forced to play "home" matches on neutral territory.

The World Cup final in Calcutta late in 1987, and surrounding events, gave cause for another rambling essay:

Faraway Farewells

EDEN GARDENS, Calcutta on November 8 was meant to see the joint farewell to big cricket of Sunil Gavaskar and Imran Khan, two of the giants of world cricket for the past dozen years. It was not to be. The World Cup semi-finals success of Australia and England saw to that. Not that Gavaskar was likely to have gone to Calcutta, having vowed never to submit to that crowd's frenzied barracking ever again.

I gave both these champions more than passing thought on the way out to India. England had said goodbye during the MCC Bicentenary match at Lord's, when they batted together. Not always is the public aware of the impending passing of a star performer. But there was no mistaking this time, even if it was suspected that General Zia might "lean" on Imran to persuade him to change his mind and have another Test series or two.*

Remember when they first toured here? Imran, with a pudding-bowl haircut, slanting his great inducers into leg slip's gut, Gavaskar, also in 1971, jet-black hair and college-boy looks, both long odds bait to punters on the lookout for colts who might one day be record-breakers.

In the years ahead they both waded into controversy and they both became idols of heroic stature. They became the pride of their respective nations and of their governments, and they became captains and ambassadors. They also happened to become wealthy, as was their just reward for physical and temperamental gifts.

Now, in cricketing late middle age, it was time to go, Imran with 311 wickets and 2770 runs in his 70 Tests, with victory in England the crowning achievement, and Gavaskar with an awesome 125 Test appearances for a supreme 10,122 runs (51.12) and 34 centuries, 13 of them tellingly against West Indies. He also clung to 108 catches. They both had a special dignity about them which some of their team-mates would have done well to emulate.

I sat in my wicker chair in the old Taj Mahal Hotel in Bombay and watched every ball of the first World Cup semi-final, the Arabian Sea stretching beyond the TV set. Upset No.1 was Australia's victory in that contest, and Imran's Cherokee countenance was as inscrutable as ever, his bowling and half-century almost having saved his side. That was it. What a waste that he should now be hanging up his international boots.

You can soon be forgotten in this game. At the nets the Indian kids clamoured for Tim Robinson's autograph. They were too young to recognise and acknowledge the old bloke with him, a Yorkshireman [Boycott] who scored 8114 runs for England.

And so to the giant Turkish bath called the Wankhede Stadium, and that memorable campaign of sweep, sweep and sweep again by Gooch and Gatting. In went India to get that 255 which would land them in the Calcutta final. And out went Sunil Gavaskar for four, bowled neck and crop by DeFreitas. He trudged off, with that long-familiar waddle of his, but any similarity between his farewell and that of the man whose records he had surpassed, Donald Bradman, was non-existent. Applauded lovingly all the way back, Bradman knew where he stood in 1948. Gavaskar, Bombay's own son, who had been conceived only a month or two later, was booed, even by some of the so-called aficionados in the members' enclosure. Poor sod.

I began to wonder, as I sat in the world's best cricket press-box [Eden Gardens, Calcutta], how many people could now claim to have seen every World Cup final. The number must have shrunk dramatically with its removal from Lord's. And this was the most thrilling of all. Afterwards Mike Gatting, to the background cacophony of a firework display, gave a press conference, subdued as a cruiserweight just revived from a knockout. To add to the unreality of it all, the legendary Mushtaq Ali, old but erect, and Vijay Hazare passed across the chamber and slipped off into the darkness.

The banquet at the Calcutta Oberoi Grand after the final was memorable for the multitude of cricket identities. N.K.P.Salve [chief organiser] managed to hide his grief, as did the British Sports Minister, who had landed with his entourage ready to be carried shoulder-high by a victorious Gatting. Instead, it was Allan Border, good old battling AB himself, who was the new monarch of world cricket. Simon O'Donnell had been introducing anybody who passed to "our cup", and later led the team on stage – respectably clad still in blazers and ties – in rounds of songs which had kept them going through the tour: *Billy Don't Be a Hero* and *Australia Will Always Be My Home*. Most of the Indian dignitaries in the hall looked on askance, and Bob Simpson, by the far doorway, was signalling urgently but perhaps not too seriously for them to vacate the stage. The boys purposefully failed to see him.

Then it was up to the team room for more songs, Tim May doing his bleary best to keep up with journalist Mike Coward's Gene Pitney impression, and Craig McDermott, resplendent in leather strides, forward-thinking enough to express enthusiasm for next season's stint with Gloucestershire [which failed to materialise]. Unbelievably, home in Australia the millions had had no direct telecast of the second half of the World Cup final, apart from those who had access to Tooheys pubs, where the Sky channel was beaming its exclusive picture.

I UNWOUND from all this with a few hours of tennis-ball cricket with the youthful editorial staff of the Calcutta-based *Sportsworld* magazine at the sports complex where they had all grown up together, and it was here, witnessing their sacred code of honour (when you're out, you're out; and half-volley catches didn't count), that I felt some faith returning in the future of the game in those parts.

Later, Mudar Patherya and Barry O'Brien presented Australian manager Alan Crompton with the ashes of a World Cup bail, housed in a small urn, hoping they would be adopted as the One-Day Ashes for ongoing competition between England and Australia. After all, the margin in the final, seven runs, was the same as in the immortal 1882 Ashes match at The Oval.

Now it was time for a whirlwind week in Australia to promote my little book *Pageant of Cricket* [640 pages]. Thirty-four interviews in four days seemed to get the message across, but more enjoyable by far were two sessions at Sheffield Shield matches: NSW v South Australia at Sydney, where the ball hopped about on a rain-affected pitch in such a way that the players had never seen before. They looked disbelievingly when told that this exciting variation once used to be a regular occurrence. Geoff Lawson, back from the dead, had learned how to bowl on it by the second innings and took six wickets. Bill O'Reilly could scarcely contain his pleasure.

At the vast Melbourne Cricket Ground, again before only a couple of hundred spectators, Dean Jones hammered an elegant 191, and in the evening another ghost from the past came out to bat, one Brian Davison, forty, captain of Tasmania.

All too soon it was time to wing back to base. Apart from an eleven-hour delay in take-off (3am is a lovely time to depart), no hot water or inflight movie, headphones that didn't work and food that was largely indigestible, it was an excellent Alitalia flight.

* Not only did Imran rescind his decision to retire: the next World Cup ended with him triumphantly holding the trophy aloft after the final at Melbourne.

Wisden Cricket Monthly, January 1988

A serious wobble cast a shadow over the Australia v England Test match at Sydney which was part of the former colony's Bicentennial celebrations:

Matters of Guilt

ENGLAND'S Bicentennial cricket gift to Australia was not the Test match victory for which they yearned. Gatting's men won four of the five days' play. The gift instead was an adoption of the guilt the southern nation had uncomfortably been persuaded to face during the early weeks of its year of celebration. A society founded on imported felons and guilty of abominable treatment of the indigenous people was being told that shame was the principal emotion on the menu for 1988. It was a time for navel study.

And then came Chris Broad.

Suddenly Australia was incensed, momentarily freed of all guilt. This Pommy was committing an unpardonable sin. Not only had he whacked his stumps over – regrettably no unique sight in latterday cricket – but he did it after having scored 139 and not even being the victim of a dodgy decision. The spotlight had swung unexpectedly to another villain, and Australia was innocent and appalled. Clever move by England, the model guest, anxious to please.

Broad, who had stood his ground and caused a furore in Lahore, now looked silly in Sydney. The England management fined him £500 – almost enough – on the spot, and he later apologised for his violence upon the stumps. It remains to be seen whether Bob Hawke's government will reward the Notts left-hander for diverting feelings of guilt, uncertainty and indignation away from the celebrating country onto the slate of the Old Country.

For the year-long birthday party to be a success it was necessary not only that little plans like Pat Cash's intended winning of the Australian Open tennis should reach fruition but that the Bicentennial Test match should have an appropriate outcome: i.e. victory for Border's XI, and preferably by an innings. Ah well, fifty years from now the 250th anniversary of white settlement may bring more appropriate results, even if the Australian Test (or all-pervasive one-day) team may be largely of Asian origin.

The vintage-car parade of Living Legends went well during the luncheon interval on the second day, though Boycott's car broke down, and some small boys had to enquire of their fathers which ones were the legendary A.C.Smith, R.Subba Row and J.J.Warr. Sir Donald Bradman led off, the leader, as of old, in a 1911 Rolls-Royce. The applause was almost desperate, after the wide lap of honour, as he disappeared into the shadowy tunnel, arm aloft, smiling broadly – if the adverb be permitted. Later in the procession came Bill O'Reilly, currently reporting his last Test match. Not only, therefore, was probably the greatest of all bowlers on view alongside the greatest of batsmen, but a truly precious apotheosis of Australian genius was there for a privileged audience to behold. Englishmen in the crowd applauded as heartily as their hosts.

Then, back to the cricket, and the old intense rivalry, and the trading of tongue-in-cheek insults. A local fan decided that Bill Athey's slow batting had earned him an amendment to his name: A-pa-they. British fans on the Hill (or now semi-Hill) waved their flags with a good deal more gusto and aggressive intent than the officers and Jack-tars on Captain Arthur Phillip's landing two hundred years ago.

As the match was turned around and saved, and Australia's self-respect restored, the national confidence, so fragile a commodity at the best of times (as the currency speculators would testify), lifted most visibly. Gatting kept Dilley on in the gloom, and Dilley bowled a bouncer, and the umpires called it off. Another generous English gesture was registered.

Might the gentle drift of the game away from England have marked another of those cricket analogies, this one the symbolisation of how the young nation has gradually distanced itself from the older?

Thank Heaven we have the residual Anglo-Australian cricket challenge, with its triumphs and tragedies, even its odd spot of guilt. It's only a game. Or is that to sell it short? See you next year, Australia, when you're 201.

Wisden Cricket Monthly, March 1988

The centenary of cricket writing's "patron saint" warranted a commemoration, albeit one of a searching nature:

The Truth About Cardus

JUST AS I was ruminating on whether it was worth entering secondhand bookshops ever again – there seems to be nothing on their shelves to entice one who has been collecting cricket books for over thirty years – the value of this custom was recently reaffirmed by the casual sighting of a copy of James Agate's *Ego 7* (Harrap, 1945).

Agate, one of the legendary dramatic critics, died in 1947, having published nine volumes of letters and diary entries under the generic title *Ego*. Like his close friend Neville Cardus, he belonged to Manchester first and England's cricket grounds and London's West End second. Witty, eccentric and of dubious sexual disposition, Agate has his name revived here because of his friendship with Cardus and the interesting "new" light his writings throw on the Patron Saint of Cricket Writing (for Cardus is nothing less than that, having influenced every serious cricket writer of the past sixty years).

We have grown used to the modern deflationary assessment of Cardus as an inventor of dialogue and embellisher of personality, and we accept (most of us) with a smile his explanation so often tendered in his final years, when he realised he had been twigged: "Ah, but it's just what Dick Tyldesley *would* have said!"

Agate tells of a flight of fancy personally witnessed: "Neville Cardus once wrote of Woolley's off-drives that they were 'like butterflies going into the flame'. But he was writing for a public which had not seen Woolley's innings. I had been with Cardus at Lord's that afternoon, and what he said was not 'Look at that butterfly going into the flame!' but 'Well played sir!'"

There was an adulatory flavour about Cardus's letters to Agate. Jonathan Cape sent Agate the manuscript of Cardus's *Ten Composers* to vet, and apparently Cardus absorbed some fairly cutting criticism of it: improvements in foreign quotations, spelling and punctuation corrections, even instances in which Agate, while declaring the book "sound", "satisfying" and "brilliant", claimed that he had "made the clumsy felicitous". In a postscript, he wrote: "It beats me how, in the Australian bush, you can have produced a book so essentially accurate in all that matters." Cardus happened to be living, in self-imposed wartime exile, in the exclusive Sydney harbourside area of Potts Point, where kangaroos and aborigines appeared only in paintings hanging on the walls in Chelsea-style drawing-rooms.

Cardus next wrote to Agate that he was working on his autobiography. It was to run to many impressions and make Cardus real money, a rare bounty for him in retrospect as he looked back on his longish life from his basement rooms in Bickenhall Mansions, off Baker Street. Back in 1944, he told Agate that some of the autobiography "seems to me astonishingly good". He was reverential towards Agate to the point of writing: "I read everything you write." He wanted the new edition of Agate's novel *Responsibility*: "I read it from street-lamp to street-lamp while I delivered insurance policies in Manchester." In Cardus's *Autobiography* he declares his awe towards Agate from the time he first came close to him in the early and humble days of employment on the *Manchester Guardian*. A sad irony was that Cardus eventually returned to England a day or so after Agate died in 1947.

In *Ego 7*, Agate continues to lean teasingly on the middle-aged Cardus with a throwback analysis in a letter to George Lyttelton. He recalled Cardus's famous passage on Tom Richardson's heroic fast-bowling marathon in a losing cause at Old Trafford in 1896: "About Richardson. Yes, of course he legged it to the pavilion quicker than anybody. I saw every ball of that last Australian innings, and my account isn't nearly so good as Cardus's in spite of the fact that he was seven [*eight*] years old at the time, and if he saw the match at all saw it from his nursery window seven miles away!"

Cardus had written in *Days in the Sun* not that Richardson "legged it to the pavilion" but that "a companion led him to the pavilion, and there he fell wearily to a seat". Believe the version which appeals to you more. Let us now leave James Agate . . . after one final extract of considerable amusement and interest: C.B.Fry's views, in a 1944 letter, on Hitler: "I knew him and had talks with him in Berlin in '34. He was courteous and quiet and a *very* good listener, and a *compact* talker. *But* he is a *fanatic* like Mohammed – "sword or Koran" . . . what struck me was that he – like all Germans – *had a bit of the brain wanting*."

It was first revealed in *Wisden Cricket Monthly* (Dec 1985) that Neville Cardus was not born on April 2, 1889, but, as his birth certificate shows, on April 3, 1888. Therefore, not only may we drink a toast to his centenary a year earlier than would have been the case, but an extra bumper is in order by way of celebration of the fact that this favourite among cricket writers does not after all share a centenary year with the aforementioned Bodyline bowler Adolf Hitler.

Andrew Lamb's *WCM* feature left one feeling that, as far as his early days went, Cardus's autobiography might just as easily have borne Clive James's title, *Unreliable Memoirs*. Moreover, some latterday writings on Cardus might just as easily be so classified as well.

Born John Frederick Cardus, the lad was brought up by his young Aunt Beatrice and his grandfather rather than his own flighty unmarried teenage mother Ada (who married three months after his birth). Let the enigma remain. His books live on, and fortunately much of his work has been republished in recent years.

There are those lucky enough too to remember the man, who was taken from us in 1975 at an age we now know to have been eighty-six. He was frail, somewhat impish, but no pushover. Towards the end, having spent himself wordwise a generation previously, he would hold court in the Lord's Long Room with his back to the play, propped against one of the great tables, reminiscing with acquaintances, ever nostalgic, ever gentle.

He promised to write a foreword to my proposed biography of Trumper. Neither the foreword nor the book was ever written. The last time I saw him was in his favourite eating-place, the London Steak House in Baker Street. I had been charged with the job of getting his signature on a bat for its owner, a citizen of the real Australian bush. Neville was seated with a cellist, a lady, who also happened to be Australian. He was as courteous as ever, though his later years were not comfortable.

News of his passing rocked the cricket world. "A member of the natural elite," was how J.B.Priestley saw him, "a man who brought style and nobility to his daily journalism, who has left us in his books so much to sustain us through a bewildering, menacing time."

Geoffrey Mather, recalling Cardus's remark that "the only thing I made up my mind early about is that I was not going to work for a living," asserted that "he never did work for a living; he made living work."

Wisden Cricket Monthly, April 1988

Neville Cardus, patron saint of cricket writing.

National heroes seldom lead completely unblemished lives, but the public tend to be tolerant. Sometimes, though, patience is stretched just a little too far:

Fallen Hero

THERE WAS a rumour on the second or third day of Ian Botham's "Hannibal trek" that even his elephants had walked out on him. His popularity was about as low as it could get, his image soiled in such a way as would have been unimaginable in the heady days of 1981. His behaviour in a Tasmanian dressing-room and on an Ansett flight to Perth had stretched his record of misdemeanours to such a length as to rival and perhaps overshadow his prodigious Test match performances. And now, as the likes of Allan Border, Greg Chappell and Ron Archer turned their backs on him in disapproval, those who had been glad to see him leave Somerset were donning "I told you so" masks.

Botham has chalked up almost as much time in the courtroom as on the Lord's pitch batting for England. Wonderful as his fund-raising walks are, nothing can save him from going down in history as a challenging, brave, aggressive cricketer . . . who was respected little off the field. Yes, he would probably have won a VC if he'd gone to real war. Posthumously. No, he did not grow up after reaching the age of thirty. No, like the skipper who had most early influence on him, Brian Close, he knows not the meaning of contrition, and has no knack of reconsideration.

Botham knows precisely where each charity walk is to end, but the path of his life seems less clear-cut, more threatening. Where will repeated excesses lead, and how do they rest beside the claims of family devotion? Cricket has more than enough sad cases – drunks, vagrants and melancholics – in its annals already. Sport has shuddered at the sight of shambling, brain-damaged boxers, a jockey and a footballer in prison, obscenity-screeching tennis players, barbaric rugby players. Though we in turn shudder at the prospect, there seems every likelihood that a champion all-rounder and national hero will always be beyond hope when it comes to the power of self-control. And the thought makes those of us who have known him since he was eighteen, and have endured his playful violence, feel sick with disappointment and foreboding.

Where stand the Test selectors in all this? If public demand, while not necessarily unanimous, comes into account – and it has occasionally affected selectors' thinking – then Botham will play for England this summer, unless his early-season form is wretched. If the selectors, on the other hand, feel that the new statute on discipline has to be implemented, they will be influenced heavily against Botham: who will no doubt utter a loud oath or two if his series of Australian court and cricket-authority fines is compounded by sanctions at home.

The long-awaited century against West Indies would put much of the problem to rights, at least for the time being, should the selectors grant him the opportunity to rehabilitate himself. His presence would hardly reduce gate takings. Almost three times as many people watched Queensland's Sheffield Shield matches this season as against the previous.

What Botham does off the field is, strictly speaking, a matter for him and his victim and the owners of damaged property and the police only. He did not bring cricket into disrepute in that dressing-room and on that flight. He brought I.T.Botham into disrepute, and, amazingly to many non-Australians, turned a nation against him.

Within a few weeks, he could be the toast of his own nation again if he does his Biggles act on the field of international cricket. There – as in "civilian" life – he is to be judged on deeds.

This being 1988, maybe we should take the popular line and blame his parents and his schoolteachers, or junk food, or the high unemployment figures, or too much sex and violence on television. Or merely accept the man, when *not* in England colours, for what he insists on being, and lower both our expectations and esteem.

Wisden Cricket Monthly, May 1988

As it turned out, Botham had little Test cricket left in him. But who then would have believed that twenty years hence he would be Sir Ian, riding high on lucrative commercial contracts, and in the television commentary box?

Another England player who got into difficulties as the turbulent 1980s drew to a close was Mike Gatting. His challenging book Leading From the Front presented the reviewer with plenty upon which to chew:

A Stubborn Little Bloke

I REMEMBER Mike Gatting's first press conference as England captain most vividly. Minutes after being invited to take over from David Gower, he came into the writing room at Lord's and proceeded to answer the gentle questioning in a soft, shy and slightly squeaky voice. Scarcely once did he lift his head. It was as if he were staring at that old oak table like a fortune-teller, trying to extract glimmers of the future. We now know how it all ended, messily, steamily, heartbreakingly.

The "barmaid business" occurred as the book was being released. But the Pakistan rumpus is here, revealing hardly anything not already known. That chapter was penned, rather clumsily, by Ms Patmore, and may – unless the TCCB hits Gatting over the head with his tour contract – point the way for other players who want to put something recently controversial in their books. He may have got round the prohibition, and it might well be argued that he, of all people, ought to be allowed his public utterances in that squalid affair.

"Gatt" has always been one for coming to the point, so it is no surprise when he states clearly on page 1, for anyone in doubt, that even as a kid he was a "very angry, naughty, stubborn little bloke, and very very determined". Some of those qualities have been greatly to England's advantage as he has piled up those nine Test centuries after such a tentative start. The little bruiser who won bronze medals for the quickstep and waltz at the Neasden Ritz first got slightly drunk at fifteen, but at nineteen he went to play for Balmain, in Sydney, where his motivation was strengthened and maturity came fast.

The story then unfortunately lapses into potted descriptions of almost every match he has played: "then I managed to get 141" sort of thing, with "Brears" and "Rad" and "Ernie" performing alongside. His views are bluntly honest: Willis was no fan of his, and he felt hostile towards Gifford and somewhat exasperated about Edmonds. He is honest enough to own that Sikander was not really out at Headingley in 1982, and is at pains to portray his softer side: he cried when Mitzi the dog died, and sheds another tear or two when certain music and films come his way.

His OBE he found "embarrassing", and that anger wells up again when he thinks of the boos at Old Trafford in 1986 and the unfair criticism at Edgbaston in 1987. And, of course, Faisalabad later that year. Most of all he misses his little sons when away playing cricket. Even now this accident-prone cruiserweight may be gazing at the old oak tabletop, wondering what the next two years are about to reveal.

Wisden Cricket Monthly, August 1988

One of the greatest sources of pleasure was being with old cricketers with stories to tell. None was more genial than jolly Bill Johnston:

Whatever Happened to Bill Johnston?

IT MUST have been thirty-five years since I'd last had a conversation of any length with Bill Johnston. Then, at the back of the Sydney pavilion, the jolly Victorian had signed his name, chuckled a bit, and passed a few comments on the day's play which left a lad aglow all the way home on the train.

Bill was a member of the legendary 1948 Australian team under Don Bradman which toured England undefeated. Modest enough and realistic enough to acknowledge that many of a later generation will not have heard of him, Bill was the tall, gangling one, missing some tufts of hair, a swinging, seaming left-armer, with a "t" in his surname, unlike off-spinner Ian Johnson.

Always it is "Lindwall and Miller" when thoughts of the '48 invasion drift back. Yet Johnston took 27 wickets in the five Tests, the same as Lindwall, while Miller took 13. In all first-class matches Bill took 102 wickets (16.42); no Australian has taken 100 wickets on an England tour since. In his 40 Tests between 1947 and 1955 he took 160 wickets at 23.91. A bouncing, bucking, rubbery figure, bending the ball in at a sharp pace or cutting it away, he was highly respected by all batsmen, and is a bowler for whom Australia would gladly trade a large chunk of her worldly goods to have back today in his prime.

But Bill is not in his prime. He is sixty-seven and recently weathered successful surgery for stomach cancer, the operation lasting longer than a full day's play – even when West Indies are bowling. He's lost a lot of weight, but not his ready sense of humour, and I was thrilled to find him living only a few miles away from my Queensland holiday home. After those thirty-five years, we spoke to each other again, and his voice on the telephone was welcoming.

A few days later we sat by his pool, scrapbooks on the table. Big Bill from Beeac, son of a dairy farmer, was nicknamed "Tate" by his schoolmates, and developed not only as a cricketer but as a baseball pitcher, breaking the then junior world record with a throw of 125 yards. At seventeen he left his 19/6d-a-week job as a clerk and went to Melbourne's big smoke. He joined Richmond, together with brother Allan, and was in the first team by the end of his first season.

Having been informed of his selection for Victoria on December 4, 1941, he was denied his debut when the Japs raided Pearl Harbor. Match cancelled. He joined the Royal Australian Navy, transferred after a year to the RAAF, and after twelve months in aircrew he went to North Queensland and Darwin (after the first bombing) to man defence radar. He was briefly in the same training camp as a dashing young airman also from Victoria, future Test team-mate K.R.Miller.

A tragic telegram to the Johnston household brought news of Allan's death after his Halifax crashed in Ireland, and when war ended, Bill was left to resume his cricket alone. He was to visit his brother's grave during the 1948 tour, and still has his flying log-book.

Don Bradman was urging the new discovery to concentrate on the faster stuff, just as old Jack Ryder had done in the Colts nets, the former Australia captain saying, "Come into this net, Bill, and bowl me a few fast ones." "I almost knocked Jack's head off!" Bill recalls with a fond chuckle.

He took 16 wickets in four Tests against India (11.37), and when omitted from the Adelaide Test he sampled for the first of many times the sympathetic communication qualities of Bradman as a captain: "I want you to know that we're satisfied with your form." This was a pointer to his having been pencilled in already for England.

The 1948 tour, now golden in memory, brought triumph to the unlikely-looking matchwinner. He had rich hauls against Yorkshire, Lancashire and Hampshire before the first Test, then Somerset and Scotland, land of his forebears. The greatest thrill of his entire career though was taking 5 for 36 and 4 for 147 at Trent Bridge in his first English Test. He adjusted quickly: "I found the ball cut away more on English pitches, so I added this to my natural inswinger. Sometimes, with a shiny ball, I had to aim wide of first slip!"

"The general reception we got from the English people was unforgettable, and very touching," he says. "It was one of the best times of my life, seeing places I'd only ever heard of, seeing historical places. We were presented to King George VI in the Lord's Test, and we ourselves were treated like royalty everywhere we went."

We turned the pages of the scrapbook, compiled by his uncle. There was the front page of the Melbourne *Sun News-Pictorial* the day after his English Test debut: "MILLER AND JOHNSTON WRECK SIDE", with portraits of the wreckers. There was a reminder of his home-town's "bob-in" fund which raised £210 for him before he sailed. This triggered the recollection that they were paid £937.10.0 each as a tour fee in 1948 – increased by £12.10.0 for the next tour of England, in 1953. Was it enough? "Yeah!"

Here was an envelope with a one-and-sixpenny Australian stamp on it, adorned only with a map of Britain and the words Big Bill Johnston. As was obvious, it eventually found him. Here was a picture of the Australians strolling over the grounds of Balmoral with the royal family. "A good day, that. I was with Princess Elizabeth some of the time." Then came a reminder of the Essex match, when the Australians hit 721 at Southend in a day's play. Bill remember making 9, a precious little knock in that it saw Ron Saggers to the fourth century of the innings. "Then I got ticked off by the skipper. He said you should never throw your wicket away!"

Still, he insisted, Bradman was the best captain of all, even though his choice was queried recently by his staunch friend Lindsay Hassett, who piped up with mock indignation: "What about me?"

The joke about Bill Johnston's second tour of England, in 1953, was his batting average of 102, the product of 17 innings, 16 of which were undefeated. Skipper Hassett arranged a certain amount of protection for him in the closing stages. Neil Harvey, whose four wickets (10.75) put him at the top of the bowling, might have enjoyed a dual honour but for Bill. Harvey charmed 2040 runs (65.80), but had to settle for second. They were room-mates, but Neil "lost some of his sense of humour then!" Bill remembers the stroke off Jack Young at Hastings which brought up his aggregate 100. He never scored an individual century in any form of cricket.

The 1953 tour was really a disaster, for Bill damaged his ankle in the curtainraiser at East Molesey and missed important matches. As we talked, the right knee, another trouble-spot, below his shorts displayed a long scalpel mark. With his skill and experience, Australia might have saved the Ashes in '53. "We were the greatest people in the world because we lost!"

His two home series against England lifted his total of England wickets to 75. But he also did well in South Africa, even though he remembers that tour principally for a nasty car crash. Returning from a function, he ran the car up an unlit railway embankment, having dozed at the wheel. "It looks as if your player is dying," manager Chappie Dwyer was told. He could taste blood, and says he had "a nine-

Bill Johnston manages a characteristic chuckle as he discovers insect damage to his memorabilia after years of oversight.

iron divot in the top of my skull". They dabbed him with friars balsam and sent him home. That night Ray Lindwall had an accident too. He "ran into a drunk". Manager Dwyer was glad to get back to the cricket.

What about that sensational one-wicket victory at Melbourne in 1951-52, when he and club-mate Doug Ring made 38 frantic runs at the end to frustrate West Indies? "I felt no pressure. If I got out, no-one had expected runs from me. Don had always said to practise your batting because it could be useful one day. He also said that class batsmen got cracks on the *inside* edge of their bats. That's where mine always chipped! I'll show you later."

Bill said that Ramadhin left the field in tears, and there were several "captains" on the field, all giving orders to each other. Johnston hit the winning single: "Umpire Ron Wright said Worrell bowled it at middle stump, and I hit it through square leg! Anyway, I was abused afterwards by people who'd lost money on the result!"

Three years later he and Harvey went some way towards what would have been an even more sensational win at Sydney against England, whose express man Tyson had almost blown Australia apart. Bill told his senior partner "I think we can tire Tyson out", but the Typhoon kept bowling at his legs and eventually, after they had put on 39 of the 78 runs needed, he was caught behind by Evans – off the inside edge of course.

A few months later, in the Caribbean, Johnston broke down again, and was finished. He ran into a boundary gutter and twisted a knee.

He looks back at his major opponents, and finds Compton the most interesting: "If he went outside the off and hit you through square leg you didn't mind. He hit it so well." May: "Good player, very elegant." Hutton: "Lovely player. Didn't give you any encouragement." Wardle, who got stuck into him once or twice: "You changed the field and he still found gaps. Miller'd keep coming up to offer advice, but that didn't help at all!"

He watches cricket today mainly on TV. He deplores the spate of no-balls, mainly from the West Indians, and cannot understand Richie Benaud's constant criticism of the front-foot law. "All the bowlers bowl from a fair distance now. We used to be taken off if we bowled two no-balls!"

His wife, Judith, having made us another cup of tea, my pleas to open those old cabin trunks in the garage finally came good. What followed, I would rather not have witnessed. Revealed to daylight for the first time in years, the historic contents were home to a family of cockroaches and those other detestable enemies, woodworm. Bill could scarcely conceal his horror. The 1948 Australian blazer had its collar eaten away. The cap was badly soiled. Most of the letters had survived, and Brian Close's England cap was OK. But Everton Weekes's West Indies cap was in a bad way, and one of the Australian sweaters had copped it. A boot seemed intact, and some of the bats were passable (the mended inside edges still visible). Probably there was still enough to make a worthwhile parcel for the auction-room. Another year would have doomed the lot to extinction.

Bill and his wife have sold their house and have to decide whether to move north to Noosa, south to Port Macquarie, or only two miles away. Selfishly, I hope they choose the latter.

Wisden Cricket Monthly, February 1989

Bill Johnston died in May 2007 and his passing was widely mourned.

The intensification of sanctions against South Africa brought satisfaction for some, but there was still an uncomfortable feeling that a certain amount of irrational dragooning was taking place:

The Hidden Debt

CRICKET, THE sacrificial lamb, has had its throat cut at the altar of political expediency. Short of some politician's intervention or change of heart – and who ever heard of such a thing? – the South African problem has been resolved . . . well, not to the satisfaction of the South African Cricket Union, admittedly, or to those who believe that England has caved in against the forces of blackmail. And on the twenty-fourth anniversary of Churchill's death, too.

England (the TCCB) did vote for the ban. They did not abstain. Their delegates may have hummed a paraphrased theme tune: *You made me ban you, I didn't want to do it, I didn't want to do it.* Short of the agreement being tested in court or of Caribbean and subcontinental politicians getting up to their old tricks, the deal has been struck and should hold. But for how long, and at what cost?

Nothing seems more certain than that mature players from England and other countries will be available in adequate quantity when South Africa renews the "rebel" tours to stimulate the game in its official isolation. Test cricket will be weakened accordingly. That will be the awful cost, though some regions may take gleeful advantage of such a situation. Should England be forced to send a virtual 2nd XI to West Indies early next year, it takes little imagination to foresee the outcome. In such circumstances, the TCCB should take similar steps to the Australian Cricket Board when the ACB sensed the futility of the projected 1987-88 tour of West Indies and called it off. But the TCCB almost certainly wouldn't, and another 0-5 would go into the record book, even though keen cricket-followers would regard such "Tests" as being no more credible than some of the contests of ten years ago, when

Test cricket in Australia and West Indies in particular was gutted by Packer defections.

Test cricket, we have been told, is being protected by the adoption of a minimum ban. But unanimity came at a price, and the bill is being picked up by the unluckiest diner at the table of twenty-five, England. Perhaps it was symbolically fitting, for the "children" have been feeding off the Mother Country ever since the game was born in those various farflung lands.

What sort of "mother" is she? Might she not have got tough with her offspring, especially the noisier ones, some of whom wanted to bundle her off to an isolation home of her own if she didn't toe the line? But she evidently considers herself to be a kindly, tolerant old lady. She has put restraints on herself while allowing all others their voice and their wish. Foreign players may continue to play in England as mercenaries – even alongside the detested South African imports – improving their game, taking salaries well in excess of those doled out to young English players. Further, Mother England will continue to welcome all Test teams in rotation, paying them fat guarantees which will provide the lifeblood of their respective treasuries.

All of which leaves the prospect of a severely depleted England XI, unless more money can be found to ward off the seniors' temptations. County clubs may find it, with greater effort, or the sums paid to visiting Test teams and to individual foreign players could be reduced. Much extra revenue has to be generated now to keep the seniors happy and the young ones, accustomed to coaching in South Africa, fitted out with alternative off-season employment. It was too much to hope for that Bangladesh, Bermuda, Fiji, Canada, West Africa and others should back their opposition to that Cape involvement with the creation of coaching posts by way of substitution. They clearly felt no such obligation.

English cricket thus faces its future alone and with a familiar worry: money. The roast sacrificial lamb tasted good to some. The English delegation must have buried their helping with mint sauce to render it edible.

Wisden Cricket Monthly, March 1989

The full chaotic effect of this legislation became apparent some weeks later when there was a sizable exodus of "rebel" cricketers from England's Test ranks onto a handsomely-paid tour of South Africa.

Before then, I availed myself of the invitation – issued to several hundred people around the cricket world – to visit South Africa on the occasion of the country's Test centenary. It was never going to be celebrated with the innocent joy of England's or Australia's a decade previously, and yet it had a more profound meaning for those who had a first-hand inspection of the country and its cricket set-up nineteen years into isolation:

Where Hypocrites Fear to Tread

MIKE PROCTER, the world's greatest cricketer fifteen years ago, turned his chubby face to the centre of our distinguished gathering and levelled his blue eyes with all the deadly sincerity observed by hundreds of hapless batsmen as "Procky" used to turn at the end of his long, long run-up.

"We need help," he said. "The outside world *owes* it to us now. People should come here, see what we've done, what we're doing. Why doesn't Ian Botham come here to see? Why not Viv Richards? And Clive Lloyd?"

It was well past midnight, and the only answer any of us could find was "Fear": fear of reprisal from the entrenched preachers of hatred, fear of interference to subsequent freedom of movement, perhaps most of all of discovering that South Africa was not as they had been led to believe.

Norm O'Neill was so angry that he wanted to bring his wife and son and grandchildren to the Republic immediately to lend weight to the coaching movement in the black townships and to the riptide of multi-racial sporting brotherhood which is gradually eroding apartheid thought and structure.

Bob Cowper, elegant Test triple-centurion, now Monaco-based and Australia's ICC representative in London, had been visibly moved by the South African Cricket Union's coaching schemes in the formerly no-go regions of black townships. His report to the Australian Cricket Board would be emphasising the absurdity of the Australian government's sanctimonious stance against South Africa – particularly in view of the enormous trade figures that accompany the sports ban.

Denis Compton was almost speechless with exasperation at the "new world" which dawned after the ICC bans were drawn up in January. He echoed Procter's question: why were some cricket identities so afraid to come to South Africa to see for themselves? Were they really content to believe the distortions circulated by the protest groups who seemed to value emotion more highly than fact?

Ian Meckiff had not seen the place for over thirty years, and could hardly grasp the changes which had taken place, the progress which had been made. Within the week, as P.W.Botha laid claim to a resumption of power after illness, Nationalist leader F.W.de Klerk had been airing thoughts of further reform. Remaining targets included the Group Areas Act and the Separate Amenities Act, the last barriers, apart from the universal suffrage claimed to be so simple and beneficial in achievement only by those who lack an understanding of South Africa's complex history. Black and white players *can* now drink together as well as play cricket together. Power-sharing will come.

A notional graph could be drawn from the views of those who had not visited South Africa for some time. Lindsay Hassett, Ian Johnson, Ray Lindwall, Keith Miller, Neil Harvey and Bill Johnston were all seeing the place for the first time since 1950. It was a different country. They could not then have gone to jazz pubs like Jameson's or Kippy's in Johannesburg and found diners and drinkers of all races mingling in happy harmony. They could not have played against a cricket team of mixed race either.

Dennis Amiss had not been there for seven years, since the English rebel tour. He noticed further emancipation. Graham McKenzie moved back to Perth only two years ago after seven years' residence in South Africa. Even he sensed a continuing trend towards liberalisation.

As for myself, I had not seen South Africa since 1975, and one of the remarks I published then was considered by some to have been naïve. I even accepted this for a time. Was it not glib to have written that South Africa was not the only country to have slums and shanty-towns?

No: neither glib nor naïve. I have seen all the Test cricket countries of the world, and none is free of shanties and slums. There is no dignity in making comparisons in squalor, but I sometimes feel shame myself at the sight of the twilighters living in cardboard boxes at Charing Cross and Waterloo. At least, in Alexandra, a sprawling black township just outside Johannesburg, the shanties are being bulldozed away and replaced by blocks of flats.

In the bush outside Cape Town, Hylton Ackerman preaches cricket to the young blacks, living among them, camping out, assisting character formation, spreading happiness. "Clive Lloyd should see the hundreds and thousands of black kids playing the game," he says. "Some can't even speak English, but say 'cover-drive' and they'll move into that shot – and usually play it well." Like Procter and like Bob Woolmer, who is still coaching enthusiastically at Avendale, a mixed club in Cape Town, Ackerman devoutly believes the outside world now owes South Africa something for the defiance shown by its cricket movement.

The buses crunched their way out to the Zulu compound at Aloe Ridge. There the Phumangena villagers frenziedly danced themselves to exhaustion, and one of the West Indian representatives said, "Man, if only Viv could be here." Viv Richards often talks of his ancestry. What would he have said to these happy people? What could he do for them?

The Zulu beer, made from sorghum, was like a delayed explosion in the brain. If there was a place for swelling emotions, Alexandra township was it. Maturing black cricketers watched their father figure, Eddie Mmatli, receive the Ted Dexter Trophy from Peter May. Mmatli later explained that if the world squeezed South Africa any harder, the blacks would suffer. "But we are tough, and we could withstand the increased hardship," he said. "The whites are wealthy and are proof against sanctions." Would further "rebel" tours be welcomed by the black community? "A West Indies tour would give the black kids heroes to admire – though we would support South Africa against West Indies this time!"

The first of the two Centenary banquets, attended by over 1200, was held at Alberton, a black-tie affair with a dazzling array of former Springbok cricketers and overseas guests. The personal reunions as well as the speeches were sublime in their intensity. Captains abounded: R.E.S.Wyatt, eighty-seven, an MCC tourist sixty-one years earlier; George Mann and his South African-born wife; Peter May; Mike Smith; Clive van Ryneveld; Jackie McGlew; Peter van der Merwe; Lindsay Hassett; Ian Craig; Ali Bacher; Walter Hadlee, John Reid, Bert Sutcliffe and Merv Wallace from New Zealand. And broadcasting doyen Charles Fortune, now into his eighties.

The fiery Eric Rowan, on the verge of his eightieth birthday, ground on about the lack of recognition for his captaincy when he took over from Dudley Nourse at Nottingham in 1951 and led South Africa to victory. (Nourse had made a minor contribution of 208, with a steel pin in his fractured thumb.) Russell Endean was ghostly pale from an English winter. "Stodgy" Steyn, one of only three survivors from the 1931-32 tour of Australia, carried his eighty-four years nobly. Bruce Mitchell, eighty, looked worried, as he did even when he was past 100 and into his fifth hour at the crease. And then came the unexpected pleasure of handing "Ossie" Dawson a copy of *WCM* in which he features in Cricketers Brave.

J.J.Warr, proposing the toast to South African cricket, noted the presence of the vastly accomplished Bob Crisp, who, he said, "won the Desert war singlehanded – with help from John Wayne and Errol Flynn", and proceeded to a Freudian slip in referring to Clive "Race". Peter Pollock, now a preacher, replied stirringly, saying, "I hope we'll rise up – and without resentment." He won applause with the comment that "when the tongues go out, they don't go out to us who support cricket; they go out to apartheid." It might be remembered that the Pollock brothers walked from the field at Newlands in anti-apartheid protest as long ago as 1971.

A "royal" touch came with the recitation of a warm greeting from Sir Donald Bradman, who no longer travels. The message concluded with words which clearly inspired the hosts: "Keep up your good work in the interests of the game of cricket. It will ultimately bring its reward."

Joe Pamensky assured the mass of guests that their presence represented "an enormous fillip to those of us who have long been determined to move independently of government, to allow cricket to do for young South Africans what government hasn't yet done, to bring all young South Africans together in cricket, to raise their expectations, to build their ambitions . . . . We know our problems here. We don't need outsiders to preach to us. And we know we've done better than outsiders give us credit for. We know also we've not done enough, but we proudly say from a cricket viewpoint there is almost no way we could go faster." He referred to the fact that South Africa had satisfied all the requirements imposed on its cricket by the outside world, and satisfied them ten long years ago.

It was a privilege one night to sit with that fieriest of fast-bowling duos, the suave Neil Adcock and his archetypal Boer partner Peter Heine. Like two big-game hunters, they discussed injuries inflicted on opposing batsmen, and they discussed the changes that had overtaken the game and society itself.

ANOTHER EXCURSION took a handful of us up the coast to Durban, an inflated kind of Bournemouth, the main target being the third and final Golden Oldies match, at the lovely Kingsmead ground, setting for the 1939 "timeless" Test and Gladwin's leg-bye thriller ten years later – and, of course, Graeme Pollock's record 274 against Australia.

One moment I was gazing at the old team photos, the next I was responding to David Pithey's invitation to don the garish gear and field as substitute for the International Wanderers. Ashley Mallett needed a rest after his nine overs on a dodgy hip, Woolmer was already off with a twisted ankle, Ken Shuttleworth had strained a rib muscle, and Norman Gifford, twelfth man, was already on and bowling, with Barrie Meyer helping in the outfield.

I clad myself in Denis Lindsay's billowing red pants, someone else's jazzy top, and Pithey's size 7 footwear – without noticing that the left shoe had only two spikes, and those at the toe end. I went on with the drinks trolley and Mallett limped off. Keith Fletcher sent me off into the distance, and so, representing cricket fanatics and faded players everywhere, I began my stint in the full glare of the floodlights before 7500 people, undecided whether I wanted to stay out of trouble or intercept one of Procter's cannonball pulls or drives.

Within minutes I was chasing, picking up, turning, throwing and falling all over the place as the toothless boot failed to grip the dewy turf. The crowd loved it.

The overs slipped by, Graham McKenzie and Lance Cairns bowling fairly tightly, Bruce Laird holding his third outfield catch, and the crowd strewn all over Castle hill free with their banter. A few recently-acquired words of Afrikaans came in useful. One further misfield and a couple of safe pick-ups were all that befell *WCM*'s editor in the last hour of the innings. No catch to rival Copley's and Fletch ignored my pleas to send down a couple of match-deciding overs of leg-spin. Sweat poured out in rivulets.

When it was over, the kids swarmed on and demanded signatures on bats and magazines, staring quizzically at the resultant scrawl. After supper with the teams and a soothing shower, I went back to the sanctuary of the press-box, where "Chucker" Griffin was a surprise inhabitant.

Later, when the Oldies' wickets began to topple following a nostalgic partnership by Fletcher and Edrich, it was suggested I might be needed as a batsman, so I wound my way casually and nonchalantly into the vicinity of the players' enclosure, where Gifford eventually volunteered me his place. I hadn't batted at No.11 since 1958,

The menu cover for the main banquet during South Africa's Test centenary celebrations featured many a long-forgotten hero.

and *never* in red trousers and under lights. When the ninth wicket fell about 60 runs were needed off three overs, with Alan Kourie tossing the ball high. Procter must have miscounted, because Kourie would be bowled out with one over still remaining at his end. All he had to call on for that over was either Garth Le Roux or Vince van der Bijl. We had the match sewn up!

With Cairns's mighty bat in my hands, I was halfway down the steps when it was realised that Mallett, who was hard of hearing as well as colour-blind and clumsy, had not grasped that he was supposed to tell everyone out there that there was a batsman to follow. Mike Procter, however, must have seen me coming out; and he still allowed the stumps to be pulled, kindly explaining in the dressing-room that he did not want the match to "finish in farce". I could appreciate his trepidation; he probably saw I had Cairns's six-hitting wand in my grasp. Ah well, next time. I shall remember Durban.

THERE JUST remained a birthday to celebrate, launched perfectly with some serious cricket on the hotel tennis court with some Aussie journalist friends. This time I did get a bat, and they let me win. Later that day I was overwhelmed by a birthday chorus to which six Test captains contributed as we drove to the airport. They had probably all noticed, with anticipation, the uncorked bottle of port in my hand.

We winged our way from Port Elizabeth back to Johannesburg, and the following day saw the final departures as the celebratory, investigative fortnight drew to a close and the guests headed off in all sorts of directions. On the last gathering, a splendid dinner in Port Elizabeth at which the victorious Eastern Province players were honoured, Mann, Hassett and Sutcliffe (bandaged hero of the 1953 Johannesburg Test) had spoken touchingly on behalf of the guests after some ribaldry from Dakin and Trueman, and on second thoughts another informal "parliamentary" session in the early hours was cancelled. Few were not exhausted from the constant debate.

Time, of course, will tell whether the tut-tutting of the outside world will give way to a more realistic desire to examine South Africa and coax it into complete reform. The movement is under way from within, and for this, cricket, the brave advance corps, has much in which to pride itself.

Wisden Cricket Monthly, May 1989

It is not only at Test level that cricketers of interest abound:

Jack Simmons

WHAT I like about Jack Simmons' seemingly never-ending career at first-class level is that they all said nobody could stay in the modern throw-yourself-about, ultra-athletic game beyond the age of say thirty-six. Old Simmo is therefore a throwback to the game of days gone by, when talented cricketers played on into their forties, employing their wealth of experience in such a manner that the fading eyesight, the creaking joints and the thickening waistline are adequately compensated. Further: he's a spin bowler. And the world needs all of that species that it can get in this age of pace fanaticism.

Further: he didn't walk away from cricket, counting his cash, as some do, the moment he'd received his huge benefit proceeds: he loves the game and wanted to keep on playing. Further: he's a nice bloke, and cricket can't have too many of them. Maybe he'd be wise to put that faded old cap of his into the Old Trafford museum and get a bright new one. That would alter his image somewhat and kid the new generation that there's a plumpish new boy on the playing staff.

Apart from the wealth of affection for Jack in Lancashire, Tasmania would have him back any time. Come to think of it, that was a flashback in history too: Ted McDonald, in the 1920s, went from Tasmania (via Victoria) to Lancashire. The favoured adjective for the Australian fast bowler was "saturnine". In contrast, Jack Simmons' merry countenance radiates friendship and warmth. Long may it beam over our green fields.

The Twelfth Man (Wombwell Cricket Lovers' Society, 1989)

Australia regained the Ashes with some ease in 1989, the clincher coming at Old Trafford in the fourth Test, when the visitors chalked up their 100th victory in the 267 contests between the two countries since 1877:

The 100th Triumph

MERV HUGHES insistently asked to nurse the perfect replica of the Ashes urn, but he had to be denied. The little urn would surely not have remained perfect for long in the giant's beefy grasp. The celebrations in the Australian dressing-room centred on hairy Merv, clad only in a towel. He treated everybody to personal showers of lager and ice-cubes, and introduced a speciality act into Ashes history by squashing a full can of beer with such power that the contents spurted out with the force of a fire-hose. The Ashes replica, brought in for photographic purposes, would have been squeezed to dust in seconds in the fast man's fist.

Allan Border wanted to buy the urn on the spot, expressing the frustration of an entire nation: the 106-year-old trophy had been recaptured (for the first time in England since 1934) and yet it would stay sealed in its glass case at Lord's. Just as well big Merv's not going back to St John's Wood before the tour's end.

Beyond the confines of Australia's jubilant Old Trafford dressing-room, England was in mourning twice over. Not only had the Ashes been lost, but sixteen of her cricketers, nine of whom had played in this series, had signed to go to South Africa, barring themselves from Test cricket for years to come. The only consolation was that the Test selection panel would now surely be forced to call up younger players in a rebuilding process publicly craved ever since it became obvious that Border's side had the measure of Gower's. The British public's anguish was now intensified after a run of 23 Tests since late 1986 of which only one – against Sri Lanka – was won, with nine lost. Cremation time again.

That England's fading grip on the Ashes lasted into the month of August was mainly Jack Russell's fault. The little Gloucester man, in for his supreme wicketkeeping skills, showed those above him in the batting order what concentration, judgment and courage were all about as he went to his maiden first-class century, hauling England away from the second-innings degradation of 59 for 6 on the Monday. Thank God, said the Lion, that the South African Cricket Union got neither Russell nor that other batting saviour Robin Smith.

The heatwave had receded as the fourth Test match got under way on the thirty-fourth birthday of Border, whose noticeable haircut deprived him of none of his strength . . . .

Wisden Cricket Monthly, September 1989

From the many hundreds of books reviewed some stand out for their unusual nature. Such a one concerned John Scott's "Caught in Court":

Cricket Criminals

REVIEWING CRICKET books can be a wearying process nowadays. So much matter is recycled – anything but in the interests of conservation. It seems that every corner of the game and its history has been exposed and re-exposed. And then along comes a book like this. Solicitor Scott has gathered together bundles of legal cases involving cricket and cricketers down the ages and pink-taped them into chapters which categorise them into murder, libel, divorce, taxes and wills, assault, etc, etc. Packer, Boycott, Botham and Sid Barnes have chapters all to themselves, while the "Libelled XI" includes May v Wellings, Wheatley v Beaverbrook, the Test selectors v Parkinson, and Clive Lloyd v all sorts of people.

The author only occasionally lapses into legal gobbledegook as embezzlement, manslaughter, political protest and streakers emerge, years on, from forgotten headlines. West Indian fast bowler Leslie Hylton was hanged for the slaughter of his wife, and never has so much detail from the case been gathered before in a cricket book. Two of cricket's numerous divorce cases are retraced: the Coningham sensation in Sydney in the 1890s, and the English fanatic in the 1980s who had cricket "for breakfast, dinner and tea", and naturally enough missed the court case, being on tour in Devon.

Wisden is also included: in 1896 the company was found to have offered Duke's No.4 balls for sale as top-quality No.1 balls (Alfred Lyttelton was Wisden's junior counsel), and in 1921 there was a strike over a wage dispute at Wisden's factory.

And there we were, thinking that the lawyers had only started to make a living out of cricket since 1977.

Wisden Cricket Monthly, November 1989

Queensland Laughter

THIS HILARIOUS chronicle was a long time reaching us: it came from Central Queensland, where time may not exactly stand still, but moves with a reluctant shuffle. Charlee Marshall, calling himself A. Bannerman Starr in these forty chapters, is a bush schoolteacher turned farmer – but most of all a cricketer, a fast bowler who regularly topped the averages and annually sent his clippings to the Queensland Cricket Association down in Brisbane, hoping for higher recognition. It never came.

He's past it now, and the closing pages poignantly display the grief felt by every active cricketer overtaken by the years. Yet even this is handled with a sly humour. The writing throughout is of high class, the early stuff touched by flavours of Just William, Huckleberry Finn, and Holden Caulfield. Starr the man hints at a bush Thurber. He leaves his beloved outback for a brief dash at teaching – and cricket, naturally – in Brisbane, and later there are excursions to Papua New Guinea and the Philippines, an unlikely outpost for cricket, but still "Starr" finds it – in a very tender episode.

Quickly, though, the tempo returns to the rumbustious and irreverent and outrageous, with bouncers flying, sixes sailing into the scrub, or further, and an astonishing parade of characters from the locality and the outside world. The facts are surely bent, Clive James' *Unreliable Memoirs* fashion, but this is no reference book, and human entertainment must always be a sacred priority. This down-to-the-dusty-earth document cries out for a wider readership. It is good for the heart.

Wisden Cricket Monthly, January 1990

HARSH NEW WORLD
1990 ONWARDS

There was an unusually expectant – even ominous – feeling all around as a new decade dawned:

Into the 'Nineties

WELL, HERE we go, into the 1990s, with hopes high that cricket will be elevated in appeal as it was when the 1880s gave way to the 1890s. There is barely any similarity, of course, between the cricket of the last decade of the 19th Century and that which we're likely to see in the ten or eleven years ahead. There were only 32 Test matches between 1890 and 1899, only a few more than are staged in a year nowadays, when countless one-day internationals are also attached to their coat-tails. It has become a truly global game, with inevitable international and inter-racial tensions intruding. If there is one pressing need above all others it is that the newly-rigged International Cricket Council should meet problems of discipline, scheduling and the way in which the game is played with firm and fair administration.

For English cricket-lovers the past four months have been fallow. Such news as there has been has principally come from abroad. New Zealand and Sri Lanka batsmen have made runs off an Australian attack that blew through England last summer like a mini-hurricane. The batting of Taylor, Boon, Jones, Border and Waugh, though, continues to pour runs into the national kitty, auguring well for the 1990-91 Ashes confrontation and the Caribbean expedition to follow. Geoff Marsh, with his 355 not out for Western Australia, and successions of big innings by Lehmann and other promising youngsters seem to confirm that Australia's latest golden age of batsmanship is 24-carat.

Any day now the strength of English cricket will once more be put to the test. The scores will bring pleasure or despair to the several million who care whether England, where the game was devised, can walk with pride among all other competitors. Success in Zimbabwe would be no more than expected. Success by Gatting's "rebels" would be poignant in that they remain the "legion of the lost". Success by Gooch's intrepid patrol in the Caribbean would be as big an upset as anything in cricket history. Success on all three tours would be a miracle without compare, following on from ten years in which England won only 20 and lost 39 of their 104 Tests.

Not only will England's cricket-playing talent be spread representatively as never before, but the media requirements will see news journalists joining, most particularly, the South African tour, in expectation of civil disorder and violence. Cricket, the proud leader in the drive against apartheid, may need its sturdiest helmet, gloves and pads to withstand orchestrated local opposition now that demonstrations are permitted. Much depends on the ability of the South African police force to restrain its wildest retaliatory instincts which otherwise would play into the hands of a cynical outside world.

Meanwhile, there could have been an urgent little rush around Britain to buy satellite dishes in order to pick up the Sky ball-by-ball television transmission from West Indies. Should Sky follow the pattern of Australia's Channel 9, with its relentless brainwashing commercials and trite commentary, this inspired advance in ratings would be short-lived. Sky has a golden chance to prove its worth both to cricket financially and to the viewer in terms of enjoyment. The prospect of all major cricket being beamed commercially leaves a queasy feeling, nonetheless, unless the restraints from which Channel 9 is now freed are firmly applied to satellite transmission.

There is so much for which we must, as ever, wait and see. The vista is much wider than that known to our ancestors . . . .

Wisden Cricket Monthly, February 1990

All these years later we know the answers: the world's cricket schedules are hopelessly cluttered; South Africa is back; and television – damagingly limited in Britain only to commercial satellite coverage for live action – symbolises the administrators' blind adherence to the belief that mountains of money are everything.

At long last South Africa's struggle ended:

A Better Tomorrow

DAY BY DAY – unless it's all a tragic illusion – the world is becoming a better place. While the vision of a reunited Germany happened to coincide eerily with terrifying nights of lashing gales and crashing trees, reminiscent of the black and fearful nights of the Blitz itself, in so many parts of eastern Europe, the Soviet Union and Africa democratic freedom was bursting through the walls of repression. President F.W.de Klerk released from prison, at long last, the Christ-like figure of Nelson Mandela, while reminding his countrymen and the world at large that his government's commitment, carried on the mandate given it in 1987 by a majority of the white population, was "that the system must give Class A citizenship to all South Africans, irrespective of race or colour".

Anybody querying what all this has to do with cricket should know better. Cricket has suffered the bullying of political activists for all too long. Nine months ago it was clear that reform was on the way in the Republic, but few would listen. Indeed, for some it will be somewhat frustrating, for their familiar target will have shrunk dramatically: which fact will still not persuade them to suspend their fire. The sanctions/boycott proponents and those who maintained contact and gave support to the reform groups within will all claim their share of the credit.

Meanwhile, linked as it was with unedifying scenes of provocative protest and inexcusable, hotheaded police violence, the tour by Gatting's team was seen not only as unnecessary but as a positive provocation in itself. Dr Bacher and the SACU were fully entitled to arrange the tour, which was conceived in a more stable climate eight months ago. The English players were fully aware of their expulsion from Test cricket, and have received large fees by way of compensation (and also as "danger money", since justified). They broke no laws by going. Their profession is cricket. They and the SACU aimed to further the game. It took courage to see it through as far as it went, even though history will see it all as something of a pitiful shambles.

In the mood of reform, the South African cricket authorities must fight hard firstly for unity among themselves – even though old grievances will die hard – and then for readmission to international cricket. Fairly soon now the howls of protest will be taking on a distinctly phoney ring.

Wisden Cricket Monthly, March 1990

Re-entry to mainstream international cricket came a couple of years later.

Meanwhile, England entered another battle in the Caribbean, while an eminent figure was farewelled in Westminster Abbey:

Westminster Reveries

IN THE heavenly hush of old St Margaret's Church, Westminster Abbey, the full meaning of cricket was evident. At Sir "Gubby" Allen's memorial service were to be seen a field marshal, an archbishop, a former prime minister, England captains from Bob Wyatt to Mike Smith and captains of industry, lords and men of Lord's, a Cricketer Brave, media men, umpires, high commissioners, humble cricket-lovers, J.Paul Getty II, and Spike Milligan. They all honoured the memory of a man who gave a lifetime to cricket and never in that life did cricket the slightest disservice. Swanton reading Cardus in that wonderfully preserved "sealskin" voice was an additional delight.

But of all the sweet and stirring words that day, none could have been more appropriate than those uttered by the Vicar of St John's Wood. His prayer began: "O Father of all, who hast made thy children to delight in play, give to all those whose livelihood or recreation is in the world of sport the joy of skill without arrogance, competition without rancour, partisanship without hostility." If the Revd John Slater's words could have carried across the Atlantic Ocean to the battlegrounds of the Caribbean, they would almost certainly have fallen on some ears that are deaf.

The savouring of the cool spring sunshine and the crystal web of fellowship came in between two acrimonious Test matches which contained some of the worst possible excesses of cynicism. In Trinidad, West Indies, so petrified at the thought of defeat, did everything but refuse to bowl. They were saved by rain coupled with their own iniquitous time-wasting under the direction of stand-in captain Haynes, who presumably still had the gall to wear his "Live, Love, Laugh" necklace throughout. How popular will *he* be on the county circuit this summer?

The series turned in that Test with the one ball which broke Gooch's left hand. "Fortune favours the brave" is another proverb you can safely tear up.

Then, in Barbados, England's over rate was little better. Those who condemned this retaliation may be naïve in the rules of war. Still, it was a question of degree: had they abused the over rate as badly as did their opponents in the previous Test, a draw may have been salvaged on the last day. England expired around half-an-hour short of safety. Anybody who thought they ought to have been racing through 20 overs an hour on the fourth day should, in cricket terms, be certified. Competition without rancour? Partisanship without hostility? Not on this campagn, Reverend.

What fatally soured the Barbados Test was the bad decision against Rob Bailey on the fourth evening. Accepting that Mr Barker was not intimidated into raising his finger, no-one could help but notice the antics of the West Indies captain, all dignity cast to the wind as he displayed his "ceremonial dance", orgasmic gesticulations every one of which was a denial of the belief that this is a game for mature, controlled men. All this from a self-proclaimed Christian – and on a Sunday, too. As Richards gave vent to his provocative atavistic urges the eye craved sight of a Headley or a Worrell or a Sobers, equally proud men, who never once caused embarrassment to players or spectators.

The West Indians got their victory, gained in part by brutal bouncers bowled around the wicket at an impotent No.11 batsman. But the cricket played under fearful pressure by gallant little Russell and those sons of Englishmen, Lamb and Smith, will remain forever in the memory. They return home, all of them, as heroes.

Wisden Cricket Monthly, May 1990

From time to time a cricketer makes his first real mark in the Test arena, and it is always a pleasure to pinpoint such a significant moment. The Trent Bridge Test match of 1990, England v New Zealand, was one among many:

Roses in the Rain

MONDAY BROUGHT all but a complete day's cricket, but few bothered to come. Those who did, however, saw the first major Test match offering of a batsman who will probably bestride the 1990s. Atherton batted throughout the day, for around 5½ hours, to finish 78 not out, having given an exhibition of smooth copybook batsmanship without ugly baseball stance or one-day shots or cheap mannerisms. It was refreshing as rose-water, and comforting to see such determination and courage from a young man who, having read medieval history at Cambridge and absorbed such salutary works as *All Quiet on the Western Front*, would probably not answer his Queen and country's call – or so he apparently told an interviewer recently.

WATCHING A Test match which has nowhere to go, fragmented as it was by poor weather, really can be a calming experience, particularly when some of the treasured old values are restored. Trent Bridge 1990 will remain long in the mind for the picture of a rosy-cheeked young man, slightly shy and blue of eye, tousle-haired, modest just as in those fictional tales in boys' innocent books so long ago. Michael Andrew Atherton, may you always remain correct and uncomplicated as you fight for your country out there on the cricket pitch.

Wisden Cricket Monthly, July 1990

Atherton finished with 151 in over eight hours, against an attack led by Richard Hadlee, and a distinguished career was now into top gear. By his retirement he had earned a record number of caps as England captain.

Out of the blue, a knighthood was draped over a player just as he was about to play in a Test match – at Lord's of course. Richard Hadlee, a superb and famously serious cricketer, was a popular choice:

Sir Richard of Marylebone

THE TIMING that went into Sir Richard Hadlee's straight six off Small with the new ball on the fourth day was rather better than that which accompanied the announcement of his knighthood. It might have been anticlimactic if left to next year's New Year Honours, but its arrival in the middle of a Test series caught a few folk off-balance. Team-mates responded with jubilation tinged with reverence and predictable good-natured mick-taking; the Lord's secretariat (responsible for the scoreboard and scorecard terminology) and the media took no chances, lacing the event heavily with "Sir Richards", even though the names of knights – and lords, come to that – customarily remain unembellished in film and television credits; and the subject himself, single-minded as ever, merely cloaked his shyness with the time-honoured modesty which has been chillingly accompanied by the kind of determination associated with assassins. Hadlee's skills with ball and bat earned him, yet again, the Man of the Match award – if, in his case, that is the correct expression.

As in the first Test at Nottingham, this one was blighted by the weather, though not as severely. A result was still an outside possibility as New Zealand took a first-innings advantage. But the pitch and the England batsmen's nerves held firm, and the sixth successive draw between these two countries was sealed, leaving all to play for on Edgbaston's smooth pitch.

Wisden Cricket Monthly, August 1990

The second half of that summer saw an astonishing performance at Lord's against India by Graham Gooch, who broke the ground record and also the mark for most runs in a Test match:

Dreams Are Made of This

SUNLIGHT PIERCES the curtains. The eyes blink open. My angel asks if I have been dreaming. Yes, I reply. I was at Lord's, and Graham Gooch scored over 450 runs in a Test match. Allan Lamb and Robin Smith made centuries too, as did the tall, upright Ravi Shastri. The Indian captain, Mohammad Azharuddin, then charmed a century off 87 balls of classical wristwork, and when his side were threatened with having to follow on, Kapil Dev hit the necessary runs, 24 of them, with four sixes around the sightscreen. Then, as England ran up a huge advantage, seventeen-year-old Sachin Tendulkar scuttled across the outfield and stuck out a hand knee-high to catch a lofted Lamb drive.

Some dream. Or might it really have happened?

That England were in for a big one was obvious by the end of the first hazy day. They were 359 for the loss of Atherton early and Test returnee Gower in mid-afternoon, for a patient 40 cruelly ended by a "bat-pad" catch which almost assuredly had none of the first-mentioned as an ingredient. Down the second half of the day, Gooch commanded the field, driving in his strictly non-classical style, tucking away the singles with huge professional know-how, and landing Shastri for leg-side and off-side sixes. The blue-eyed Essex giant had limbered up for his 10th Test century, and 13th in all cricket this season, with 177 off the slightly more demanding bowling of Lancashire at Colchester, and it really seemed – deceptively of course – that batting was just about the easiest function he could now be asked to perform in public. Hirwani turned his leg-breaks and googlies too slowly to be harmful, and the seamers were ordinary in appearance and effect.

Any chance, then, simply had to be accepted, and when More put a straightforward snick from Gooch, off Sharma, down when he was 36, it was to incubate into one of the most catastrophic errors in Test history. Gooch made almost 300 further runs before his innings ended: another nightmare among the rosy dreams.

Gooch was 117 by tea, his century having come off 172 balls, and just before the end, Lamb reached his hundred with the day's 50th boundary, joining Gooch in an exclusive club of two who had made as many as four Test centuries at Lord's. Some of Lamb's shots were verging on contemptuous, and it needed a stout heart to bowl a full length on this slumbering pitch to the heavyweight Gooch and his pocketsize near-replica.

Their third-wicket stand of 218 swelled on the second day to 308 (278 minutes), a record for any England wicket against India, before Lamb's square-drive was smartly scooped up in the gully by Manjrekar just before lunch. Lamb's 12th Test century was his highest at 139, a curious record.

By now Gooch had sailed into his third hundred. A hundred and ninety-four overnight, he had experienced some discomfort when the new ball was taken at the start, but an on-driven three off Prabhakar took him to 201 off 303 balls, the 10th Lord's Test double-century, and Gooch's first in Tests. It was still overcast and humid as the solid-as-oak figure in the white helmet began passing great, long-revered milestones: Hammond's 240 before lunch, Bradman's 254 after. With Hick's achievement of 50 centuries recently chalked up at the tenderest age, how many Bradman records remain? Only a couple of hundred of them probably.

Gooch reached 255 in 493 minutes; Bradman's 254 in 1930, the nearest to perfection of all his performances, lasted 339 minutes, and he faced 376 balls. Gooch had so far faced up to 381, so he was up with The Don in productivity, though the *frequency* of balls bowled to him was only 69 per cent in ratio to Bradman. Offsetting this is the fact that Gooch had no Allen, Tate, White, Robins or Hammond bowling to him. What Bradman might have done to this Indian attack might be the subject of another colourful dream.

Gooch works on the Ken Barrington principle that you get runs while you may, for tomorrow could bring a duck. Hirwani came on late on the second day, and Shastri later still (3pm). It remained overcast, but Gooch and Robin Smith batted on in their own little pool of sunlight, the skipper passing his previous highest in first-class cricket (275), and even though a tabloid had concerned itself that morning with the legality of Prabhakar's action, all the bowlers came alike to him. The heavy foot went out with certainty and the heavy bat scythed through. At tea he was 299, Smith 77, and spectators might have felt they were being taken on a tour of the rarefied Himalayas. There stood the total at a massive 589 for 3 – ten hours having seen three wickets fall, of which one was dubious – and under the gaze of England Test record-holder Sir Len Hutton, Graham Gooch re-emerged after the break and tucked Shastri to fine leg for a single first ball: 300 in 594 minutes (454 balls), with 40 fours and two sixes.

Shastri missed a caught-and-bowled at 306, and Gooch showed who was boss next over by hitting the spinner for four and then six into the scaffolding, moving past Hobbs's ground record. Drizzle sent them off for twenty-five minutes, but the dullness made a declaration pointless, for Malcolm would not have been permitted to bowl in such light. So Gooch marched on, the anticipation as he approached the world Test record mark of 365 being feverish.

He had been at the crease for the time it takes an accomplished runner to win four marathons when he missed with a drive at Prabhakar at 333 on the stroke of 5 o'clock. The epic was over, and as he carried all those records and honours back with him to the pavilion, Graham Alan Gooch, just thirty-seven and implacably modest, may have blushed, though it was impossible to tell from the already flushed face behind the stubble.

That evening, Gooch told of his initial disappointment at getting out when he did, and said he became nervous around 292, when, having gone that far, he didn't want to get out. His ear infection had responded to the antibiotics, and he'd had breast of chicken and a roll at lunchtime and nothing for tea. It had all been an "endurance test". And he repeated: "I might get nought next time!"

That fear was to prove very wide of the mark.

After a century from Shastri, a glorious 121 by Azharuddin, and an explosive 77 from Kapil Dev which saved a follow-on by India, England had to go in again 199 ahead. Graham Gooch made further history:

GOOCH AND the barely-noticed Atherton now proceeded to structure an amended assault, and in the passage to their record 204 for the first wicket, Gooch climbed up from the one individual record to another: past Hutton's 364 in a match and Greg Chappell's overall record of 380. Azharuddin missed him at cover soon after that one, when he was 57, but he was soon pulling Sharma into the Mound Stand and straight-driving Shastri for six. Drizzle forced an early tea, after which Gooch back-cut Shastri to the Tavern rope to bring up his hundred off only 95 balls in 121 minutes.

The umpires had been kept busy warning the batsmen against running up the pitch and the Indians for roughing up the ball, but the crowd, in the main, were in euphoria, more so when Gooch hoisted Hirwani for six, and did it again. Only one more record seemed there for the taking: most runs in any first-class match, 499 by Hanif Mohammad.

Who could condemn Gooch if he got out through fatigue after 774 minutes at the crease in this match? Suddenly he drove at Sharma and was gone, his 123 having come off 113 balls, his side – always his paramount consideration – well placed now to launch a final assault.

England eventually set India a target of 472 and went on to win by 247 runs. The closing stages on the fifth day were rather anticlimactic:

LEWIS, NOT unlike a youthful Wes Hall, bounded in and had Prabhakar lbw with a painful yorker, so that by lunch it was just a matter of time: 158 for 6, the boy Tendulkar gaining further useful experience and Kapil Dev perhaps about to do something remarkable again. This time, though, Hemmings had him caught out at midwicket. Tendulkar, having got the feel of Lord's for a further hour and a half for future reference, was taken at slip by Gooch off the merciless Fraser, who then had a protesting More lbw. Sharma's boundaries before the final wicket fell were not only in keeping with the adventurous Indian spirit, but took the match total beyond the 1930 Lord's Test record aggregate of 1601. He was eventually run out by a direct hit at the bowler's end. The fieldsman – Man of the Match too – scarcely needs naming. Mr Gooch had started this match, dominated it, and finished it off.

Was there any other way of ending this extravagant dream?

Wisden Cricket Monthly, September 1990

When my pre-eminent English cricket hero, Len Hutton, died on September 6, 1990, I was locked into the process of getting the next edition of WCM to press. This traumatic event prompted me to add four pages and to work halfway through the night to pay tribute to the man who had had such impact on my younger self as model batsman and high-scoring idol:

Sir Len: Gentle Hero

THE LASTING grief following Len Hutton's death will touch those who saw his delicate artistry on the field and those who knew him for the quiet, slightly poignant figure he became as an older man. While he was the world's best batsman, his slight, elegant figure and distinctive broken nose were overwhelmingly familiar to cricket-followers, particularly the young, who had in him the perfect model. The cover-drive was a classic sculpture, with the steady head, usually becapped, perpendicularly in line with front toe-cap and finely-controlled wrists. The leg-glance, whether off his insubstantial chest or tickled off the half-volley, was a thing of touch and beauty. His defensive play was an art-form, and a back-cut to the base of the Hill at the Sydney Cricket Ground off a rising ball from Ray Lindwall glows in the memory still. His batsmanship sprang from genius, though the weight of responsibility carried by Hutton in the Tests undertaken by England in the 1940s and 1950s caused many of his efforts to be laboured. So often, particularly when Denis Compton's lavish skills failed him, Len Hutton stood alone.

His achievements had not the Hitler war interrupted his career must have become supreme. Not only was he among those who lost six first-class seasons and some overseas tours (he was twenty-three when war broke out) but damage to his left forearm during commando training in 1941 left it a couple of inches shorter. It was thought at one time that he would never be able to play first-class cricket again. When he did, the added difficulty of coping with the fast, lifting ball was obvious.

Len Hutton still finished with a set of figures matched by very few: 40,140 runs at 55.10, 129 centuries (eighth in the list), 19 of them in his 79 Tests (in which he scored 6971 runs at 56.67). The world record Test score, 364, was his for almost twenty years from 1938, and his 1294 runs (despite three consecutive noughts) in June 1949 remain a record for a monthly aggregate. He passed 1000 in August of that year too, the summer of his benefit, which raised £9713.

He was marked down as a great batsman in the making when he was no more than fourteen. George Hirst and Herbert Sutcliffe were taken aback by his poise and concentration. Born in Fulneck, a Moravian community near Pudsey, on June 23, 1916, into a cricketing family, Hutton passed rapidly through the Yorkshire ranks and began his first-class career just before his eighteenth birthday, registering a duck (run out by J.G.W.Davies) against Cambridge. Before that initial season was out he had shown his worth with an innings of 196 at Worcester, and although 1935 and 1936 brought him only one century each, by 1937 he was ready for an England cap. Opening with Jim Parks snr against New Zealand at Lord's three days after his twenty-first birthday (which he had marked with an opening stand of 315 with Sutcliffe against Leicestershire at Hull), he was bowled by Cowie for a duck. In the second innings he made 1. But, spared for the next Test, at Old Trafford, he made 100.

His debut against Australia came in 1938, at Trent Bridge, where he scored 100 again, posting 219 for England's first wicket with Charles Barnett, and the final Test of that summer elevated him to a pedestal which was to bring mixed blessings for Len Hutton for the rest of his days. There was no time limit to that Oval match, and when Hammond won the toss, his batsmen were under instructions to make 1000.

They nearly got there, only serious injury to Bradman and Fingleton persuading England's leader that 903 for 7 was enough. Of that dizzying total, young Hutton made 364, as generations of schoolboys have known, in 13 hours 17 minutes, falling to a catch at cover by Hassett off O'Reilly on the third afternoon. With fellow Yorkshireman Leyland he had put on 382 for the second wicket, then 135 for the third with Hammond, and after Paynter (0) and Compton (1) had threatened collapse, Hutton and Hardstaff took the total to 770 – a stand of 215 – before Hutton's epic closed. The cut with which he took his score past Bradman's Ashes record 334 is no film rarity, and nor is the historic handshake from The Don, whose 1930 innings of 334 at Leeds the fourteen-year-old Hutton had watched.

A national hero now, and surging with confidence once his stamina was restored, Hutton swept all before him, after a moderate (in Test terms) 1938-39 tour of South Africa, during which he was knocked out by a ball from Eric Davies in the Transvaal match.

In 1939 he exceeded his 10 centuries of 1937 with 12, and raised his highest score for Yorkshire from 271 not out to 280 not out, putting on 315 at Bramall Lane, Sheffield for the first wicket with Sutcliffe (again) and helping to finish Hampshire off with 4 for 40 with his leg-spinners. That summer, against West Indies he made 196 at Lord's (248 in 140 minutes for the fourth wicket with Compton) and 165 not out at The Oval. If ever war brutally derailed a career, this was it.

The worldwide curiosity as to how readily Bradman would adapt to post-war Test cricket was just as eagerly addressed to Hutton, with his reshaped arm. A century in the Lord's "Victory Test" in 1945 was a comfort to all. He went with MCC to Australia in 1946-47 and gave the crowds some idea of his class, many of the onlookers having had to make do with night-time wireless descriptions and newsreels before war had broken out. Now, he treated the spectators at Melbourne, Adelaide and Sydney to centuries, the last in the final Test, when he had to retire at 122 because of tonsillitis. His 37 in the second Test, also at Sydney, had older men comparing him with Trumper, and even the locals were sad when he hit his wicket in trying to negotiate an evil lifter from Keith Miller.

The Lindwall-Miller combination, one of the most testing in all cricket history, made for some stirring encounters between them and their English adversaries, and Hutton, who, with his Lancastrian opening partner Washbrook, always had to withstand the hottest bursts, often later implied that it was Miller's unpredictable hostility which taxed him most. Their duels were to be continued in 1948.

In 1947, generally listed as the year of Compton and Edrich, Hutton went past 2500 runs for the third time, averaging 64, with 11 centuries, including another huge one, 270 not out, against Hampshire, this time at Bournemouth, and twin hundreds at Southend off Essex. A quiet Test summer was illuminated by his third round 100 in Tests on his first international appearance on his home ground at Headingley, against South Africa. That winter, rested from the tour of West Indies, he had to be flown out as a reinforcement, and made a couple of hundreds against the territories. Soon it was time to face the Australians again.

The 1948 Ashes rubber was one of the most action-packed, and Hutton contributed much to the last two Tests after being at the centre of the sensation of the year when he was dropped from the third Test, his only omission by England in an eighteen-year career, prompted by a certain fretting reaction in the face of the Lindwall-Miller barrage. Back for Headingley, he made 81 and 57, putting on 168 and 129 with Washbrook. There was a rare absence of Hutton Test centuries this season, but in the Oval Test, Bradman's farewell appearance, Hutton was first in and last out for 30 when Lindwall demolished England for 52, Yardley's 7 being the next-highest score.

Hutton made nine centuries for Yorkshire in 1948, and one for the Players against the Gentlemen at Lord's, launching him to South Africa that winter, where he added two more Test centuries in a successful campaign, his 158 at Ellis Park, Johannesburg being part of a record opening stand of 359 with Washbrook.

His peak years – the rebuilt left arm almost forgotten by marvelling admirers – continued with 1949 (another 12 centuries, two of them – one a double – in the New Zealand Tests and 3429 runs in all) and then came a precious winter of rest. He crowned a quieter 1950 with 202 not out against West Indies at The Oval, carrying his bat through an innings of 344 and holding at bay this time the spin examination of Ramadhin and Valentine.

There was a shining magnificence about Len Hutton's achievements on the 1950-51 tour of Australia which somehow sets it apart. England lost the first four Tests, two quite narrowly, and won the last, at Melbourne, the first victory since Hutton's Oval match of 1938. He averaged 88 in the series, miles ahead of the rest, and began by showing his rare talent for survival on a rain-damaged pitch in the opening encounter, at Brisbane, where Freddie Brown decided on a strategy of holding Hutton back to No.6 in the first innings and 8 in the second (when he made an unbeaten 62 after going in at a score of 30 for 6). A gritty 156 not out in the Adelaide Test saw him carrying his bat through an England innings for the second time in six months, and his contribution to that emotional victory at Melbourne, with "mystery man" Iverson almost tamed, was 79 and 60 not out, which ended sublimely with Hutton making the winning run – after teasingly playing a ball back to bowler Hassett when all six stumps had been ripped out as souvenirs while the ball was still in flight.

Bill O'Reilly, one of the toiling bowlers at The Oval in 1938, now proclaimed Hutton a better batsman twelve years on. "His footwork is as light and sure and confident as Bradman's ever was," stated "Tiger". "He is the finished player now . . . one cannot fail to be impressed with the fluency and gracefulness of his strokemaking . . . His control of the game is masterful. And his concentration, which has always been a salient feature of his batting make-up, is unimpaired." While expecting Hutton to make yet another tour of Australia in four years' time, he concluded: "He can rest assured that many young Australians are already setting him as their pattern – such was the profound impression he made in this country."

This writer will vouch for that – though, in the classroom, a finger pressed constantly against the nose failed to give it the shape of Hutton's.

Hutton's name was linked, untypically, with sensation during the 1951 season, though it was only through becoming the first batsman to be given out "obstructing the field" when he instinctively sparred at the ball as he imagined it to be falling onto the stumps – just as wicketkeeper Endean was about to make the catch. England won that match at The Oval against South Africa to take the series and continue the building of a new Test side as the post-war recovery continued. Peter May had just made his Test debut, and England's long-awaited fast bowler was on the verge of being launched.

By now Hutton had become the thirteenth batsman to make 100 centuries, narrowly missing the mark in the Manchester Test victory (98 not out), but making certain with 151 at The Oval – surely now his favourite ground – in the Championship match against Surrey.

The first Test against India, at Headingley, in 1952 might well be remembered more readily for the visitors' scoreline of 0 for four wickets in their second innings, and the new speed sensation Fred Trueman's seven wickets, but in social terms its significance was immense in that the amateur-captaincy tradition was abandoned – not by universal agreement by any means – with Len Hutton, lifetime professional, becoming captain of England. "When I'd put the phone down I wondered what I'd let myself in for," he later recalled.

The Lord's Test saw the new leader in a perfect light: winning for the second time, scoring 150, and meeting the young Queen in the first summer of her reign. Another century followed at Old Trafford, and an 86 at The Oval. Captaincy, although Yorkshire were to continue to cling to the amateur belief, was not disagreeing with this introspective and sometimes pessimistic man.

He made nine other centuries that season for Yorkshire, and was still regarded unequivocally as the world's best batsman. Could he rise still further in popular acclaim by leading England to an Ashes victory in 1953, Australia having held the little urn since 1934?

One of Len Hutton's many great moments: victory over Australia in Australia, 1955.

He fought hard, and it was a long time coming, but in the year of the Coronation and the conquest of Everest, when the Glorious Gloucesters did their stuff in Korea and Stanley Matthews at last won at Wembley and Gordon Richards at last won the Derby, Len Hutton led England to victory in the final Test at The Oval, having made important runs in every Test bar the fourth, where a stunned-silent crowd at Headingley saw Lindwall bowl him for a duck. He had endured a dismal crowd reaction at Lord's, after his catching had several times proved fallible, and then gone on to piece together a patient, chanceless 145 that had the members standing. It was his fifth and final century against the old enemy, and sustained England's hopes to the last Test, where his 82, compiled while wearing his 1938 cap (which a Lindwall bouncer once removed), and shrewd use of Laker and Lock led to an eventual triumph greeted almost on the scale of VE Day.

Far away from the home crowds, and unconveyed by any such thing as satellite television, Hutton, now thirty-seven, gave his all for England in a torrid series in the Caribbean that winter. Put upon by a pompous politician, challenged by the sudden crisis of a riot in Georgetown, blamed in some quarters for the unruly behaviour of a couple of his young players, Hutton braved the intense heat and showed the vice-like concentration of old to weld innings of 169 to set up victory in the third Test and 205 at Kingston in the last, squaring the series (Bailey 7 for 34). There were some to say, despite all his other efforts, that *this* was Hutton's finest hour.

His strength was receding, the lengthening strain taking its toll. In 1954 he had to stand down, and David Sheppard became captain of England against Pakistan for two Tests. But the frail Yorkshireman with iron in his soul came back for the Oval Test (which England contrived to lose) and was deemed the man to lead England in defence of the Ashes in Australia in 1954-55.

It could hardly have begun more dismally. Seeking early assistance from the pitch for his all-pace attack, he put Australia in at Brisbane and saw them run up, with the help of dropped catches, 601 for 8. England were beaten by an innings. At Sydney he boldly dropped Bedser (unfortunately without remembering to tell him to his face) and put his pace plan into action again, Tyson now running in off a shortened run, and Statham, as ever, bowling tirelessly and accurately into the wind. With May and Cowdrey maturing with every innings, England took control of the series, maintained a phlegmatic over rate, won the middle three Tests, and retained the Ashes, Hutton, after having had to be persuaded to take part in the Adelaide Test, making 80 there to help maintain England's mastery.

His final innings against Australia, at Sydney, was ended by his respected adversary Lindwall for 6, and for the last over of this drawn match, Hutton walked the length of the field and took the ball himself, bowling Benaud as he aimed a huge hoick. It was a whimsical ending to an extraordinary seventeen-year participation in England v Australia Test cricket. He had won the Ashes again – and "without leaving a smell" as he so graphically put it.

He played in the two New Zealand Tests, finishing with 53 at Auckland, and one of the greatest of Test careers gently closed. His back pained him, and he felt generally run down in 1955, when it began to seem that time was running out. He had been appointed as captain for the five South African Tests, but had to withdraw. In June, just after he had entered his fortieth year, he stroked his final first-class hundred, 194 against Notts at Trent Bridge, the last 94 coming in little more than an hour. That year he was made an honorary MCC member, unique among playing professionals. The announcement of his retirement in January 1956 may even have saddened his admiring opponents.

Four more first-class innings followed in random matches in 1957 and 1960, and for Col.L.C.Stevens' XI against Cambridge University at Eastbourne in July 1960 he ended his career as he had begun it: with a duck.

Thereafter, having moved south to Kingston in Surrey, though having left a large portion of his soul in Yorkshire, he concentrated on his work for J.H.Fenner of Hull, wrote beguilingly for the *Evening News* and then *The Observer*, and added to his autobiographical *Cricket is My Life* (1949 and reprints) and *Just My Story* (1956) with the reflective *Fifty Years in Cricket* with Alex Bannister in 1984. In it, he wrote: "I sometimes wonder if it was not the second-worst happening of my career to become a record-breaking national celebrity at an age when I had just qualified to vote." A full-length biography by Gerald Howat was published in 1988.

His knighthood, conferred in 1956, was only the second, after Sir Jack Hobbs's, to go to a professional cricketer, and was deemed to have been thoroughly well earned, especially by those who had "been to war" with him over the years. With it went no "side". He wore the honour as graciously as he had batted or made his somewhat reluctant speeches as skipper.

In 1975 he became an England selector, but resigned a year later. The modern players did not find it easy to "relate" to him. To them he seemed more enigmatic than ever. Sir Leonard lent his full support to the Save The Oval campaign, and in 1987 he was president of the Forty (XL) Club. In 1982, the University of Bradford had given the city's distinguished son an honorary degree, and recently he responded to Yorkshire CCC's call by accepting the presidency of the club, though having not the slightest desire to become involved in the political infighting that has bedevilled it for so long. In 1988 he was guest of honour, and enjoyed, a gala dinner in Leeds to commemorate the fiftieth anniversary of his marathon 364.

Sir Len Hutton attended Godfrey Evans's gala seventieth birthday dinner only thirteen days before his death. He was suntanned in later life, in contrast to the pale-faced troop who had blocked the path of Yorkshire's and England's cricket adversaries. But he looked careworn, older than his years, his conscientious work – for that is what it was – of the early and middle years surely having taken its toll. Nonetheless, he seemed pleased to sit again with Miller and Bedser and Compton and the irrepressible Evans, discussing old times in his soft, thin voice, and, as usual, doing a lot of listening, his eyes expressive as ever.

He died in Kingston Hospital on September 6 after surgeons had fought to save him from a ruptured heart artery, and he leaves a widow, Dorothy (sister of Frank Dennis, the former Yorkshire player), and two sons, John, forty-three, and Richard, the former Yorkshire all-rounder, who played five times for England and on whose forty-eighth birthday his father died. Sir Len's funeral took place at St Peter's Church, Kingston-upon-Thames on September 13 and was followed by private cremation.

Wisden Cricket Monthly, October 1990

While missing the real devil's number (111), commentators for years have babbled on about "87" being Australia's unlucky number (for which there is no plausible evidence). Having bumped into Keith Miller at Len Hutton's funeral, I discovered that he had an authoritative view on the matter:

That "87" Nonsense: Keith Miller Explains

KEITH MILLER was back in London, doing the social rounds, watching a bit of cricket, going to the track, cursing the stick he had to use to help him through an attack of shingles around the thighs. Unexpectedly and very sadly he was called upon to attend the funeral of his revered old adversary Len Hutton. Then, three days later, off he flew, home to Australia, unstoppable at seventy after extensive chemotherapy for ear and jaw cancer – but with an unusual grievance bugging him. He has never been an irritable chap; not when flying with the RAAF in Europe during the Second World War or when he was winning matches for New South Wales and Australia in the 1950s, a swashbuckling, handsome hero far too grand in scale for any sensible lad even to start to try to emulate.

But now he was growling discontentedly about this myth which has grown around the score of 87.

"These commentators rant on about this supposedly Australian superstition over the number 87, and they really don't know what the hell they're talking about!" If he'd had a cricket ball in his hand, it would have taken no fortune-telling genius to reckon on what Miller's next delivery would have been.

So how did this 87 thing come about? "I'll tell you," says our hero confidentially, and a little breathlessly.

"When I was a kid, I went to the cricket all the time, to the Melbourne Cricket Ground. That was in the days when Don Bradman was making 100, 200, 300. The scoreboard at the MCG used to be a bit slow in those days. The numbers sometimes went up a bit late. You have to keep that in mind."

Compton, Evans and Australian High Commissioner Doug McClelland were gesturing to him to head for the limousine which was to take them back to London from the Kingston church. "Righto, I'll be with you; just a minute; just got to get this story out." The "tosh" these commentators had been putting out was obviously a prime irritant to the man who, it was about to emerge, was at the root of the superstition.

"Anyway, I'm just a kid in the outer, watching The Don bat for New South Wales against Victoria. Christmas 1929 I think it was [it was]. So I'd be, what, ten [he was]? Anyway, Don's seeing the ball as big as a football. But suddenly 'Bull' Alexander bowls him! I'd looked up to see his score just before 'Bull' got him, and that score – 87 – stuck in my mind. I couldn't get it out of my mind. Every weekend I'd look through the club scores, searching for more 87s. It became a sort of fixation.

"Even a few years after, when I began to play for South Melbourne alongside Ian Johnson, I was still conscious of this 87 thing. I always tried to avoid it when I was batting, but Johnno got out for 87 once and I said to him, 'That's bloody funny: I saw Bradman get out for 87 once.' It was a sort of cult, a superstition.

"Anyway, after the war, into the early 1950s, Richie Benaud and Alan Davidson and some of those blokes picked it up, but they didn't really know what it was all about. And more years later I heard Paul Sheahan on the radio talking about this superstition being based on 87 being 13 less than 100! What a load of bull!"

His friends waited patiently by the church gates, but the story had to be finished. There was more to come.

"I checked the thing out with Bob Radford at the NSWCA one day, just to refresh my memory. And there it was: Bradman bowled Alexander *89*! It wasn't 87 after all. The scoreboard had been slow again. And all these years . . .

"The commentators still rattle on about it. You listen."

I'd rather not.

"And another thing. They've got this ridiculous superstition about 111, which they call triple-Nelson . . . Righto, I'm coming!"

Wisden Cricket Monthly, November 1990

Melbourne 1954-55: Australia all out 111; Adelaide 1954-55: Australia all out 111; Headingley 1981: Australia all out 111. 'Nuff said?

Queensland's Gold Coast and its mountain hinterland was one place where one could get away from it all, though there was a bit of a disturbance when the England team passed through:

Frith Down Under – Part I

THE IMMEDIATE problem, notwithstanding Iraq, was to track down Andy Sandham and shoot him. Readers who were around this time last year will already have nodded knowingly and said, "Ah, yes. *WCM*'s tired old editor is on another of his winter sabbaticals in Queensland, with nothing better to do than chase cane toads."

Half-true.

The ugly, venom-filled cane toad has succeeded Ian Botham and Viv Richards as Australia's public enemy No.1. It threatens wildlife with its poison glands. It is spreading menacingly southwards and westwards. They come out only at night. Australian television is so ineffably awful that it becomes a matter of convenience as well as duty to go outside after dark with a torch and loaded air-rifle. Those readers who are even *more* clued-up will have guessed that "Sandham" was victim No.325. The numbering and naming of the little monsters holds boredom at bay and keeps a man's cricket brain statistically nimble.

Eight cane toads later, I don't know if I was patrolling in search of Duleepsinhji or Gooch.

The Brisbane Test was flavoured with perplexity, but a further month's reflection out on the cane-toad trail does no more than confirm that England batted nervously and shamefully. There was one further horrifying revelation, and that was that Allan Lamb, who was to be dismissed by Alderman in the first over next day, was sighted at Jupiter's Casino, on the Gold Coast, after midnight. It was alleged, in a front-page story, that David Gower and Tony Greig were with him, and that they entered the high-rollers' room around midnight, with one Kerry Packer.

Now if . . . *if* . . . Mr Packer had offered to take me to Jupiter's, Test match or not, I'd have been inclined to accept. That is to say, as long as he offered to float me for a hundred thousand dollars at the tables. Lambie, lucky little fellow, was not seen to take a drink by any of the pimps who obliged the newspaper reporters: otherwise team manager Lush might have had to put him on the next aircraft home. Poor Lambie. He ran out John Morris and Stewart junior on December 13 and then himself on December 15, having had facial skin cancers removed on December 11. What a tour.

And to think that while I was watching the deciding Rugby League Test in the early hours in my Brisbane hotel room, the England acting captain was down the coast having a flutter at an establishment you can see from the top of the road leading up from the cane-toad killing-fields.

The biggest joke of the month had to be the ludicrous near-hysterical indignation rattling from certain sections of the English press bandwagon when Mike Gatting assisted Gooch and his men at the nets. Not that cock-eyed logic was anything new in some of those columns, which have a helpless tendency towards pack instinct.

It was stimulating to drive down from cane-toad country (kookaburras, lorikeets, magpies and possums also abound, I should add) to Carrara. There a few dozen people turned up to watch a club match which, while not as low-key as a game of beach cricket further down the road at Surfers Paradise, was not exactly of world interest; except for one thing: the batsman considered by many to be the best in the world was playing for the locals, the Gold Coast Dolphins. Graeme Hick batted at No.3, with John Stephenson of Essex opening (and still blinking at the abruptness of his discharge from the England camp after being called in to assist at practice – and signing some team bats!).

The small gathering was distinguished by the presence of another once rated No.1 in the world, Barry Richards, who is now the QCA's chief executive, and also by a member of Bradman's legendary 1948 side, Sam Loxton, a local resident now like fellow Victorians Bill Johnston, George Tribe and Ernie McCormick. Sam gave us a potted reminiscence of that other absurd Brisbane Test match, that of 1950-51, when he held five catches and was one of three Australian batsmen out before a run had been scored in their second innings of 32 for 7 declared. Those who call for the return of uncovered pitches and the capricious events that must follow might do well to reflect, even so, that the current England side, during the first half of this tour at any rate, have been quite capable of capricious performances on good pitches, thank you very much.

I had to leave Carrara before Hick batted (under lights). There was some business to attend to up in the hills. Big devil, too, nearly the size of a dinner plate. But for

211

the further four months of his qualification period, Hick himself would have been at the Gabba with England, perhaps xylophoning the boundary in answer to Dean Jones's intimidating 145.

Soon, to Sydney in the hope that the series is balancing towards a thriller, leaving the cane toads to regroup, thereafter to return and seek out Hutton [364] and, next victim, Sobers [365], then Bert Sutcliffe [385], and No.499 Hanif, if they keep coming. Who knows? If I stay up late enough and the infestation is persistent enough, A.E.J.Collins [628] might cop it one dark night before it's time to abandon the campaign for another year.

Wisden Cricket Monthly, February 1991

There soon followed one of the more unusual I Was There experiences:

Frith Down Under – Part II

THREE MILES from the cool and placid Pacific, with the picturesque Nerang, Beechmont and Wunburra Ranges six miles to the west, Carrara Oval was a restful place to be. Robin Smith had just reached his rehabilitation century against almost the best State bowling attack in McDermott, Rackemann, Hohns and Peter Taylor. John Morris had just finished his maiden hundred in England XI colours; the globules of spectators, some from England, slumped dreamily in the pockets of shade around this football stadium. The horrifying events in the Middle East might have been on another planet. Here, it was warm and seemingly eternally sunny, and the common wish was that time would not move on too swiftly – or even at all.

The idyll was, as they say, suddenly shattered. Out of the azure sky whined two Tiger Moths, one just above the level of the towering floodlight pylons, the other some way below. Batsman Lamb looked startled and batsman Smith play-acted with his bat, turning it into a Kalashnikov, braced at his shoulder. Off the biplanes zoomed, high into the shimmering blue sky, and the cricket match continued, the small crowd and the cluttered press-box left to chuckle and wonder.

Then, within seconds, one of the English photographers called to me: "Have you got a car?"

"Yes."

"Where is it?"

"Over there. Why?"

"Can you drive fast?"

"Fast as a '76 Celica will allow."

"Let's go, then! Gower and Morris were in those planes!"

The cameraman recoiled from the hot blast emanating from the small vehicle as the door was flung open, and with thousands of poundsworth of equipment clattering against glovebox and gearstick, we bumped over the gravel pathway to the exit and thence a mile along the road to the little airstrip where even now the Tiger Moths were touching down.

"Is this as fast as you can go?"

"Yes! And I'm not going through a red light, even for a scoop picture! I copped a $50 seat-belt fine last month!"

We skidded into the airfield and pulled up in billows of dust just as the flyers were emerging from their machines. Obligingly, Messrs Gower and Morris climbed back into the cockpits, smiling not unnaturally with exhilaration. "You haven't lived till you've been up in one of these!" quoth the Derbyshire man.

The local paper had had an early tip-off and their photographer was already there. The three of us took about five reels between us: the two cricketers in the cockpit, leaning on the wing, standing by the propeller (surely the switches were off?), peering through the struts. All the Biggles allusions began to trip off the tongues of those privileged to be at hand.

Back at Carrara Oval, the cricket writers were reluctant to accept the story now going the rounds. They were even more sceptical about Gower's claim that he had planned to drop a water bomb on the field, if only he could have laid his hands on a plastic bag. This, after all, was the Gold Coast, the Fun Capital of Australia.

The England manager and coach and captain Gooch all professed to have had no prior knowledge of the escapade. It all began to overshadow England's growing ascendancy in this Queensland match. All that most people seemed to want to talk about was The Biggles Adventure.

That evening, John Morris rang David Gower, who was dining with his editor up in the hills. "The management wants to see us at eight in the morning," said "Animal". Gower topped up his glass of Geoff Merrill 1987 McLaren Vale Chardonnay and waited for tomorrow to take care of itself.

Wisden Cricket Monthly, March 1991

The two players were fined £1000 each and censured by the TCCB.

A Touch of True Genius

FOR ALL Gooch's glorious batting double at Adelaide, the romantics will see to it that the match is remembered first and foremost for the Test debut innings of 138 by Mark Waugh. It was conceived out of the same kind of crisis as faced those other young Australian blades Archie Jackson, Neil Harvey, Doug Walters and Greg Chappell when they first went to the crease against England, Jackson on this very same Adelaide Oval. They all made centuries and became part of their country's sporting legend. With Waugh – he of the 464 stand with his twin brother in Perth – there was perhaps less surprise, since his class was already proven in both countries. Indeed, in 1990 he scored over 3000 first-class runs, leaving most of those overthrown bowlers to absorb his great first-up Test deed with no great sense of surprise.

Four minutes younger than his brother Steve (no more time than it takes a modern bowler to complete an over), Mark Waugh displayed not the slightest inhibition – a pronounced Australian characteristic – although he was observed by those close at hand as being dry of mouth and slightly uncertain of step when the battle-call came. From the first ball he was all poise and straight bat. His timing was pure Cowdrey, his range wide, his balance perfect, his running brisk. The more one watched, the greater the temptation to see in him true genius. How many Test runs will he have made by the end of the 20th Century?

AND, IN passing, the series provided further fuel for the raging concern over miscarriages of justice in split-second run-out decisions. To nominate but one, Boon (49) was thrown out by Malcolm when only 5 in the first innings at Adelaide. Millions saw the reality of the well-earned dismissal, but umpires – most of them – insist on relying on the naked eye – a preposterous state of affairs – and so the batsman stayed, and the match was distorted, quite needlessly. It is already well past the time when umpires should be sitting down and giving this matter the deep consideration it deserves. The authorities, we understand, will be more than glad to give the system a trial, possibly in one of the limited-overs competitions this summer.

Wisden Cricket Monthly, March 1991

Here lies a clue to the problem of resisting the notion that the truth should prevail by examination of replays: the majority of umpires, evidently content to continue to look foolish when errors are displayed on the screen to a vast audience, were seeing video as a threat to their "authority". The people who were supposed to be in authority as guardians of the game's best interests (the administrators) should have been informing the umpires that technology was being brought in whether they, with their myopic stance and often bulging egos, liked it or not. Nearly twenty damaging years were to pass before that technology was to be fully utilised.

As for Mark Waugh, he made over 8000 runs in 128 Tests, with 20 centuries, and held 181 catches with the most magnetic and soft hands ever seen in the slips (mostly), and when he was persuaded to retire I felt a rare chill of disappointment.

Wicketkeepers tend to be an agreeable breed, for some odd reason. This tribute to one of them reached also to some others of the brotherhood:

'Keepers: a Fascinating Species

WICKETKEEPERS are an interesting species. They come in all shapes and sizes, though mainly welterweight to middleweight, and project a fascinating range of personalities. The ancient adage that you had to be both brave and slightly mad to stand behind the stumps has lost some credibility since 'keepers have taken to standing well back to all but the slowest of bowlers. But nerve does come into it, and one should never be fooled by the swagger of a Farokh Engineer or the balletic grace of a Jeff Dujon. They hold down the key position in the field. Every ball.

I've known a lot of wicketkeepers, from Herbert Strudwick, who kept for England not far short of a hundred years ago, to Bruce French, who performed for county and country with just the same kind of perky and yet gentlemanly manner as little "Struddy". In between, there have been the businesslike Leslie Ames, the complete professional; Godfrey Evans, the most flamboyant of the lot and the best cheerer-upper the game has known; and Alan Knott, yet another from Kent, who was frighteningly close to perfection. The neat and patient Bob Taylor preceded Bruce French into the England XI, a world record bag of victims being his on retirement: a target Bruce might contemplate reaching perhaps?

Of the overseas performers, I actually saw Bert Oldfield keep when he was fifty-seven, and still silky-smooth of movement and attired like something out of *Tailor and Cutter*. Traditionalists usually select him as the finest of Australian wicketkeepers, though the tall, craggy-faced Queenslander Don Tallon still has a lot of support. Another from that hot and steamy state, Wally Grout, has a glowing reputation and the statistics to support it, though images of his predecessor Gil Langley linger more readily because of his paradoxical physical untidiness and generally efficient glovemanship. Gil's protruding belly-button must have startled many a new batsman.

Rod Marsh eventually topped the Australian and world lists, his rugged style, aggressive moustache, flaring nostrils and billiard-table legs leaving an unforgettable impression. What a contrast Ian Healy makes, with his Oldfield-like fastidious clothing and preference for footwork rather than the desperate dive.

Of the rest, Don Brennan of Yorkshire was the worst natterer; Kiwi Ian Smith had the most gremlin-like personality; "Kiri" Kirmani of India was the baldest; Springbok John Waite seemed the tallest; John Murray combined neatness and ritualism in unique fashion; Paul Downton was the most "invisible" – which is intended as a compliment; David Bairstow was easily the most florid.

As for the central character in this particular publication, it has been a joy to watch him in action. Boyish, never flashy, beautifully competent, Bruce French has been a credit to the art, an elegant addition to the species.

Bruce French Benefit Year 1991

Inevitably as new names appear the old ones fade away. One of the most distinguished died on April 6, 1991:

Farewell, Bill Ponsford

HE WAS colour-blind, had a sizable rump, and crouched anxiously over the bat. Yet had there been no Don Bradman it is feasible that today we should be referring to Bill Ponsford, who has died aged ninety, as the best batsman the world has seen.

The judgment would have been strictly quantitative, for "Ponny" was no oil painting. He remains the only batsman to have reached 400 on two occasions*, once amassing 1013 runs in four consecutive innings, held the Sheffield Shield record with 1217 runs in a season, and was the first among Australians and Englishmen to score centuries in both his first two Test matches. His scores for Victoria as well as his side's aggregates during the 1920s resembled misprints: 429 out of 1059 in 1923, 352 out of 1107 in 1926, 437 out of 793 in 1927, all at the Melbourne Cricket Ground. He was thus the world record-holder, having twice upped Archie MacLaren's 424 at Taunton in 1895.

Then along came Bradman with his 452 not out early in 1930, and from then onwards Ponsford was satisfied with mere double-centuries.

Not that he was overshadowed when he and Bradman batted together for Australia. Cautious without ever wishing to waste a scoring chance, Ponsford drove either side of the wicket with heart-breaking confidence, and cut with huge assurance. Destructive bowlers such as Verity and Ironmonger always felt he gave them even less chance of dismissal than did Bradman.

The pair had some colossal partnerships for Australia: 230 against West Indies at Brisbane, 388 at Leeds and 451 in the following Test at The Oval in 1934, a world Test record until Martin Crowe and Andrew Jones put on 467 against Sri Lanka at Wellington two months ago.

Terrifying though the Bradman-Ponsford liaisons were to English bowlers, Australian cricket folklore places another pairing on an even higher plane: Woodfull and Ponsford, the two Bills, "Mutt and Jeff", were the twin fortresses from which many a Victorian and Australian tall total was established.

To Australia's immense satisfaction this duo provided a proud retort to England's celebrated opening pair Hobbs and Sutcliffe. They had eighteen century first-wicket stands for state and country, the biggest being 375 against New South Wales, in a mere 225 minutes, Victoria steaming on to 1107, with leg-spinner Arthur Mailey taking four wickets for 362.

Ponsford's bat, known as "Big Bertha", seemed so wide that an umpire one day put the gauge on it and found that the spread down at the "meat" had flattened it beyond the legal 4¼ inches. Against the fury of Larwood and company's bodyline attack he often turned his broad back, collecting bruises galore, but making an 85 in the Adelaide Test that impressed for its great courage. That and a speedy 110 in the 1930 Oval Test ranked, alongside an unbeaten century in a Shield match on a treacherous, rain-ruined Melbourne pitch in December 1930, as Ponsford's finest three innings, irrespective of the thirteen double-, triple- or quadruple-centuries he carved out.

He scored 110 in his first Test and 266 in his last ten years later. He was one of the quietest men who ever played the game at top level, and even dropped his head when a camera approached, such was his shyness.

* Brian Lara later emulated him in this distinction.

The Guardian, April 9, 1991

Our television viewing was broadening fast, with satellite television covering big matches all around the world with ever-advancing technical gimmicks. An invitation to assess it was too good to resist:

Reach for the Sky Button

THE CHOICE of television cricket-watching is now so broad as to tempt a man to remain ensconced in his armchair not only throughout the winter but most of the summer too. Further, watching Test highlights from West Indies without prior knowledge of the run of play has been a new experience. Having kept well clear of all news bulletins during the day, I have programmed Eurosport's highlights from Jamaica, Guyana and Trinidad after midnight and watched them first thing next morning. The tension was intense – when it did not rain. It can be very wet in the Caribbean, though not always when you want it to be.

The pace of the Sky TV highlights differs greatly from the ungenerously- parcelled BBC half-hour, which usually embraces a mere twenty-odd balls, all producing boundaries or dismissals, ponderously stretched out by slow-motion replays. BSkyB has been heightening the degree of expectancy by including the occasional "dot ball", so that no forward assumption can ever safely be made by the viewer.

Then, with the opening of the Sky Sports channel in mid-April came a change in domestic routine. Live transmission from Barbados was viewable from 3pm until some time in the early evening. The story was then completed in *two hours* of highlights from 10pm.

Allowing that the cameras at Kensington Oval had a kind of two-way fixation for the simpletons jigging around and banging their drums in the wooden stands, the pictures were excellent. All the dreadful lbw decisions against Australia came across clearly, and Curtly Ambrose's smiles, sneers and arm-waving made for vivid television.

The symmetry of Mark Waugh, the grim determination of Boon and Taylor, McDermott's menace with the ball and receding reserves of intestinal fortitude with the bat, Merv Hughes's miniature nervous breakdown when he dropped that Richardson hooked catch – it all came through in sharp detail. Malcolm Marshall, mopping his brow, increasingly resembles Louis Armstrong, while the facial range of Greenidge throughout his 11¼ hours at the crease was a study for watching psychiatrists.

Viv Richards, who shocked us all when he first removed his cap, glowered and glowered. My good lady thought she had caught me watching the cartoons when she entered the room and glimpsed a close-up of the West Indies captain chewing furiously. Poignantly, whenever Patterson and Walsh grimaced or smiled we were reminded of that long-forgotten image of the joyous West Indies cricketers of a bygone age. They show those brilliant teeth nowadays only when wickets fall, which admittedly is with fair frequency.

Domestic English cricket is dull fare in comparison. The Sunday League and B&H matches, over their short courses and with the drama now more *Coronation Street* than *Carmen*, owe more, in entertainment terms, to the commentary team than to the comparatively tame pictures. Henry Blofeld, who always sounds as if he is calling down a dubious line from Ootacamund, is as kindly as Geoffrey Boycott is mean and professional. Thus: HB – "Phil Neale, rather unlucky not to have played for England?" GB – "Not really. He's a good *county* player."

Bob Willis, meanwhile, has had treatment for his flat tones by developing a new delivery based on the tonic solfa, faithfully finishing almost every sentence on the high doh, which contrasts merrily with the basso profundo on the Caribbean telecasts of Michael Holding, who makes Paul Robeson sound squeaky. Funnier than many a professional TV comedian, David Lloyd, with his rich Accrington vowels, loves a laugh and gives many away. I could hardly focus the next ball for laughter vapour after he had referred to a full bunger as a "boon-gurrr". "Bumble" is one of cricket's treasures.

It is all very chatty, and a glorious mixture of dialects. They give fervent plugs to the hotels where they are staying, but the paid-for commercials are, as yet anyway, less relentlessly frequent and brain-bruising than on Australia's Channel 9 coverage.

The somewhat over-effusive anchorman, Charles Colvile, sits propped up in the studio, pumping out platitudes, and seemed to relish the closing stages of the Barbados Test, when West Indies thrashed Australia, who had recently demolished Colvile's dear England, who are about to be steamrollered again by his much-admired West Indies.

Even a gust of joviality from this earnest presenter failed to loosen the rigid backcloth of terror from the countenance of the studio expert, Roland Butcher. Little Roly, of course, knows better than most that West Indies have brought fast bowling to an art form – even if it most closely resembles Picasso's *Guernica*.

Here and there, BSkyB slips in one of its harmless "Tetley Tales", with the bright-eyed Blofeld introducing cricketers and others who, seated in a pub set, utter humorous anecdotes. Pam Ayres and Peter Richardson are among the best, but if these episodes are to have a real usefulness, BSkyB might consider them as fillers while the West Indian fast bowlers dawdle back to their marks.

The Times, April 30, 1991

For some years West Indies had been all-conquering but not easy to watch, for their success was based on an army of fast bowlers who bowled little else but short-pitched stuff throughout their opponents' innings. Most of the more attractive strokes were simply impossible to play, and the over rate was cynical, sometimes scarcely touching ten overs per hour. It was disappointing that the TCCB had actually invited them back a year early this time:

An Unappetising Tour

ANOTHER INVASION is upon us by a West Indies team which is the most fearsome, the most successful, and the most unpopular in the world. Their game is founded on vengeance and violence and is fringed by arrogance. The only mercy is that they're not bringing their umpires with them.

Images of their gamesmanship early in 1990, when they warded off England's challenge, have been overlaid with new and equally unsavoury tableaux of Desmond Haynes menacing wicketkeeper Ian Healy after he had appealed for a catch in the recent series against Australia. The same Haynes, who appears to be next in line to captain West Indies, was later seen with Merv Hughes blowing acidic kisses at each other, degrading a game which was already up to its armpits in cynicism. The illegitimate running-out of Dean Jones will forever be a blot on Caribbean cricket history. It was some consolation that two "nice guys" topped each team's batting: Richie Richardson and Gus Logie, and Mark Waugh and Mark Taylor.

How incredible it was to learn that when the series had ended, the West Indies captain, Viv Richards, "demanded" that the world's cricket authorities clamp down on intimidation and abuse. Thus spoke a man who was supposed to be in charge, and yet who is invariably at the very centre of the war-dances. "People should be made to realise," he says, "that no individual is bigger than the game." How true. How very true.

Richards even claimed that this sort of thing was happening everywhere in cricket. From where he stands it might appear thus, but in fact such ugliness does not perpetually soil England's matches with Australia, New Zealand, India or Sri Lanka, or many another contest. West Indies, for their part however, have become embroiled in one sour series after another.

Their supporters will insist that bitterness arises from the fact that West Indies have been so steadily victorious. This may be close to the truth, but there is a vital additional factor to be identified, and that is that these matches have long since become manifestations of the racial tensions that exist in the world outside the cricket-ground gates. Just when the cricketers of both sides should be teaching ordinary folk how to co-exist and enjoy honourable sports combat, a damaging counter-image emerges.

It has not been uncommon of late to hear cricket-lovers talk of ignoring this summer's one-day internationals and Test matches in favour of county cricket. The visitors' over rate will be poor (and the TCCB are letting them get away with it). This, tactically, will almost certainly be matched by the home side. There will be no variety in the West Indies attack, with no slow bowler of Test class in the squad. And we have seen it all oh so many times before. What on earth persuaded the TCCB to invite them back a year early?

At least play will cease at 7pm, even if West Indies, in seven hours' play, have bowled only 75 or 80 overs. By capitulating on that point too the TCCB at least have curtailed everybody's inconvenience. West Indies cricket needs this tour urgently, having suffered another financially disastrous home series. And yet they have also outbluffed the TCCB completely by refusing to accept controls over bouncers and fast, high full-tosses. So it is left to the umpires: and we know well enough how lacking in the right stuff they usually turn out to be.

No new, more attractive image is likely to materialise across the face of West Indian cricket while the present senior players prevail. The game is left to hope that from those islands will come another Worrell or Sobers, to bestow the grace under pressure which is true genius.

Wisden Cricket Monthly, June 1991

It became necessary to add something a month later after an hysterical and appallingly inaccurate feature on that editorial was splattered across a tabloid paper:

Just to Clarify

NOT SIMPLY because England had not beaten West Indies for twenty-two years, but the world looked a different place a month ago. Since then, parts of our June Editorial, which expressed dissatisfaction with aspects of the West Indian approach to Test cricket, have been appropriated by a tabloid newspaper and distorted into a lurid article which was then gleefully "syndicated" and abetted by other media personnel – some of whom ought to have known better – as far away as the smallest Caribbean island. The end product was barely recognisable from the original. Feelings were hurt and rationality became an extremely elusive commodity. Such is the structure of the communications world that only comparatively few of the readers of and listeners to the warped and mischievously construed versions of *WCM*'s words can be reached to be appraised properly of the statements made here, statements which are the only ones for which we can be held responsible.

In essence, *WCM* claimed that West Indies were the most unpopular team in the world. This was a critical comment with which some might, and indeed did, take issue. The belief that the team the world's Test countries least fancy playing against is West Indies has been challenged. So too has the theory that crowds come to England's small Test grounds principally in the hope of seeing the world champions beaten.

The statement that West Indies' success has been based on "vengeance and violence" seems almost deliberately to have been misunderstood in certain quarters. In refuting the "vengeance" comment ("retribution" might equally well have been used), some West Indian cricket supporters have firmly rejected the notion, in the same breath pointing to the living hell served on the 1975-76 West Indians in Australia (so vividly described in Viv Richards' new book). This was precisely the point. West Indies, mainly in the person of Clive Lloyd, decided that never again, if at all possible, would West Indies be outgunned by the opposition. The evolutionary four-man pace attack had arrived.

There is nothing new in the vengeance/retribution type of motivation in sport; nor is it the exclusive province of West Indies cricket. When Lillee and Thomson were pounding England in 1974-75 they were, in the eyes of many, exacting "revenge" for the Tyson and Trueman bombardments of the 1950s. Trueman had been the long-awaited response to the sometime terror tactics of the late 1940s by Lindwall and Miller, who had been seen as the payers-back for the "sins" of Larwood and Voce (in the 1932-33 Bodyline series), who had been England's retort to the torment inflicted by Gregory and McDonald as Australia rode roughshod over England in the early 1920s. And so on. Restoring the balance; getting even; paying them back. Name your own favourite euphemism.

"Violence" is an emotive, awful word, even when used in a strictly cricket sense, but the bouncer may reasonably accommodate several adjectives, "violent" as appropriate as any. A ball aimed at scaring a batsman, driving him back, restricting his response to considerations of physical safety or, at cavalier best, a risky hook shot, is no gentle chess move. Dealt out in abundance, especially at tailenders, the bouncer is cricket's implement of violence, as opposed to the intellectual challenge of flighted spin, or the batting spadework demanded by solid old medium-pace.

Representatives of the West Indies camp have taken exception to what they have seen as an implication that they alone were responsible for the unpleasant atmosphere arising from the recent West Indies v Australia series. Again, it is time not only for exceptionally careful wording but equally thorough comprehension and digestion.

In suggesting that West Indies' matches have become "manifestations of the racial tensions that exist in the world outside the cricket-ground gates" there was no intention to lay the blame on any particular team. It is known – through the remarks of Viv Richards and others – that West Indies' opponents sometimes have engaged in unacceptable verbal provocation. One view that seems to unite West Indies and England is that Australia have proved to be the biggest problem for both of them in the matter of "sledging". The cricket world lives in hope that the forthcoming introduction of match referees and the more intensive training of umpires will stamp out this painful and enraging tactic once and for all.

It has never been *Wisden Cricket Monthly's* aim or desire to offend readers, West Indian or otherwise. That sensibilities have been pricked is regretted; but the fault is surely less in transmission than in interpretation and magnification, the removal from context and the bending of tone. John Arlott wrote of *WCM*'s editor in 1975 that he had "considerable feeling for West Indian cricket". In that same year this same editor received a letter from the MCC secretary commending him for an article critical of the physical and verbal excesses of Dennis Lillee. Cricket's welfare was then and is now the central consideration.

It so happens that the one-day internationals and opening Test match have been played in the best of spirits, a fact owing much to the familiarity of both sides with each other on the county circuit. The fires of emotion seem to have been damped down. Hallelujah!

Wisden Cricket Monthly, July 1991

West Indies' fifteen-year reign of terror coincidentally ended with this 1991 series against England, and as Caribbean talent – bowling at least – dried up and the administration lurched from one crisis to the next, the early years of the new century were to find some people actually yearning for a revival of West Indies cricket as defeat followed defeat. The tide turned and the decline began to show firstly in the one-day tournament:

The Latest English Models

THESE ONE-DAY series which traditionally precede the Tests are so often referred to in disparaging terms: a "glorified net", "junk food", "crowd-pulling crash-bang-wallops". Perhaps they are, in reality, rather like the Motor Show. Picture the 1991 reconditioned models Botham and Lamb, and the beautifully preserved vintage Gooch, the bright young Atherton and Illingworth, the comfortable old family roadster Pringle, the dashing new Fairbrother, the sporty DeFreitas, the fast but dubiously reliable Lewis, the trusty Russell, the exciting new Ramprakash, the bouncy horn-blaring Lawrence, the swift and businesslike Reeve. And then there was Britain's latest, classy, imported model, the Hick.

The build-up had mounted over some years, and the young former Zimbabwean, at the crunch, had the good fortune to find that much of the media attention was deflected by his team-mate, "The Legend". Botham was back at thirty-five, a re-riveted supertanker now, still the nation's favourite, fresh from some wickets and a big century against the West Indians at Worcester. The Motor Show was on, and the queues grew long.

West Indies, lacking Haynes with back trouble, departed from the third and final encounter in thoughtful mood. The series had been lost by three widening margins partly because a fifth bowler of reliability was lacking, while only Richards and

Logie had managed half-centuries. The tourists had seen new boys Hick and Fairbrother make runs with ever-growing confidence after Lamb had served a reminder of his lingering skills and Atherton of his growing maturity. The Tests were certainly going to be longer and more realistically contested, but nearly all the orders at the "Motor Show" had gone into England's book.

Wisden Cricket Monthly, July 1991

England's revival continued in a memorable Test match at Headingley, Leeds in June 1991:

Dancing on the Moon

WHEN TODAY'S middle-aged were just boys and girls, speculation about man's stepping onto the Moon seemed far-fetched. But in 1969 Neil Armstrong made it. Since 1969, the vision of England's beating West Indies has become almost as certifiable. But in Kingston in 1990, Graham Gooch made it happen (away from home) and now, at Headingley, he has done it again, breaking that embarrassing twenty-two-year drought.

Gooch's youngest player, Mark Ramprakash, was seven weeks short of entering the world when Ray Illingworth led England to that distant last victory on English soil, and the *Something in the Air* that Thunderclap Newman sang about – at No.1 in the pop charts of July 1969 – certainly had nothing to do with level competition with Caribbean cricket opponents. Five Anglo-West Indian series in England were to pass without a trace of English victory, destiny waiting patiently for the young London Schools cricketer who toured East Africa in 1969 to reach a formidable maturity. G.A.Gooch, in the past fifteen months, has become a towering figure in world cricket, and talk of a knighthood is less far-fetched than our childhood doubts about that Moon walk.

Headingley was cold and dull almost throughout this unforgettable contest, and the pitch could never be trusted in that it always assisted movement off the seam and continued to mix the degree of bounce. Viv Richards said afterwards that England's bowlers weren't favoured; his own men benefited too. They were, after all, experienced county players. Baseball cap perched on head and fat cigar between his fingers, the West Indies captain was generous in defeat, though defiant when looking to the continuation of the series: "We gotta knock these guys down, y'know," he said of Gooch's victorious England XI, "not in the sense of bouncers though!" Much laughter.

It was a match which sponsors Cornhill will have cherished more than most, and it will be relived in many an anthology to come, by authors as yet unborn. From the beautifully-appointed new press-box the 100th England v West Indies Test match was a tense thing to behold from start to finish. Former *Yorkshire Post* cricket correspondent J.M.Kilburn, now eighty-one and blind, launched the new observatory with some charming words, but any dreams of a strident beginning by England next morning were shattered when, put in to bat, they lost four wickets before lunch.

[England scored 198 (Robin Smith 54), then bowled West Indies out for 173 (Viv Richards 73). With the match thus poised, Graham Gooch in the second innings played one of the finest innings in Test history.]

Memories of England's recent second-innings collapses began to haunt those of a nervous disposition. With England 47 for 3 at lunch, the twitches were spreading.

Atherton had stewed for 17 balls before scrambling his first run, and soon fell to

In one of the strongest batting performances in cricket history, Graham Gooch at Headingley showed the West Indian bowlers that enough was enough. He even declined an offer to go off for poor light. (PA Photos)

an acrobatic Dujon catch. Hick, having played the short stuff with an immaculately straight bat, elbow skywards like a Moon rocket, was out, again for 6, when an Ambrose yorker outside off struck an indecisive, loosely-held bat and cannoned into the wicket via boot. Next ball Lamb was caught at slip, and Ambrose had taken 3 for 1 in 10 balls. Ambrose, Ambrose, Ambrose: it was dance-time again. When this flagpole of a man finds his rhythm there seems no stopping him from taking eight wickets, or even all 10, as was tipped on this occasion, as he proceeded to double his take to six later in the day. Just why Richards chose to pamper him by keeping him out of the attack after the lunch break will long be debated. Curtly E.L. Ambrose could have wiped England out between lunch and tea.

As it was, no wicket fell in that session of 32 overs, eight of them from the harmless Hooper and Richards, the first slow bowling of the match. No liberties could be taken with Marshall, Walsh or Patterson as Gooch and Ramprakash built towards a telling lead. The youngster took a nasty full-bunger from Walsh on the wrist, and was three-quarters of an hour (33 balls) on 6. Gooch, when 44, was thought by the West Indians to have touched one to Dujon, though the ball merely brushed the pad, and the veteran and his apprentice took their stand beyond 50.

Tea brought an end, Ramprakash giving Dujon another virtuoso one-hander. And when Robin Smith was lbw first ball, the balance had swung back West Indies' way. Then the tense Russell was adjudged caught behind from the thinnest of touches, and it was 124 for 6, 149 ahead. England's little keeper was one of eight players in the match who were out for under double figures in both innings; 25 of the 40 dismissals were for less than 10.

If Ambrose towered over the match now, with 6 for 36 in 21 overs, Gooch was in the ring with him, trading blows, avoiding the knockout attempts, scoring points with courage and consistency and the fiercest concentration. What emerged was actually one of Test cricket's greatest performances.

Ambrose came off. No risk of exhaustion was being taken. And in a defiant tactical gesture, Gooch declined the offer to go off for fine drizzle. Before long steady rain drove them off anyway, but England had retrieved a slender initiative at 143 for 6, 168 ahead, significantly with their commander-in-chief still unbeaten with 82.

Headingley's first-ever Sunday of Test cricket therefore presented an exciting prospect, even if the weather was still uncharitable. The prospect enticed 6000 into the ground, and they first saw the Essex lads, Gooch and Pringle, hold fast for the initial, crucial half-hour until rain drove the players off. Ambrose, against expectation, added no more to his six wickets, and just before lunch Gooch pulled Walsh for four to post his fifth Test century against West Indies, all of them brave and skilful, none more useful. If Richards had had an Alderman at his disposal how different it all might have been. But this fearless EastEnder, in common with the heroes of the classics, is at his best when the demands are most severe. Like the Victorians, whether serving the Queen in Punjab or Natal or policing the village – for such comparisons have often been made – Gooch is inspired not only by the obligations of his profession but by visions of "England, home and beauty".

This century came in 5½ hard-fought hours, from 240 balls, but his task was a long way from finished. In the most telling partnership of the match, he and Pringle went on to add 98 in 140 minutes, the pitch now perhaps slightly less capricious but still demanding unrelenting vigilance. A beautiful delivery from Marshall ended Pringle's resistance after 94 balls, and immediately an offcutter from Walsh caused Gooch to jack-knife – and to reflect, doubtless, that it was in England's interests that this pitch should remain "alive".

Richards was still rotating his bowling somewhat mechanically, with the greatest threat, Ambrose, sending down only seven of the 28 overs so far this day. After a longish delay following heavy rain, groundsman Keith Boyce having attended to a leakage from the covers halfway up the pitch and to one side, the tense rivalry was resumed. Marshall bowled off a shortened run, but it was Walsh who gained the eighth wicket, winning an lbw decision against DeFreitas with the total 236, and England lead of 261.

Watkin and Malcolm soon went, leaving Graham Gooch unbeaten with 154 of his side's 252, having carried his bat, as far as he could recall, for the first time in his life. Whatever he did last year – and that amounted to 1058 runs in his last 10 Test innings in England – Hadlee, Hirwani and all, this was *the* innings, against the bowling of the world champions on a bowler's pitch. When that white helmet was eventually removed, he confessed to feeling that these important runs had been a "great thrill" because they came against the best in the world. But he stressed – and who could blame him? – that the game could still go either way.

That was after Simmons had chopped the first ball of the final innings into his leg stump, and West Indies had finished at 11 for one after a disturbed day of only 48 overs. Perhaps England were slightly more eager for rain-free conditions on the final day.

It was some day, Monday, June 10. There were 5000 present, 2000 of them taking advantage of free entry after the previous day's short ration. It was blowy, overcast, and unpredictable. For the superstitious the early omens were grim for England, for Ramprakash missed a hard chest-high catch at point from Haynes, and Richardson was looking for the initiative, punishing the wayward Malcolm and unleashing hooks and drives with the businesslike certainty of a Weekes. Haynes seemed plumb lbw to Pringle, but umpire Bird shook his head. Memories of Lord's 1984 surfaced: of course, all was vanity: West Indies would sail to victory.

Three balls after the big shout, however, Haynes was out, gloving to short mid-on. Steve Watkin, the twenty-five-year-old from Maesteg, now swung the match with three wickets in consecutive overs of generously-pitched bowling in a "howling gale" (Gooch) against which sorry liberties were attempted. Hooper nicked to slip; Richards, after only ten minutes at the crease, sent a terrifying skyer way over Gooch, who took it over his shoulder at deep mid-off; and the England captain then grabbed a thick edge from Logie with an outstretched left hand. Some of the decorum of the press-box was temporarily flung aside with West Indies 88 for 5.

[England went on to win with some comfort after all, by 115 runs, their seamers doing the job.]

"Four-nil, four-nil, four-nil, four-nil!" Yorkshire's massed youngsters chanted below the pavilion balcony. Many of them no doubt expressed themselves as being "over the Moon" at the result. How close to the reality this really seemed, thinking back to that long-ago summer of 1969. At last England had found their Neil Armstrong in Graham Gooch. Now, could Mars and Jupiter be reached?

Wisden Cricket Monthly, July 1991

It was much closer than that: West Indies went ahead with victories at Trent Bridge and Edgbaston, then England won the fifth and final Test at The Oval to level the series two-all.

The summer of 1991 was momentous in other ways. South Africa's long banishment from "official" international cricket came to an end:

Twenty-One Years and 122 Days

TWENTY-ONE YEARS and 122 days elapsed between Ali Bacher's catch to complete a 4-0 whitewash against Australia in the 1969-70 series and his emotional appearance in the Lord's Long Room on July 10, 1991, as managing director of the United Cricket Board of South Africa upon his country's return to full membership of the International Cricket Council (though without its original founder-member power).

The catch at St George's Park, Port Elizabeth, as soon became obvious, sealed off eighty-one years of Test cricket by the whites-only Springbok side. The 1991 ICC readmission vote came after more than two decades of protest, intrigue, desperation, hypocrisy, and – from liberal politicians and sportsmen of conscience – much brave action and utterance. Small wonder that Dr Bacher initially could barely speak to the gathered media at Lord's, so overwhelming had been the emotional build-up over all those years.

His energetic efforts to break down apartheid in cricket and to keep the game alive in his ostracised country are well enough documented. There were many moments of doubt and anguish along the way, and the eventual breakthrough could never have come had not the African National Congress given the cricket bodies its support in the wake of the messianic President de Klerk's reforms across the Republic. The campaign for recognition then became a strictly political exercise, representatives of numerous governments around the world joining in discussions at venues far and wide.

The mood of impending acceptance mushroomed, as did the desire to foster recognition of and global membership for the multiracial South African cricket body. Cricket-loving heads of state played their part, some of them hardliners from the days when South Africa's reforms had not gone far enough. During the recent Nottingham Test match there were still reservations about the intent of Pakistan and West Indies, but a clearer portrayal of what had been going on in South Africa evidently satisfied Pakistan at the eleventh hour, leaving only the West Indies Cricket Board in negative mood. Its president, Clyde Walcott, was the subject of the most curious quote of the year. After two decades of posturing and shrugging and protesting that they could not go against the various Caribbean governments' hard line, the Board's stance now was that "cricket in the Caribbean is not necessarily the slave of politicians' dictates". Might another liberation, equally monumental to South Africa's, have slipped through with scarcely anyone having noticed?

Cricket's Berlin Wall has thus been dismantled, and a somewhat undignified scramble begins to book all kinds of tours by and against the new-edition South Africa XI. Participation in the World Cup early next year seemed a distinct possibility in the first few euphoric hours, but the resistance to undue haste asserted itself twenty-four hours later as the historic ICC gathering concluded its business. At the same time, Mike Gatting and his team which toured South Africa in 1989-90 learned that, slightly illogically, their ban would not be lifted for at least a year. Visions of Broad, Gatting and Foster in the forthcoming Edgbaston Test against West Indies were thus speedily aborted.

It will have given the South Africans particular pleasure to have been led back through the forbidden gate by India (proposers) and Australia (seconders), both former hardliners. As the faces of Ali Bacher, Geoff Dakin, Krish Mackerdhuj and Steve Tshwete are planted indelibly into history, cricket-lovers everywhere (who had also to absorb the concurrent news that Yorkshire are to break with tradition and sign up an overseas player: an item almost lost in the excitement over South Africa's readmission) will anticipate with relish a photograph of South Africa taking the field in a Test match once more, to go alongside the sad and fading picture of Procter, Pollock, Richards, Barlow and Bacher vacating it.

Other ICC decisions were to restrict bouncers to one per batsman per over; to brand a "beamer" head-high or above as a no-ball; to impose "harsh" fines on over rates below 15 per hour in Tests; to appoint match referees at international matches; and, for financial reasons, to defer the matter of instituting a panel of "third-country" umpires. A new "code of conduct" is to come into force from October 1.

Wisden Cricket Monthly, August 1991

In December 1991 my closest friend in cricket, John Arlott, died. This greatest of broadcasters and estimable writer had become a substitute father, wielding colossal influence on me. Now, once again, it was time to sit down and try to do justice to a special person:

John Arlott: the Mighty Oak

A GREAT English oak has come down, and the landscape seems bare. John Arlott had been part of cricket's setting for so long that the very thought of his departure seemed invalid. Those who knew him well will grieve forever. And yet countless thousands who never even met him are feeling the loss as if he were a brother or a favourite uncle.

As the years aggregated, the ambitious poet and bon viveur of the 1950s, thought brash by some, matured into a reassuring paternal figure, compassionate, calm, worldly wise, himself scarred by the losses of a baby daughter, twenty-one-year-old son, and forty-three-year-old wife.

Broadcasting, the main thread of his life, had begun in earnest in 1947, the golden Compton-Edrich summer, when South Africa toured England. The thread came to an end in 1980 with the Gillette Cup final, following the more readily-remembered Centenary Test match, when he took his leave matter-of-factly, while being toasted by the entire Lord's crowd, the England and Australia cricketers down below, and goodness knows how many faithful listeners across the land and even across the seas. From the commentary-box, down the wretched stairs he went, along to the Warner Stand, and up more stairs, finally to plonk himself down, mop his brow with the red handkerchief yet again, and gaze somewhat blankly at the far Mound Stand. Breath regained, he continued to keep his emotions under control. Almost. A sheet of paper was clicked into the old typewriter, and the *Guardian* report soon began to take shape.

John was less composed, it has to be recorded, when Basil Easterbrook, on behalf of the cricket writers, presented him with an antique watch as a retirement gift, making a neat little speech. For once, Leslie Thomas John Arlott was speechless. Out came the red hankie again, with, minutes later, an anguished utterance at having been rendered temporarily incapable of response.

It was a memorable summer, 1980. He had announced early that he was retiring, and everywhere he went people and organisations wanted to show their appreciation of him. Whether he liked it or not, he did belong to the people. But he was seen little after that long and rousing adieu, for he left Hampshire, having chosen to retreat to his adored island of Alderney, where his spacious home (so grand that the German commandant had used it during the Occupation) sat almost at the centre of the one-mile-by-three, sea-slapped, rocky mass within sight of the Cherbourg peninsula. He had his reasons for going there – romantic sentimentality, clean air, absence of both juggernaut vehicles and vandalism, light taxation – but this most gregarious of men now faced an enforced reduction in live contact with his vast circle of friends, such were the complications of journeying down to the Channel Islands with any sort of frequency.

As the 1980s advanced, John's health declined severely. His trips to the mainland were brief and strictly for medical emergencies. Towards the end he could not travel at all. His isolation intensified, and it was left to Pat, his wife, his sons Tim and Robert, and a handful of local friends to keep him company – plus one other highly distinguished part-time Channel Islander, Ian Botham, whose friendship was greatly cherished.

John Arlott thus had much time in which to reflect upon a full life. Born in a cemetery lodge in Basingstoke on February 25, 1914, the only child of Jack and Nellie, he was not truly acquainted with his father until he came back, in khaki, from the Great War. A scholarship took John to Queen Mary's School for five years' secondary education; through his mother's Liberal Party activities he encountered (very shyly) Lloyd George, and was moved ever closer to an abiding commitment to Gladstonism. Two attempts to become an MP, in 1955 and 1959, were to turn into creditable failures, sparing him for cricket, to the gratification of his listeners.

From school, Arlott had taken an office job in Basingstoke's planning office, an institution he was to curse in later years for what it did to his hometown. Soon he was a £1-a-week "diet clerk" in a local mental hospital, where he worked for four years before joining the Southampton Police Force in 1934.

Cricket had already bitten quite deeply into him. His first Test match, at The Oval in 1926, viewed while in London on a family holiday, made the kind of decisive impact that such an experience often does on twelve-year-olds searching for direction. There followed an ever-deepening affection for the Hampshire county team, which was then the XI of Tennyson and Mead and Newman, coupled with a wide curiosity about all the other good things which life offered, not least the writings of Thomas Hardy.

John was to be a policeman for eleven years, marrying a nurse in 1940, enduring the uncertainties and horrors of wartime England, the intensive night-time bombing not only of the docks in Southampton, and finding relief in extensive reading. He began to give lectures and write verse. His *Cricket at Worcester 1938* was published by Cyril Connolly in *Horizon*, and he was on his way.

A son was born to John and Dawn in December 1944, a "handsome, gracious and generous" boy they named Jimmy, and who was to die in a road accident twenty-one years after, by which time his parents were divorced. The father thereafter was to wear no neck-tie but a black one.

While still a policeman, John had begun to broadcast. BBC Bristol gave him his first opportunity, producer Geoffrey Grigson prophetically pronouncing him a "natural broadcaster". His emerging talents and confidence next raised him to the heady task of delivering a peacetime message on behalf of the police to King George VI on Victory Night in 1945, shortly after which the upwardly mobile detective-sergeant found himself taken on as a literary programmes producer for BBC Overseas Services, and rubbing shoulders with the likes of Dylan Thomas, George Orwell, John Betjeman, E.M.Forster, and Laurie Lee. It also meant living in London, which was then a purely exciting matter.

Then came the first cricket commentary, the 1946 Indians at Worcester, scene of his role as Hampshire's substitute fieldsman in 1938 when they had run out of twelfth men and he, an ardent camp-follower, was enlisted, only to run himself ragged as Worcestershire piled up 413 for 3. He used to recall with amusement that, having seen Learie Constantine's acrobatic fielding in 1933, he tried to emulate him that day on the third-man boundary, got his legs in a tangle, and finished up in a startled female spectator's lap.

His commission of six broadcasts in 1946 did the trick. Soon he was discovering England and meeting more people – how he loved people – and making the wireless medium his own natural habitat. With further wonderment, he moved in among famous cricketers, talking and dining with them, leaving behind his own modest attempts to play the game (as a "slow and dull" batsman who once carried his bat for 9, and an off-break bowler of dubious action) in favour of a far more rewarding world of high craft and celebrity. His first tour book, *Indian Summer*, a slim but sweet volume printed on poor post-war Indian paper, followed.

He identified most strongly with the English county cricketer. The freemasonry and inherent honesty (as it then was) of that band of professional sportsmen captured his imagination most powerfully. Breakfasting with them, talking technique, sipping the evening away in a rural hostelry, absorbing cricket history was all John Arlott's heart's desire. And now he was being paid – though at first not hugely – to do this, and it stretched his credulity to the limit. In 1967 he was to become president of the Cricketers' Association, the county cricketers' "trade union", an honour which meant even more to him than his OBE (1970) and honorary MCC membership.

The Head of Outside Broadcasts having noted his "vulgar voice" and "compensatingly interesting mind", he was offered regular cricket commentary next summer, 1947, the "golden, vintage" summer when his voice became part of most British households. Meanwhile, he composed further sonnets, made further friends, began to dress almost dandyishly and stepped delightedly onto media's main highway.

Compton made his thousands of runs while Arlott, tall, handsome and imposing, spent some of his time protesting that, no, he was *not* Denis Compton. The euphoria was intense, but never such that he lost sight of the fact that there was more to life than cricket. Literature, gastronomy, aquatints, engraved glass, wine, and now travel – the first venture into Europe – swept him away from the village ethos, though he was ever to be prone to the nostalgic glance back over his shoulder to his origins. He developed skills as a host which were to leave deep impressions on all who ever crossed his homely threshold, firstly in London, then in the halcyon days at the Old Sun in the Hampshire village of Alresford, and finally, in his autumn days, on his "exile" home of Alderney. That old oak table could just as easily have been set in 19th Century Hambledon, when the minute-book recorded: "A wet day: only three members present: nine bottles of wine." Except it was an unusually quiet day at the Arlott household if only three diners were present.

After the big year of 1948, when Bradman's Australians conquered England, John made his first overseas cricket tour, to South Africa. It was an enthralling expedition, but his observations away from the cricket grounds bred a fierce indignation at apartheid's wicked injustices and stirred him eventually to be a key spokesman on that towering issue. If he was to be remembered for anything, he often asserted, it should be for his role in helping Basil D'Oliveira to settle in England, a move which was to set off a dramatic train of events that sealed South Africa's agonised isolation and contribute, however peripherally, to the eventual unlocking of that convoluted society. His unscripted speech on the matter in the Cambridge Union Debate showed

John Arlott (right) in his heyday: the most famous and best-loved voice in England.

what Parliament had missed.

John Arlott did not tour during future winters – apart from Australia in 1954-55 and again, briefly, in 1977 for the Centenary Test – for he loved England in all its seasons and hated tropical heat. He also had much else on his plate. For years he enjoyed watching and writing about football, until the game's morality soured. He built up his collection of first editions, aside from a burgeoning cricket library. It was an entertainment to walk with him through the arcades of Portobello Road and to see him greeted like a brother by the antiquarian booksellers. Charing Cross Road and Cecil Court were also on his beat, and dealers who sent him lists were usually contacted by return.

It must have seemed that he was turning into some kind of polymath when a fellow BBC producer asked him if he would care to write some hymns. His Harvest hymn took off all around the world, and made him more money per word than anything else he was ever to write. It was sung by the congregation at his funeral. His early religious faith had seemed scarcely to have survived his later personal losses, but there had in fact been communion in the final months of his life.

Snatches of Arlott commentary, had he but known it, were already easing themselves into the archives for rekindling years ahead. Few, however young, have not now heard his description of Bradman's final Test innings, when he was stunningly out second ball: ". . . pushes the ball gently in the direction of the Houses of Parliament . . . Hollies pitches the ball up slowly and – he's bowled! . . . and what do you say under these circumstances?" A tape exists of the frantic Gladwin leg-bye victory at Durban a few months later. Much else has scandalously been allowed to be destroyed, but posterity should understand what all the adulation is about if it refers to many of the later recordings which have survived.

The early Arlott voice, captivating though it proved at the time, seems harsh and over-earnest against the later tones, which were deeper, more slowly unfurled, timed with the touch of an Olivier. No-one can ever have been so much at home with a microphone or more compulsively in love with the medium of wireless.

As the busy summers passed, his work-rate manifested itself in further books on Test series, an ever-deepening interest in wine, and regular newspaper writing. His second son, Tim, had been born, and in John's own words, around this time he "hardly knew whether he was on his head or his heels". After his years as general instructor at the BBC Staff Training School, he gave up his pensionable job and wrote for the *Evening News* until 1955, became wine correspondent to the *News Chronicle* until its closure in 1960, and wrote football for *The Observer* before the most telling of his journalistic appointments came as cricket correspondent to *The Guardian* in 1968, in succession to Denys Rowbotham. To undertake the role once occupied by Neville Cardus thrilled the Hampshireman utterly.

He was lucky to have survived to take this plum offering, for only at the last minute had he been withdrawn from Manchester United's European journey in 1958 which ended in tragedy on the runway in Munich. Don Davies, who went in his stead, was killed. In that same year had come the "horrid" and "highly distasteful" business of divorce. But he was a much-changed man by now, master of the microphone, having, at Valentine Dyall's insistence, left the rusticity in his voice undisturbed by elocution coaching. The popular broadcaster may well have been polished by self-education, but the prime characteristic, the voice, remained raw, a trademark as resounding as the St Bruno tobacco advertisement in which he appeared.

With the domestic move back to Hampshire came the arrival of son Robert in 1963. For a year or two yet John was a radio panellist, connoisseur of cheeses, upon which subject a slim book was produced, and of the increasingly popular wine, which led to several weighty and learned volumes.

By the time he retired to Alderney in 1980, worn out by travelling and declining health, married now to Patricia, a former Lord's secretary, following the traumatic loss of Valerie, his second wife, he had written and edited dozens of cricket books, not only on Test series but mini-biographies of his idol Maurice Tate and a number of Hampshire beneficiaries, *Alletson's Innings*, a booklet about the first Test (1877), the charming little *Picture of Cricket*, and, more substantially, *Rothman's Jubilee History of Cricket*. He poured all his love and admiration of Jack Hobbs into a biography in 1981 (having founded the Master's Club in his honour in the sparkling year of 1953); but many consider his 1971 biography of Fred Trueman to have been his finest hardback. The long list under his name in *A Bibliography of Cricket* is testimony to his industrious effort across the years. For forty years he reviewed the books – and invariably generously – for *Wisden*.

John never refused an invitation to write a foreword, and may have set a record in the number he did, all warmly worded and delivered promptly. His own autobiography, *Basingstoke Boy*, which appeared in 1990, was condemned in some quarters, mainly because of its slightly unnatural third-person format. He probably left the venture too late, but it is still a rewarding and moving book.

As retirement loomed, the honours kept coming, an honorary MA from Southampton University high among them. Upon the establishment of *Wisden Cricket Monthly* in 1979 he became the senior member of the magazine's editorial board – having already engineered the Editor's entry into English cricket journalism some seven years earlier. John Arlott wrote for almost every issue of *WCM* over the twelve-and-a-half years' association, and was greatly valued as consultant as well as bosom friend.

Having sold most of his gigantic collection of cricket books and wine, and staged a farewell from the Old Sun which ran for days and nights, he took himself and wife Pat off to Alderney, where he soon found it necessary to dispose of most of his aquatints too, the salty air having threatened treachery to them, So intense was his sense of exhaustion that he toyed for a while not just with staying put on the island but taking up residence on Raz Island, a small outcrop cut off for several hours each day by the tide. But the need for people around him – how he loved that word "companionable" – soon reasserted itself.

He returned to the mainland from time to time: to film his sequences at The Oval and in the Bat and Ball pub and on Broadhalfpenny Down at Hambledon for the *Benson & Hedges Golden Great Batsmen* video; to do the public address at The Oval when the old England and Australia cricketers squeezed into flannels, and the sight of sixty-one-year-old Ray Lindwall struggling in to bowl, from the same end as in 1948, choked him and made him for once almost incomprehensible; to Basingstoke for his final public speech, when emotion did finally stop him in his nostalgic tracks; to Forest Mere health hydro, where he managed to smuggle in forbidden food and drink, with the complicity of friends; to Hambledon again for the *Times* bicentenary celebrations, when he raised himself in the low-beamed Bat and Ball and recited Nyren to a spellbound gathering.

The matchless conviviality of the October Alresford Fair golf days was no more, and the uproarious Christmas luncheons in Winchester were never the same without his presence. John Arlott was a completely civilised and compassionate man, exasperatingly modest, genial by natural disposition though not lacking in that crucial faculty where people were concerned. There were those – some eminent – of whom he heartily disapproved.

Members of his "court" were appreciated best when they engaged in honest, stimulating argument or, better, debate, with a generous and mandatory allocation of laughter, though his smile, indeed his entire range of facial expression, was somehow touched by a barely discernible essence of sadness which vanished only when the full Rabelaisian chuckle engaged gear, thick eyebrows raised high. His friendship was enormously enriching.

I was his final visitor from the mainland. He suffered during his final two years. By the cruellest irony it was the voice, that famous voice, which, far from simply weakening with age, could sometimes barely be summoned at all, so merciless were the emphysema and bronchitis. Forced to listen, with little strength for response, he would smile his crinkly smile, and wink by way of reassurance. His doctor, wife, sons and friends kept him going almost to the point where he was a medical marvel.

He asked, in his boredom and frustration, to be taken for a drive, for the second time that morning, and we rolled down the narrow road, round a rocky mound or two, and perched looking out to an angry grey sea that lashed the craggy shoreline with a wintry fury. He asked me to pour him a brandy from the flask in the glovebox. It went down in true Arlott style.

"I shan't live much longer," he whispered. And for once there was not a great deal this inadequate could offer by way of response to his ailing seventy-seven-year-old surrogate father.

He accompanied us next morning over the short distance to the airfield, and gazed expressionlessly ahead through the windscreen after we had said goodbye. I said I'd get over again next summer. He looked so diminutive now.

Three weeks later I was back at that spot, one of a planeload there for his funeral. The wind howled, but the sun glimmered through the windows of St Anne's Church. Among the close circle were Ian Botham and Mike Brearley, who both loved and understood him, and Leo Harrison, Hampshire wicketkeeper and friend of half-a-century. But pushing even further back through the years was seventy-eight-year-old Jack Donovan, a gentle eighteen-stone hearty, who had been a schoolfriend of John Arlott's sixty-seven years previously. He did what few in that church could have done: he held to his course throughout a loving address, wavering only at the very end, as he said, "Rest in peace, John. Goodbye, old friend." The man of Hampshire was then borne to his final resting-place.

Seldom can there have been such determinedly happy sounds after a funeral – an English one at any rate – as the gathering adjourned to the church hall for three hours before dispersal, many back to the airfield. The friend we had all lost was central to the anecdotes. The universal feeling was that "this is what he would have wanted" – an end to the tears, no maudlin shaking of heads. The suffering was over.

Thanks to recording technology, John Arlott's voice will be heard at the touch of a switch and his kindly face can be called up on the screen for ever more. For this we must be thankful.

There falls across this one December day/The light remembered from those suns of June . . . .

Wisden Cricket Monthly, February 1992

Another World Cup, this time staged in Australia and New Zealand, left the chronicler exhausted – yet again:

Every Four Years is Enough

TIRING, WASN'T it? Thirty-nine World Cup matches in thirty-three days, all monitored closely: watched live or on TV or via highlights nocturnally recorded, with intermittent radio support. Who slumped over the office desk after viewing through half the night? Who overshot his station, deep in nightmarish sleep, with Wasim Akram belting the ball clean off the screen and into the china cabinet? Was the reversal in England's form and fortunes – like a lift falling down the shaft, its cable snapped – too much for your wrought-up emotions?

Well, spare a thought not only for the players, who cumulatively travelled 1.4 million miles, but for a chap who wanted nothing more than to recover gently from the rigours of 1991, pottering around on his little bit of Queensland, murmuring Banjo Patterson's tender, evocative *Clancy of the Overflow* as he tugged at the elephant grass, sorted out the loathsome cane toads, and trimmed away at the eucalypts which threatened the life-enhancing view of the Pacific.

The problem was that without the Banjo volume propped on a fence-post, it was necessary to remember the verse. And with a head full of strike rates and batting averages, of match starting times, interstate time zone differences (*five* of them at one point), and vital thoughts on each country's prospects of reaching the semi-finals, it was exasperating to get no more than halfway through a verse before drying up; even if the audience was merely a kookaburra and two lorikeets.

> *I am sitting in my dingy little office, where a stingy*
> *Ray of sunlight struggles feebly down between the houses tall.*
> *And the foetid air and gritty of the dusty, dirty city*
> *Through the open window floating, spreads its foulness over all.*

Such fear of the metropolis might almost deter a man from pursuing his job, but the time came for braving the highway to Brisbane and the traffic jams around Woolloongabba. And, ultimately, the hell on wheels known as Sydney and the unusually clamorous Melbourne, which one seems to get to see only when that city welcomes the world. You could hardly move in the jam-packed streets of Melbourne in 1977 when the Centenary Test was played in the midst of the Moomba Festival, with Abba also in town, and a royal visit – by Her Majesty the Queen.

"She" was there this time too, of course, in the person of "comedian" Gerry Connelly, who succeeded in extending Prime Minister Keating's blundering division of the country. Offended, Gooch and Botham walked out of the World Cup dinner on the eve of the final, prompting shoals of letters, both of eager approval and scathing condemnation, to newspapers across the land. "I love my country and I can't put up with that sort of crap," explained Botham, who clearly is no regular viewer of *Spitting Image*.

I wrenched myself away from Queensland early one bright Sunday, to be wafted south on a smooth 106-seat high-wing British Aerospace 146-300 (Martin Crowe's World Cup batting average?) that completed a typically easy flight through Australian skies – to land in a Sydney dark under rain-clouds, with the mood soon to be unimproved by the refusal of the dustcoated attendant on the SCG members' gate to acknowledge the ACB World Cup media pass. Patience triumphed in the end over the temptation to defy the bristling moustache and jump the turnstile, as Sid Barnes and Denis Compton both once did.

> *And the hurrying people daunt me, and their pallid faces haunt me*
> *As they shoulder one another in their rush and nervous haste.*
> *With their eager eyes and greedy, and their stunted forms and weedy,*
> *For townsfolk have no time to grow, they have no time to waste.*

All the compelling cricket of that England-South Africa semi-final is doomed to be forgotten beneath the furore surrounding the rain-wrecked finish. England would surely have choked South Africa's final charge before the rain came, and South Africa would surely have found 22 off 13 balls once the ball had become slippery. The umpires were surely right to have observed the rules as written. It was the last instance of rain interference in the competition, the system of target adjustment after time lost having been fiercely condemned throughout. The method must not be repeated. Rumour had it that the scheme was Richie Benaud's brainchild, and many of those who had watched Channel 9 with the volume up claimed that he alone raised no objection to the cruel distortions it sometimes imposed. Importantly, no country claimed to have objected to it before the World Cup started.

Hours down memory's avenues with Jock Livingston, the old New South Wales and Northants left-hander, now retired in Sydney; a brief chance meeting with the last of the great commentators, Alan McGilvray, now eighty-two, in good shape; and a cheerio call to Bill O'Reilly, eighty-six, housebound since he lost a leg but still fiery in his condemnation of one-day cricket and all its absurdities. "I suppose you won't know what's hit you when you watch your next Test match and they're all wearing white instead of these technicolor pyjamas?" he snorted.

Then on to Melbourne for the big one. The best kind of build-up had to be a stroll around the city, savouring the anticipatory excitement, careful to avoid a messy end to the daydream under the iron wheels of a tram. Then came the first shock: a young man with shaven head entirely whitewashed, cross of St George across his face and across the back of his flat head, shirt strung to his belt. Others similar were spotted, and once more arose within the revulsion that only extremist partisan supporters can generate – soon to be matched by shrieking flag-brandishing Pakistan supporters. It can have a heavy bearing on whom one wishes to see win.

To be there was everything. The new edifice known as the Great Southern Stand stretched up to the sky and the hubbub was of battleground proportions. [Pakistan 249 for 6 beat England 227.] It is no small privilege to have been present at all five World Cup finals. Maybe only a dozen of us have managed it, perhaps including Sir Colin Cowdrey, who handed the costly and breakable trophy to Imran. The former England captain, representing a statelier age, stood only a few feet from the spot where he made the first of his many Test centuries. It happened on a pre-1956 Olympic Games MCG, pre-Packer, pre-Great Southern Stand; and, come to think of it, pre-limited-overs cricket, an era from which Imran himself happens to be a relic.

And now it was deepest, darkest night, another poorly supervised press conference having come and gone, and the walk back to the hotel was long, the air fresh, the mood deflated. It had been a long tournament, a long season, with greed again taking cricket up the wrong track.

To a symphony of twanging hamstrings the World Cup had run its cluttered course. Everyone, it seemed, loved South Africa. West Indies' "sins" of early 1991 seemed forgotten or forgiven. But the naked hatred flowing to and fro across the Tasman Sea was dreadful to the ear and eye.

With the "a" having snapped off my typewriter, I was probably more concerned that West Indies should play in the final against anyone bar ustr li , New Ze l nd, P kist n, South fric , or Sri L nk .

Clatter of suitcase and hasty exit from Melbourne at dawn on a flight only hours after the nocturnal press conference, remembered for Imran's command performance. An Eastwest 727 this time flew right across country direct to Coolangatta.

And he sees the vision splendid of the sunlit plains extended,
And at night the wondrous glory of the everlasting stars.

Wisden Cricket Monthly, May 1992

Sportsmanship Test

SOMEWHAT UNEXPECTEDLY Pakistan land in England for their Test and one-day international tour as one-day champions at the 50-overs game. They are also, of course, now challenging for the title of world Test champions, having recently drawn a series with West Indies, who are undergoing the painful process of regeneration. England, runners-up in the World Cup, also levelled a Test series against West Indies only months ago, so even and competitive series of five-dayers and one-dayers are in prospect.

The deeper significance, however, concerns relations between the two countries following the ill-natured 1987 series in England and the downright acrimonious series in Pakistan in 1987-88, to be remembered always for the shocking images of England captain Mike Gatting in heated conflict with umpire Shakoor Rana and for the perpetual hostility that soiled the series.

Imran Khan may perhaps have heard of Bill Woodfull, Australia's highly respected captain during the 1932-33 "Bodyline" series. Does he realise how history is about to repeat itself yet again? In 1934 Woodfull, a man of solid integrity, led the Australians on a "bridge-mending" tour of England, when cricket's greatest need was for the bad tastes of '32-33 to be cleansed from everyone's mouth. Good, sportsmanlike, honest, attractive cricket was urgently needed. Just as it is now.

It is therefore heavily incumbent upon Imran, or whoever leads the Pakistanis, and Graham Gooch too, to see to it that all their vast experience and good sense are brought to bear on the conduct of the 1992 series. Knowledgeable cricket-lovers recognise that there is an enormous potential for admiration of the Pakistanis: their stylish, aggressive batsmen, their fleet fielding, their fast bowling, their leg-spin variations. They may have the collective ability to shape as one of the finest teams of all time. But none of this hope will come to anything if there are managerial outbursts or misbehaviour on the field.

Some may wonder what right Ian Botham had to warn Imran to "pull his players into line" in order to avert a nasty atmosphere in the forthcoming series. Whatever one thinks about England's bulky *enfant terrible*, he could never legitimately be accused of being unsporting. He saw from close quarters a blatant attempt to cheat him out during the 1987 series with Pakistan, and in last month's World Cup final he and other England batsmen were subjected to foul language unbecoming of cricketers of any persuasion.

Botham spotlit Aamer Sohail. This talented cricketer had already forked out $A250 for stupidly letting his mouth off in the Australia match at Perth, where his fine was oddly coupled with the Man of the Match award. Also fined in that World Cup match – which happened to mark the upturn in Pakistan's performance – was wicketkeeper Moin Khan and over-earnest Australian fast bowler Mike Whitney. Moin struck most observers as being a lesser wicketkeeper than David Boon. But his relentless chattering, commonly confused in the modern game with "professional commitment" (were gentlemanly Jack Hobbs or genial Patsy Hendren uncommitted?), seems to appeal to his captain. It is time his captain appealed to him: to *shut up*! Or will it be left to the umpires to curb the tedious "Catch it!" cry, uttered every time a ball is played – even along the ground. Then we should doubtless hear the bleatings about officious English umpires once more.

If the Pakistanis are smart they will resolve to play like real champions, letting their batting, bowling and fielding do the talking for them. Crowds the length and breadth of England will then accord them the credit and the acclamation they crave, joining with the thousands of expatriate Pakistanis in the enjoyment of quality cricket from the old brigade and the new.

Wisden Cricket Monthly, May 1992

Too much to hope for, alas. Tempers frayed and hostility, physical and verbal, marred the series. As for the childish cry of "Catch it!", far from being curbed, it wormed its way into everyday procedure in the field of play.

A book called England Expects, written by Mark Peel, brought reminders of one of the most popular of English cricketers. I was glad of the chance to review it:

Living and Dying for Cricket

HARDENED TEST cricketers seldom openly weep at the loss of a colleague, but many did when Kenny Barrington died, during that dreadful tour of West Indies in 1981. As coach and confidant, a father figure, he won the respect and often the love of the generation of cricketers with whom he worked, just as in his own playing days he was revered by Surrey and England supporters for his ceaseless conscientiousness at the crease. That dedication sprang from ambition, of course, and also from the insecurity of a man whose background was unpretentious and God-fearing. He was neat, conservative, superstitious. He was endowed, alas, with a fragile nervous system, so that the strain of it all caused a build-up of neurosis that triggered one heart attack to end his playing career and another a dozen years later that ended his life. Ray Illingworth was surely not exaggerating when he said that Barrington "laid down his life for cricket".

How he could ever have bowled leg-spin so successfully with his fraught temperament is a marvel in itself. But then anxiety is an imponderable menace. The early runs were made aggressively, but initial failure in Tests forced a resolve to tighten defence and give nothing away. His final Test average of 58.67 (6806 runs) was considerably higher than his first-class average. But what a price he paid. He took a physical battering, particularly from the West Indian fast bowlers, and because he was convinced that he threw he had a phobia about Charlie Griffith. He thus became a marked man. Walter Robins told him it was because he antagonised the fasties by doffing his cap after evading a bouncer (Randall used to infuriate Lillee in this way); Barrington, though, was only being his naturally jolly self. He scarcely knew *how* to take the mick. The image of him sobbing at night as he nursed his physical and psychological wounds is heart-rending.

The 1961-62 tour of India was the making of him. The crowds loved his clowning, and he confirmed his ability to sweat it out for hour after hour. Two years later his 256 at Old Trafford was one of the longest innings ever mounted against Australia. Elsewhere, his fierce determination not to get out led to a suspicion of selfishness, and, in 1965, to his being dropped for the funereal pace of his Edgbaston century against New Zealand. He was badly stung at the time, but later, being the reasonable chap he was, he saw it as reasonable.

One of his greatest knocks was the 143 at Port-of-Spain in 1968 – this after he had reached breaking-point in 1966, only to come back with century after century in the 1967 Tests – but he still found touring the Caribbean a fairly distasteful affair, as revealed in his letters to his wife: "We're being taken for the biggest ride . . . the umpiring, the crowd and Charlie . . . it is downright cheating . . . I must be bloody mad to come out here."

He was a very loving, caring husband, and it was a blessing that, as his active cricket ended, after fifteen years of marriage the Barringtons had a son. Had Ken not been beset by peculiarly worrying tours as England manager/coach, that small family might have been spared such early grief. The final few pages are painful reading.

Had the man [John Major] who wrote the foreword been at No.10 in those days he would doubtless have seen to it that this cricketer who displayed such honourable patriotism and high personal standards was given some decoration or other. Too late now.

Wisden Cricket Monthly, August 1992

Ken Barrington, a true Brit.

Zimbabwe's politically-motivated election to Test status in 1992 alarmed sceptics everywhere:

Come in, Dear Weaklings

ZIMBABWE, ACCORDING to the former Prime Minister of Rhodesia, Ian Smith, is "going to the dogs". Seeking clarification from one who should know, we are told that Mr Smith is short on pessimism. Zimbabwe, we are told, has *already gone* to the dogs. What a fillip for that nation, therefore, is its elevation to full Test match status, as granted by the International Cricket Council in July.

It also happens to be a disastrous blow to Test cricket's normally well-guarded sanctity as the supreme form of the game's expression. Zimbabwe's election to the top shelf cannot properly be justified, and renders future results and averages farcical. Their team is not as strong now, nor its future as bright, as when previous applications were rejected.

So what has changed? Did that one-day victory over England at Albury in the World Cup swing the voting? If so, let's have Holland in. They have beaten Australian and English teams in their time. Was a complex deal struck in the Lord Harris Gardens? Let Zimbabwe in, and England can stage the next World Cup and have its South African tour "rebels" freed by Christmas? Might South Africa's continuing claims to the next World Cup be nothing more than a clever cover? They in turn will be glad that Zimbabweans now have no need to try for Test representation by moving south.

It is some years since it became generally if reluctantly accepted that sport and politics cannot be separated. Zimbabwe's elevation has about it a pronounced aroma of political engineering. The cost to cricket will be the diluting effect it has on Test cricket. It is tedious enough to have to append footnotes to certain records springing from the county game, explaining that they were arrived at by contrived cricket. The addition of this weakling to the family of Test nations will see them merely tolerated as non-profitable visitors, lower on the scale even than Sri Lanka, who are still awaiting a first invitation to play West Indies after ten years of Test status. Runs and wickets secured against Zimbabwe may be qualified in italicised footnotes by the discerning, but they will still assist someone, in all probability, to overtake Gavaskar's and Hadlee's overall Test records.

It adds a huge oddity to the history of cricket that while President Mugabe (who once acknowledged that cricket civilises people) snatches agricultural land from Zimbabwe's whites for minimal compensation, and with the drought turning much of his land to dust, a former Test cricketer from the region, Jackie du Preez (South Africa 1966-67), says unequivocally: "We are simply not good enough. I am afraid we will be slaughtered and embarrassed. The ICC and Zimbabwe are taking a very long gamble."

That gamble may not be unconnected to the old England-Australia veto power, which has never been employed but still offends the newer Test nations. What chance the ICC meeting of 2020 being in Harare, with England's delegates struggling to justify retention on the full Test panel?

Wisden Cricket Monthly, September 1992

There was worse to come. Bangladesh, an enthusiastic but essentially feeble cricket country, were given Test status, and the ICC dithered over umpire referrals, gave a "World XI" match in Sydney Test match status, forfeiting more of its credibility with every passing year.

Further trouble had come during that summer of 1992, causing a distraught editor to pen yet another anxious leader while wondering what had happened to the joys that cricket had once brought:

Who's Doing the Tampering?

CRICKET ONCE again finds itself in agonised contortions, and all because of muddled thinking by those charged with the running of the game. Fear of something – preposterous legal action, perhaps, or a holy war in the streets of Bradford? – persuaded the ICC officials to stifle the matter of the ball replacement by the umpires during England's one-day international against Pakistan at Lord's on August 23. *WCM* has established that the ball was replaced under the terms of Law 42 (5) (Unfair Play). Match referee Deryck Murray's statement was castrated before publication. It read, finally, only that the ball had been changed. The immediate conclusion can only have been that had the ball been changed merely because it was out of shape or had gone soft (Law 5), such a clarification could easily have been made public. That it was not has left a cloud of suspicion over Pakistan's bowlers.

Why should the chairman of the ICC be seeking suggestions from member countries as to means of combating ball-tampering when a precise procedure is already laid out in the Laws, supported by the ICC's own Code of Conduct? And what went wrong in 1991 at The Oval, when umpire John Holder warned the England captain that, in his opinion, there had been untoward damage to the ball's surface? There was no refutation, and the ball was not changed. But that vigilant umpire was "rested" from the Test panel this summer, and was therefore unable to direct his eagle eye onto proceedings. Those umpires [John Hampshire and Ken Palmer] who did so at Lord's in August acted only after their attention had been drawn to the ball's condition by Allan Lamb, who has since paid a heavy price for his "They gouge the ball" claims in the *Daily Mirror*.

Now former cricketers are queuing up to confess to the things they once did to cricket balls. We are all the wiser for these tales of scientific seam-lifting and surface-gouging with fingernails, bottle-tops (sometimes secreted inside wristbands) and carpenter's nails. Even before George Hirst and Bart King perfected swing/swerve bowling at the turn of the century, Peel and Peate knew how to pack mud onto a ball to make it misbehave, and in Lumpy Stevens' time, in the 18th Century, the underhand bowlers had it so much their own way that they could legitimately select their own – and understandably the roughest – pitch. Why not now, some argue, allow bowlers to do what they like to the ball? The answer has to be that cricket is already quite capable of turning into farce, without adding the monstrosity of a charter for gouging.

We have seen the sort of swing from Pakistan's fast bowlers which would have delighted Benny Goodman. If it yet transpires that the movement has been emphasised by illegal "dimples" on the rough side of the ball, then their achievements would be discredited. This would be sad, as truth often is. The answer lies with that ball locked away in a TCCB cupboard at Lord's. The mystery may well yet deepen should that ball conveniently go missing.

Wisden Cricket Monthly, October 1992

It came as little surprise when no trace could be found of that ball. It later became clear that administrators and match officials were terrified at the prospect of an international incident, though there were those, including third umpire Don Oslear, who fearlessly stood by the assertion that ball-tampering had occurred. There were instances in other matches too, and similar cover-ups. The traditional joy of cricket was under sustained bombardment in this hard modern world.

Welcome light relief came with David Lloyd's book G'Day Ya Pommie B...... and Other Cricketing Memories, reviewed in the autumn of 1992:

Clever Quips

"THOMMO" GAVE "Bumble" the title for his collection of funny stories, shortly after bouncing one of his 99.88mph deliveries into the Lancastrian's throat. But it is not a violent book. It is very, very funny; which is why we ran an extract in our September issue. It helps if you can "hear" the text in Lloyd's rich Lancashire warble. Even if not, the snips are health-enhancing. Take his response to Alec Bedser's proud claim that he was fit enough to bowl 45 overs a day: "You can't have been bowling so well, then, if you had to keep bowling 45 overs every day. Couldn't you get anyone out?" There are some ball-tampering tales, topically, the classic being umpire Bill Alley's utterance after detecting some sharp fingerwork on the seam by a Lancashire bowler: "If you don't get 7 for 20 with a ball like that I'll report you to Lord's."

Wisden Cricket Monthly, October 1992

An invitation to reflect on the days of first-grade cricket proved irresistible:

And I Look Through My Tears

CRICKET HAS swallowed me up during the twenty-odd years I've worked in England as an author, editor, film-maker and collector, but the best years in so many ways remain those seasons when I knew the high tension of first-grade cricket in Sydney.

I'd grown up with the St George club alongside fellows such as Norm O'Neill, Warren Saunders, John Cope and Reg Gasnier. But it took a switch to Paddington to get me into first grade. We hardly ever won a match, for Arthur Morris and Ron Archer were on their last legs and there was not much talent coming through; but it was a great privilege to play home matches at Rushcutters Bay and Trumper Park, which would always stir the history-minded.

But one match tends to stand out across a span of what I'm horrified to see is already thirty years. It was Paddington's away match against Western Suburbs at Pratten Park, which I knew well enough from my schooldays at Canterbury Boys' High. It was a one-dayer, just after Christmas 1962.

And was it any wonder that an ordinary cricketer such as myself felt an extra edge of tension at the prospect of facing Alan Davidson, who was then not only in his prime but aiming to prove his fitness for a place in the Test team in the midst of the Ashes series against Dexter's team.

The first problem was Bob Simpson. He made 134 not out and showed that *he* was OK for the next Test. I remember skidding to the grass time and again at mid-on as Simmo's on-drives proved incompatible with my short spikes. Ken Muller, one of Harold Larwood's sons-in-law, made 38, and Jim de Courcy, his Test career ended not so long before, hit 59 before the declaration at 3 for 251.

Davo, Les Ellis and Johnny Watkins then swept our top order away, the first six batsmen, including Davo's cousin Peter and our best bat, Ted Cotton, making only 44 between them. Now our skipper was David de Carvalho, a man very strong on theory and always effusive when it came to giving instructions. As I grabbed my gloves and bat, he told me to walk very slowly to the middle, for every minute counted. The follow-on was a distinct danger, and since our batting was proving inadequate we needed to come on strong with the time-wasting.

Well, I took "de Carbuncle" extremely seriously and must have taken three or four minutes to reach the middle (no "Timed Out" in those days; now it is firmly embedded in the Laws).

And there, gathered on the pitch, was a reception committee. This is too genteel a publication for me to reiterate the harshness of the greetings. All I'll say is that the sight of de Courcy's snarl, his teeth back in the dressing-room and only his "fangs" showing, did nothing to relax me. Davidson bowled; I nudged and nicked and played and missed; Simmo spun a few, as did Watkins.

Somehow I made 31 – only a thick-edge single off Alan Davidson, if I remember right – before wicketkeeper Theodore caught a glance off Les Ellis's deceptively fast bowling. We went away with the "triumph" of merely a first-innings defeat.

I drove my little green Morris Minor down Canterbury Road, a hero returning to his wife and three little children. Debbie was busy cooking; the boys were knocking a ball about in the yard; so I gave a ball-by-ball account of my afternoon adventure to my four-month-old daughter. To spare her any nightmares, I mentioned nothing of de Courcy's fangs.

A belated apology, Wests, for my gamesmanship. But it's not as if it cost you the premiership. Saints won it again.

Now let me think: how long did I take to reach the wicket against them?

The Magpie Monitor: Western Suburbs Cricket Club, October 1992

One of the game's greatest and most colourful figures died late in 1992:

Was He Not the Greatest?

LIKE JOHN WAYNE, he strode in from the West, six-foot-three, eyes gleaming and quizzical, a throaty chuckle ever ready to crack the awed silence. "Tiger" O'Reilly, best described as a *spin* rather than *slow* bowler, was not of the Mailey or Grimmett mould, trading in patient, gentle guile and flight. His was more the mentality of the fast bowler, naked aggression marking his run-up, delivery and facial expression. With his huge hands he imparted great spin – as much from the off with his steeply-bouncing googly as from leg – his strong wrist whipping in the overspin. Even if his bent-kneed delivery slightly lessened his height advantage, his bowling brought prolific results and made him the severest challenge a batsman could know during the 1930s.

Was he the greatest bowler of all? England's S.F.Barnes and George Lohmann once seemed to have been the only rivals for the title, all things considered. Some of the moderns, especially Lillee and Hadlee, have come into such discussions. O'Reilly quietly knew his own worth: when asked if he had ever run out a non-striker who was backing up too far he laughed and said that when he was bowling, no batsman was ever that keen to get to the far end. Any speculation about supremacy goes a long way to being settled by Sir Donald Bradman's statement that O'Reilly was the best bowler he ever faced or saw.

William Joseph O'Reilly was born on December 20, 1905 (R.G.Menzies' eleventh birthday) in White Cliffs, in the far west of New South Wales, "where the crows fly backwards to keep the dust out of their eyes". His grandfather, Peter O'Reilly, had emigrated from Ballyconnell in 1865, and Bill remained deeply proud of his Irish ancestry. In 1917 the family moved to Wingello, where Bill's interest in cricket was fired sufficiently for him to take a seven-mile walk along the railway track in his ever-lengthening stride. His first "cricket ball" had been a banksia root, chiselled into shape, but the decisive day came when his brother Jack returned from a visit to Sydney with the "secret" of Arthur Mailey's googly. Young Bill soon mastered it with a tennis ball, and his fate was sealed.

Cricket sometimes seemed an unduly tough game, as when he played at Bowral in 1925 and bowled unavailingly while a diminutive seventeen-year-old named Bradman carved out an unbeaten 234 on the matting-over-concrete pitch. Bill always claimed that the Don was dropped twice by an overweight slip fielder who was busy lighting his pipe at the vital moment. The romantic ending came a week later, when the match was resumed (at Wingello, such were the rules) and O'Reilly bowled the embryo world champion immediately with a beautiful leg-break, behind his pads.

His first-class debut came in 1927-28, but after two further matches for New South Wales he was given a teaching post in the bush. He fumed at this interruption, which, in retrospect, he reckoned cost him a place on Australia's 1930 tour of England.

In his first Test, in 1931-32, he took four South African wickets at Adelaide for 155 off 81 six-ball overs in a match dominated by Grimmett (14 wickets) and Bradman (299 not out). O'Reilly instantly relished the "glorious company" he was keeping.

It took him, he said, about fifty years to get over the 1932-33 "Bodyline" series. He believed that Australia should have retaliated to England's hostile leg-stump attack. No great batsman himself, he swished left-handedly or ran for cover when his turn came. But his role as bowler was grandly fulfilled, his 27 wickets in the five Tests being next to Larwood's 33. Though he seldom changed his opinion on anything, he was to admit in later years that the once-hated Jardine was, in the confines of the press-box, quite likeable.

The first of his nine-wicket hauls came next season against Victoria, and then came his first overseas tour. Australia's sweet success in England in 1934 owed much to Bradman and Ponsford, who both averaged 94, and to McCabe (60), but the bowling responsibility rested with O'Reilly (28 wickets at 24.93) and Grimmett (26 at 26.72). Affording the English no aesthetic pleasure with his lumbering method, "Tiger" used his pace-change and spin variety to mop up 11 wickets in the opening victory at Trent Bridge, his second-innings 7 for 54 becoming his Test career-best figures.

In the third Test, at Manchester during a heatwave, he shocked England with the wickets of Walters, Wyatt and Hammond in four balls. Hendren and Leyland centuries brought massive recovery (627 for 9), but O'Reilly toiled bravely on to take 7 for 189 in 59 overs. "Never say die" is a cliché which could have been coined for him.

He still had a regret. Had his impulsive batting not let him down in the Lord's Test, Australia might have saved the follow-on and *he* rather than Verity (15 wickets) would have had access to a pitch nicely gingered up by the rain.

During the tour, O'Reilly topped the list with 109 wickets at 17.05. His wizened little mate Grimmett also took 109 (19.81), hardly ever removing his cap, unlike O'Reilly, who was unabashed at his baldness.

The tour produced his best-ever first-class analysis in the Somerset match: 9 for 38, five of them lbw. With the stumps flying and short leg taking catches off the splice, it was as if another "demon" after Spofforth had come to haunt England.

By 1935-36 he was off on tour again, this time taking South Africa by storm. He (27 wickets at 17.04) and Grimmett (44 at 14.59) demolished the opposition, setting up a 4-0 victory which sealed it as a tour which became, for O'Reilly, "by far the most pleasant experience of my cricket career".

Not unexpectedly, he proved to be Australia's most penetrative bowler again in the thrilling 1936-37 series against England, taking 25 wickets at 22.20. The discontent now was internal. He, his cherished team-mate Stan McCabe, Fleetwood-Smith and Leo O'Brien were hauled up before the Australian Board on fuzzy and flimsy charges relating to behaviour but almost certainly not related to a barely tangible religious divide which had evolved in the Australian side. O'Reilly remained not only mystified but unforgiving, but he went on to take 5 for 51 and 3 for 58 for his country in the fifth and deciding Test at Melbourne.

In grade cricket he did what S.F.Barnes used to do at non-first-class level: devastated the opposition with few exceptions. He topped the Sydney grade averages 12 times in 14 seasons. Firstly for North Sydney and then St George, he took 814 wickets at 8.35. He could be paternal not only to promising young St George players such as Arthur Morris and Ray Lindwall but to opponents as well, provided they showed guts as well as skill. He was probably only once rendered speechless and that was when the teenaged Sid (S.G.) Barnes stretched up to pat him on the shoulder as they left the field for tea and condescendingly told the world's best bowler that he thought he'd bowled pretty well.

Barnes was one of O'Reilly's team-mates on the 1938 tour of England. "Tiger" never pretended to recall that venture with anywhere near the same pleasure as 1934. Grimmett was missing, for a start, and although O'Reilly's five wickets in each innings at Headingley set up a victory which ensured retention of the Ashes, he never quite forgave the Oval groundsman for England's world record 903 for 7 in the last Test, when his 85 overs of sweat and toil brought him 3 for 178, including weary Hutton's wicket at 364. That and the Trent Bridge pitch were, he growled, "dosed up to the eyeballs".

Apart from the "oddity" Test at Wellington after the war, when he took 5 for 14 and 3 for 19 on rickety knees in Australia's two-day victory over poor relation New Zealand, that was the end of Bill O'Reilly's Test career. In 135 first-class matches he took 774 wickets at 16.60. (In 133 matches S.F.Barnes took 719 at 17.09. Dare one suggest that the Australian operated, in general, on firmer pitches and against stronger opposition?) He dismissed England's supreme champion Hammond 10 times in 19 Tests. Suggestions that left-hander Leyland had his measure annoyed O'Reilly, who would defiantly point out that he got him nine times in 16 Tests. As for Sutcliffe, Bill got him six times in nine Tests, and his bellowed lbw appeals were about the only thing ever to ruffle the cool Yorkshireman.

After the war he began writing for the *Sydney Morning Herald*, guided initially by the aptly named Tom Goodman. His offerings were direct, though crafted from a broad knowledge extending well beyond the cricket world. He sometimes became emotional, especially when a young spin bowler arrived on the scene. He championed the likes of Kerry O'Keeffe and David Hourn, and saw from the start what a talented player Steve Waugh was. His detestation of limited-overs cricket – the "pyjama game" as he named it – with its spirit of restriction and denial and absence of subtlety, was expressed at every opportunity.

He scoffed at coaches, never forgave English cricket in that "the English couldn't handle leg-spin so they decided to destroy it", and never lost his schoolmaster's instinct insofar as a letter of complaint from Geoff Lawson at the harshness of something O'Reilly had written about him was returned copiously marked with corrections to grammar. Here, after all, was a man who had met the great Australian literary figure Henry Lawson in 1914.

Early in 1988 came his final stint in the press-box, high in the Noble Stand at Sydney. It was one of life's unimagined privileges to sit with him throughout that match. He described the placements of McCabe's hooks and pulls during his 187 in the Bodyline series. Interruptions were frequent. Every journalist in Australia wanted to interview him and photograph him. He was, after all, one of only three cricketers named among the 200 Greatest Australians to mark the Bicentennial.

O'Reilly's name was to be immortalised on a grandstand at North Sydney Oval and later at the SCG. It must at last have seemed that losing his left big toenail seventeen seasons running had been worthwile after all.

Sir Len Hutton, who mastered him with the bat but could never break his will, said: "Every ball that O'Reilly bowled was a potential wicket-taker. He didn't bowl what they call 'rest balls'. Every time that ball left his hand it was O'Reilly's intention to get somebody out. I enjoyed batting against him. He helped me to concentrate a great deal." Enough said?

Wisden Cricket Monthly,
November 1992

"Tiger" O'Reilly, spin bowler with the temperament of a quickie.

The Right of a Writer to Criticise

EVEN A public rebuke by the Duke of Norfolk failed to silence E.M.Wellings when he felt that the attitude of Ted Dexter and his England team in Australia in 1962-63 warranted criticism. His response, in print, was to the effect that he was "unrepentant and would risk incarceration in the Tower of London to uphold the right of a writer to criticise in matters of public interest".

It was not unknown for readers of the *Evening News* to threaten withdrawal of their patronage as an expression of their outrage at Wellings's views. But they were often misjudging him, for his attacks on the game's adverse trends and ill-conceived pieces of administration were the compulsion of a man whose regard for cricket was unusually deep. He had played it well, with and against most of the pre-war household names, and was an outstanding analyst. He was also a solitary man, especially so in the twilight of his life. He died in hospital in Basingstoke on September 10, aged eighty-three, his last years blighted by arthritis.

There were those – whose own turn undoubtedly will come – who accused Lyn Wellings of living in the past. In fact, he had been living in the past for a long time. In 1968, having had lunch with him and J.M.Kilburn during the Oval Test, a young journalist [me] departed quite dejected, temporarily convinced that cricket had ceased to be worth watching with the departure of Woolley, Verity and Hammond.

Born on April 6, 1909 in Alexandria, Egypt, where his father was an executive with Lipton's Tea, Evelyn Maitland Wellings was sent to prep school in Bournemouth at six, proceeding to Cheltenham College and thence Christ Church, Oxford.

At Oxford, coached by J.T.Hearne and G.A.Faulkner (whose coaching staff he subsequently joined for a time), he secured Blues in 1929 and 1931, having fallen foul of the ruling faction in 1930. He won another Blue for golf. He took 5 for 118 in the 1929 Varsity match and 5 for 25 with off-spin on a helpful pitch in 1931, when Oxford, given a lead by Pataudi's 238 not out, won by eight wickets.

His best figures were 6 for 75 against Leicestershire in 1931, but his best *bowling*, he always felt, was 3 for 93 against mighty Yorkshire, when he bagged the prize wickets of Sutcliffe, Leyland and Mitchell. Even at eighty, Wellings brushed his ear with a high arm as he demonstrated his long-ago method.

In 36 first-class matches he took 108 wickets (30.15) and scored 836 runs (20.39), his sole century coming at Eastbourne in 1933, an "excellent" 125 for Leveson Gower's XI v Cambridge. Four of his matches were for Surrey in 1931, though without distinction. Yet that season afforded him "the nicest thing that ever happened": as he took his place in the cover field, his idol Jack Hobbs smiled and chatted to him. Those who knew Wellings in later years might be surprised that this flinty character was also "smitten" by Woolley (whom he once had lbw for 95).

Having watched his first Test in 1926, at The Oval, where another schoolboy debutant spectator, John Arlott, also happened to be a particle of the crowd, Wellings was to start reporting on Tests while still a young man. He served the *Evening News* from 1938 until retirement in 1973. He reported over 200 Test matches and toured Australia nine times, his match notes always meticulously compiled. The 1946-47 venture remained his favourite.

From the peaceful, dignified press-boxes of the 1930s, Wellings learned to live with changing standards, though never uncomplainingly. He once hurled his typewriter from the enclosure; denied the assistance of a copy boy, he once let his half-hourly dispatches pile up beside him until a telephonist was frantically sent; incensed at the intrusion of a television camera as he sat in the front row of the press-box at Lord's, he diverted its scrutiny by sticking a rude word on the window.

When the 1970 South African tour of England was threatened by political forces, Wellings had some brass Springbok badges minted, to be sold for three shillings in aid of a Save the Tour fund. Thousands of the little pinned emblems were found in his study after his death.

He castigated those (not least *Wisden* and its editor, the irascible Norman Preston) who misguidedly awarded Test status to the 1970 Rest of the World matches, a Lord's-backed decision mercifully short-lived.

Truly an individualist, in 1958-59 Wellings led the attack on Australia's ranks of illegal bowlers, and he defended Ray Illingworth in what became almost a class war among English writers during the 1970-71 tour. He was "trenchant", "outspoken", even "bitter" and "vitriolic", "the world's most controversial writer". Australian columnist Frank Browne, of all people, named him "the tycoon of the bilious typewriter". Wellings gave every impression of enjoying his infamous reputation.

Five of his seven books were on Ashes series.

During the Second World War, Wellings served in the Officer Cadets Training Unit until, with the rank of captain, he was invalided out in 1944 with colitis. He had been horrified by the blunders and mismanagement. He declined to accept a pension, feeling that the country could ill afford it. His younger brother Donald, who won a DFC at Dunkirk, was killed while serving with the RAF.

After retirement from Fleet Street, Lyn Wellings and his second wife lived in Spain for seven years. Upon his return to England he made a cricket-writing comeback with *WCM*, to which he contributed articles with all the old concern for cricket, upholstered with the traditional Wellings fire and brimstone. He also wrote a column for the Hampshire Cricket Society newsletter – until "banned" by the county club chairman.

His widow, observing his instructions, cast his ashes into the English Channel.

Wisden Cricket Monthly,
November 1992

Wellings: truth before popularity.

At tortoise speed the cricket authorities began to awaken to the possibilities of – and the desperate need for – the eradication of umpiring blunders by using video evidence:

Justice is Done (in Part)

FOR WHAT in particular will 1992 be remembered? The World Cup? The Great Ball-Tampering Scandals? The thrilling Lord's Test? The passing of Bill O'Reilly? The fuss kicked up by certain MCC members (described not all that unreasonably by one eminent columnist as "demented") over the omission of David Gower from the tour of India – a tour which is threatened by yet another outbreak of fanatical religious carnage on the subcontinent?

In terms of cricket's beneficial development, the introduction of video evidence during televised matches towers above everything else. The South Africans took the honours for bravery in becoming the first to try it out. It was instantly successful. The historic first verdict took less than half-a-minute, and Sachin Tendulkar, who would probably have survived given a naked-eye decision, was rightly given out. Countless TV viewers already knew he had not safely made his ground, but this time the most important viewer was an umpire [upstairs], and his decision was *accurate* to the last centimetre. It is a jarring little detail that the green light was chosen as the signal for dismissal. Red would have seemed more appropriate, marking the stop to an innings.* There was, of course, no amber light. The result of the scrutiny of the replay was precise. Justice was done. All cause for bitter dissent was removed.

It was surprising to learn that the dwindling body of opponents to video-assisted umpiring for line decisions had as its chief spokesman in Durban the Hampshire captain. Mark Nicholas was not alone in not having thought the matter through, for he illogically argued that the system would be too expensive if TV had to be installed into all first-class matches.

There will continue to be bad decisions in *untelevised* matches, *but only a handful of players will be party to the miscarriage of justice.* And even then it will be discontent based on the recall of a split-second of action, beyond proof if unphotographed. There will not be millions of TV viewers pouring scorn on a wretched umpire. Mr Nicholas has clearly forgotten that if video assistance had been permitted at Southampton in Hampshire's 1985 NatWest semi-final against Essex, Graham Gooch would have been given run-out and the match would almost certainly have gone Hampshire's way. It would be discreet not to raise the subject with any Pakistani of Gooch's run-out escape in the Headingley Test seven years later!

Further resistive argument has it that if you can't resolve *every* close decision – lbws, bat-pads, caught-behinds – then why sort out only the run-outs and stumpings? This is quite illogical. It might just as well be claimed that if a doctor can cure a man of a bad cough but not his wife of diabetes, then the poor chap will have to be left to go on coughing and hacking.

The West Indians at Brisbane will have regretted that the system has not yet been adopted where they happened to be playing, for Brian Lara was wrongly adjudged stumped. The video replay proved he was not really out. A year hence the practice should be universal, and cricket will be so much the better for it. If only it was this simple to determine criminal guilt in a court of law.

* This was soon remedied.

Wisden Cricket Monthly, January 1993

Tim Tremlett, member of a distinguished cricket dynasty, requested a contribution to his benefit booklet – gladly supplied:

The Nearly Men

EVEN DON Bradman was a Nearly Man. Four more runs in that final Test innings and he'd have averaged 100. Thirty-three more by Graham Gooch at Lord's in 1990 and he'd have taken the world individual Test batting record. Tough luck. But when you think of Nearly Men you tend to reflect on those who showed promise, won perhaps one or two opportunities in rare company, but slipped back into semi-obscurity.

The first I recall from a personal point of view was George Ronald Thoms. Never heard of him? Well, he became a doctor, settled in England, and married a girl from *Emergency Ward 10*. Not a bad fate, perhaps. But he nearly became a regular Test cricketer. In January 1952, Thoms, together with youngsters named Colin McDonald and Richie Benaud, was blooded by Australia in the final Test of a series against West Indies which had already been won. I sat up in the Sheridan Stand at the SCG and watched Thoms and McDonald labour away at an opening stand of 39 in 100-degree heat (Lord knows what the temperature was out in the centre).

McDonald, who was to carve out a brave and prolific Test career, was first out, for 32, with George a "glum" 7. Gerry Gomez eventually bowled him for 16, made in almost an hour and a half. That opening stand was described by Harold Dale as "the most dreadful exhibition of opening batsmanship which can ever have sullied the fair field of Sydney".

Thoms and McDonald were just as cautious in the second innings, when our hero raised his highest Test score to 28 before treading not only on his stumps as he tried to pull a short ball from Worrell but out of Test cricket, had we all but known it, for ever and ever. This chap Benaud scored 3 and 19 and took only one wicket (West Indies No.11 Alf Valentine) so there was probably little chance we'd ever see him again in Australia's colours either . . . .

What George Thoms had that few of us can claim is some green flannel tailored into a baggy green cap, with the coat of arms on the front and his name in the lining. I still can't quite make out whether he was the Nearly Man or the description better fits us thousands and millions who never managed it as far as Test cricket.

Well over a thousand men have played Test cricket, and quite a few of them never made it to a second appearance. They froze with nerves or performed badly or simply were unlucky. A lot of them were lucky to get that Test cap in the first place.

On the subcontinent, kinship with Board members is no great disadvantage when the time comes for team selection. In England, it used to be the amateur-professional divide that cost many a good man his due reward. Nowadays, it almost seems that principle has been reversed in that one player of "amateur" disposition, at any rate, is shunned by the hard-heads who plan England's Test campaigning. A certain Hampshire left-hander nearly crashed into a pylon while Tiger Mothing in Queensland; nearly didn't break the England runmaking and Test appearances records, and nearly failed to captain Hampshire to victory in the NatWest final of 1991. Jon Ayling fixed that one up.

The more you think about the word "nearly" the more frightening it seems. Our worthy beneficiary is no Nearly Man. Tim Tremlett has been a decent, solid county all-rounder and is now a greatly respected coach, and he is not even the son of a Nearly Man, for Maurice, his dad, played three times for England.

The Year of the Trooper: Tim Tremlett Benefit Year 1993

A third generation followed when Tim's tall son Chris was capped by England in 2007, though a sustained Test career did not follow – as in the case of grandfather Maurice.

Cricket people have the same day-to-day worries as the rest, although Geoff Howarth's seemed more serious than most:

Love Must Wait

WHEN FORMER New Zealand cricket captain Geoff Howarth arrives back this month to take up his new job as coach of the New Zealand side, he will be leaving behind his partner of four years, Kate Hammersley. After years of touring, Geoff is no stranger to leaving loved ones behind for months on end, but after his retirement he thought it was an ordeal he would no longer have to face. Now, amid the excitement of his appointment, it is a problem both he and Kate are facing bravely.

"We are both mature enough and strong enough to face this separation," says forty-two-year-old Geoff. "I guess we'll have a few long and expensive phone calls!" says Kate, a former model who was widowed. She has three children, who all adore Geoff. It is Kate's determination to avoid upheaval for them at this critical stage of their education that keeps her in England.

In the meantime, Geoffrey Philip Howarth, OBE, is bracing himself for the challenge of taking over as New Zealand's cricket coach, and also working in the field of youth cricket development, based at the cricket academy in Christchurch. Naturally Geoff regards the job that lies ahead as a more pleasurable prospect than a bitter English winter.

He first ventured to England at the age of eighteen, a talented youngster just out of Auckland Grammar with a yen to play cricket for a living. His brother Hedley, now a shellfish exporter, had toured England that year and played in his first three Test matches. Two years later, in 1971, Geoff made his debut in county cricket with Surrey, starting a career during which he was to score more than 15,000 runs, 2531 of them in Tests for New Zealand.

He rose to be captain of Surrey and of New Zealand, leading his country on a tour of England in 1983.

Geoff's parents came from Oldham, Lancashire. His father died in 1989, on the same night Geoff and Kate met for the first time. His mother Anne, eighty-one, still lives in Auckland and is thrilled that Geoff will soon be back in New Zealand.

Not that he has been overseas for all that long at one time. As his career blossomed in the 1970s, he returned to New Zealand in the English winters to play for Auckland and then, from 1974, for Northern Districts. "I really don't know whether I'm an Englishman or a New Zealander!" he jokes. "I love it over here. Until now, my premier job has been with Surrey County Cricket Club. Those were formative years, and I made a lot of friends, at the same time losing track of my Auckland schoolmates."

He admits he couldn't enjoy living in either country if he felt he would never see the other again. But there is no doubting his keenness to succeed in his new job.

The current New Zealand side – young, confident and talented – has enormous potential, and it is his job to tap that talent. The calmness which marked his six Test centuries (two in one match against England at Auckland fifteen years ago) will apply. And the circumstances of his appointment were not smooth in that his predecessor, former Kiwi wicketkeeper Warren Lees, based in Dunedin, did not want to relinquish the job.

Geoff's serene demeanour veils a past probably more bumpy than average. He's been divorced twice, has a son by his second marriage and another from a liaison in Tauranga. He knew all about taking the rough with the smooth during the richest span of his playing days, when he was hit on the head by a Botham bouncer in the 1978 Nottingham Test and was forced to retire, only to score 123 at Lord's in the next match.

Then, in a famous Test at Dunedin in 1980 – won by one wicket against the exasperated West Indians – victorious captain Geoff Howarth was twice hit on the skull by fast bowler Michael Holding, his helmet being torn off both times. Geoff retained his dignity throughout an acrimonious series, and scored 147 at Christchurch in the following Test to ensure that New Zealand kept their advantage.

Even in his last Test, in Jamaica in 1985, his bravery was conspicuous as he carved out an innings of 84 against a no-holds-barred West Indian pace attack. He has been there and done that, as they say.

New Zealand's new coach faces a torrid initiation: a tour of Australia later this year, a Pakistan tour of New Zealand after that, and then a New Zealand tour of England next May. Geoff – and Kate and the family – will enjoy that. Then there is a tour of South Africa with, perhaps, a tour by the New Zealand Under-19s somewhere in between.

Geoff and Kate opened a bottle of champagne after receiving the midnight call from New Zealand Cricket Council chairman Peter McDermott telling Geoff he had the job. But there'll be no more champagne – except perhaps in a winning New Zealand dressing-room – until Kate rejoins Geoff for Christmas. In between there will be many airletters floating to and fro, and many a plaintive long-distance phone-call.

New Zealand Woman's Day, June 8, 1993

The 1993 Ashes series went resoundingly Australia's way. They won four of the first five Tests before losing at The Oval. Two victories were by an innings, the first here at Headingley in the fourth Test:

Aussie Landslide

GRAHAM GOOCH was born under an unfavourable star. On the very day, July 23, 1953, when Rose Gooch presented husband Alf with a 9lb 2oz son, the Australian fast-bowling maestro Ray Lindwall dismissed Len Hutton and Denis Compton for ducks in the Headingley Test. Gooch's fortieth birthday saw Border's Australians advance from 307 for 3 to an Ashes-safe 613 for 4 by the end of the second day's play. Life – as a Test captain – thus ended for England's best batsman at precisely the time when, to non-cricketers at least, it is thought traditionally to begin.

It was another slaughter. As at Lord's, Australia lost only four wickets against England's 20. The English hopes which rose tentatively out of the Trent Bridge encounter were flushed away with broad, flashing bats and nagging, spinning deliveries. It seemed futile to go on believing that there was really not all that much between the two sides.

Australia, confident, spirited, hell-bent, did it this time with only one wicket going to leg-spin wizard Warne in his 63 overs, and after knowingly having "gone off the boil" in the longish spell between third and fourth Tests. They were now back close to 100 degrees Centigrade, and looking for a 5-0 ultimate margin.

Wisden Cricket Monthly, September 1993

England did manage to snatch a consolation win in the final Test, but we were seeing an Australian side which was perhaps the most formidable in history. It was to dominate world cricket for years to come, and England were to be starved of the Ashes from 1989, when they last conceded them, until 2005.

Credit Where It is Due

THE WARMLY acclaimed victory by England at The Oval saved the 1993 Ashes series from entering the annals as a complete rout, but it scarcely wiped away the memory of four Australian successes – plus a Trent Bridge draw which seemed to underline the paucity of English skill and imagination.

There was much to relish about the "new" England XI's approach and performance under their young leader on the south London ground which is now unrecognisable from the field from which the Ashes sprang in 1882. M.A.Atherton, with his pink schoolboyish countenance and taciturn nature, has disabused more than one set of opponents who deemed him easily put upon. It is to be hoped most of all that the captaincy issue, so often wastefully argumentative, now vanishes for a generation, and that the squad that Atherton takes to the Caribbean does its homeland proud.

Among the final thoughts on the 1993 Test series, it is apparent that the months of painful self-examination and the perpetual rounds of mournful inquest into England's poor showing blinkered the majority from a true and proper appreciation of Australia's performance. How sad it always is to hear people groaning as their own team is defeated, when, as in this particular case, that defeat is the result of brilliant batsmanship from a newcomer, Slater, and determined play by the expressionless Boon, lyrical performances by Mark Waugh and granite resistance by his brother, and true Test-match batting from Taylor and Border, who both stand on the "sinister" side of their bats. How often have wicketkeepers coupled high-class movement behind the stumps with three scores of 80 or more in front of the stumps during a series, as Healy did?

But most of all, what chance did there seem earlier in this decade, when fast bowling dominated the game, that a leg-spinner and an off-spinner would hold the stage for match after match, plying guile and stamina and control for hours at a time, showing the young that there can be far more to cricket than short-of-a-length fast-medium bowling? Warne and May will be remembered even when visions of the battering-ram of Hughes and the "English" method of Reiffel have faded.

So, underappreciated though they may have been, the Australians took all the major awards. England, however, stole the final fanfare, and it will be a matter of great interest to see what shape the Test team will be in when it lands in Australia a year hence.

Another summer of cricket is thus gently transposed for all time into a paper record. The overseas seasons get under way, with Test match scores coming in from all parts of the world. On with the sweaters, up with the thermostats. *O, my Malcolm and my Fraser not so long ago . . . .*

Wisden Cricket Monthly, October 1993

Cricket books and memorabilia were now a boom industry. But it wasn't always so:

Tender Ted

TED BROWN, the doyen among cricket booksellers, died on August 15 in Liskeard Hospital, Cornwall, at the age of eighty-two. He was greatly respected for the care and integrity displayed in his buying and selling, and occupied the premier position in the field after purchasing the huge stock of Epworth Secondhand Books upon Leslie Gutteridge's emigration to Canada in 1967. No longer was the City Road shop the mecca for those who wanted to build a cricket library of quality. Now, postal transactions with E.K.Brown in Cornwall were the order of the day, short of undertaking the long journey to peruse his sagging shelves. As David Smith wrote in an interview in 1990, "he would not be rushed; he was always discreet, and was determined his new venture would combine pleasure with business". He handled the movement of a number of major collections, including those of G.Neville Weston and John Arlott, and became UK agent for a cluster of overseas cricket publications.

A Warwickshire man by birth, the tall Brown was a promising all-rounder while at school and in the local league, but in 1946 his career as a headmaster took him to Duloe and thence Liskeard. He retired in 1968 and dealt full-time in cricket books for a further seventeen years, during which time the "industry" expanded to attract a host of younger dealers. He witnessed the pronounced rise in prices with amazement and the sharpening in business attitudes with some despair. From one of his catalogues, in 1968, come offers which illustrate the modest level of values then as compared to now: Chevallier Tayler's *Empire's Cricketers* for £10.10.0 (£10.50), Farnes's *Tours and Tests* £1.10.0, R.S.Holmes's *Surrey Cricket and Cricketers* fifteen shillings (75p), and *Cricket: A Weekly Record of the Game* £1.15.0 per volume. *Wisdens* from the very first (1864) were offered, subject to availability, at modest prices that would make today's purchasers at auction swoon with disbelief.

Wisden Cricket Monthly, October 1993

And ever more steeply prices continued to rise over the years ahead.

The difference between war and sport has seldom been more clearly defined than in the words of the charismatic Australian cricketer Keith Miller, who scarcely ever gave a formal interview. For one who had watched him in the 1950s and had known him across the years it was a memorable experience to spend the day with him:

Keith Miller: Airman, Cricketer and Anglophile

"I BELIEVE you're the man who runs Lord's?" said the elderly MCC member, addressing Lt-Col. John Stephenson, the secretary, by the pavilion door. "No," said the Colonel, with that familiar twinkle in his eye, "I'm not." Then, pointing to Keith Miller alongside him: *"He* is!"

The statement was true insofar as Miller claims lovingly that "when I walk into Lord's I feel I own it." He has long been an honorary life member of MCC, and the main purpose of his 1993 visit to England (which is about his fortieth since he first came in uniform in 1943) was to sit for a portrait commissioned by MCC. Now, for the last of fifteen sittings, he sat in the artist's paint-splattered little studio only a giant six hit from The Oval, where Miller made his final Test appearance in England in 1956. By choice he wore his RAF tie, and first glance at the canvas revealed an inspired touch: background photographs of Miller the batsman and Miller the bowler. The batting photo was the favourite of many a cricket-lover, most notably of late Australian prime minister R.G.Menzies, who hung it in his study in the 1950s.

This was Miller's first sitting for any artist. Was the restless soul a good sitter? "Oh yes!" said Michael Corkrey. This must have been helped by the constant flow of classical music? Miller cut in: "I *demanded* it!" We then chatted about Neville Cardus, with whom he had such a rapport, and Sir John Barbirolli, the great conductor.

But Lord's Cricket Ground was the recurring theme. Although the famous arena struck Miller as a "crummy little ground" at first sight in 1943, when he was also bemused by its pronounced slope, it grew on him. It might also be said that *he* grew on *it*, for he began to score heaps of runs there in wartime Services matches, including three centuries in first-class matches in 1945, two in "Victory Tests" for Australia against England and an amazing 185 for Dominions, when one of his seven sixes deposited a Hollies delivery onto the roof of the old broadcasting box above the England dressing-room.

His Test matches of 1946 to 1956 hardly feature in his reminiscences, the memories being foggy and somehow less important than those generated during the dramatic years of war. "Of all the cricket I ever played," he asserts, "the wartime cricket at Lord's was the best and the happiest. There was no niggling. People were just glad to be alive."

K.R.Miller the Fearsome Fast Bowler also sprang out of the wartime contests at Lord's. At Lord's last summer Miller was teasing his old friend Bob Wyatt, ninety-two-year-old former England captain, whom he dismissed twice in 1943. "I call Bob 'my bunny'. Got him off two paces with my first ball!"

Australian Services wicketkeeper Stan Sismey said that Miller "got quicker as the war went on", recalling Denis Compton's question as he took guard: "What does this chap do?" Sismey could only offer that "he's only a change bowler, but he's a bit quick". The first ball whistled past the startled Compton's nose. The Miller-Compton friendship, of course, became that of blood brothers, with torrid Ashes battles followed by rousing off-field social pleasures that not even Botham could surpass.

Miller was now punching out the recollections as fast as those runs often came, cricket overlapping in a blur with the frenzy and emotions of war. There was the time he hopped a lift in an aircraft from RAF Ouston, Newcastle, down to Northolt. The humble flight sergeant's request was met warmly by the RAF officer: "Come on then, Aussie!" Over Northolt they circled for ages. It was so busy in the sky. Miller felt dizzy. Then they approached the runway – only for a Spitfire to scream in under them to make an emergency landing, engine overheating after a glycol leak. The officer was soon goodnaturedly dismissing the young pilot's apology. Miller meanwhile was clearing his throat and asking how he might find a place called Ruislip. The officer offered him a lift: in a staff car no less.

That officer was Wing Commander "Laddie" Lucas, legendary much-decorated airman, golfer, author and MP. "I idolise him," says Miller, proving that even heroes sometimes have heroes.

It was turning into a merry revel of namedropping. Miller used to play golf with another wartime hero, Douglas "Tin Legs" Bader, and Gubby Allen. Their last round was played only a couple of days before Bader died, and Keith, revealing himself as an old softie after all, kept the golf ball.

In cricket, Miller only ever had one hero, Bill Ponsford, and claims to have read only one book right through: M.A.Noble's *The Game's the Thing*. He therefore refuses to make comparisons between cricketers.

What about that crash-landing? "Well, one of the engines caught fire, but I managed to hit the right button to extinguish it." He had read in *Flight* magazine about an experienced pilot who tried three times to land on only one engine before perishing in the fourth attempt. Consequently, when Miller, despite a changing wind, touched down, going much too fast, he yelled "Button up!" to his navigator and collapsed the undercarriage ("I'm down, I thought, and I'm staying down!"), belly-landing the aircraft and writing it off. An hour or so later he joined in a soccer match, this Aussie Rules star, but his nervous system suddenly gave way and he collapsed. Worse, he had suffered spine damage which was to hamper him throughout his cricket days.

Some of his missions were to destroy V1 and V2 launch sites across the North Sea. Once, he landed his Mosquito with an explosive drop-tank still partially attached to the wing. Miraculously it dropped off without a murmur as he touched down.

Although losing many friends, Keith Miller had what might be termed a charmed war, never more so than when he went off to Dulwich one Sunday to play cricket. When he returned to Bournemouth he found the town barricaded off after a German raid. A Focke-Wulf had bombed and strafed , and a church spire had collapsed onto the Carlton pub (where the *Bournemouth Echo* offices now stand), killing eight of his mates. Cricket had saved Ft Sgt Miller's life, though, in the absence of a leave-pass list, he was posted as missing too – until he strolled back.

"I came from Melbourne," reflects Miller, "where crowds at the MCG were close to a hundred thousand, so I was amazed at how cramped Lord's seemed. But it grew and grew on me. I walk into Lord's and I know them all – the girls in the shop and on the switchboard and the fellas on the gate, and the printers too. It's small but comfortable. It's kind of intimate."

He rates the Sydney ground, as it used to be, Hill and all, with its cushy outfield, as the best to play on; but the best for atmosphere, he insists, is Lord's. "Don Bradman and I actually agree on that!"

The batsman immortalised in that photograph used as a comfort in times of stress by Bob Menzies was tall, animated, usually elegant, the outline topped by flopping, shiny, dark hair. The slips fielder was inert, chatty, then swiftly acrobatic. The bowler was electrifying in his hostility, but prone to the mischievous grin. This, he knew, was always meant to be a joyful *game*, far removed from the grim realities of life.

He was getting fed-up sitting in this chair. The artist was almost at the end of his long labour. It spurred another tale, about his return to peacetime Melbourne: "The big boss, who had been sitting on his bum throughout the war, said he had a nice job for me down in Yarraville. I said No thanks! So he sent me up to the personnel officer, who told me I'd been away long enough and it was about time I got in and did some work! I told him to stick it."

He joined his mate Sid Barnes in a job in Sydney, selling liquor. "No good – hard to stay sober! Then Dick Whitington got me a job at the *Sun* in Sydney." His wife, Boston-born Peggy, had sailed to Sydney during the 1946-47 Test series, and listened silently while the ship's captain complained about "that fellow Miller" who kept bowling bumpers at Hutton, who had had an arm badly injured during the war. Peggy, noted for her tolerance, didn't let on.

A day with Keith Miller was an emotional undertaking: the oil painting, the note-taking, the wartime reunion – and memories of watching him in his prime.

It was his determination not to leave his young wife alone in a strange country that prompted him to turn down an offer to play league cricket in Rawtenstall – though he must have signed some paper or other, for a representative of the club confronted him during the 1948 Lord's Test. Miller referred the matter to "Plum" Warner, who replied, "Is that so, Keith? Well, we have judges, KCs and solicitors sitting out there among the members. Take your pick. Which do you prefer?" One of the legal gents dealt with the claim during the tea interval, and £50 settled it.

And now it really was time to go. He reached not for a bat but for his aluminium stick, and we made for the car. I was to drop him off in Lambeth for a cup of something with the girl driver who used to see him and the rest of the boys off into the sinister night at RAF Great Massingham, Norfolk half-a-century ago.

"I was hospitalised and homebound for months before coming over this time, you know. I *wasn't* very well. I looked like something out of Belsen or Buchenwald. But I've built myself up and I feel ten times better now."

A quick tale about his jockey mate Scobie Breasley; a thought for John Arlott (who once wrote that Keith Miller seemed to be "busy living life in case he ran out of it"); emphasis on the most admired of his thousands of friends – Laddie Lucas, Jim Swanton, John Woodcock, and the late Billy Griffith ("He was at Arnhem, you know"); and while conceding that it will be good to see Sydney again (besides a wife and four sons, he has, at the last count, seven grandchildren – one half-Thai) he makes brusque response to a final pair of questions. Australian republicanism? "Next question?" The Australian flag? "Next question?!"

Sydney may be home, and he did captain New South Wales for years, but while there are Miller Rooms at the MCG and The Oval, and now a painting of him at Lord's, there is nothing commemorative about him at the SCG. "Not even," as he puts it, "a bit of graffiti!"

Flight Driver Jean Slater not for the first time had wondered if she would ever see "Dusty" again. But now, in 1993, within autumn shadow of the Imperial War Museum, the sparkle shone in the Aussie airman's eyes, and he looked and sounded like Gary Cooper once more, though the years had slowed the Errol Flynn swagger.

The symbolism of Lord's as a tribal meeting place for England and Australia was spelt out by wartime Australian prime minister John Curtin. His words are quoted in the 1945 *Wisden*: "Lord's is to Australia what it is to this country," he told a City of London gathering. "We are defending the City of London and those twenty-two yards of turf which we hope will be used time and time again, so that the Motherland and Australia can decide whether the six-ball over is better than the eight-ball over."

Wisden Cricket Monthly, November 1993

Keith Miller died in 2004.

Coping with Loss and Change

AS THE new year unfurls, Britain drowns and freezes, Australia blisters and burns. And the burghers of Sydney had the hide to talk about "disaster" as the Australian cricket team collapsed to lose by five infuriating runs against South Africa. (Forget 87: the devil's number for Australia has long been 111: Melbourne and Adelaide 1955, Sydney '79, Headingley '81, Sydney '94.)

There are at least two worlds – the sheltered world of cricket, and the often more turbulent world outside the cricket-ground gates. Even though the latter will always influence the former, cricket remains the secure treasury of history, statistics and personalities.

But there is inevitable ongoing change. It is the result of gains and losses – not the mere losses of Test matches or county games, but the losses of better qualities. There used to be more visible humour on the field. There used to be more overs bowled per day. There used to be less short bowling. And though this modern shortcoming seems well on the way to being rectified, there also used to be more spin bowling.

The losses which are most deeply felt, however, are the men who gave so much shape and form to our pleasures. For those of a certain age, the deaths of John Arlott, Len Hutton, Bill O'Reilly, Freddie Brown and Lindsay Hassett, to remember but five from recent years, has spelt loss on a painful scale. To the pantheon now goes Brian Johnston, doubtless cracking awful jokes all the way. Very few in and even beyond the cricket world remain untouched by his departure.

A strange quality among cricket's favourite luminaries is that the men and women who watch them or read them or listen to them develop a sense of familiarity and friendship with them, so that their final going seems an acute personal loss. A little of yourself dies with one who has been such a significant part of your life, albeit a voice oozing good cheer from a radio. All those leavings of balls outside off stump; all those strokes to the boundary; all those catches and misses: you have shared them down the years. Someone else will now do the calling, but somehow it is like trying to get used to a new pair of shoes.

It is argued, of course, that each generation has tastes only for the modern and has no need of or desire for old styles and practices. Anyone aged seventeen or less cannot have listened comprehendingly to an Arlott commentary, and therefore cannot mourn its demise. The time will come when folk will fail to understand what it was about "Johnners" – entertainer more than commentator – that so warmed the nation.

Therefore, it may be as well to accept that life is best conducted under the viewpoint that old books are closing and new ones are opening every single day of one's life. We can do no more than treasure each good moment. Look ahead, backward glances indulged only sparingly.

And on that basis, the prospect of Australia's attempt to square the South African series at Adelaide and of Atherton and his young blades entering the Caribbean cauldron with everything to gain refocuses the attention wonderfully well. The preparations and predictions are about to give way to action.

Wisden Cricket Monthly, February 1994

An extraordinary event took place in Brisbane early in 1994, underlining the course which cricket was now taking into full-blown showbusiness:

Barry Richards Bats Again

JUST WHEN you think you've seen it all .... A New Zealander bowling underarm to an Australian; a batsman with a camera on his helmet and wires trailing from his torso; and Rod Marsh bowling the biggest wrong'un ever recorded. It was all part of a fun day at Brisbane's Gabba ground: the Allan Border Tribute Match, an event which filled the ground and reminded us all that the game can be – and usually is – taken too seriously.

Mind you, when it was all over there was a gentle yearning to watch some fair dinkum cricket again. Deliberately dropped catches, especially by the likes of Ian Healy, are not all that savoury a sight, and the succession of wides bowled by a footballer proved tedious not only to the Channel 9 director who was dying to bung on another ad.

The attractions were there from the first enticing billing: Barry Richards, Sir Richard Hadlee, Mike Procter, Doug Walters, Greg Chappell, Joel Garner, Rod Marsh, Geoff Lawson, Jeff Thomson: they all creaked out onto the turf again, creating a minor orgy of nostalgia.

"I played against Barry in all his four Tests in '69-70," squeaked Bill Lawry, "and he never played that once!" It was a play-and-miss against the grey-haired Thommo that the former Australian left-hander was referring to. And when the bespectacled Richards, QCA chief executive now and a stone or two over his old playing weight, cut a half-pace McDermott to the rope, Channel 9 replayed the shot over and over.

Meanwhile, Hansie Cronje, Richards's young South African partner, was wandering round like some disorientated spaceman, seeking ease from his embarrassment by chatting to umpire Tony Crafter, who was smartly decked out in cable-belt around his waist and mini-camera on his head. The resulting on-screen images had limited appeal, for they reflected the normal movements of the head, which are frequent and not always directed towards what a viewer would wish to see: Cronje spent some time studiously surveying the turf. The stump camera has already proved an asset. We now know that the helmet apparatus has no future, except perhaps in the case of the umpire.

The umpires, of course, have already given the authorities their opinion on such an innovation; which is why it is not worn in conventional matches. Here, Mel Johnson, a man of singularly strong will, was having nothing to do with the gimmick technology. He it was who gave John Dyson not-out in the Sydney Test of 1982-83 when he was out by a yard.

Doug Walters had to down his playing-cards and trudge out to the middle twenty-eight years after first doing so in a Test match. In 1965, just before his twentieth birthday, he spun together a debut innings of 155 against M.J.K.Smith's England attack on this very ground (though it was charmingly "under-developed" then, with red-flowering poinciana trees everywhere). Dougie's touch is still there, though he was soon puffing and red-faced. A couple of great pull shots peeled back the years, and there was a leg-side six off a Border full-toss.

When McDermott hit Marsh's fleshy body with a couple of bouncers, he could hardly continue for laughing. Now *that's* not something you see all that often in Tests.

Procter, once the greatest cricketer in the world, quietly gathered 29 off 27 balls, patiently tolerant of the Tony Greig chitchat which came through his earpiece. In came Sir Richard [Hadlee], using the same bat he used when he retired three years ago – and a slightly revised coronary structure. For a time his partner was a tallish chap who is studying accountancy in London, one J.Garner. Between them they have taken 690 Test wickets.

The arrival of Greg Chappell gave Sir Richard the chance he probably thought he'd never get: mock revenge for the infamous Trevor Chappell underarm, at the direction of his brother-captain, at the MCG thirteen years ago. It skidded along the turf and Chappell put a boot to it to try to get it to sit up so he could hit it for six. The ball disobeyed, but he still banged it through the covers for four. Kiwi-Kangaroo relations have long been at a low ebb, but this will have raised them a fraction.

It all helped pass the time. At least there had been massed ranks to watch the fun, in contrast to the thin attendance at the recent Gabba Test.

Wisden Cricket Monthly, February 1994

Soon the brutal West Indies fast-bowling attack was at work once more, with pitiful absence of intervention by the umpires. This and brattish behaviour elsewhere made it a depressing era in many ways, with administrators leaving themselves open to charges of limp management and weak influence:

Too Good to be Spoiled

ANDREW LANG once enthused: "How much good cricket there is in the world!" There still is, of course. But the dear old boy would have spluttered into his dram had he somehow been able to see on the yet-to-be-invented television some of the ugly pictures beamed into our homes in 1994. They were not just ugly. They were obscene.

In the Jamaica Test match, intimidation went unrecognised by umpire Ian Robinson, thus exploding, at the first time of asking, the ICC's belief that "third-country" umpires would bring relief to a contentious issue. This was not a question of any suspicion of impartiality. It concerned efficiency – coupled with courage. Many umpires have refrained from stepping in against intimidation by fast bowlers because they themselves have been fearful of intimidation from various sources. Zimbabwe's Mr Robinson simply wasn't up to it. And yet those who appointed him cannot have been unaware of the challenge he would face.

Courtney Walsh, he of the flailing, malevolent right arm, backed by his acting captain Desmond Haynes, took cynically to bowling around the wicket and dropping the ball short against the inept, shortsighted England No.11. Most of the great fast bowlers would have terminated Devon Malcolm's innings quickly and by skilful means: an outside edge, a yorker, a slower ball. Not so Mr Walsh. Just as he had brutalised the England captain and his partners on the third evening, he displayed no conscience in the matter: he would go as far as the umpire would let him: and the umpire failed the great game.

This had less to do with the one-bouncer regulation than the original (and never superseded) Law 42.8. Umpire Roy Palmer knew what he was doing when he invoked this law against Aqib Javed at Old Trafford in 1992 when the same hapless Malcolm was being targeted: *The bowling of fast short-pitched balls is unfair if, in the opinion of the umpire at the bowler's end, it constitutes an attempt to intimidate the striker.* Reference is then significantly made to the striker's relative skill.

Walsh's excess in Jamaica was roundly condemned. Many of the local spectators looked concerned, and even Clive Lloyd spoke against it. Messrs Gower, Holding and Willis were not prepared to excuse it, and Graham Gooch, who was now talking all day instead of batting all day, came out against the bodyline assault.

It raised an echo of brave Bill Woodfull's remark when the mealy-mouthed England manager Pelham Warner went into the Australian dressing-room at Adelaide after Woodfull had taken a pounding from Larwood: "There are two teams out there, Mr Warner; one side is playing cricket and one is not. This sort of thing is ruining the game, which is too good to be spoiled."

The glib will crow that cricket is "a man's game". So is boxing, but even that often barbaric sport establishes initial equal rights for both combatants. Malcolm was forced to become a sitting target, and even as he hedged away, the ball continued to seek him out. No equal rights there. Cricket's moral Rules of Engagement had been broken.

Meanwhile, in New Zealand, a Pakistan player sustains a head injury from a bottle thrown by a cowardly spectator, and in South Africa, Australia's erstwhile match-winning bowlers, Warne and Hughes, bring further disgrace on the game by losing control and abusing opponents. The pictures of Warne, the gifted leg-spinner, screaming hysterically at the departing batsman, Hudson, might have come straight from that discredited game soccer, and turned the stomach. That Warne and "Big Merv" were fined only £200 and "severely reprimanded" by the match referee generated further despair. Was Mr Carr not aware that Hughes had transgressed twice before, and that Peter Kirsten had been fined much more heavily at Adelaide a month previously for comments to an umpire which were much more of a private nature? If he was aware, his leniency was inexcusable. If he was not aware, why? Full marks to Alan Crompton, the Australian Cricket Board chairman, for being as good as his word and acting independently by adding sizable fines against the offenders.

All of which leaves insufficient room for adequate congratulations to that upright, smiling sportsman Kapil Dev, who stayed on his legs long enough to reach the untouched heights of 432 Test wickets. Like all the truly greats, he did it by skill and perseverance. Cricket really is a pursuit "too good to be spoiled".

Wisden Cricket Monthly, April 1994

Another invitation to write something for a benefit booklet was keenly met for a very affable chap from Essex:

"Charlie" Childs to Viv Richards

ALL OF ten years ago, John Childs came with us on a pro/am cricket tour of Barbados, as part of the Wisden All Stars, a collection of half-a-dozen county professionals and some keen club cricketers who enjoyed themselves in the Caribbean.

John, then with Gloucestershire, was a late recruit for the tour, but without a doubt a precious addition, for he gave the paying customers just what they expected, thoughtful coaching and plenty of pleasant chat by the poolside. "What a thoroughly nice bloke" was the frequently-heard remark.

The thoroughly nice bloke with the charming sense of humour was going places, had we but known it. In 1985 he was reborn with a move to Essex, in '86 he was a Wisden Cricketer of the Year, and in '88 he was eventually capped by his country.

In his Test debut he bowled with the same flight and accuracy as on the Barbados tour, only this time he was bowling to the rampant Viv Richards. In fact he temporarily paralysed the West Indies skipper. For twenty minutes he wove his spell, then Viv launched into a cow shot which brought four fortuitous runs and Childs was taken off. I glared in anguish at the ceiling of the press-box.

It was no way to treat a slow bowler, and yet "Charlie" just smiled and strode off. I don't think there was even a shrug of the shoulders. Phil Edmonds would probably have grabbed the ball and refused to give it back.

It was terribly anticlimactic, and yet, being the philosophical soul that he is, John most probably travelled home from Manchester (1 for 91 off 40 overs in the end) doubtless feeling a warm glow at having been awarded an England cap which no philistine could take away from him.

He's had a lot of success since for Essex, and has come close to adding to his two Test caps, but I have an everyday reminder of his skill, skill of another kind, when I see the "Wisden Cricket Monthly" notice he painted for us in 1984 for the office front door, as like the great Australia leg-spinner Clarrie Grimmett, John is a qualified signwriter. A casual request for the office sign was met with an immediate smiling response.

Is it any wonder: the keenness to pay tribute in his benefit brochure? But I do wish the England skipper had kept him on longer that day at Old Trafford.

John Childs Benefit Year 1994

England's captain in that Old Trafford Test match – if you're wondering – was John Emburey.

A somewhat legendary figure who had put a little work my way in the early days died in the spring of 1994:

Reg Hayter of Fleet Street

PROPRIETOR OF British sports journalism's largest school of apprenticeship, Reg Hayter, who died in hospital in Northwood on March 13, aged eighty, had a deep love for cricket and football which fuelled his long working hours and rewarded him with innumerable friendships. The legions of young, aspiring reporters, many of whom graduated to enviable positions in national newspapers, regarded Hayter's Agency, tucked away in successive offices behind Fleet Street, as anything from sweatshop to academy. Reg, of the warm heart and occasionally stern eye, picked out the best of them and eventually fed them to recruiting sports editors.

They came from the towns and the provinces, and at least one from Sydney knocked on his door. You didn't do it for the money. The aim was to embark on something money couldn't buy: experience. The fee covered petrol and sandwiches but little else.

"Fact is sacred, comment is free," Reg used to preach. It was only later that I discovered that this lovely credo had been minted many years earlier by C.P.Scott of the *Manchester Guardian*. It was Reg (now there's a sentence-beginning of which he would have disapproved) who was drafted in, with his squad, when my editorship of *The Cricketer* came to a sudden end in 1978. He would have been appalled at the mis-spelling ("Heresay") in 48-point lettering on their first front cover, and no more amused by the three dozen errors within.

He looked after the affairs of Denis Compton, Basil D'Oliveira and Ian Botham, to name but three sportsmen from separate generations, and he instigated many a ghosted book, putting his name also to a handful of his own. He had started out in 1933 with Pardon's agency, and was soon the Press Association's chief cricket reporter, writing for *Wisden*. After the Second World War, during which he had helped start the fund-raising British Empire XI which played all over the country, with as many star cricketers as could be found, Hayter went on several England tours before, in 1955, buying Bert Long's agency and realising a long-held dream. He was still putting in devoted hours until shortly before his death.

He was a regular in El Vino's in Fleet Street, and ran his own merry touring cricket team. For decades he was attached to Stanmore CC, floating the new ball down when into his seventies. He could make light of his stammer, joking that the BBC had knocked him back because he was "too tall". He spoke at Stanmore's dinner only a couple of days before he died, having been toasted grandly by many of his countless friends three months earlier at an eightieth birthday gathering. Reginald James Hayter, born in Paddington on December 3, 1913, left a widow and five children from their fifty-four-year marriage, one of whom, Peter, is the *Mail on Sunday's* cricket correspondent.

Wisden Cricket Monthly, May 1994

Always there is a craving to know more about cricket's major performers. Occasionally significant evidence comes up in the auction room:

Hammond Revealed

WALLY HAMMOND was possibly the greatest cricketer England has ever produced. He was certainly one of the more interesting characters: alternately brusque or charming, icy or helpful, often reclusive, even secretive. It may have been the lonely boyhood; it may have been, quite simply, in the genes. Those of us who collect letters know that one by Hammond is hard to come by. It was therefore amazing news last year that a whole cluster of them, written to his first wife and oozing with personal expression, was about to come onto the market. They came in one large batch of thirty-two, and sold for £2682.

Lightning then struck again. Vennett-Smith, the Nottingham auctioneers, offered forty more Hammond letters in their March sale, and this time they came in single lots: a chance for everybody.

They were written, most of them, to Kitty Hall, a Folkestone girl, while Hammond was a bachelor in his early twenties. The content makes it clear that they were very close, and historians at last have an opportunity to peer into the mind of the batsman who was to bestride county cricket for a dozen glorious years and give England something almost to match the firepower of Australia's supreme Bradman.

Hammond's books are readily available and reveal the public face. These letters illuminate the private man: "Don't worry about them [his affections for her] for I am not in the habit of showing them everywhere. I don't seem to be made like that, but I have plenty, believe me . . . You know it would be very nice to be sleeping in the next room to you and have you tuck me in, yes! . . . I wonder if you want me as

Wally Hammond, perhaps the finest cricketer ever produced by England. His human frailty was revealed in his letters.

44 Ravernake Road,
Hampstead,
N.W.3.

Thursday

My Dear Litty.

Just a short note to ask you if it would be humanly possible for you to come to London monday midday or tea time and spend an evening with me also to stay the night in town and go back on

Tuesday, you of course know what I mean. If of course it is impossible just then me a line to the above address, and say so Then we shall have to leave it until I come again to Folkestone. With heaps of love in haste

badly as I want you . . . spend an evening with me, also to stay the night in town and go back on Tuesday, you of course know what I mean . . . [from the Waldorf Hotel, London]: For Gawd's sake be careful. Mother has made her presence very uncomfortable and I can't get rid of her . . . [on Armistice Day]: I am going to spend the first half in church and the second half enjoying myself . . . Could you find a nice sporty girl to make up a four if I brought down a friend? . . . [from Cape Town]: I have been the perfect model of a good boy out here." And then, in July 1927, he writes to say it's all over, though he hoped they would remain "pals".

Does this not prove, once and for all, that letters are what really count? Autographs (signatures) are common currency by comparison.

These letters had quite high reserves placed upon them, and estimates of £100-200. Only around half of them sold. Truly the Recession must still be biting.

Elsewhere in the sale, a West Indies blazer went for only £45 and a South African Cricket Union flag (now where did that come from?) made £35. Lord Harris's signature fetched £100. A George Geary benefit booklet, one of the earliest at 1924, made £72, and a W.G.Grace letter cost a keen buyer £145. A letter from Bert Oldfield to the South Australian Cricket Association (and where did *that* come from?) went for £55, and some early cigarette-cards realised good prices.

Wisden Cricket Monthly, May 1994

Having taken the world Test record with his astonishing 375 against England at the Recreation Ground in Antigua, West Indies left-hander Brian Lara was soon coupling it with the highest score ever made in first-class cricket:

Too Much to Absorb

THESE ARE times of major social, political and military significance. Cricket history, too, is being made on a scale seldom known before. Captains everywhere will be compiling dossiers on Brian Lara, scanning his rare dismissals and re-examining the mode in search of clues to likely weaknesses. Fieldsmen and wicketkeepers who have downed the infrequent catches Lara has offered will be fighting against the urge to slit their wrists. Even exhaustion cannot be relied upon to take care of this phenomenal run-maker, for a day after scoring his incredible half-thousand he overcame fatigue and the reactionary shakes (to say nothing of the wearing demands for autographs and interviews) to bump off a quick 70 against Surrey to steer Warwickshire to the B&H final.

The older one is the harder it is to absorb what has happened. Inside fifty days, Lara has swept away names such as Sobers, Hanif, Bradman, Macartney, Richards, Bert Sutcliffe, Frank Foster and – though, to their shame, many would not have heard of him, and care even less – Percy Perrin. "Swept away" is, of course, too strong a term. These names have simply been pushed further down the records column. But there's nothing like being top. It is that very belief that drives the champions on past what mere mortals regard as a decent performance. Would it not have been more "natural and normal" to have been satisfied with a double- or even triple-century? But that is the thinking of the unimaginative, the unromantic.

It is not as if Brian Lara has made his 277, 372 and 501, and all the mere centuries in between, mostly off moderate English bowling, in grinding style. He is a flashing strokemaker, whose appeal, as Sir Garry Sobers said in Antigua, stems from the fact that he wears pads only to protect against the rare ball which eludes his punishing bat. There seems to be not a negative thought in his head. He now puts immense pressure on bowlers, sorting out those who will wilt before his reputation and those who will be fired up at the prospect of taking his richly-prized wicket (at least before he has reached 250).

All this has squirted a vivid smokescreen across the image of another pretty useful left-hander, Allan Border, who stepped out of Test cricket midst discordant noises. The Australian Cricket Board wanted to plan ahead; AB was tempted by the upcoming Ashes series but would have wanted to miss the tour of Pakistan. Thus the sudden announcement of retirement which not only surprised the Board but miffed Channel 9, the "cricket channel", for he gave the news to a friend at Channel 7.

But Border's deeds are carved into the granite: his 1989-1993 Ashes triumphs which wiped away the grisly memories of the 1981 series, even if the BBC continued, to the end, to nark him with replays of it; his unsurpassed toughness of approach, never lessened by even half a degree when the West Indies headhunters were at it; and his set of figures which, even five years ago, would have seemed, like Lara's recently, to be beyond the reach of man. Well played, AB. Happy retirement.

Wisden Cricket Monthly, July 1994

Cricket on Television

FOR THOSE who continue to believe that cricket is England's national summer game, the report by the National Heritage Committee will have brought cheer, for it seems to point to some protection for the televising of the game in this country. Despite its superb coverage of overseas series, BSkyB satellite television will never reach into as many homes as does BBC TV, which beams Test cricket into almost every residence in the UK, should it be wanted. It does it, too, without the brain-addling commercials between every over and at the fall of each wicket. But there has been an erosion in past summers. With a sense of timing worse than that of batsmen Tufnell, Such and Malcolm, the BBC programme directors allow extended weather waffle and other pointless interferences to blank out crucial viewing, such as Gooch's arrival at 300 in the 1990 Lord's Test. The National Heritage Committee probably has rubber teeth, but it should see the job through by insisting that the Beeb restores truly comprehensive coverage. The temperature in Tunisia can never be quite as important as Darren Gough's last determined over before lunch.

Wisden Cricket Monthly, August 1994

Little over a decade later television coverage of cricket in the UK, having first reverted to Channel 4, was greedily handed to BSkyB for pots of money which bolstered the county clubs and supposedly supported "grass roots" cricket. Some of the millions undoubtedly went towards expanding cricket's "government". But, meanwhile, only a fraction of the community could afford a satellite system. People who had loved cricket all their lives were now denied it in their living-rooms, and countless school-age potential cricket-lovers were no longer "exposed" to the big matches and would inevitably be lost to football, which drowns the land for almost the entire year.

Bert Oldfield, Australia's wicketkeeper in the 1920s and 1930s, was a key figure in encouraging my commitment to cricket as a youngster. The centenary of his birth could not be allowed to pass without a fond memoir of recollection:

A Little Aussie Gentleman

IN A HOUSE cluttered with cricket books and relics, one item has a special sweetness. It is an Australian Test blazer, almost boy's size, from the 1930 tour of England, given to me by Bert Oldfield in 1954. It was given freely and without calculation by an old-world gentleman who was said – so I heard – to be a tight-fisted businessman.

It was a presentation made, perhaps, in recognition of fervid enthusiasm shown by a seventeen-year-old for a game which unites men of all ages and nationalities. That shop, W.A.Oldfield's, was already a shrine; it now became a magic temple.

It was in Hunter Street, Sydney. There was a lifesize enlargement in the shop window of the classic Hammond cover-drive, with Oldfield himself in perfect position low behind the stumps. Around this giant cardboard cut-out were bats and stumps and brilliant red cricket balls, and inside the shop were stacks of boxes full of boots and sprigs and sweaters in the colours of all the Sydney grade clubs, including the red stripes of my beloved St George.

These everyday items could also be obtained from Stan McCabe's shop in George Street or Alan Kippax's rather impersonal establishment in Martin Place. Mr Oldfield (he was "Bertie" or "Cracker" only to his own generation) went back a lot further. He used to talk of fellow Glebe cricketer "Tibby" Cotter, a turn-of-the-century boyhood hero of his. There was a huge enlargement of Cotter by the staircase. He spoke of his fine athletic build and beautiful skin, and of his death in the Great War.

I did the right thing on one visit to the shop, lashing out on an Oldfield Test Perfection cricket bat. He threw the tin of linseed oil in for nothing and wrote a letter wishing me luck with the bat. Any wonder I went back as often as I could.

Upstairs was the reclusive Charlie Macartney, who emerged once just long enough to sign my autograph book. It was a place to meet all kinds of cricket people. An early visit, during the 1950-51 MCC tour, coincided with a call by English cricketers Trevor Bailey (with his Lindwall-broken thumb in plaster) and Reg Simpson, who patiently listened to the meaningless outpourings of a star-struck teenager. The talented New South Wales batsman Ray Flockton worked in the shop and it was exciting to talk to him only days after he had taken 85 off the West Indian attack at Sydney.

But the chief draw was always the proprietor, Bert Oldfield, capped 54 times by Australia, holder of 78 catches behind the stumps, with an amazing 52 stumpings to go with them. And he made more than 1400 Test runs. He would, Ray Robinson once wrote, "have made a fine courtier in Louis XV's day. You could picture him in the ballroom at Versailles, with powdered wig, gleaming shoe-buckles and snowy lace at his wrists". In complete contrast to the muddy shape retrieved from a shell-hole in Belgium in the First World War, his head broken, the Bertie Oldfield of the 1920s and 1930s was an elegant vision in cream and white.

And now, in the 1950s, he moved with brisk dancer's steps around his shop, head high, wide smile, meticulous speech, waistcoat perfectly fitting, starched white collar gleaming. This was the man who would have caught you or stumped you almost apologetically and sent you on your way with a sympathetic smile and a word of consolation. The battered fingers were the only clue.

I once saw him keep wicket. He was in his sixtieth year and he had agreed to turn out in a match in honour of the Pakistan High Commissioner. He seemed to crouch not quite as low as in the old photographs, but he moved with supreme grace and ease, and I went home proud and satisfied.

He would talk of Hobbs and Sutcliffe and Hammond, and of England and its castles and theatres, and of the Royalty he had met, and of the many kindnesses extended to him in the Old Country. Once he gave me a lift to the Sydney Cricket Ground in his car. It was like gliding along in a Heavenly carriage. I remember giving in to one brief fantasy as the vehicle cruised down Macquarie Street. I was off to the SCG to open the bowling for Australia, and my driver was my wicketkeeper: Bertie. Hope Jack Gregory's in good nick today. I don't want to show him up for pace. Expect Bertie will scoop a few up off the edge while the ball's new. Amazing how he never seems off-balance, never dives or cavorts around like this Evans chap

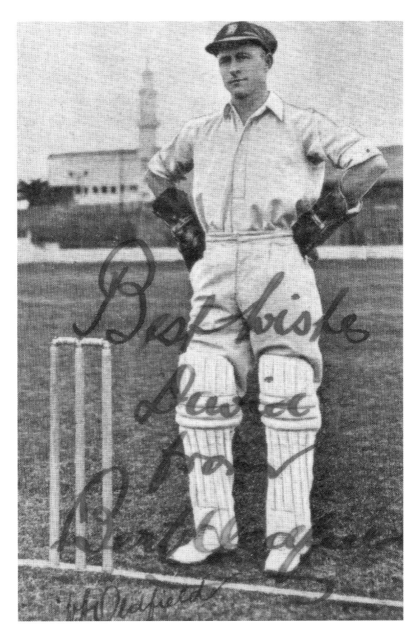

W.A.Oldfield, elegant and sweet-natured.

Mr Oldfield must have braked sharply. I was back in the 1950s. Moore Park was up ahead. I had to leave the car before it entered the members' gate into the holy of holies. I knew I could see him again in the shop some day. I've forgotten the day's play, but not the transfixing effect of that ride.

It was many years later that, having been resident in England, I walked into the new Oldfield shop in Sydney. He took me to lunch at his club. Afterwards, as we crossed the street, he did an old-fashioned thing. He linked arms with me, the way sportsmen used to do so uninhibitedly so long ago. And I was so *proud*. Had a speeding Holden descended upon us I should gladly have put myself between it and this antique little cricketing treasure who had once kept wicket for Australia.

I took my sons to his house in Killara. We had a blissful afternoon tea and hours of talk, not all cricket. He gave them a cricket bat, lovingly signed. Later they could not decide whose it actually was, so I sorted matters out by adding it to my collection. That and the 1930 blazer are on daily view, a kind of immortality I suppose, even though this dapper, almost delicate, little wicketkeeper died in 1976. September 9 marks the centenary of his birth. All who knew him will salute him.

Wisden Cricket Monthly, September 1994

After a generation in the cricket wilderness South Africa returned to play a Test series in England in 1994, and took Lord's by storm, beating England by 356 runs:

Another Spion Kop

THIS WAS the day that might never have come. During the years of rude and humiliating ICC rebuff to South Africa's crusading cricket delegates, this day seemed beyond expectation. While demands were met only to be replaced by new and greater demands, South Africa's rehabilitation became a faint and forlorn prospect. The resilience and optimism and hope of the committed took on a desperate and at times seemingly absurd hue. No South African team would play at Lord's this century, surely?

Not only have they played here – thanks to the broad vision and creative thought of the de Klerks, Mandelas and Bachers – well before the end of the 20th Century, but they have performed with a thrust generated out of years of frustration. There was a passion about South Africa's play such as only a new nation might know, matching the collective purpose of domineering sides like Australia, West Indies and Pakistan, all of whom are continually fired up in a way which makes stabilised, stale, old England scratch its head uncomprehendingly.

Of course, South Africa's record-breaking Lord's victory, achieved in four days, received much less than its due recognition – by non-South Africans at least – because of the Atherton Affair. The hysteria and self-righteousness triggered by the England captain's pocketful of dust saw to it that for days afterwards South Africa were as absent from the average mind as at any time during their twenty-nine-year lock-out. One joker even suggested that it was all a deliberate diversionary manoeuvre by Mike Atherton so that folk would not dwell on the thrashing administered to what had been regarded as an England XI hot on the revival trail.

Wisden Cricket Monthly, September 1994

With turbulence continuing seemingly on all fronts, the latest hoo-ha came with the England captain's dirt-in-the-pocket affair. So an editor clamped his teeth and embarked on yet another protest at the cackhanded running of the game and the

Atherton Defended

IF MIKE ATHERTON had poisoned the MCC president and run off with the treasurer's wife there would have been scarcely more acreage in the newspapers than came his way after the incident at Lord's. Absent-mindedly, it seemed, he placed his dusty fingers on the ball, and although the umpires – one from Australia, the other the most experienced in the world – decreed that the ball's surface condition had not been unnaturally altered, Atherton was seemingly "done" on suspicion.

If sentences were dished out daily merely on grounds of suspicion, the streets would almost be deserted.

The chairman of selectors optimistically hoped to settle the matter quickly and cleanly by taking £1000 off Atherton for withholding a complete explanation to the match referee, and another £1000 for "having soil". It is – to put it conservatively – unusual to carry earth in one's pocket, though it does save bending down and it does save time. Crucially, the practice does not contravene any rule, regulation or law. A refund of the soil-in-pocket penalty somehow seems a moral obligation.

The avidity with which the majority of English cricket writers – many under the direction of their sports editors – fell upon the England captain made one's stomach turn. Without a shred of unquestionable evidence of misdemeanour they demanded Atherton's resignation. As successful batsman and iron-willed captain he is the best thing to happen to English cricket for years. He has led the side out of macabre shadows into days of hope and occasional Test victory. His success seems to have brought out that least attractive of traits that persuades people to slash the stems of poppies which they perceive as being too tall.

None dared to call Atherton a cheat, but the inferences were obvious. It was, once more, the day of the pious soapboxers. From the childhood days of early memory into adulthood, none of the sanctimonious critics can have escaped, at some time in his life, The Challenge of Authority: a question from a parent: "What are you doing in that larder?" Or a schoolmaster in the laboratory: "What the devil is this in your test-tube?" Or a traffic policeman: "And what speed do you think you were doing, sir?" Human instinct is to reply succinctly and negatively, even when there is nothing to hide.

ICC match referee Peter Burge asked the England captain if there was any "substance" in his trouser pocket. Mike Atherton was unable to summon the sort of grinning defiance used by a Mick Jagger. "Substance"! Resin? Lip-cream? Or did he mean bottle-top? The real explanation – the dirt – sounded too absurd. The fleeting panic and hesitation, as when one tries to duck a bouncer, proved costly.

The hounding of the captain then began in a spectacular way and in a manner unique to England, where perversity close to perversion sees to it that the captain of the national cricket team shall be the prime target of an insatiably bloodthirsty press. Millions who might not have known their Kirkstall Lane from their Vauxhall End then pronounced learnedly and noisily on Atherton's "guilt", "shame" and "disgrace". They deserved to lose him.

Stronger than another vilified young captain, Kim Hughes, of Australia, Atherton emerged after days of introspection and uncertainty, and eventually, in soft voice, he made reference to "the gutter press" after his poignant 99 in the next Test. Among the journalists who recoiled at that remark were some fairly big fish who will be bent on savaging their prey further. Atherton, tough and resilient, will probably see them off.

Wisden Cricket Monthly, September 1994

Roses in December

"GOD GAVE us memory that we might have roses in December," J.M.Barrie once wrote. Thus, the English winter is made less chilling. Imprints on the mind of sunlit days from Taunton to Scarborough will have as warming an effect as cherry brandy.

But God has also now given us satellite television and radio, and for the lucky ones who can afford it, Jumbo aircraft which will transport them to where cricket is played between October and April. It need not be all memories of the past season and painful longing for the next. Cricket goes on in a handful of other countries: and to such an extent that there are many more Tests and one-day internationals than ever before, making the five months of the English season seem sedate in terms of activity.

Of course, the cricket-lover will show selective interest where his own country is not involved. Even so, it would have been few Englishmen who did not feel acute interest in the excitement of the short Pakistan v Australia Test series. Fifty-odd for the tenth wicket to snatch victory and a winning/losing leg-break which passed the wicketkeeper and launched a thousand grim nightmares for him showed that the vision of global accessibility to "live" or even recorded TV pictures is a long way yet from fulfilment.

Then came Salim Malik's double-century and Damien Fleming's hat-trick at Rawalpindi. Such cricket deserved a much wider audience.

At least there are instantaneous photographs, which is more than our forebears had a hundred years ago, precisely, when Stoddart's English team ploughed across the ocean to take on Australia in five remarkable Test matches. We approach, too, other anniversaries. Seventy years ago Arthur Gilligan's English team sailed in *Ormonde* and played a spirited Ashes series, losing four Tests, one, at Adelaide, by only 11 runs on the seventh day, and winning at Melbourne by an innings, a result that warmed English hearts back home, for Australia had not been beaten for twelve years.

A greater number of folk will remember what happened forty years ago. Len Hutton's side were thrashed at Brisbane in the opening Test, only to find a cohesion that made them winners over a fading Australian combination.

Yet another anniversary is the twentieth of the ill-fated Denness expedition, when Lillee and Thomson pummelled the 1974-75 England batting unmercifully, breaking bones and spirits and proclaiming an abrasive new era which culminated in the Packer revolution.

So variegated are these Ashes series of 1894-95, 1924-25, 1954-55 and 1974-75 that we are entitled to expect something new again from the 1994-95 rubber. It may not be two-all with one to play, as it was a hundred years ago, but expectation is high that England will not be easily over-run this time. The Ashes tradition demands a competitive series now after the last three lop-sided encounters since 1989.

To dip again into the faithful book of quotations: "History is a pact between the dead, the living, and the yet unborn" (Edmund Burke). Atherton owes it to Stoddart, Gilligan and Hutton to get the best out of his troops. Then England's shivering supporters will have *real* roses in December – and January too.

Wisden Cricket Monthly, November 1994

There were not to be many roses for England that winter, or – in Ashes Tests – for another entire decade, so while hope continued to sustain Englishmen everywhere, it was just as well that there was no clear vision of the future.

Late in 1994 the biggest name in English cricket committed himself to an autobiography. It was the long-promised "real" book on his life and embodied some torpedoes aimed at people who had annoyed him:

Botham's Book

I MAY HAVE been the first ever to interview I.T.Botham: Taunton, June 12, 1974, I ventured down into the dark dungeon-like dressing-room after this eighteen-year-old had dismissed the world's best batsman (Richards, B.A.), had one and a half teeth knocked out by Andy Roberts, and then smashed Somerset to an absurd victory in the B&H quarter-final: there he slumped, utterly spent, dragging on a small cigar, eyes glazed. "Excuse me, but how do you actually pronounce your name?" Was it Both'm, Bo'thm, Bot-ham? What was his date of birth and birthplace? Usual procedure when somebody new appears on the scene. He answered wearily, patiently.

Had it struck me to ask if he thought that over the next twenty years he would play in 102 Tests, take 383 wickets and score 5200 runs, have his name in scandalous headlines, raise millions for charity, and become a star of pantomime and television*, he would probably have said, "Of course!"

His self-belief has been phenomenal. It has been the secret of much of his success as well as several of his aberrations, and gave his team-mates and his millions of admirers cause for joy as he pillaged his way to victory for his counties and for England. The Headingley, Edgbaston and Old Trafford Tests of 1981 will be recalled until the film fades, reassuring those who had begun to feel that England's post-Churchill exhaustion could never be dispelled.

And yet from there, target of jealousy and victim of paranoia partly self-induced, he began to trip over.

There have been books about him and ostensibly by him, but he was often heard to say, "You wait until my *real* book comes out!" This is it, and he blazes away in a style which is totally unsurprising. He mocks Dexter, comes clean on his reasons for declining a South Africa tour, recounts his set-to with "nonentity" Ian Chappell, vituperates against a succession of selectors for not restoring him as England captain and for dumping him prematurely, justifies his wild strokes, expresses contempt for MCC members, condemns Yorkshire for not clamping down on racist barracking, hammers the Durham administration, disapproves of Australian sledging and Gooch's "obsessive" training, accuses the Pakistanis of ball-tampering, and brands the Lord's authorities unfit to run the game, saying they do not have the spirit of cricket at heart. And all this by way of the barest outline. It's a big book, and the moans mercifully are interspersed with dollops of fun.

His debt to wife Kath is repeatedly acknowledged in what is almost a tome of apology. She has had so much up with which to put. And so have the kids. They are stuck, no doubt proudly, with a man whose philosophical gems include: "Life is too short to be forever wondering whether you did the right thing." And yet he shows remorse at hurting Kathy not only by making her jealous of his friendships with Viv Richards and Tim Hudson but through the marijuana episodes. She has long endured "the exhausting business of being Mrs Ian Botham".

Illy cops it; Imran is branded a "self-confessed cheat"; Gooch is lampooned; Roebuck is also dealt with: "identity crisis", "a sad case", "smell the man's ambition", "fanatical desire to rule Somerset".

Yes, this is the *real* book, a high proportion of its contents utterly familiar, the rest full of six-hits off people he despises. "I have always been a man of action first and foremost," he writes. Exactly. The young fella, with the short haircut which suited him so well, had so little to say for himself. His bat was his tongue. Perhaps it is Man's fate to become intolerant and loquacious with the passing years.

* Let alone becoming Sir Ian

Wisden Cricket Monthly, November 1994

I.T.Botham, cricketer whose fame and exploits won him a starring role in the outrageous Spitting Image series on television.

By now it was patently clear that in Shane Warne the cricket world had thrown up somebody very special. A dozen years later he would have been many people's selection as the finest spinner of all time:

Wizard Warne

SOME YEARS ago, public opinion on who was the greatest bowler that cricket had ever seen was divided simply between England's S.F.Barnes and Australia's Bill O'Reilly. It is no longer that straightforward.

Over the past forty years further names have suggested themselves. No more competent off-spinner ever lived than England's Jim Laker. Australia's fast bowlers Ray Lindwall, Dennis Lillee and Jeff Thomson often looked unplayable. From West Indies have come fast men galore, the thoroughbred Michael Holding and the awkward beanpole Curtly Ambrose being the pick of the bunch. Another skilful paceman who customarily gave batsmen little hope of long life was New Zealand's Richard Hadlee; while from the subcontinent came the crippled genius Chandrasekhar, with his fizzing, bucking googlies and leg-breaks, and Pakistan's ace trickster Abdul Qadir, with pacemen Wasim Akram and Waqar Younis doing things with fast cricket balls which have seldom if ever been done before.

Statistics inevitably come into it, but there is more to it than that: otherwise Kapil Dev, the [current] Test leader, would be top of the list – or Wilfred Rhodes, with his supreme tally of 4187 first-class wickets.

That bowlers win matches is a maxim repeatedly demonstrated. At the Gabba on November 29, Shane Warne completed an Australian victory over England which was initially shaped by McDermott, a bowler of a different temperament and technique. "Wizard" Warne once again came into his own in the later stages of a match, when the pitch was uneven from the constant pounding and scraping of the bowlers throughout four days. Much of Warne's damage was launched from around the wicket, leaving the batsman with no sensible alternative but to block the delivery with pad or body. It was therefore, in a sense, *negative* leg-spin bowling, which is almost a contradiction in terms. Warne's spiritual ancestor, Arthur Mailey, attacked non-stop, tossing the ball high from over the wicket, dipping it with top-spin, turning it this way and that, chuckling as he was belted for six, lighting up with his Irish grin as his over-confident opponent met his demise.

Warne, like Mailey, believes that laughter is permissible on the Test cricket field, and that is an endearing characteristic. But he is less inclined to "buy" his wickets. There is more of O'Reilly about him, a belligerence more usually associated with the fast men. Mailey, Grimmett, O'Reilly, Benaud – none of them would have turned into a screaming madman as Warne did in Johannesburg last March after his dismissal of Hudson. But Warne deeply regrets "cracking" in public, has apologised repeatedly, and asks how many times does he have to be "hung" for this deranged exhibition.

Reputation restored, the Wizard now looks capable of taking at least 40 wickets in this 1994-95 series against England. He continues to spin the ball extravagant distances, with the widest range of variations known to man, all controlled with extraordinary accuracy. Importantly, he is supported by a highly skilled wicketkeeper in Ian Healy and a crowd of close fielders who miss hardly anything. At times, one's sympathy for the batsman as he seeks to live in this hostile environment is heartfelt.

Warne bowled 50.2 overs in England's second innings at Brisbane, and was as bright as a button at the conclusion. His 8 for 71 removed another by the name of

Keith from the top of the best-bowling table in Ashes Tests in that city; Keith Miller, who turned seventy-five during the match, and, to judge from the verdicts of Len Hutton and other batsmen, merits inclusion among the luminaries listed above.

It seems, therefore, that Shane Keith Warne is close to being as lethal a bowler as any that cricket has seen. At Brisbane, he slipped past O'Reilly's total of 144 Test wickets, and it is food for thought that at the Wizard's age (25 years 77 days) the Tiger had not yet made his Test debut. At the rate at which Tests are played now, Warne could end up with 100 caps, and that might bring him 500 wickets. How many Tests might he win for Australia in that time? He has taken 61 wickets in nine Tests this year, following 72 in 1993.

The lip-cream gleams whiter than white; the creamy-yellow hair spikes up in disciplined rebellion; the blue-green eyes sparkle in unison with the diamond ear-stud; the personal pride and joy ooze boyishly. The challenge to England – indeed, to the world – is to find broader pads, broader bats even, and some kind of strategy (apart from winning the toss) which so far remains undiscovered. Even Ambrose needs rest after 10 overs. Warne, it seems, cannot be worn down.

Wisden Cricket Monthly, January 1995

Those seemingly bold projections were exposed, a dozen years later, as actually being too conservative. Warne went on to pass 700 Test wickets, and then retired in favour of Twenty/20 treasure when Australia would have benefited from his continuing service.

The Gabba, November 1994: Warne scuttles Alec Stewart in England's second innings on his way to figures of 8 for 71. (PA Photos)

I'd always promised myself that if ever I had a son I would name him after the world's leading batsman at that time. The first Frith junior, born December 1958, was thus named after Peter May. (Some clever-dick friends have since remarked that perhaps it should have been "Garfield" or even "Hanif".) It was with great sadness that the following was penned upon P.B.H.May's somewhat premature death days before his sixty-fifth birthday:

Farewell, PBH

PETER MAY was the archetypal clean-cut Englishman, tall, square-shouldered, erect, slightly stiff of movement, self-effacing and taciturn, shy of smile but steely in reaction to adversity. At Sydney in 1954-55, he strode to the wicket in a second-innings crisis and built, with Cowdrey, a bridgehead to victory, which Tyson's thunderbolts eventually secured.

Even at twenty-four, May looked like a schoolboy magnified. Bat-face towards his pads in the stance, he drove powerfully through the on side and straight, while his square-drive unfurled beside a long left pad, the strong shoulders imparting unusual velocity to the bruised ball. A forward defensive against Lindwall, Miller, Johnston or Archer was a barn-door.

But he could crack the short ball cross-batted through midwicket with the best of them.

Four years later he returned to Australia with the burden of captaincy upon him. The team looked as strong as England had ever sent to Australia, but the result was as bad for England as this current 1994-95 Ashes series threatens to be. Peter May was saddened by the underperformance of his own players, by the dubious bowling action of at least one of the Australian bowlers, and by the intrusion into his personal life after his fiancee joined him in Australia. His Melbourne Test century, though, was a joy for this particular admirer, who had named his first-born after the England captain twelve days earlier.

Last spring, we talked for the last time, gazing from a Tavern Stand box across an almost empty Lord's. In his

P.B.H.May, England's master batsman of the 1950s.

273

delicate, nasal tones he commented on the recent England tour of West Indies, and affirmed his hope that a revival would stir. At sixty-four, he still seemed extraordinarily boyish.

His years as chairman of Test selectors caused him heartache. "PBH" was not the sort of man who enjoyed being lampooned by the press. He grew touchy. At different times he poured scorn on the use of the word "pressure", and, though he was never disposed to wag his finger, it was as if he were doing so when he once pointed out with gentle vigour that he never changed his mind about anything. When asked privately how broad was the brief of the new England manager/coach Micky Stewart, with a suggestion of that angled grin May responded: "He did as he was told as a player, and he'll do so now."

It was that sense of discipline which made him the great batsman that he was. Two Peter Mays now would put England right.

Wisden Cricket Monthly, February 1995

A gathering in Sydney early in 1995 ranks above almost every other cricket occasion because the chief guests were first-class cricketers who had also served in the Second World War. They were warm, friendly men who knew the true values in life:

Remembering 1945

AUSTRALIA'S COMMEMORATION of the end of the war in Europe and the Pacific fifty years ago this year kicked off with a reunion dinner in Sydney on January 4 at which members of the Australian Services cricket team of 1945 were present. Most of them played in the "Victory Tests" in England, three at Lord's and one each at Bramall Lane and Old Trafford. Among those present who had served in uniform but were unable to take part in the "Victory Tests" were Ray Lindwall and Bill Brown, while New Zealand's Martin Donnelly, who played at Lord's for The Dominions (and scored a century which was quickly overshadowed by Keith Miller's hurricane 185), was also present, dapper as ever at seventy-seven. Miller was too ill to attend, and poor health prevented Bob Cristofani from travelling from England. The late Lindsay Hassett, captain in 1945 and "12th Man" in perpetuity, was represented by his widow, Tess.

There never could have been an evening quite like it as the veteran Servicemen/cricketers supped at the Cricketers Club of New South Wales, some, such as Colin Bremner and Stan Sismey, with the wives they first met over half-a-century ago while stationed in Britain. Proceedings, which were hosted by ABC Radio's Neville Oliver, began with some newsreel footage of the 1945 matches and a recent interview with the popular and whimsical Hassett.

Some of the guests of honour then reminisced at the microphone, A.G.(Bert) Cheetham (NSW pre-war) recalling his sense of privilege at the scoreline marking his debut at Lord's: c Hammond b Wright 0. Cheetham, who bowled the opening over in that first Victory Test, was less thrilled at his second innings, when his partner Cec Pepper ran him out for the same bare score.

Perky Ross Stanford, who won the DFC while bombing German rocket-launching sites with 617 ("Dambuster") Squadron, sang a few wartime ditties, including *Along Came a Bloody Blackbird*, to which the Aussie airmen had London's high society rocking and bending in their tiaras and tight dresses. The Lancaster pilot, who scored 416 not out as a schoolboy in 1931, then laughed about his first-class debut, at Adelaide in 1936. Don Bradman made 369, but when Stanford joined him at 533 for 4, the eighteen-year-old was so nervous that he pushed his first ball to mid-off and bolted. The Don's hand was firmly raised and the throw ran Stanford out.

They talked about their glorious failures on the cricket field, but they were good players to a man, as well as war veterans who treasured the true significance of sport in a way that few young men could understand. Norm Stocks is still seeking a 1946 *Wisden*, just to prove that it all happened. Larry Maddison, the team physio, whose skills were valued particularly on the India leg of the tour, confessed that his own muscles weren't as full and taut as they used to be. Reg Ellis still wants to write a book about his adventures in '45. Eddie Williams looks not much more than half his eighty years.

Australia Remembers 1945-1995 – this event having been co-ordinated by Sgt Grant Pinder – thus received a warm-hearted launching, thanks also to Stan Sismey's thoughtful narrative about the unit's formation. Dead comrades were remembered, but above all it had the feel of a joyous thanksgiving. The testimony back in 1945 had been convincing enough, with many thousands of war-fatigued spectators at Lord's eagerly watching the soldiers and airmen from Britain and Australia as they pushed the six-year tragedy behind them.

Wisden Cricket Monthly, March 1995

Early in 1995 the long period of West Indies supremacy (they were unbeaten in 29 series) ended at last:

End of West Indies' Domination

FOR THOSE who prefer commonsense to computers, Australia are now champions of the cricket world. Forget the one-day stuff, which is so often a lottery. Forget Pakistan's Test claims, too, for they are now in total disarray. The writing on the West Indian wall is now flashing in neon. Their long, long term as "unbeatables" came to an end not merely in series defeat but in a humiliating innings loss that had some of their players weeping. VJ Day took on a new meaning for younger Australians: Victory in Jamaica.

Now it's up to England to balance some of the "blackwashes" of recent years and to push West Indies further down the world league. The players are there. Might it be too much to expect that Graeme Hick, who has been lampooned for his difficulties against the short ball, will emulate another who has been targeted and ridiculed – Steve Waugh – by working his way to a double-century?

It is to be hoped that the crowds in England will be spared the kind of revolting display turned on by Ambrose at Sabina Park, when he loped down to within a couple of feet of Waugh to deliver a mouthful. Ambrose's captain tried in vain to pull him back. What might a Peter Burge have made of that as match referee? Ambrose was most fortunate that the lenient Majid Khan was presiding. In cricket as in civil law, there is no consistency.

One thing guaranteed to West Indians, as ever in England, is generous applause for whatever their batsmen, bowlers and fieldsmen achieve, though this time there will be some patriotic stirrings from the "Barmy Army". The Australians were stunned by the habitual silence which greeted their batsmen's boundary shots. So much for the allegedly "knowledgable" and "cricket-loving" spectators of the Caribbean.

Reflect on the uncertainties experienced by Richie Richardson as the rival Caribbean territories nibble away at him in their outrage and jealousy, and compare it with the unbending and universal support given to Allan Border and, in turn, Mark

Taylor by the entire Australian community. There might just be some justification for the backbiting in Richardson's case, for he is in charge of a combination from a number of independent countries. Atherton surely has no such handicap (despite the foreign-borns in his ranks).

Wisden Cricket Monthly, June 1995

The 1995 England v West Indies series was drawn two-all; West Indies' position at the peak of Test cricket was now past, and grim and often humiliating years lay ahead.

The running of county cricket has long been the subject of heated discussion and to a host of manoeuvres and adjustments. The modern world was moving at a hectic and sometimes panicky rate, so the proposals to do this and that to the established structure came thick and fast. Interpretation was not always easy, but it was worth a try:

Reaction v Revolution

COUNTY CRICKET is beautiful. That is the opinion expressed by a contributor to the latest issue of Kent County Cricket Supporters Club's periodical booklet, and it is expressed in defiance of the threatened major surgery on the English domestic game, surgery that we are assured will lead to more England Test victories.

The heartfelt assertion by "The Boy on the Boundary" does not surprise, for it comes out of a corner of England which may be seen as a heartland of traditionalism, a county which has suffered lacerations by the Channel Tunnel rail link almost comparable to that administered by the Luftwaffe. Kent also happens to be a non-Test-match county.

The six gentlemen who drew up the *Report of the Test Match Ground County Clubs Working Party into the Future of English Cricket* are all employed by county clubs which are privileged to stage Test matches, and they therefore consider themselves to hold the real power. A notable absentee is any representative from Lord's, be he from MCC or Middlesex, though agreement is expressed with certain restructuring recommendations detailed in MCC's Griffiths Report of early 1994. An oddity is that two of the authors, from Surrey and Yorkshire, work for clubs which are only tenants at The Oval and Headingley respectively, just as Middlesex are at Lord's. The thirteen first-class counties not represented on the self-appointed working party include several which could just as easily have become "Test match proprietors" in the time of our Victorian forefathers. They will need convincing that the present structure is not the best.

The working party's initiative in preparing the discussion document must be applauded, for without it the TCCB would presumably have done nothing to satisfy this country's craving for an investigation into England's increasingly disappointing performances. It is this problem which was the driving force and which was listed as Item 1 among the Objectives. The feeling seems to be that if everything is right with the national team, everything will be fine in county cricket and at lower levels.

By the same token, if things are not right at Test level, many administrators seem to fear that support for the English game will dwindle. It is an unsavoury fact, however, that the support they fear losing is not that of the county members but of sponsors and those fine fellows who swill wine all day in the corporate hospitality areas.

Based on last year's Championship table, Lancashire and Yorkshire would be in any new Second Division. It is reasonable to suppose that they would quickly buy themselves out of it, recruiting top players, redoubling efforts to raise money, and utilising what could be a guaranteed £750,000 annual grant from central funds (surely the first hard proposal on the distribution of the next four years' riches from the new TV contract). Beyond the four years? More fear: that more England defeats will reduce the drawing-power of television and its support advertisers.

So it's all about money, and that should surprise no-one. Would the current England side be any stronger and more competitive had it sprung out of the two-division system? Would there be more players of talent vying for jobs in first-class cricket? No to the first, yes to the second; but it's anybody's guess.

It is not all to do with numbers and cash. The tiny island of Barbados once had a team that might have beaten other countries of vast populations. Cash cannot buy the sort of passion displayed by Test teams such as Australia when they strut out into the arena.

So what if the main thrust of the "Big Five's" paper is adopted and six years from now England are still in the lower reaches of the world Test table? County cricket by then might not be quite as "beautiful" and the deckchairs at Canterbury, Hove, Cheltenham, Chelmsford, Northampton, Grace Road and Chesterfield might mostly be empty. Never was it a trickier time to balance reaction with revolution.

Wisden Cricket Monthly, July 1995

The men in suits went on their irresistible course, tinkering, devising, compulsively rearranging. The County Championship was divided into two divisions; central contracts for a Test squad were introduced; and as the new century unfurled they fell to their knees before the cash cow that was Twenty/20 cricket. As for England's Test team, they were to continue to have some good years, some bad ones. How could it be otherwise?

Here is another book review that had special meaning:

Philpott on Cricket

PETER PHILPOTT, former Australian Test leg-spinner and coach, knows as much about wrist-spin as anyone alive or dead. And I say that not simply because he got me out twice in one afternoon in a grade match in Sydney many years ago (I'm still smouldering over the lbw). He has, also, the precious gift of communicating lucidly and kindly, a legacy of his schoolteaching days. Like all lovers of this most difficult of arts, he is thrilled that far from completing its headlong dive to extinction, leg-spin and its variations is popular again, a bouncy blond Victorian leading the revival. Some philanthropist ought to buy up huge quantities of this manual and distribute it to schools and clubs all over the land. Even if only one Doug Wright emerges, the exercise would be worthwhile. The observations are thick on every page and even in the picture captions: for instance, Ian Salisbury has a "stiffness and military precision" about his action which compares unfavourably with those who have "fluid grace". Like artists of the brush, only the lucky few are born to prosper. But study of this book will usher in both fun and improvement. It may just be the best ever written on the subject.

Wisden Cricket Monthly, July 1995

Having published a contributor's article which examined the thorny territory of national identity and commitment by foreign-born cricketers – a feature which sent some people into paroxysms of indignation – I found myself writing an editorial on the subject as pertaining to one particular cricketer who was to have a colourful career as an Australian Test and one-day player. His personal dilemma at this early stage of his career, when he had already set a new world record for sixes hit in an innings and a match, was painful to behold:

Symonds's Dilemma

IN WHAT has become cricket's Year of National Identity, it was hardly surprising that the 1995 English season should end on a note of farce. Midst a maze of rules and regulations, speculations and declarations, the career path of Andrew "Roy" Symonds has become a *cause celebre*.

The young man from Queensland may be forgiven for feeling slightly bewildered at the invitation to tour Pakistan with England "A", chosen on the basis of his English birth qualification and his assertion earlier this year that it was his "desire and intention" to represent England. This statement, while not quite a legal affidavit, permitted him to join Gloucestershire. The county, having seen promise turn to spectacular reality, naturally want him back (Jack Russell said "preferably for the next twenty years") – though preferably without the encumbrance of an "overseas" label.

Symonds is to be congratulated for politely rejecting the "A" tour invitation. He knows, having spent the past 90-odd percent of his life in Australia, that the birth qualification is little short of a joke. Like another brilliant cricketer, Mike Procter, who suddenly became "English" in 1980, he recognised the classification as little more than an expedient. Procter felt it would have been absurd for him to have turned out for England in a Test match. He was South African. That was his national identity. Gloucestershire were his employers in the game he loved and at which he excelled. Nothing more.

Now, despite the advantage that usually accompanies a birthright, Symonds, an Australia Under-19 player and now the world champion six-hitter, will have difficulty in gaining acceptance by the TCCB in future years as anything other than an overseas player. Selection by Australia this winter, even in a one-day international, would prove conclusive of course.

Once again, this complex matter would seem best funnelled into one criterion: where did a player learn his cricket? While this may not always be easily a matter for certification, it would have prevented the Symonds fiasco – and also, incidentally, Roger Twose's transition from a native England fringe prospect into a "prefabricated" player for New Zealand.

Then again, perhaps none of this matters? The ICC has its Qualification Rules and allows for countries to tighten them further if they wish. If a cricketer is, to summon John Woodcock's notorious words at the time of Tony Greig's 1977 defection to Packer cricket, not "English through and through", does anyone really care? If either a foreign-born but genuinely UK-resident or a British-born but overseas-raised player keenly wants to play for England, does it matter whether it was his heart or his wallet that persuaded him?

Groomed at Australia's Cricket Academy, Symonds, who has not even been certain of a place in the Queensland XI, has responded to the signal from his heart. His adoptive parents, who emigrated from Birmingham with baby Andrew in 1977, and his friends and team-mates on the Gold Coast have told him – perhaps without even opening their lips – where he belongs. In identifying his Australian preference, Symonds had to resist not only the blandishments of the England selectors and his county club but of the Cricket Writers Club, who gave him their coveted Young Cricketer of the Year award (even if several members voted for him out of a playful sense of mischief), and of the Professional Cricketers Association, who made a similar award (while also demanding that he be reclassified as an overseas player).

If there was a further ironic side to it all, it was that certain players who themselves once turned their backs on England were now critical of the young man for refusing the England "A" offer.

In Andrew Symonds's particular case it was an agonising decision. But it was the right one.

Wisden Cricket Monthly, October 1995

Society's behaviour continued to be reflected in cricket, not least in lower levels. First-hand observation prompted the following letter to a leading magazine:

Game Scarcely Worth Playing

SANDY MITCHELL (Comment, August 17) spotlights an all-too-real sadness surrounding cricket today at its lower levels. Television sees to it as never before that the game, as Neville Cardus was among the first to observe, reflects society. At top level it is played almost completely without chivalry, but with meanness, greed (the product of insecurity), and sometimes brutality. Inevitably, those who watch then go about their weekend aspirations in emulation of what they have witnessed.

As I stumble through my forty-fifth playing season, I am usually deafened when batting by fieldsmen incessantly clapping – not my strokeplay, I hasten to state, but in their ritualised attempt to gee up their fellows. We even have a chap in our ranks who bellows "Keep at it!" from the first over, as if our concentration and "commitment" were likely to begin to fade after three deliveries.

One opposing captain recently proposed, when play was impossible on a rainy Saturday, that scores be fabricated so that more points might come the way of both our teams. Dishonest shouts for catches and leg-befores are now the norm. And when players have to stand in for absent umpires, cheating is rife. The game is, quite simply, scarcely worth playing in such circumstances.

I am not alone in wondering if the days of clean, competitive cricket are past, and it is time to find a gentle "friendly" on a Sunday. Or do even those games resound to clapping and shouting all afternoon?

Country Life, September 7, 1995

The 1995 England v West Indies series might easily have gone West Indies' way had not Richard Illingworth supported Mike Watkinson in a tenth-wicket stand lasting an hour and a half in the penultimate Test:

Cricket's Cobra Quality

CRICKET HAS a cobra quality. It sways dreamily, lulling all around it into a trance. All is timelessness. Muscles, eyes, senses relax. Warmth embraces. Thoughts wander. Then the snake strikes.

Such was the fifth Test at the hospitable, historic Trent Bridge ground, a contest in which the pattern fooled some seasoned cricket-watchers into asserting, even in the tense fifth day, that this was an "inevitable draw". Yet when Mike Watkinson spooned a catch to Sherwin Campbell midway through the final day, England were 214 ahead with about three hours remaining. Lara might have knocked off that target almost off his own bat.

Instead, the catch fell from Campbell's grasp, denying Walsh his 300th Test wicket, and England's tenth-wicket resistance lasted a further 24 overs before the "inevitable draw" became just that.

Not that all the engrossing cricket came on this gripping last day. Throughout the match, as throughout the series, the battle was hypnotic.

Wisden Cricket Monthly, October 1995

England went on to draw the Oval Test too, leaving an absorbing series tied two-all.

Brian Johnston had been just about the most popular figure in cricket. A 1995 biography was reviewed with some keenness:

Searching for the Inner Man

THERE IS, of course, no shortage of Johnstoniana. Over the past twenty-odd years Brian Johnston himself was responsible for piles of books and tapes, and soon after his death a compendium predictably entered the bestseller list. What, then, could Tim Heald add?

It was his aim to discover the inner man, the *real* Johnners, the persona. What lay beyond the beams of warmth and jocularity? Was he any different in private?

Two key areas beckoned to be explored: the drowning of his father and remarriage of his mother when Brian was ten, and his receiving the Military Cross in 1944 while serving with the Grenadiers. Were these the major influences in the construction of a personality that charmed a nation and left it – or a vast proportion of it – inconsolable when BJ died in 1994?

The jury is still out. It is no new theory that, as with so many comedians, his daily objective was to shut out the cruelty and ugliness of the world. The author didn't know him for long, but he is skilled at enticing people to rack their memories and trot out their recollections. Thus Lord Runcie believes that a large portion of Brian Johnston's emotional life was kept carefully suppressed, while the author himself concludes surely with accuracy of touch that the laughter and the smiles were "always keeping the dark side of life at bay".

The book may well be "authorised", but wisely the warts have been dotted in: his humour was often, to be frank, lavatorial; transcripts of his cricket commentary "seldom stand the test of time" – future generations may find it hard to understand what all the fuss was about, though importantly, as John Arlott pointed out, he made pomposity in the commentary-box impossible; and occasional indiscretions could only be described as clumsy.

His political incorrectness was endearing, and any man who is reduced to tears by *Carousel* just *has* to be a good man. That he drove himself too hard in his final years was a tragedy that was perhaps inevitable. At eighty he was performing his roadshow. It was not particularly profound stuff but *entertainment*, delivered with a "deft professional touch". And it was punishing. Heald believes it to have been probably the "most extraordinary thing he ever did" in his extraordinary life.

The most accurate summary might have come from a blind listener, who said: "He was a friend to those who never knew him, eyes to those that cannot see, warmth to those who were alone and depressed."

As for the man behind the man: what was there? Judging for yourself could be a lot of fun.

Wisden Cricket Monthly, October 1995

Soon, Wisden Cricket Monthly, the magazine I had founded, reached its 200th edition. It was a time to look back in reflection and plan for the next decade:

Taking Fresh Guard

PLEASANT THOUGH it would have been to have highlighted our 200th edition with an account of a thrilling reunification Test match in South Africa, it was not to be – though Mike's [Atherton] Miracle of Johannesburg will amply suffice. Yet again, England's cricket community can indulge itself in a wry smile at those from afar who habitually scoff at the rain that is alleged always to fall exclusively on English cricket grounds.

Our pleasure as our double-century edition comes up is nonetheless heartfelt. While a 200th issue is not exactly a bicentennial in years, it represents a triumph of survival in an age in which competition has been fierce and financial stability generally precarious in most areas of business.

WCM's foundation in the spring of 1979 coincided not only with the election of Britain's first female prime minister but also with the liberating peace pact between established cricket and the Packer revolutionaries. Cricket had lost its innocence – such as it was. It was a sacred game no more, and perhaps we were fools for even having believed that it had been.

As a new-born member of the time-honoured family of Wisden publications, the magazine was given a gratifying reception – almost everywhere. It was clear that a need was being answered. We have not merely talked about "facing cricket's major issues": we have tackled them head-on, interpreted them, absorbed and reflected the opinions of the game's followers – our readers – the body of people without whom cricket would be no more significant than ludo.

Our compact staff have met admirably the demands of working both at considerable speed and to a high level of accuracy. That level might easily be confused with pedantry, but in reality it is intended to recapture long-lost standards.

Through many of *WCM*'s years it was not only difficult to keep Botham off the front cover but accommodating all that warranted inclusion has caused many a headache, eased slightly by the enlarged editions of recent years. Some of the hardest letters this particular editor has to write are to would-be authors, trying to explain the seemingly inexplicable: that there is simply no room for their offerings. It is a tribute to cricket that so many people want to express themselves in its cause.

John Arlott, the founding spirit, led a contributors list over the years that was all an editor could ever have desired. Then, once every month, the editor himself has had to get steamed up over some contemporary controversy. These mildly irate outbursts later brewed as frequently as fortnightly as the game's agonies and contortions multiplied. But there was pride, too, in such matters as more informative scoresheets, with the innovative crediting of run-out fielders, and the campaign – all ten years of it – for video-assisted umpiring, the adoption of which [line decisions only at this juncture] has cleansed one of international cricket's darkest corners. Should we ever conjure a solution to the problems surrounding the murky matter of adjudging lbw, *WCM* readers will be the first to know.

We listen to our readers. The periodic surveys have ensured that our endeavours are on course to satisfaction: county cricket covered in depth, the ever-increasing global game reported informatively, minor (parochial) cricket acknowledged where it has broader interest, a quota of historical matter, the employment of photographs not commonly available. The baptismal pledge of 1979 has continued to be honoured.

A cricket magazine is unique in format and presentation, and builds up into a collection which finally outweighs even the heaviest of books (eight million words and ten thousand pictures so far in our case). But the years have brought change: broader newspaper coverage of cricket, the introduction of radio and television "magazine" programmes, and more random printed ephemera than ever before have all conspired to restrict the growth of the art-paper colour monthly. Whether *WCM* will survive through next century, when CD-ROMs and other electronic wizardry will also be aimed at keeping cricket-lovers well-informed and happy, only time will disclose.

Aluminium bats, the acceptance of helmets, pirate players, spectator assaulting player, player kicking player, underarm deliveries, streakers, political grandstanding, county club upheavals, revered old records smashed, pot-smoking allegations, West Indies' unprecedented bouncer-based domination, Sri Lanka's and Zimbabwe's entry at Test level, purposeful book reviews, obituaries of the great and good – all of this has been recorded in *WCM* in the past sixteen years and eight months. We can only guess at whether the years to come will throw up so much of the unexpected. It will surprise if they don't.

So, Merry Christmas and Happy '96, dear readers and advertisers, and thank you for your ongoing support. We take fresh guard at 200, and aim to reach 300 with the attention to detail of a Bradman, the attractiveness of a Lara, and, wherever possible, the jollity of a Compton.

Wisden Cricket Monthly, January 1996

Six weeks later I was dismissed.

Unexpectedly, the chance had arisen to write an autobiography. With my life spread across England and Australia, it was natural that the book should be called Caught England, Bowled Australia. Here is a passage describing my enmeshment by cricket in the early 1950s:

Caught in Cricket's Lovely Trap

CRICKET HAD now well and truly taken over. Old Mr Doust across the road was telling me tales of Trumper and Bardsley and Collins; I was playing at school and at weekends and with Keith across the road whenever the rain let up, and crouched over one of the table-cricket games when it was too dark or wet outside. When nobody else was available, I'd put a cricket ball into one of Mum's cast-off stockings and tie it to the clothes-line and bop-bop-bop-bop-bop until I felt the off-drive was as good as Hutton's. Conveniently, there was the deserted school playground across the road, where a tennis ball could be hurled forty-five yards towards a chalked wicket (how was I to know I was about to start a forty-odd-year career perched at slip?). Then, throwing the ball from fifteen yards, one could bat against the rebound. Who needed anybody else? The imaginary teams were brilliant, Trumper followed by Bradman, Hobbs and Hammond opposing them. Soon I had whipped up a cricket jamboree such as no kid before me, surely, had ever known.

When I was exhausted I would climb one of the gumtrees by the school perimeter, with cicadas screeching, and look down on the empty playground and quiet street, wondering if I would ever be good enough to play in a Test match, and wondering whether to face up to the certain truth that of course I never would. Even if my technique continued to improve, perhaps one day touching the perfection of a Hutton or a Lindwall, I sensed that my temperament would always be an insurmountable handicap. I even got nervous playing against myself up against that school wall.

All kinds of variations presented themselves. I tried a golf ball against the wall and it came back so fast I almost lost an eye. But it assisted the development of the hook shot – as did the join in the matting in the middle of our Saturday-morning pitch. An elephant of a fast bowler, left arm over, dropped on the join one day, and had I not got my first real hook stroke to it it would have killed me. And already I was hearing the odd soul say that cricket was a slow game.

There was, of course, another kind of cerebral cricket. I spent all spare cash on cricket books at Dymocks, the old, high-vaulted shop in George Street, Sydney. The first was *Elusive Victory*, E.W.Swanton's book on the 1950-51 Ashes series, of which I could claim to be part, having watched one day's play and listened to almost all the rest on radio, clinging to each word uttered by the friendly Johnny Moyes, Alan McGilvray, Arthur Gilligan and Vic Richardson. Then came the first *Wisden*, an incomparable delight to handle for its chocolate binding and esoteric small type. And then came Cardus.

I lashed out 12/9d for *Good Days* and 4/6d for *The Summer Game*, and tried to work out, as the train rumbled me to school or back, what was meant by Grimmett's name penetrating "to the quiddity" and what sort of batsman must George Gunn have been if, as Cardus says, "his bat was a swift rapier used not for warfare but just to tickle the ribs"? This Woolley must have been something if some of his innings "stay with us until they become like poetry which can be told over again and again". As for MacLaren, my old teacher Mr Hawkins' favourite too, what a vision of him glowed from the page: "His bat swept down and, after his stroke, it remained on high, and MacLaren stood still, as though fixed by the magnificence of his own stroke." To my credit, I hope, I never tried this. Such florid batsmanship is associated with the English amateur rather than the down-to-earth and usually victorious Australian batsman.

There was not a spare minute. Off to the SCG to see Sheffield Shield cricket; playing cricket wherever the chance arose; reading about it; listening to radio commentary (no television then); back into Sydney to see the English cricketers at the hotel before they went home, having won the fifth Test in the wake of all those painful defeats.

I worked out a good way of compiling a scrapbook on the 1950-51 Test series. The local butcher used to ask for old newspapers, so I offered to stack and tidy them for him, while cutting out the cricket pictures. A nice coloured portrait of Compton out of *Sporting Life* crowned the front cover beautifully.

With every day that passed it became more obvious that cricket and I were made for each other. There was something supernatural about its grip on me. Every single day my diary entries carried the evidence though there were only around thirty-five words pencilled in. In November 1951 the entries tell it all: "Saw Bert Oldfield at his shop. Saw 1st day of NSW v West Indies. Spoke to Frank Worrell on the fine-leg fence" – "Did not go to school. Went to see West Indies v NSW. Got autographs. West Indies are stubborn but got 4. Came home with Ray Lindwall in his car. A great experience" – "Went to the Test match. Doubtful weather on and off all day. West Indies got a good start, 6-286. Got 4 autographs" – "Went on to Test match.

Sixteen years old, and striving to bowl like Lindwall and bat like Hutton.

Very crowded. Hottish. Went to dressing-rooms after. Only got three autographs. Went into stand and saw the photo gallery" – "Went to last day of 2nd Test. Took Mick. He was a devil. Aust won by 7 wkts. Stopped behind after. Only got 2 autographs and Worrell signed photo. Warm all day. Went to Bert Oldfield's in the morning. Got cap, bat oil and bat grip."

I framed the Worrell picture and hung it up. He was so charming, and his entry to the arena, white gear gleaming, red cap bright in the sunlight, black skin fascinating, was to be an enduring image.

Interest in cricket history was fanned by public film shows at Sydney Town Hall where, on a giant screen, the 1920s were recaptured as Jack Gregory thundered in again to bowl, with whimsical little Arthur Mailey twisting his leg-spinners down at the other end, and Hobbs and Sutcliffe, revered England batsmen, manoeuvred their grey bats to place the grey ball across the silver-grey outfield. All this plus film of the 1901 Federation ceremony and the diggers marching to war: a great shillingsworth.

And at last I got my first real cover-drive away. Having made it somewhat timidly into the school 1st XI, I went out to open with the deep-voiced extrovert beanpole, Rod Barton, who was to make a name for himself as a baseballer. The setting was the tree-ringed Chatswood Oval, where Macartney used to hit the ball over the railway line. Sick with nerves, as usual, I did Rod's running for him, pottered about a bit, and then found the glistening red ball coming along at a tempting width and rather a generous length.

What would Len Hutton have done? Put his left foot across, let the bat swing down easily, keeping the head steady, eyes glued to the ball. Crack! Away it journeyed, smacking into the white pickets, and the umpire expressionlessly signalled four. I too tried to show no emotion. But inside I was exploding with ecstasy.

Caught England, Bowled Australia: A Cricket Slave's Complex Story
[Autobiography] (Eva Press, 1997)

Poetry has never been a predilection but some time in the 1980s I felt disposed to dabble after a disappointing afternoon on the field:

Irredeemable Hours

Along green lanes;
Signposts to the afternoon
Of sport; and tight breathing
In the visions of what triumphs are to come.

And hours afield, from a lifetime, irredeemable,
Run down to the dusk,
When deep shades of unfulfilment
Dim the mind, and the soul
Is pressed low in dreams of what might have been.

Caught England, Bowled Australia (Eva Press, 1997)

Still playing league cricket at the age of sixty, I now found just as much pleasure in charity cricket, mostly with David English's renowned team the Bunburys:

Wet Wet Wet!

OUR LEADER, Captain English, is good at rounding up star attractions to play for his Bunburys cricket team. So how come he failed to sign Wet Wet Wet for the Puttenham match? In almost half-a-century of playing cricket, I have never encountered such flood conditions.

The cloudburst broke at precisely the time we were supposed to be taking the field against the British Comedy Society at this charming ground in the depths of Surrey. Up came the water level. Down went our spirits. So much had gone into the organisation, as always.

When the rain eased up there was idle, silly talk about playing after all. Players wandered out, their boots disappearing beneath mud and pools of fresh water. Then came a note of urgency. Our leader put us on full alert. Though we could hardly stand in the slush, the game was on!

The villagers descended on the waterlogged arena as word got round, and the event was saved. For the best part of three hours the players slipped and skidded and splashed in as bizarre a game of cricket as could ever have been staged. Tony Murphy, wise man, bowled off half-a-step rather than the dozen paces Surrey and Cheshire fans once knew. Boxer Gary Mason, distracted by his forthcoming wedding, gripped the red bar of soap and still endeavoured to bowl his Shane Warnes. Dave Beasant got some bounce. Leslie Grantham got some wickets, knowing the deadliness of the straight ball. Muggins here kept wicket – and later found that several washings failed to get rid of the mud stains from sweater and trousers. Local police have launched an enquiry into the contents of Puttenham Cricket Club's top-dressing.

Freddie Finn's record number of flights on Concorde (600-plus) was no good to him now. He set another record this day for the number of times he slipped aileron-over-tailplane. We feared for his safety. Which helped take our minds off our own.

We chased our target manfully – or it might have been more like dolphins, Robert Duncan finding the boundary with some lusty hits. Frith nearly ruptured himself with some ambitious hits before Andy Sinton (his batting partner, not a fielder) ran him out. As usual, this left the guilty one in need of reparation, and he duly played some shots which showed how football's gain was cricket's loss.

We were nearing our target but losing wickets. Beasant's dismissal was serious. But then Dave English smacked some good'uns to bring us within two runs of victory as the final ball came. Cluck! Away went the ball for an easy single. Scores level. But the winner had to be attempted, and the man running back to the danger end was Gary McDonald, of *EastEnders*.

He saw the incoming throw from the corner of his eye and desperately hurled himself through the air like Superman. Down he came, chest-first, to body surf all of fifteen feet, a glorious muddy spray proclaiming his progress. We had no access to video replay. Gary reckoned he had made it. The umpire didn't. It was a tie, and everyone was happy. Well, perhaps not Gary.

So we had pulled it off: played in defiance of conditions that would have had Test and county players on their way home hours ago. The crowd were especially appreciative, which made our commitment all the more enjoyable. As with all Bunbury matches, you finished with a warm glow. Plus, this time, unsavoury brown stains all over your clothing and pads.

It therefore came as a bit of a shock when, a month later, we descended upon rural Hampshire for the last match of the '96 season to find dry conditions. How would we handle them?

No such luck as a tie this time. Robin Smith's Hampshire side overwhelmed us at Clanfield. But, of course, everyone had a great time. And "Judge's" benefit benefited.

The England star arrived in style, by helicopter, and Ian Wright bowled for the Bunburys and batted for Hampshire, which confused scorer and statistician Vic Isaacs. And Fraser Hines, after coaching from me in the art of the flipper, bagged a cluster of wickets. Neil Foulds showed what we suspected already: that he could handle the red balls. And Smithy got into trim for a century next day against Nottinghamshire with a few trademark shots. Will Kendall, also about to make a hundred next day against Notts, registered a duck against the Buns now. Poor Paul Whitaker out-statisticked the lot by managing a duck now and another on the morrow.

Liam Botham batted, bowled, kept wicket, flew in the helicopter, and had a beer or two to prove whose blood was in his veins, and as darkness fell we chatted to our esteemed team-mates Neal Radford and Paul Pollard, and all worried about the whereabouts of "Buddy Holly", whose group were successful on the cricket field and were now ready to inflate the marquee with their marvellous music.

I never found out if Buddy turned up. Dark memories of 1959 came drifting back. Then it was off into the night, down the unlit Hampshire lanes, yet another cricket season ended, but in the nicest possible way: among my happy mates the Bunburys. Thanks, Dave.

The Bunbury Cricket Club Official 1997 Magazine

The Captaincy Debate

WAS THERE ever a time when the England captaincy was settled for more than a few months at a time? Years ago, when the skipper was always drawn from the ranks of the unpaid players (until Len Hutton's appointment in 1952), there was speculation as to whether Cowdrey or Dexter or Sheppard would lead the next touring team.

The appointment of hard-nosed Ray Illingworth to lead the 1970-71 England tour of Australia upset Cowdrey's supporters. Later that decade came the switch and swap of Denness and Greig and Brearley. In the 1980s, Gower, Gatting and Gooch were the participants in an undignified round of musical chairs.

At least with the appointment of Mike Atherton in 1993, when Graham Gooch tossed in the towel, there came hope that a young man with exceptional powers of self-discipline and poise would usher in a settled period of stability, when the captaincy issue would give way to more constructive matters, such as building a winning side by spotting talent and consolidating team unity.

Atherton has led from the front and has played many a memorable innings from the hot spot of No.1 in the order – none more stirring than his defiant 185 not out in almost 11 hours which saved the Johannesburg Test in December 1996. He has taken all that the ferocious West Indies bouncer merchants can fling at him, and has even worked out ways of existing for long periods against Shane Warne's leg-spin torture.

In Atherton's four-and-a-half years of Test captaincy, though, he has been forced more than once to "consider his position". When the world turned against him for rubbing a bit of soil on the ball in a Lord's Test in 1994, he wanted to chuck it in, feeling he was being treated with exaggerated hostility. Only his father and a couple of close friends persuaded him to carry on.

Then, at the end of last summer, when England's hopes of winning back the Ashes were dashed, he wondered if he should continue. He took his time, and surprised the pundits when he emerged from his meditation with fresh determination to carry on. He was now England's leading captain in terms of Tests, having passed Peter May's record of 41. Ahead loomed the Caribbean challenge, with England fancying their chances as never before in recent memory. The new administration was more clear-minded than its predecessors, and all seemed set for a co-ordinated England campaign.

Then what happened? Atherton spared himself the trip to Sharjah. Adam Holltoake, Surrey's tough and bold skipper, took over the England reins and pushed and pulled his side to glory, winning the Champions Trophy.

There it may have ended. Holltoake had done all that was expected of him – and more. But wait a minute! This aggressive Australian-born pocket Botham had hit the winning runs in all three one-day internationals against Australia a few months earlier, so why not fall in line with the new fashion of having a tailor-made one-day side apart from the Test side, with, if it should make sense, a separate captain? After all, Australia had broken with tradition by sidelining Test captain Mark Taylor and appointing Steve Waugh.

Here, as throughout history, England's selectors viewed matters differently from their Aussie counterparts. They stuck with Atherton.

There is an interesting similarity between Taylor and Atherton. Test captains of roughly equal experience, they both open the batting and make their runs at no great rate. It's not expected of them. They are anchormen, both of them. And yet Atherton has batted well in one-day cricket, making plenty of runs at a reasonable rate. So has Taylor for Australia, and his fans, who went on believing in him when the knives were out for him a year ago, are indignant that he was sidelined for the one-day tournament. It is not as if his successor, Steve Waugh, made lots of runs (he didn't) and won nearly every match (he didn't) and shone out as the on-field "general" (he didn't).

England, then, seem to have made the right decision in sticking with the same captain for Tests and one-dayers, and Holltoake has absorbed any disappointment he might have felt, knowing he still has a big role to play as a No.6 who chips in with inventive bowling, brave fielding, and a sometimes noisy "psychological" input.

He may yet lead England in next year's World Cup, for he is nothing if not dynamic.

Whether Mike Atherton cares to lift his performance in the field as far as being demonstrative goes remains to be seen. But it is unlikely. He is an undemonstrative person, highly intelligent, a tinge on the shy side, often sceptical, barely short of cynical. Like Holloake, he enjoys a really good laugh ("laff" as he would put it, in his Lancashire tongue; to Holloake's residual "laaaf"). But both are fiercely competitive. And what truly professional modern cricketer would not covet every honour within reach? That's why Holloake's disappointment should not be underestimated. All the talk before the announcement was that he would resume the England one-day captaincy at the end of the Test series in West Indies. That would have been an upward move of great significance beyond the Sharjah triumph, which was not even televised in Britain. The Caribbean series is very high-profile.

Adam Holloake will be as loyal as the rest of the England team. He has the same respect for his captain as they all have, including that other sometime media claimant for the leadership Alec Stewart. Just to play is the great honour. The pride, remuneration and spin-offs are beyond compare.

Atherton has endured many disappointments during his captaincy, and when he looks ahead to a fearfully busy schedule he must wonder how he'll be feeling when it's all over. After the Caribbean come the South Africans and a Test against Sri Lanka, then another Ashes tour of Australia, followed by the 1999 World Cup. In the circumstances, England must consider themselves fortunate that so much top captaincy material is available.

For my money, it's A.J.Holloake for England's World Cup challenge a year from now.

Cricket World (India), March 1998

Adam Holloake played on for Surrey until 2004, leaving the club as yet another of the many disenchanted. Atherton extended his England career after relinquishing the captaincy, and stepped off the field into a lucrative media career in which his articulacy surprised and amused those who could recall the taciturn figure who used to sit glumly in the hot seat during press conferences.

A special commemoration came with the summer of 1998 for what would have been W.G.Grace's 150th birthday. Among the publications to mark the event was a solid biography which the Telegraph asked me to review:

WG's Big Birthday

THIS SUMMER of the 150th anniversary of W.G.Grace's birth was ushered in less than civilly. *Wisden's* curmudgeonly essay "WG: Champion and Rotter" toed the modern trendy line of inconoclasm, the contributor seemingly distant from a full understanding of his subject.

In stark contrast, Simon Rae's biography of WG seems the most detailed and rounded picture so far of the Great Cricketer; the friendly, cheerful, bucolic athlete who, unencumbered by excessive intellect, chalked up not only batting and bowling records galore but also thousands upon thousands of uncomfortable rail miles.

WG was a man of action, not words, an utterly uncompromising adversary on the cricket field and at the negotiating table, and unquestionably the most notorious exponent of "shamateurism". But, as Rae makes clear (as did *The Memorial Biography of Dr W.G.Grace*, edited by Lord Hawke, Lord Harris and Sir Home

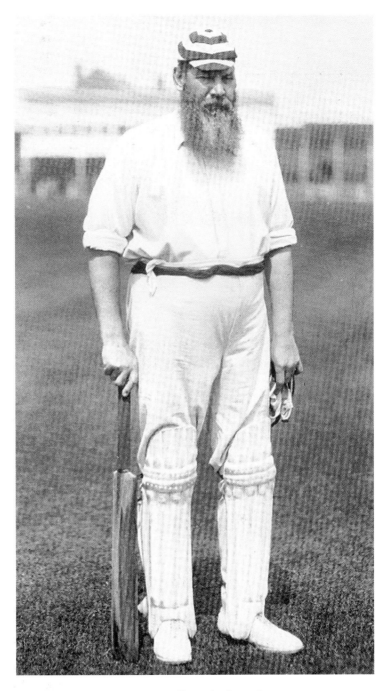

Dr William Gilbert Grace, still cricket's mightiest image.

Gordon in 1919), all who knew WG well revered him. He was uncomplicated, extraordinarily modest and warm-hearted, dominant in stature and attitude (in spite of his squeaky voice). He was also immensely clubbable.

All the familiar stories are here, newly wrapped: the apple-pips of raucous competitiveness among older brothers and relations (and dogs) in the Gloucestershire orchard; his amusingly halting speeches in North America and Australia and at the numerous banquets in England; his "kidnapping" of the padded-up Midwinter from Lord's to rejoin his native county; his sleepless night in the middle of a double-century innings as he tended a woman in childbirth (he chose to work as a GP in a poor district, treating the humblest of his patients free of charge); his umbrage at Kortright's throwaway "Surely you're not going, Doc? There's still one stump standing"; his sequence, when aged twenty-eight, of 344, 177 and 318 not out, the Yorkshiremen about to confront him in the last of these innings having proclaimed loudly that he would surely be spent after the first two giant innings at Canterbury and Clifton.

Furthermore, what ought to please the Englishman of today is that WG habitually upset Australians (it is claimed that he was the most "unpopular and vilified" English captain before Jardine) – although he had some treasured friendships, too, with his colonial brethren.

This is the weightiest of all books on Grace in wordage. Rae has indicated his sources for even the most obscure references, and has also found a way of recounting WG's match-by-match exploits over fifty-odd years without becoming tedious. The pictorial selection contains some pearls, and the text errors are few. The only recurring irritation is the reference throughout to *the* MCC. Otherwise, it is from start to sad conclusion a smooth and compelling read.

As the six-page bibliography suggests, the author has scanned so broadly that there is a surprising amount of fresh material, some of it concerning WG's ancestry; some of it on his and Agnes's "shamed" housekeeper (an unwed mother of two); we also learn that WG once had a marriage proposal rejected because of his high-pitched voice; and snippets such as the salmon-coloured drawers the young WG wore in sprints and hurdles sustain a vivid narrative.

There is no attempt here to excuse WG's inclinations to get physical with several who upset him, but, like some rugged schoolyard tearaway, he was usually ready to apologise for his over-exuberance and occasional "unparliamentary language". If Lord Harris, as well as his lowliest professional team-mate, admired him so fervently, he must have been fundamentally good. He was so popular and had cricket so thoroughly at heart, according to Harris, that his excesses were readily forgiven. Remind you of any particular modern cricketer?

Yet, despite WG's high profile at Lord's, he was probably never entirely "one of us". He seems to have cared little, but having to wait until he was forty before being asked to captain England's Test team must have stretched his patience. As for a knighthood or peerage, his chance seems to have flown in 1895 – his last golden summer – with Rosebery's succession by Salisbury as Prime Minister. Any such honour might not have sat comfortably with him. At that time, anyway, he was preoccupied with attracting the shillings into his three testimonials, which closed at the equivalent of £500,000 today.

This 560-page volume ensures that a national treasure's status is upheld in the face of myopic disbelievers. With the July 18 birth commemoration looming, let the toasts and celebrations begin.

Daily Telegraph, June 27, 1998

W.G.Grace re-entered the mind when passions were inflamed by the debate over whether MCC's membership should be opened to women:

What Would WG Have Thought?

IF THE MCC committee's wish is fulfilled, and the club's first female members come through the Grace Gates at Lord's around the time of the centenary of W.G.Grace's death in 2015, it seems fair to ponder what the great cricketer might have felt?

It should be said that Grace was unquestionably a man's man, though not necessarily a male chauvinist (a term he would little have understood).

His revered mother, Martha, knew more about cricket than many men. In 1873 he married his cousin Agnes, whom he committed to a taxing cricket tour of Australia by way of a honeymoon. He was devoted to his daughter, Bessie, who died young, and was a compassionate, capable country doctor, not least in seeing children of the poor into the world.

Grace was a man of deeds rather than words. There is no evidence that he had any opinions about suffragettes even though they burnt down the Tunbridge Wells pavilion.

But the politically-inspired push for women to make themselves at home in the Long Room – unthinkable in his time or even thirty years ago – might well have had Grace reacting, as he once did when he disapproved of an umpire's decision (not against himself, as it happened): "Shan't have it! Can't have it! And I won't have it!"

Daily Telegraph, August 27, 1998

WG's scowling, incredulous ghost notwithstanding, female membership was granted by MCC and the first women admitted were to be seen in the Long Room well before 2015.

Sometimes it takes longer than expected to put matters right. An invitation to review Devon Malcolm's ghosted autobiography provided one such opportunity:

A Delayed Response

ETHNIC CLEANSING in Bosnia, genocide in the Congo, India and Pakistan at nuclear loggerheads – and people are still going on about a goddam magazine article published three years ago.

Thus wrote a friend of mine upon hearing that the notorious article by Robert Henderson in the July 1995 edition of *Wisden Cricket Monthly* was still, three years later, an obsession for a few who habitually dip their pens in pots of acid and schadenfreude. The article, you might recall, had examined the possibility that foreign-born cricketers might occasionally have problems in mustering the fullest commitment when playing for England. Several players sued Wisden, who chose not to defend themselves. There were apologies and large financial settlements. And the controversy came in useful as part of an excuse to dismiss me as editor seventeen years after I had founded the magazine.

Devon Malcolm (who was mentioned just once, in passing, in the *WCM* article) and Phil DeFreitas (who now comes badly out of his former team-mate's book) were the key beneficiaries in that affair, so it is no surprise that Malcolm gives it a few pages in his autobiography. "Even my detractors would surely acknowledge that I'd always tried my utmost," he writes. Agreed. In which case how come he feared that his reputation would be damaged by that article? Ah, well . . . .

What shocks and disappoints is that he tells two gross fibs about me. He'd rung me up – he says on page 140 – to ask why I'd published the article, and I'm supposed to have told him that the subject was a matter for legitimate debate. *I haven't talked with Malcolm since January 21, 1991*, when he declined my invitation to a meal with other England players while they were in Queensland.

Two pages on he states that I "kept making desperate calls" to him in 1995 to try to reach a compromise after the article had appeared. Equally untrue and deplorable. He has been asked to explain these distortions, but I have not had the courtesy of a reply.

The challenge of reviewing Malcolm's book is therefore unusual. I've heard it described as "sour" and "miserable". Another Henderson – Michael of *The Times* – saw it as "ghosted pap" and Malcolm as a "moderate bowler" on whom "no captain could rely". He also recreates the scene as England celebrated an amazing victory over Australia at Edgbaston in 1997: Malcolm scurrying around begging players to scribble on memorabilia for his benefit. "For goodness sake, Dev," said Atherton, "can't you just enjoy this moment with the rest of the boys?"

So by now I'm beginning to feel almost sorry for the chap. Perhaps I could find something appealing to write about the book? I'd been as thrilled as anybody by his rare five-star performances, especially the 9 for 57 against South Africa in 1994, and I'd held my head when he bowled trash. I'd also written in outrage in *WCM* when, as a clueless No.11 batsman, he had been peppered with bouncers in Tests.

The delightful Arthur Mailey used to boast that he once bowled tripe and now he was writing it. There are similarities here, though there is nothing delightful about the dubious claims which undermine Malcolm's book. His ugly spat with Ray Illingworth and coach Peter Lever was about his bowling. He rejected the notion that he should run through straighter; and yet here (p.21) he recalls accepting the identical advice given him by Michael Holding way back when Jamaican-born Malcolm was still registered with Derbyshire as an overseas player. When he toured West Indies with England in 1990, the taunts of the Jamaican spectators "was definitely putting me off", which is equally interesting.

He knows a bit about trumped-up rows too, for that is the way he describes the Derbyshire v TCCB affair, when Micky Stewart offered to go north to give him special coaching, and the club chairman took loud exception.

There are further moans about a lack of discussion with Illingworth and Atherton. But does he not have a tongue? Then he says he could have sued over the "nonentity" label given him by Lever. Why not? He had already brought the board of Wisden to their knees. Might there have been reflection that the legal success was not a universally acclaimed victory? Then comes the insistent whinge at being omitted from the Durban Test, even though the selectors were vindicated when Ilott, Martin and Richard Illingworth took 10 for 145 in South Africa's only innings.

He poured out his grievances to the *Express* upon his return, thus breaking his contract. He blames the man from the TCCB for that, for not talking him out of it, would you believe? Malcolm had also amazingly stooped to playing the race card ("I was naïve"). He says he only wanted the right of reply. Well, sometimes we're denied this; and you can only vent it all to your poor wife. We seem to have that much in common.

My annotated copy of this pathetic book might, I suppose, make interesting reading one day. "Why not give me a chance?" Malcolm bleats at Edgbaston in '97. "A bad delivery has been known to dismiss a Test batsman." This, I simply had to scribble, is something no great Test bowler would ever be reduced to claiming. And who is he trying to kid when he says that it "wasn't in my nature to make a fuss"? He seems to have done little else over the past few years.

"I never bothered reading Illingworth's book," Devon Malcolm asserts. Well, he ought to. And mine too while he's at it.

Bodyline Books Catalogue, Autumn 1998

Contributing to a player's benefit publication has always been a pleasure (though I wasn't invited to write for Mr Malcolm's). Some cricketers, such as P.C.R.Tufnell, have afforded above-average scope for fascination:

Tufnell: a Favourite Character

SOME OF us are always on the lookout for the unusual in this age of dull conformity, and when a particular post-match press conference took place after the 1991 Oval Test, I knew we had it. Journalists were banked eight deep in the players' dining-room as Tuffers emerged. His cap was back-to-front, his feet were bare, a beer-can dripped in the clasp of fingers which had just spun six West Indians out for 25 runs, and the eternal cigarette drooped from his animated lips.

Micky Stewart, the England coach, sat beside him with his hand on Tuffers' shoulder. I thought at the time that this was not only to reassure Tuffers in the face of all the media attention but more a case of hoping to engage his "pause button"

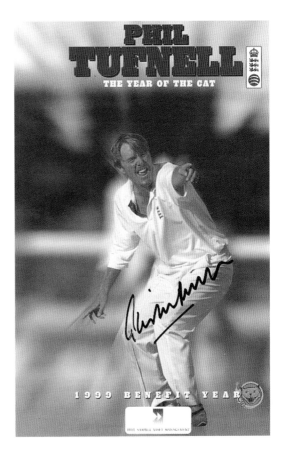

Philip Tufnell's benefit was his first big payday. Others followed when he became a television "celebrity".

293

when the need arose.

P.C.R.Tufnell laughed his way through that "conference", as he has since joked through many others, pretending not to take the game too seriously and always making it clear that he belonged to the proletariat even if he had three initials and attended a fairly posh school for a short while.

As a connoisseur of spin bowling, I was overjoyed when the Middlesex lad overcame a dismal Test debut in Melbourne to take five wickets at Sydney, coming within a whisker of claiming a hat-trick. He gave the ball a real tweak, and you prayed no-one in authority would try to persuade him to bowl tight, thereby reducing his flight. It had happened to others and at times even Tuffers was forced to resort to negative tactics. On these occasions you sensed his frustration and you felt for him.

His run-up initially caught the eye. Had there ever been a slowie who seemed to contort halfway to the wicket as if he was breaking wind, before twirling the arm and delivering a ball that curled and snapped the other way to the outside edge. Pure heaven.

The international wickets piled up: 5 for 94 against Sri Lanka at Lord's, again in 1991, and the memorable 7 for 47 at Christchurch in the thriller the following winter. Then the tabloid front-page stories began, and the England selectors became nervous about selecting him. Even in 1998 there were reservations about taking him to Australia for a third time, much to many Australians' relief. Tuffers had taken 11 wickets the last time they faced him at The Oval in 1997.

Tuffers reminds me of Tony Lock, though his batting falls short of the old Surrey and England man's. Even so, he brings rich entertainment to those watching. I remember one such occasion when a West Indian screamer veered towards his boot, causing him to yell out in advance. Unfortunately he pulled the wrong foot out of the way and the missile crashed into the remaining boot, followed by yet another scream.

Stay around, Tuffers, for another ten years, please.

Phil Tufnell Benefit Year 1999

He stayed around all right, but, alas, only as a television "celebrity" on mainly gormless programmes.

Closer to home, heartfelt support was tendered to a former team-mate:

Darren Bicknell: Giant Footprints

MY DEAR old friend John Arlott used to regard county cricketers as the salt of the earth. Never was he happier than when sharing the breakfast table with the players – preferably Hampshire, but not necessarily – as they browsed through the scores in the morning papers. Almost without exception, they felt themselves privileged to be involved with cricket for a living. An occasional ironic remark would inevitably emerge, but on the whole, warmth and generosity, even occasional sympathy, flavoured the conversation around the table.

Whether John Arlott would have felt at ease with the current generation of county cricketers will never be known, though one thing can be asserted: he would have enjoyed the company of the amiable and intelligent Darren Bicknell.

It is always a delight to witness the positive progress of a youngster into maturity. There was a time in the mid to late 1980s when it seemed possible that Guildford Cricket Club would one day supply half the England Test team. The Bicknell brothers were clearly bursting with talent. Then along came Ashley Giles, and my mate from Melbourne, John Hollioake, used to talk – as we stood patiently in the slips – about his two cricket-mad boys.

I kept wicket the day that teenager Giles switched to spin. He bowled it well, but I advised him to stick with pace, for he was built for it and bowled a mean seamer. Why not save spin for later years, when he loses that sharpness? Well, his back was already bothering him and, fortunately for him and the game, he ignored the well-meaning advice.

By now, D.J.Bicknell was already a Surrey player, having followed younger brother Martin into first-class ranks in 1987. We had been deeply impressed with his calmness and determination. As a fifteen-year-old, he had scored his first century in a club match. Everyone around him recognised his special qualities and willed him to advance, and this inevitably led to tons of "advice" being poured onto him. Wisely and tolerantly, he listened, always politely, and sifted out what seemed to make sense.

There was early difficulty against spin, and a tendency to lash out. These are the telling days for any aspiring cricketer, when brain-power, physical skills and emotions need to be harnessed securely. Young Darren did a masterful job of converting his natural powers into a method and a mentality that would serve him well at high level.

I vividly recall hearing his name on the BBC radio lunchtime round-up for the first time, when he was referred to as "Denzil" Bicknell. That was a jocular delight for all friends and family. His name soon became familiar and unmistakable though, and he now finds himself with thirty centuries in first-class cricket, and the prospect of a rewarding return to the game after major surgery which, while causing indescribable frustration at the time, will have refreshed his appetite for batting just when other thirty-one-year-olds might be creaking under the mental and physical

"Denzil" Bicknell, record-breaker from Guildford.

weight of so many years of non-stop cricket. For one thing, his wife and children know what he looks like. David Boon's daughter spoke for all professional cricketers' offspring when she asked Mummy during yet another Australian overseas tour: "Has Daddy gone to Heaven?"

There is indeed too much cricket for much of it to be absorbed seriously. But Darren Bicknell has left two giant footprints already on the game's history. In sixty years of county cricket at Guildford, his unbeaten 228 against Notts in 1995 is the highest innings*. It was also the longest at eight minutes under ten hours. And yet, a year earlier, he batted his way to the top of a very distinguished list by occupying the crease for 638 minutes in Surrey's match at Trent Bridge when scoring 235 not out. This was the longest innings ever played in a County Championship match, outlasting Arthur Shrewsbury's 10¼ hours for Notts v Middlesex, also at Trent Bridge, in 1887. Darren was pushed back to second place in 1996 when Jason Gallian batted 22 minutes longer for his 312 for Lancashire v Derbyshire at Old Trafford, emphasising the extra scope for the marathon which four-day cricket affords, these marvels of concentration pointing to Test match potential.

There is a third large D.J.Bicknell footprint, and that is the record Surrey third-wicket partnership he and David Ward established at Canterbury in 1990. Their 413 displaced the 1919 mark of 353 set by Andy Ducat and Ernie Hayes.

Future generations will feel that England must have had a fine opening pair during the 1990s for Darren to have advanced no further than England "A". And they will be right.

* Justin Langer (342 for Somerset v Surrey, in 618 minutes, in 2006) now holds the ground record.

Darren Bicknell Benefit Year 1999

There was never a friendlier cricketer than Godfrey Evans, whose obituary was one of the most painful to compose:

Genial Jack-in-a-Box Godfrey

HE WAS easily the jolliest and most spirited of cricketers, which makes it so painfully hard to say goodbye. Last summer he was the life and soul of an archive cricket film evening in Northampton, just as almost half-a-century ago he was keeping English chins up at the Sydney Cricket Ground as Australia piled up 400-plus against a bowling attack shorn of two key men. Godfrey Evans, whose death at the age of seventy-eight was announced yesterday, seemed biologically incapable of being downhearted, which was in keeping with his adventurous and optimistic nature.

Marriage at twenty was an early manifestation of these qualities, though in one biography "Godders" quietly conceded that he was never a saint. Despite the many separations while he pursued his spectacular wicketkeeping and cavalier batting for Kent and England, and through several business ventures that failed, the marriage lasted almost thirty years before it fell apart. His ebullience and eternal charm, evidenced by eyes that twinkled like the diamonds he once traded, kept not only his own intent positive but that of everyone around him too, not least perspiring bowlers and anxious captains.

He never displayed the slightest bitterness at having missed, by two runs, a century before lunch against India at Lord's in a Test match, even though it was surely only denied him by deliberate delaying tactics. Evans, who admitted to having batted with a stunning hangover, probably blamed himself for not getting on with it. After all, he was the chap who nodded in full obedience to his skipper, F.R.Brown, when it was suggested that, to win a match against South Australia, they should canter safe singles. T.G.Evans instantly forgot his promise and lashed five fours off the spin bowler's next over to conclude proceedings.

Physically he was hardly the most reassuring sight as he went out to bat. He seemed far too close to the ground, and he seldom seemed to take matters all that seriously. Even when he replaced Frank Tyson at the crease at Sydney after the England express bowler had been knocked out cold by a Ray Lindwall bouncer, he was obviously cracking little (somewhat nervous) jokes with the Australians. Modern cricketers would have found the spectacle beyond belief, for Evans was, by the dictates of the time, without helmet or arm-guard. Those thick little arms, smothered with dark hair, bore the clean, white bat which would be his salvation or otherwise.

His wicketkeeping was agile in the extreme, and showy in a nice sort of way. Like Ian Healy, he brought stylish little flourishes to his taking of the ball and passing it back. But he loved to leap. This art was the ultimate expression of his personality. It was the fulfilment of his deepest desires on a cricket field and the foundation of his great reputation in the late 1940s and early 1950s. When I sat on a panel with John Arlott and Jim Swanton in 1977 to choose England's Greatest XI of the first hundred years of Test cricket, my two seniors had one major difference of opinion, and that was over Godfrey. "Have you forgotten how many straightforward catches he put down?" probed Arlott, in one of his less charitable moods – though he cannot have had a Hampshire alternative in mind. Largely because of his greater run-making capacity, another Kent keeper, Les Ames, got in.

When a Kentish benefactor offered a financial inducement, Evans proved he could bat steadily. But even when he became serious for once, it never showed on his cheery countenance. Looking back over his many years in the sun, he became solemn when thinking of Headingley 1948, when Australia scored 404 to win on the final day, and he had a nightmare behind the sticks. "I left the ground in a hurry that evening!" he said. Time for another glass of something, and a change of subject.

Another bit of tease territory was the reminder that he set the odds at 500-1 when England seemed to be hopelessly placed at Headingley – yes, Headingley again – in 1981, and Lillee and Marsh cleaned up handsomely. It was brave of Ladbrokes to employ such a flamboyant character as their adviser. And yet he had got off to a good start, clearing up after an associate had regurgitated his drink and passed out in the press-box on that monumental day when Lord's admitted the betting fraternity after banishing it over a hundred years earlier. "I'm a publican, don't forget!" chortled Godfrey, making good the mess before the startled gaze of a couple of dozen journalists.

The heart simply lifted every time T.G.Evans was sighted. Above that perky chin was a small, whimsical mouth that was almost always set in a personable smile or, in top gear, a broad grin. The white mutton-chop whiskers came in later years, and were his trademark. "How goes it, Master?" was the usual chuckling greeting.

One morning I had a present for him, the first of a limited-edition hand-painted metal miniature, showing him reaching one-handed for a low leg-side catch. Those hands that had executed over a thousand cordial dismissals behind – and a few times in front of – the stumps gently took the model and turned it round and round. "Ken Funston, Johannesburg!" he laughed. It was misguided to have considered Godfrey merely frivolous or flippant.

Godfrey Evans, life and soul of many a party.

Only last year, at Arundel (he would drive many miles just to be among cricket folk for a drink and a chat), he got serious for once, saying how unfair it was that the commentators in 1953 had gone on and on about a catch he had floored from Neil Harvey's bat. He explained how Statham's pace was such that the edged ball "took off", in defiance of the norm. The lack of understanding and the degree of criticism had hurt all these years, though he declined to name the offending commentator.

Best not to let the grief cut too deeply perhaps. Godfrey Evans was loved by just about everybody who came into his lustrous orbit, and crammed every available morsel of enjoyment into his seventy-eight years, notwithstanding a short-lived concession to doctors' orders a couple of years back when the theory was aired that drinking was no longer advisable. It was a heart attack that caused his death.

All these years, his name at the top of the Test match table listing the longest times taken to score the first run (T.G.Evans, 97 minutes, Adelaide 1946-47) has been one of cricket's major absurdities. That he was relegated to second place last winter may or may not have pleased him. I was looking forward to checking it out with him during the World Cup. Not to be. Makes you want to believe in reincarnation.

The Independent, May 4, 1999

The birth of the greatest on-going cricket contest in the world – England v Australia – took place at the young Melbourne Cricket Ground in 1862. Surprisingly, no book on this historic venture had been attempted until I undertook extensive research and produced The Trailblazers in 1999. From the mass of detail, here is the passage leading to that first momentous ball in Anglo-Australian cricket competition:

The Grand Match

NEW YEAR'S Day 1862 marked the birth of a rich and vivid tradition. The unprecedented event, a cricket match between representative English and Australian sides, was the source of a stream that would widen and deepen into a sometimes raging river, coursing out of a period when customs and attitudes were far removed from those of today but when the conflict of affection and misgivings that exist between Englishmen and their Australian cousins was already in place.

After a cool and cloudy dawn, this historic day turned out beautifully, with an azure sky and a cooling breeze from the south. The temperature slowly rose beyond the comfort level as the day progressed, and Caffyn later described how the heat was so intense that it fetched the skin off some of their faces.

From a fairly early hour, people and traffic converged on the ground in Yarra Park, the former Police Paddock, Crown land cleared in 1853 of trees, wattle and wildflowers, a seedbed now for the future gargantuan Melbourne Cricket Ground. Pedestrians, men on horseback, buggies and all other manner of horse-drawn conveyances, and some drawn by bullock, raised clouds of the white dust which was blamed on the recent Caledonian Games. With overflowing trains discharging their eager loads, it was all a sight previously unknown and unimagined in Melbourne. Horse patrols were needed to control the confusion of traffic, and a police constable stood watchfully by every entrance gate.

All round the perimeter of the ground were traders and hawkers, boys selling cards (printed locally by Clarson & Shallard) bearing images of the players, with scorecards on the reverse, booths offering refreshment and serving thirst-quenching concoctions as fast as they could pour them. There were fruit stalls and sweet stalls, shooting galleries, Aunt Sallies (customers throwing balls at dummies) and even roulette wheels, while the odd barrel-organ was grinding away. On Jolimont Hill, another moneymaking opportunity had been seized by some men who set up a protective enclosure for private carriages.

An enterprising painter left his brushes and pots at home and hired out his ladder instead: for a shilling he would let you climb up into one of the gum-trees for a free view of the cricket. And for another shilling he would return later and help you down. Some of those already perched on branches teased the hesitant down below. Only one fellow fell out of the trees all day. He was taken to hospital.

A public holiday had been granted to Government office workers, bank employees, and the mercantile community, and doubtless hundreds of others gave bogus excuses to miss work. For this was the Great International Challenge, a chance to see cricketers of a higher calibre than had ever been available before in Australia.

The crowd was massive. With no turnstiles in situ, it was left for reporters to guess at the number, but a consensus put it at between fifteen and twenty thousand inside the ground and perhaps another ten thousand on the rising ground outside the surrounding picket fence, some of them up in the trees. Almost half those inside had paid half-a-crown (against a shilling ground admission) for accommodation in the enormous new grandstand, which stretched almost a third of the way around the eastern side of the ground and provided space underneath for several publicans, who had stocked up initially with five hundred crates of beer. Champagne was on offer at four shillings a bottle, Scotch at three shillings. And Spiers and Pond added to their astronomical income by setting up their restaurant under the stand. (The ground had its own water supply for those with less in their pockets.) Amazingly, the promoters had covered all their tour costs by the end of this [opening] match, taking £6000 in admission money and subsidiary items, and £1000 from leases which had been auctioned out to refreshment stall-holders.

It was a memorably colourful sight. Women had viewed the day as a challenge, and wore bright, elaborate dresses, and most of the male spectators, while not resembling Regency dandies, had made an effort. There were to be no problems of drunkenness or crowd disorder, the *Argus* finding as the only cause for complaint the smoking in the grandstand, which it regarded as unfair to the ladies.

The ground was a picture, and a credit to Melbourne Cricket Club, which had begun as a village cricket club in 1838 and now had about a hundred members. The smooth emerald-green turf, laid over fifty yards square by T.F.Wray in defiance of certain scepticism, had taken well, and the English cricketers were to remark favourably on it. There was simply nothing back home to compare with it. The pitch was flat after much effort with the horse-drawn roller, and the outfield had been manicured. The wooden pavilion, neatly painted and with a twin-gabled roof lending it style, provided a focus from grandstand and outer alike.

Around the ground were enough advertisement hoardings almost to have satisfied cricket's hungry commercial managers of the late 20th Century. There was a prominent Spiers & Pond board of course, and signs for many hotels.

So shaky was local confidence that it was impossible to back the Victorians even at 15 to 1. Flags were placed around the chain fence for the first time, and the ground overall "presented a gay appearance".

For the Victorian combination a team of eighteen (only two of them born in Australia) was agreed at the eleventh hour.

There was a buzz from the northern end of the grandstand. The players had arrived. At 11.15, escorted by Christopher Pond, the English cricketers, caps raised and smiling, made their way through the cheering mass. The sight caught the emotions of the *Argus* reporter, who felt that the "champions of the dear old land" were generating something greater than a welcome: he felt that the demonstration was a sign of "blood and brotherhood". He was also concerned for the players' safety as the crowd came close to smothering them as they struggled to reach the room set aside for them under the stand. It was, he declared, a triumph of emotion over good manners. The Victorian players, who had been practising, returned to their tent, and seem to have been less troubled by the fans.

The ground was cleared at 11.45, for the first day's play was due to start at noon. But at that hour there was still no sign of the Governor, Sir Henry Barkly, and his entourage. His Excellency may have been held up in traffic, but all was forgiven when he made his stately entrance into the Vice-Regal box, which was draped in blazing red, with the Royal coat of arms at its head. The national anthem, *God Save the Queen*, was played, the crowd silent throughout, and when the band ceased playing, a tremendous burst of cheering rent the air.

Having lost the toss, the Englishmen – Caffyn the first to step into the field, closely followed by Griffith and the rest, with captain H.H.Stephenson coming last, considered then to be the position of honour – had already followed umpires Smith and Wells onto the field, where they warmed up pending the arrival of the Governor. Mortlock's catching impressed in particular. Stephenson now led his men in three hearty cheers for the Governor, who graciously signalled the start of the first-ever Anglo-Australian contest. It was 12.20pm on Wednesday, January 1, 1862.

The Trailblazers: the First English Cricket Tour of Australia: 1861-62
(Boundary Books, 1999)

An attempt to clarify one of the most misunderstood terms in cricket's lexicon:

"Chinaman" Defined

WHY IS a "Chinaman" in cricket so-called?

The term springs from the clever spin bowling of West Indies cricketer Ellis Achong, who was of Chinese descent. In the Test match at Old Trafford in 1933, he spun the ball past England batsman R.W.V.Robins, who was swiftly stumped. [The ball went unexpectedly past the *outside* edge of his bat.]

He exclaimed: "Fancy getting out to a bloody Chinaman"; to which West Indies all-rounder Learie Constantine replied: "Do you mean the bowler or the ball?"

Achong was not the first to specialise in slow left-arm wrist bowling. Yorkshire's Roy Kilner and Maurice Leyland were slightly earlier exponents. Over the years Australia has produced most. They got wickets by deception, spinning the ball in from the off, then varying it with googlies (also known as "bosies" or "wrong'uns"), dropping the wrist to alter the axis of spin and causing the ball to turn the other way, towards the slips.

Confusingly, the term "Chinaman" means one thing in England and another in Australia. Most English cricket folk talk of "Chinamen and googlies", whereas Australians know they are the same. Careless usage in Britain has clouded the meaning.

Daily Mail, August 27, 1999

A major influence passed on in January 2000:

Remembering Jim Swanton

THE TWO towering figures of cricket broadcasting and writing for thirty-five years after the Second World War were E.W.Swanton and John Arlott. Apart from their imposing physical presence and their dress sense, which was often vivid, they had little in common. Swanton went to a minor public school, Cranleigh (and was thought to have nursed a grievance at being unable to attach something like "Winchester and Oxford" to his name), while Arlott went to the elementary school in Basingstoke. Swanton never disguised his admiration of the amateur, "gentleman" cricketer; for Arlott it was the professional who earned a living at the game who was the salt of the earth. History will see Swanton as a writer who also broadcast. Arlott wrote copiously too, but his Hampshire tones and poetic inclination plus his warm humour cast him immovably as The Voice of Cricket.

John Arlott died eight years ago, and on Saturday, Ernest William "Jim" Swanton died three weeks short of his ninety-third birthday, having been well and enthusiastic enough to have been writing almost to the end. In his seventy-five-year career he saw into print some eight million words on cricket, and most of them were authoritative to the point of pontifical. Readers' opinions were readily shaped.

The younger Swanton served the London *Evening Standard*, but his imperishable mark was made with the *Daily Telegraph*, whose cricket pages he led from 1946 until mandatory retirement in 1975. It was inconceivable that he would then vanish, to play golf, write his memoirs and speak at dinners, and so his weighty prose continued in the paper for a further quarter-century.

Swanton suffered two famous setbacks. In 1932 he failed to deliver an account of Sutcliffe and Holmes's record stand of 555 at Leyton speedily enough to the sports desk, and was therefore judged too risky to send on England's winter tour. He thus missed the fateful Bodyline tour. Bruce Harris, the *Standard's* tennis writer, went instead and scarcely knew how to interpret what he saw on Australia's cricket battlefields.

Swanton's other setback was more serious. As a major in the Bedfordshire Yeomanry, he was taken by the Japanese in Singapore, and consigned to the horrors and brutality of jungle captivity on the Burma Railway. His cricket lectures helped sustain morale among the British and Australian prisoners, and when the severely emaciated Swanton returned home at the end of hostilities he was somehow strengthened by his experiences. His Christian faith having intensified, he took up residence at Pusey House, Oxford.

His writing now took on a new dimension, however, and, as the summers – and touring winters – passed, Swanton's stature grew. He was not interested in frills: just solid Churchillian prose. On air, his "sealskin" voice, toffish and somehow sepulchral, recounted the details of the day's play thoroughly enough through the BBC airwaves; and in his lengthy newspaper column there was a complete absence of self-doubt. He genuinely cared for cricket and fought dedicatedly to uphold its

best qualities and traditions.

This magisterial approach appealed more to some than others. Not all England captains welcomed the freshly printed *Telegraph* cricket page calculatedly delivered to the dressing-room each morning. And Ray Illingworth became, if anything, even more determined to recover the Ashes in Australia in 1970-71 in the face of Swanton's unabashed espousal of Colin Cowdrey, who had been overlooked as skipper.

Jim Swanton was well aware that the adjective often associated with him in the public mind was "pompous". Indeed, it was thought to be a source of gratification. He was too proud to ride in the same motor-car as his chauffeur, don't you know; never stayed at the same hotel as the other newspaper chaps on tour because he was usually put up instead by the Governor; and, when a somewhat shy Aussie journalist was forced to shout his story down a defective telephone line at Lord's in 1968, Swanton, after several disapproving glares, sent a minion across to ask the poor chap to lower his voice. It was as if he felt obliged to substantiate the old jape surrounding the sudden belching of smoke from a chimney outside Lord's: "Good heavens, Swanton's been elected Pope!"

He sat on committees at Lord's, which is something no ordinary cricket writer does. He wrote lots of books, reworking original material persuasively. If *Elusive Victory* (England in Australia, 1950-51) is a favourite it is because it was the first cricket book this young fellow ever bought. Many years later I was recommended to Swanton as a prospective editor when a vacancy occurred at *The Cricketer*. My advocate was none other than John Arlott. I was scared, for EWS was good at many things, but not at making a newcomer feel at ease. "Now look heah" was one of his pet expressions. I found it useful in later years as a means of disciplining our rogue pet cat.

The Independent, January 24, 2000

NEW CENTURY
BEYOND 2000

The death on February 25, 2001 of Sir Donald Bradman brought forth a predictable avalanche of tributes and reflectives in newspapers, magazines and on television. Leaving to one side the obituary I wrote for Wisden Cricket Monthly, here is a less formal contribution, originally prepared for the symposium at Lord's in Bradman's memory organised by the Menzies Centre for Australian Studies in June 2001:

Farewell, Don

"HE REMAINED so astonishingly unimpressed by himself." Those were John Bradman's memorable words after his father died. He expressed the hope that Sir Don would not be deified but would be seen as a human being, with foibles and the odd flaw. "Never in the slightest degree," he said, "did he become his own hero."

The world has a fixed image of a batsman and captain who was as near to perfection as cricket has ever known – and by a long way too. He vigorously guarded his privacy and that of his family, and he was always very measured and precise and disciplined in his public utterances and in his writings.

The compelling fascination for me was the discovery of what sort of person he really was in the later years of his life. I enjoyed the supreme privilege of knowing Don Bradman for thirty years, during which time we met, dined and talked – and sometimes argued – at regular intervals. We also corresponded regularly – long letters each way. I recently filed his to me in proper order. There were over a hundred of them.

He never wrote idle platitudes. He displayed most of the moods and emotions known to man: admiration, scepticism, gratitude, frustration, concern in family matters (and, touchingly, about my heavy workload during the seventeen frantic years I edited *Wisden Cricket Monthly*), and humour – though not of the cynical kind. In fact his humour was simple and wholesome, revealing the bush boy that he always remained deep down.

There was the time the Bradmans and I were dining one evening in a quiet corner of an Adelaide restaurant, and the young waitress asked him if he'd like some apple pie for dessert. He directed a sparky gaze at the girl and said, "And what makes you think I'd want some apple pie?" Unabashed, she said, "You just look like a man who would like apple pie." So he said, "Right, then, I'll have some apple pie!" And we all dissolved into squeals of laughter, Don being the last to regain his composure.

I once tested his sense of humour by sending him an obituary written fifty years earlier, in 1934, when he came so close to death during the tour of England. It had been found in a drawer in a Midlands newspaper office. He wrote to thank me and coolly pointed out that there were two dozen errors in the piece.

When he read that I'd paid about £800 for Victor Trumper's 1898 silver fob watch he seemed surprised, and observed in his next letter that he reckoned he might dig up a couple of his own old wrist-watches. Around that time he found he did not have a copy of the gramophone record he made in 1930 in which he played the piano and discussed cricket. I duly made a tape copy from an original in my collection, and his reaction was: "I sounded different then. But I was fifty years younger and had my own teeth!"

Another of Don Bradman's qualities was humility. Most really good cricketers are modest. But here was the top man. He knew well enough where he stood in the history of the game. But his modesty was innate, and I don't believe you can fake humility across a period of thirty years.

He honoured me with forewords to two books I wrote – *Pageant of Cricket* and a pictorial history of England v Australia – and both times he meant it when he said he hoped his offerings were good enough. If not, send them back, he wrote. Not a trace of arrogance, supposition or greed. He actually declined payment, saying jocularly that he might need a favour from me some day. Modern "superstars" take note.

For decades a conscientious and unpaid cricket administrator himself, he deplored the decision, passed at Lord's, to make the chairman of selectors a paid appointment. And further evidence of his attitude towards money came in an aside when Greg Norman was having a rough trot: "Too much money hasn't helped his golf – he's down to my scores!"

Sir Donald was noted for his meticulous preparation not only as a cricketer but as public speaker. During the Centenary Test match in Melbourne in 1977, I was startled to get a phone call from him at the motel. He wanted to confirm that Ranjitsinhji had once scored two centuries on the same day. I was able to say that he had, but couldn't fill in the exact details since I hadn't carted my immense cricket library to Melbourne with me!

Later, when Don saw Ian Chappell's "history of Australian cricket" on video, he offered an aside: "His knowledge of cricket history would fit on a postage stamp."

Intensely proud of his standing in the game – as batsman, administrator, or perhaps as bowler too! – Don Bradman could be highly sensitive. No sooner had I sat down in his lounge-room on one occasion than he produced a piece of paper from the inside pocket of his coat and challenged me on several details in my latest book, a history of slow bowling. "You state that I bowled Hammond with a full-toss in the Adelaide Test of 1933." I nodded grimly. He then went on to deny that that ball was a full-toss. I protested that a number of players from that match had described it as such, and that Arthur Mailey almost made a pastime out of bowling Jack Hobbs with full-tosses, and that they both customarily laughed about it. But The Don would have none of it.

He was impatient too when I declined to support him editorially in his campaign to restore the back-foot no-ball law. He tried several times, and although I was delighted to give him space in the magazine to state his case, I could not subscribe to the notion myself. I felt a somewhat poor guest when the latest broadside occurred at the lunch table in his own home. I was really up against the wall when he produced his nuclear weapon: "So! [he pronounced that word in a way that I grew to love, almost rhyming it with the word for a female pig]. So, you think you know better than Dennis Lillee, Richie Benaud, the Chappell brothers, and me?"

I bowled well wide of the off stump, mumbling something about all games with white lines having them for a purpose, and we can't ever again have bowlers delivering off nineteen yards. But he was flushed, and I daresay I was too. Then his wonderful wife Jessie intervened, as she must have done on so many occasions across the years when debate escalated dangerously: "David," she said innocently, "have you written Don's obituary yet?"

Relieved at the change of pace, I claimed that I was not that well organised. And anyway, he was going to reach his century, wasn't he?

The delightful Lady Jessie was probably the only person to have had him completely in hand. When he grew that small white moustache after getting a sunburnt upper lip, he began to like it and proposed to retain it. Nobody would have had the temerity or the power of persuasion to get him to remove it – apart from his beloved wife, who said simply, "Shave it off, Don. You look like Charlie Chaplin." He enjoyed telling that story against himself.

When, in 1995, I published in *WCM* extracts from Bill O'Reilly's oral memoirs that included an accusation that Bradman once threw his wicket away in a Shield match to avoid another going-over by Ernie McCormick with the next new ball, he was very hurt. His pride was badly bruised, and he wrote two letters to me, one for publication vehemently denying the charge.

I thought that was it. But he was big enough to forgive me – on the surface at least – generously acknowledging that I must have considered it my editorial duty to run the story.

His happiest tour was in 1948, his last to England as a player. He had a fairly young team who all – even the rebellious Keith Miller – greatly respected him. On the three tours of England in the 1930s he had been a victim at times of personal jealousies and, latterly, a religious divide. It is often said that he had no close friends among team-mates, that privacy was everything to him, that he preferred his own company, rather as Geoff Boycott has done in recent times. The sense of dedication to the cause of success was paramount to both these batsmen.

But Don Bradman did form fairly close friendships within the team with men such as Archie Jackson, Tim Wall, Ben Barnett, Charlie Walker and Ron Hamence, and he took others such as Fleetwood-Smith and Sid Barnes under his wing.

One of my favourite pieces of writing concerning Don Bradman was by R.S.Whitington: during one pre-war summer the South Australia players took off to the cinema, and during the interval they went out into the side alley for a smoke and a chat. There, Whitington spotted the young and carefree Don and a pal "joking to each other and roaring with unrestrained laughter". Don was unobserved (he thought) and away from the unrelenting glare of public scrutiny. He was, for once, acting naturally. Writer and team-mate Whitington went on to remark that Bradman "became quite human after two glasses [of cold beer]".

Another slightly amusing trigger to his rare bouts of impatience was when birthday cards poured through his letterbox. "I KNOW I'm eighty-four [that "know" rhyming beautifully with "sow"]," he'd write testily. "I down't need reminding! It means I'm one step closer to the grave!"

Somewhat contradictorily he wrote after the charming former Test batsman Graeme Hole had died: "Why do so many rotters push on, while the good die young?" To my amazement, not so long ago he ended a letter: "Make the most of your youth." It was considerate advice, but while he was approaching ninety at the time I happened to be close to sixty myself.

Sentimentality was alien to him. Those letters might contain remarks about the discomforts of old age, but he was never one to hark back to "the good old days", other than perhaps to rue the poor over rates and bowlers' long run-ups and deterioration in behaviour – and the no-ball law, of course.

Linked to this was an intensely practical outlook, best illustrated by his remark in 1937 when England's Stan Worthington toppled into his stumps after hooking and was thus out hit-wicket. Somebody murmured "Bad luck", to which Don Bradman retorted: "You're not supposed to tread on your stumps."

He was no more impervious to criticism than the rest of us. But he was careful never to give his critics the satisfaction of a reaction in public. Whenever possible he simply set out to square the matter somehow – just as when a bowler such as poor old Arthur Mailey was written up in the press as having Bradman's measure. Arthur thought long and hard before turning up for Balmain's match against St George. But he did, and sure enough The Don hammered his spinners all over the oval with particular relish. It must be wonderful to be that good.

He counter-attacked in his books too when appropriate, though his reaction to O'Reilly's ceaseless criticism was restrained. Jack Fingleton was more of a problem. "Fingo's" writings embody some of the most persuasive praise of Bradman – but left the unprepared reader open to surprise. Bitterness inevitably emerged. In the inappropriate setting of his book on Trumper, Fingleton compared The Don unfavourably with Australia's hero of the Golden Age. Later, in Michael Page's Bradman biography, The Don comes out ahead of Trumper. Looking back now, it all seems a little like a schoolboy spat.

In 1980 some extremely uncharitable things were written by three eminent English writers concerning Bradman's absence from the Centenary Test celebrations in London. The despicable suggestion, among others, that he was "not willing to share the limelight" cut him deeply. He sadly referred privately to the "lust for glory" displayed by these journalists. But he refused to respond publicly. What solely prevented him from travelling to England was the fact that from 1977 onwards his wife endured a succession of terrible health problems. What his three critics had in common was that in previous years he had denied them interviews. This was consistent with his lifetime policy: "If I give an interview to one, then in all fairness I'd have to give interviews to all – plainly an impossibility."

And it was, if he was to preserve some time for himself and his family against the ceaseless and matchless barrage of attention which came at him through seventy-odd years of his life. I am glad to recall that I wrote an article in *WCM* showing up those three journalists for their tasteless and wildcat attacks on DGB. I was not firing his bullets. They were bullets of my own.

How did I become favoured by his friendship? We had,

It's January 1930, and the Boy from Bowral has well and truly arrived: 452 not out for NSW v Queensland at the SCG.

The Don with the author over half-a-century later, rifling through the memories.

perhaps, three things in common. We had both worn the St George cap – he with considerably more success than I, it hardly needs adding. He instantly identified my commitment to cricket and my almost obsessive love for it. And we both enjoyed a stimulating discussion. In fact he loved it – debate and argument on the economy, politics, cricket – with him preferably having the final word. Just like my own Dad. Just like me. Perhaps, for seventy years or so, too much wide-eyed and slobbering reverence came Don Bradman's way. He preferred direct chat, on level terms, with mutual respect the keynote.

Despite my inner feelings of awe, absurd as it may seem, I tried always to relate to him as if he were an ordinary man – which in so many ways he was. And I think he appreciated that.

I'd look at that crinkled and famous countenance, with its alert, beady eyes, and still see the young Don Bradman from the old newsreels, with the kookaburra facial profile and the crackling voice. A shiver would run down my spine. He was "Our Don Bradman" all right. Thousands – millions – had a stake in the legend. His smiling, quick-footed strut to the wicket lifted hearts – apart from bowlers' – and he was adored far and wide for twenty years.

Then his days in the sun drew to a close and he donned a three-piece suit and took to wearing glasses. His 1974 portrait in oils at Lord's shows a bank manager rather than the most efficient flannelled creature the game has seen.

To me he will always be the Boy from the Bush who made good and, bless him, elevated cricket to fresh heights.

Allan's Australian Cricket Annual 2001

307

The file on suicides among cricketers grew to extraordinary length in the Frith Archive, prompting – almost demanding – interpretation. The book By His Own Hand resulted in 1990, followed in due course by a revised and much larger volume a few years later:

Cricket Suicides: Cricket Innocent?

IS CRICKET to blame? I once thought it might well be, but I'm not altogether convinced, despite the deadly statistics. The game may sometimes rawly expose a man's inner frailties, but these were implanted mostly at birth or during adolescence. If not, they came with disillusionment in later life, when unfulfilled desires and ambitions or jealousy or fatigue or the inability to do now what could once be done becomes a lethal weapon turned in upon oneself.

Yet cricket's tragic toll suggests that there is something in there which sets cricket and cricket-lovers apart.

Cricket is only superficially a team game. Essentially it is a lonely game, one for the keen individual, with multiple odds stacked against him. In this it is a fairly faithful reflection of life. And it offers regular opportunities to achieve sporting heroism. In addition, the fellowship that reaches well beyond the boundary and beyond the confined period of one's own playing days is a great force for good. These are elements in tempting cricketers to play on and on.

One county cricketer, playing for his third county club, did not mind the fact that the grounds on which he kept wicket and batted were usually almost empty. His name was in all the newspapers almost every day and in the annuals which would line the bookshelves. His life had meaning. He shared an attitude with Vin Diesel, one of the stars of the movie *Saving Private Ryan*, who said, "I like film-making so much more than theatre. I like the immortality."

It might be argued that cricket's unduly high levels of suicide and divorce (one random statistic: in 1980 six Middlesex cricketers were all having their marriages dismantled) match those of Hollywood and exceed the national norms. But the key question remains: are the psychological strains imposed by the playing of cricket, whether as a livelihood or with amateur passion, more damaging than the everyday and cumulative mental stresses faced by milkmen, mortgage brokers or medical practitioners? And, moreover, are cricketers brought down more severely than their brethren in other sports by the drawn-out, stressful demands of the seemingly never-ending pursuit of the summer game?

Cricket's virtues are renowned. Played well, it gives thrilling satisfaction to both performer and spectator. To those who need it, it offers rich scope for fellowship and comfort. Withdraw all this and a void is created which at its worst can be fatally damaging.

The mild terror engendered by the first realistic, if long-distance, glimpse of old age and the severe limitations and discomfort it can impose stems in part from the cold reality that with the later years comes an inability to do things that once came easefully and naturally – things well beyond just bending the spine into bowling or flicking arthritis-free knuckles across a leg-break or running a quick three and facing the next ball without so much as a quiet gasp for breath. Mocking shadows replace the freedoms of choice as they fade away with the unremitting physical wind-down. "The brightness dies: the old eyes fall," John Arlott once wrote. "They see, but do not understand,/ A pursed, rheumatic, useless hand."

This must have explained the deaths of some of the middle aged cricketers in this alarmingly long cavalcade. Had Harold Gimblett remained on the farm, might he not have had a smoother and comparatively untroubled (and longer) life? If A.E.Stoddart had had children and permitted himself more of the company of his numerous old friends, would he not have come to terms with the loss of those years of glamour and hero-worship which he navigated with much grace and modesty as well as gratification, and gone on to a ripe old age – perhaps even surviving the financial jeopardy wrought by the Great War? The salvation of many of them, it seems, might only have come if some magical Peter Pan potion had permitted them to remain on stage until they chose to give up the game, as opposed to the game's giving them up.

For some, a future without cricket was unthinkable. For them it cannot be said that it was the stresses of cricket that precipitated a spiritual decline, but rather the threatened *loss* of cricket. Yet even the prolonging of a career – cheating Time for a time – may not allay depression. To try fruitlessly to repeat youthful triumphs can be as painful, physically and morally, as collapsing while trying to jitterbug with folk a third of one's age or sprinting for a train forty years after leaving school and thereby courting a coronary occlusion. It is just unfortunate that a cricketer's usefulness ends around the time that others are embarking on the most rewarding phases of their working lives.

Carl Jung's essay on the Stages of Life points to two major phases. The earlier brings an establishment of identity. Then sometimes comes a "mid-life crisis" through which we need to develop inwardly, striving for a higher maturity out of which will come the authority (and dignity) that experience ought to bestow.

Christopher Booker has written on this: "Just at the age when politicians, lawyers, doctors or teachers are reaching the top, the sportsman's career comes to a close. Much of what has helped to give him a sense of his place in the world has been snatched away, and he then faces the problem of how to rebuild his career and identity in a new way."

He then cites an elderly man who was once the most famous cricketer in the world but who now, many years after his retirement, was standing, straight-backed, impeccably dressed, "the very picture of an old-fashioned English gentleman", in no way reduced by his "obscure role" as a London shopkeeper. This was Sir Jack Hobbs. It probably helped that he had batted on through his mid-life crisis – if he ever had one – scoring first-class runs into his fifty-second year. (The need for crutch-splitting dives in the outfield today would have seen Hobbs off fifteen years sooner.) He was modest, dignified, perfectly content. Perhaps it was in the genes.

Silence of the Heart: Cricket Suicides (Mainstream, 2001)

Building a new career in the media now offers opportunities for former Test cricketers, with those in television especially picking up enormous fees. They are still asked for their autographs and their opinions. It is the rest who, while not yet middle-aged, often face the difficult challenge of making a good life after their earlier years had been tied up in cricket. Mercifully, the vast majority manage to do so.

A dark age enveloped cricket when match-fixing and bribes were indentified as rampant in certain international areas. One highly-respected cricketer emerged as the most unlikely of wrong-doers. Penance followed. Then came the tragedy of his early death:

The Tragedy of Hansie Cronje

NEVER IN cricket's long history has such a conjunction of tragedy attached to one name. Two years ago Hansie Cronje, South Africa's captain, was a figure of shame and disgrace following his stunning confessions that he took money for manipulating international matches. Following painful months of humiliation and ostracism, his appeal against the life ban imposed on him in October 2000 by the United Cricket Board of South Africa having failed (he was also refused permission to write or broadcast on the game), he embarked on a programme of rehabilitation. Commuting to Johannesburg from the home he and wife Bertha shared in Fancourt, in the Western Cape, he was making a living as a finance manager with an earth-moving company. Then, on Saturday, came the news of his death in a bad-weather crash. The cargo aircraft in which he had hitched a lift ploughed into a peak in the Outeniqua range, near George.

Thus, those who now look back on one of the most extraordinary of sporting lives are tossed by the powerful opposing currents of emotion – an on-going indignation over Cronje's greed and the serious damage it did to cricket, but also sorrow at a life extinguished at thirty-two, a life which had embraced stirring visions of batsmanship and leadership during that period in the 1990s when South African cricket was reflowering after twenty-two years of political exclusion. There should be no doubting the level of grief among those who knew him best and shared the triumphs and the dressing-room camaraderie before the tentacles of corruption worked their way into Cronje's soul.

His record as captain is impressive. Only four players have led their countries in Test cricket more times than his 53, and the results were very creditable: 27 victories against 11 losses. In one-day internationals he captained in 138 matches, winning 99.

The son of Ewie Cronje, a Free State cricketer himself, and younger brother of Frans, also a first-class cricketer, Wessel Johannes ("Hansie") Cronje was an outstanding captain at Grey College, Bloemfontein before enrolling at the University of OFS. His first-class debut for OFS came at eighteen, in 1987-88, when South Africa were still in the international wilderness. But by April 1992 his stature was such that he was selected in the first South Africa Test XI of the new epoch, playing in the inaugural Test against West Indies at Bridgetown.

Thereafter his development was in tandem with that of his country as they got the feel of competition with the outside world. The first (and highest) of Cronje's six Test centuries, 135 against India at Port Elizabeth, set up victory in the match and the series. A year later came a hundred in Sri Lanka and another against Australia at Johannesburg, both of which contributed to important wins. After an indifferent series in England in 1994, when shortcomings against pace found him out, at the age of twenty-five he took over the captaincy from Kepler Wessels and made centuries home and away against New Zealand. Cronje had the same kind of Afrikaner dourness as Wessels, but few objected so long as the successes flowed. South Africa bristled with talent which delighted not only their own fans.

Cronje's attitude to life was undergoing change. In 1994 he accidentally knocked down and killed a black girl who ran out in front of his car as he drove through a village in northern Natal late at night. Unlike many in similar circumstances, the distressed Cronje stopped, only to face hostility from the villagers, some of whom brandished knives. He and his team-mate were forced to drive away. The experience intensified his Christian belief, a commitment (which he shared notably with Jonty Rhodes) that was soon widely recognised, and which made Cronje's eventual misdemeanours – in the eyes of many – even harder to forgive.

There were similarities to Greg Chappell in style and bearing at the crease, and when Cronje improved his technique against spin – he punished Shane Warne's bowling with some big hitting to midwicket, sometimes into the crowd – he was the complete all-rounder, since his economical bowling was an important component in South Africa's strategy too. There was a calmness touching on coldness about him at press conferences, where his tone was flat and his eyes verged on the catatonic. And there were occasional hints of a driven man when the upright skipper, contrary to the terms of the Code of Conduct, suddenly bulldozed an umpire into reviewing a run-out decision against Graham Thorpe in the deciding Test at Cape Town early in 1996. The batsman was given out after a video review, Cronje received the prescribed and relatively mild punishment, and the match and series swung irreversibly to South Africa. When Cronje was filmed gouging the ball with his boot-sprigs in Australia, his image underwent further subtle change.

He played successfully for Leicestershire in 1995, the highest of his four centuries 213 at Weston. Then along came temptation. He ducked the first invitation to throw a match against Pakistan during the Mandela Trophy tournament, but in 1996 came the fateful introduction to an Indian bookmaker (former India captain Azharuddin, soon to be struck off himself for match-fixing, was the link), and Cronje accepted US$30,000 in return for giving his wicket away.

Sinking ever deeper into corruption, he asked his team if they would be interested in deliberately losing a one-day international in India. The suggestion was articulated in the guise of a joke. The players rejected any thought of it. By the 1996-97 season Cronje was picking up $80,000 for providing information about players and strategy, and the bribes and gifts were mounting up. In January 2000 he responded to a suggestion from a South African gambler by persuading the England captain Nasser Hussain to join him in forfeiting an innings apiece after lengthy rain interruption in order to set up an exciting finish in the Test at Centurion Park. England got home by two wickets. Cricket, thought the innocent man in the street, had been the winner. For his entrepreneurial efforts Cronje received £5000 and a leather jacket.

His world collapsed when Indian police tapped a phone conversation he had with a bookie in Delhi. Challenged, at first he denied everything, but, shortly after Delhi's Joint Commissioner of Police had charged him and three of his players (Herschelle Gibbs, Nicky Boje and Pieter Strydom) with involvement in match-fixing, Cronje's resolve to maintain his innocence collapsed. In the middle of the night, just before a one-dayer against Australia in Durban, he tearfully confessed to a team security officer in the hotel before ringing the UCBSA chief Dr Ali Bacher, who instantly stripped him of the captaincy. His career was over.

Granted immunity from prosecution, Hansie Cronje agreed to testify before the commission set up under Judge Edwin King. Formal enquiries had already taken place in Pakistan and India. Now Cronje bared his soul. His state of mind throughout the hearing was understandably mercurial. Sometimes he spoke with the flatness of old, sometimes he even displayed a trace of arrogance and flippancy, and at the end he wept as he was led from the room. Cricket wept with him, for the scandal automatically cast shadows of suspicion over every player and every match of importance. This was the truly poisonous afterbirth. It would need time and fresh ICC security measures before faith in the game could be rebuilt.

A contrite and remorseful Cronje was able to tell the world of his agony some months later in a media deal worth some £100,000. Not unexpectedly he spoke of suicidal thoughts – "Hansie, you've fallen so far anyway. A few more feet won't matter" – and of how Satan had entered his world when he took his eyes off Jesus and "my whole world turned dark".

It was judgment time all over the cricket world. In some areas – not least his old school, where the pupils declared him a hero – his behaviour was seen as not so very deplorable, perhaps even condonable. The world today seems bent on punishing slight perceived offences while readily offering forgiveness for even some of the more monstrous misdemeanours. Time would have determined the full scale of Cronje's redemption and rehabilitation. The greater tragedy is that we can now never know.

The Independent, June 3, 2002

The sensational 1932-33 Test series between Australia and England, indelibly branded as the "Bodyline" summer, brought a showdown between the apparently unstoppable run-maker Don Bradman and supercilious England captain Douglas Jardine and his key weapon, fast bowler Harold Larwood. Their final duel came at the Sydney Cricket Ground in the final Test of that rumbustious series:

Bradman, Larwood and Verity

AND THEN came the moment Australia's pride and joy had vowed would never come. Larwood hit him. He hit him with a short ball which smacked into his left upper arm, causing him to drop his bat. Bradman thus became the last of Australia's major batsmen to be "branded" (though he had taken a few blows on his padded thigh during the series). The crowd howled its displeasure – and again, next over, when a bumper from Voce hit Woodfull.

Fingleton thought this Bradman innings to be "the riskiest and most thrilling batting imaginable", and concluded that Larwood was not interested in hitting the exposed stumps. It seemed to be that "Larwood was anxious to claim a hit on Bradman". Might there have been a pint of beer on it – or more – with Bill Voce? We shall never know.

It was some time before the muscle stiffened, so Bradman was able to go on blazing away at everything he could reach, with Voce now straining every sinew and the pitch playing at uneven heights. Bradman's fifty, reached with a crisp square-cut four off Verity, came in only 76 minutes. The second half of the century partnership came in a mere 33 minutes, and when Larwood's new spell ended abruptly Australian hopes rose.

The stark reality for England was that Larwood now carried a very serious foot injury, and his dream of taking six of the remaining nine wickets and thus pass Maurice Tate's record of 38 in an Ashes series, let alone claiming Bradman's wicket for the fifth time in their past six Test encounters, was shattered. There was a sharp exchange between bowler and captain, for Jardine found his champion's breakdown not only unbelievable but unacceptable. To please him, Larwood had to finish the over.

It was a pathetic picture. All Larwood could do, with Jardine utterly determined to keep him on the field as long as Bradman was there, was stand at the crease and wheel his arm over. The bluff was based upon a mirage: that the injury was no more than cramp. Just as poignant was the sight of Woodfull patting back the slow deliveries; someone of a less gentlemanly disposition – O'Reilly perhaps – might have helped himself to 20 runs.

"I can't run. I'm useless. I'll have to go off," Larwood pleaded.

"Field at cover point," snapped Jardine. "There's a man covering you there. You can't go off while this little bastard's in."

Freed for the time being at least from the greatest menace, Bradman became if anything even keener to add to this wondrous necklace of runs. Having survived at 37 a "catch" by Jardine in the gully off Allen which was called as a no-ball, he had even escaped poisoning, if a barracker's wry shout was to be believed. As Jardine offered a glass to Bradman during drinks the cry came across the ground: "Make him taste it first, Don!"

Verity takes up the story. On a river bank on the rest day he had sat in his familiar state of deep meditation, thinking over what Jardine had said about the footmarks left by [Australian fast bowler] Alexander. He visualised those roughened patches and deduced that they were not much use to him as they were almost completely outside the line of a right-hander's leg stump. But he made a fine calculation that if, bowling over the wicket, he could pitch the ball on a small strip about a foot long and three inches wide, the ball would bite. Moreover, with the right field placing, batsmen (one in particular) might be tempted to exploit gaps deliberately left.

"The first two balls I bowled to Woodfull hit the spot and turned sharply," wrote Verity, "and just as sharply a midwicket conference was held between the batsmen. Don was down at my end next over, and bang! – four runs came to him through the vacant cover field. Yet another followed: but then, suddenly he was out – bowled in attempting to repeat the stroke off a delivery that pitched outside the leg stump."

The crowd groaned, for a Don double-century had been the wish – and had seemed a distinct possibility. Now he left the field, to loud appreciation and with Jardine clapping his hands to draw Larwood's attention – "Right, Harold, you can go now!" The Englishman limped from the Sydney arena alongside Bradman, neither of the two arch gladiators saying a word. It was one of the most dramatic exits in Test history, but no cameraman, it seems, considered it worth filming.

Bodyline Autopsy (ABC Books, 2002)

The nasty problem facing Australia's batsmen every once in a while during the 1932-33 Tests: how do you survive and score runs against chest-high fast bowling with this intensive leg-side field setting?

The ever more cluttered international calendar and efforts to downplay England v Australia Test cricket have caused some to wonder if the oldest of Test contests might be losing its appeal, particularly with Australia repeatedly dominant for year after year. An invitation to tabulate ten solid reasons why the Ashes matches retain all the old allure was too tempting to resist:

Why the Ashes Matter

IT SMACKS of desperation at present to assert that because Ashes cricket is the oldest Test competition between two nations it is therefore endowed with the greatest significance. How could it when England have failed to win a series since Freddie Flintoff was in short pants? And how significant is it now that Test matches are played by *ten* countries, and players and enthusiasts alike struggle to sustain interest in the face of such an intensive schedule – made worse by the teeming one-day internationals that complete cricket's calendar?

Yet this very congestion and consumer indigestion are probably a key to the appeal of Ashes cricket. Whenever it comes along, its special qualities are revealed. Its antiquity is the envy of all other competitions, and in this uncertain world its continuity underpins its appeal.

1. Notwithstanding the unpalatable fact that there are those, including some who govern us, who wish to obliterate all trace of what has gone before in this great nation, the charm of ANTIQUITY is the primary base for the truth that Ashes cricket still matters.

2. CONTINUITY is a close relative to antiquity. No matter how old you may be, you will relate this winter's series to all others in your Ashes memory bank, even if you are so blessedly young that your interest was sparked only last year – more than likely when Mark Butcher earned immortality at Headingley, bursting that unsightly balloon that bespoke of England's inability to beat Australia again.

3. Let's add UNPREDICTABILITY to the attractions of Ashes cricket. Of course, other countries have their share of caprice. But they can't point to such a vast gallery or to something as long ago as 1882, when Australia provided the first major upset by beating the Mother Country in England. That shock seven-run victory at The Oval inspired the ironic obituary announcement in the *Sporting Times* which, in turn, prompted those society belles in Melbourne to present England's captain, the Honourable Ivo Bligh, with the cute little urn which today rests in its glass case at Lord's – to the undying irritation of generations of conquering Australian cricketers.

4. The Worrell Trophy, the Wisden Trophy, the Border-Gavaskar Trophy: all admirable and all fought over with the utmost conviction by the respective countries. But the brightest jewel, the mystical trophy that quickly becomes familiar to the newest of recruits to cricket's spell, is THE ASHES, the powerful and venerable token of combat that is the envy of all outside the Anglo-Australian sphere.

5. And so we come to HEROES. Yes, the other Test countries have their impressive honour-rolls. But just as our roads are more congested each year, so the glorious deeds in Test matches around the globe are swiftly overtaken in memory as the inevitably imprecise "world championship" compels teams to play far more cricket

than is good either for them or for the distended public stomach. There used to be time for unhurried relish of outstanding performances. That is why the annals of Ashes cricket ring with the names of Grace and Spofforth, Jessop and Trumper, Rhodes and Armstrong and Hill, Macartney and Barnes, Gregory and McDonald, Woolley and Bardsley, Hobbs and Sutcliffe, Ponsford and Woodfull, Hammond and McCabe, Larwood and Voce, Grimmett and Verity, Hendren and Leyland and O'Reilly. And that's just to skim the surface only as far as the 1930s.

6. One name towers above all others: DON BRADMAN. In Bradman's career, from 1928 to 1948, he played Tests only in England and in his homeland. He collected 19 centuries against England, and when he died at ninety-two in 2001, the volume of tributes and reflective material was unprecedented not only in sport but in most areas of human activity. Since Bradman's name – now deified – is synonymous with Ashes cricket, it provides a strong guarantee that it will still matter beyond our lifetimes.

7. A further special factor is the unwritten AGGRESSION PACT "enjoyed" by Poms and Aussies. Everyone seems to have a cousin in Australia. The rivalry is unfettered by sensibilities over race or religion, so in what often seems like a family squabble the abuse is unbridled, though often softened by a grudging respect. The licence to be rude is touched by history, and sometimes politics: I recall a barracker on the SCG Hill in 1962 bellowing out, "Hey, Dexter! What about the Common Market?"

8. Several countries relish defeating England as part of the COLONIAL PAYBACK. With Australia, the effect is heightened. The English still sometimes look down their noses, Jardine-style, and refer to the clinking of convict chains, while those in the New World have a lexicon of ironic responses, such as reference to the shortage of baths in English households. This right to verbal jousting must be preserved.

9. Poor old Plum Warner, England's beleaguered manager on the Bodyline tour seventy years ago, delivered a gentle homily to Australia on TRADITION: "This modern scoffing at tradition is a product of super-democracy. Tradition is a hell of a good thing. It's what takes a regiment through hell. Good God, you fellows out in Australia have a great tradition. What is it, do you think, that makes your soldiers fight to the last man and your cricketers to the last ball? It's tradition, of course." Tradition, as most young men discover when they become old men, is what helps to secure the soul.

10. The tenth factor in rendering Ashes cricket important? Simply the frenzy of PUBLIC AND MEDIA INTEREST that gushes up each time England and Australia shape up for a fresh bout. Only global war has ever stopped it.

The Times Ashes Handbook, October 31, 2002

Ashes Test cricket was restored to full health with England's triumph in 2005, Australia's decisive recapturing of the urn in '06-07, and another England success in 2009. For the time being, it was a grippingly fluctuating contest once again.

The faster that gratuitous change gnawed pieces out of the established order the more reactionary many of us were inclined to become:

Wisden's Jazzed-Up Facade

IT MUST be time to send in the SAS to rescue Wisden. The "popularisation" has edged beyond the tolerance level for too many long-term readers. Like so many media enterprises, the House of Wisden seems enslaved by the belief that everything depends upon attracting young readers. Much depends on them, of course, but the solid base of the readership consists of middle-aged and elderly cricket-lovers to whom the Almanack is one of life's essentials. There really is no need to panic, Mr Wisden.

The acquisition of one's first *Wisden* ranks in memory with other firsts in life, such as the first shave. The 1951 *Wisden* bore the Ravilious woodcut – men in top-hats – and had about its form a solemnity appropriate in a book reverentially referred to as the sport's "bible". It afforded a feeling of reassurance. The next year I shelled out 22s 6d for the chocolate hardback, which was equally delightful to hold. Today, the limp and the hardback are identically priced. I am not alone in believing this to be a barmy piece of marketing. It is like being asked to pay the same for a weatherboard house as for an otherwise identical one constructed from brick.

The *Wisdens* of old, as we now know, were not entirely reliable statistically. Nor did they need anywhere near so many pages of international cricket, for Test matches were the preserve of deserving nations – with the possible exception of New Zealand. It was also spared today's acres of one-day cricket coverage.

The Almanack was regarded by the cricket community then as being indispensable, just as it is now. The owners are well aware of that. Yet there is this compulsion to keep changing. Not that it concerns the public, but even the traditional black-tie dinner to launch the new *Wisden* has been scrapped*. There was a time when it went ahead (at the East India Club in St James) even when some of us were in range of possible sniper fire from the besieged Iranian Embassy. That was another situation when the presence of the SAS would have been reassuring.

The continuity of *Wisden* is the core factor. It does not need gimmicks. Even Michael Vaughan's mother will buy the 2003 edition specifically for its content. Vaughan's batting in Australia enchanted most of us. But having him on the front of *Wisden Cricketers' Almanack*, just as he has been depicted already on the covers of magazines and brochures, is a pretty ordinary move. What if Vaughan is again the world's outstanding batsman next year? Does he feature again? Or will the second-best be depicted? Or will some overseas player have to go on to prove something else that does not need proving: that *Wisden* is international? Maybe a bowler instead? Or a woman? Why not Sir Mick Jagger, one of the earlier Getty entourage? If it is to be Vaughan again in 2004 it is to be hoped that he is shown playing that rapturous cover-drive rather than displaying one of the most obnoxious of modern symbols of sport, the clenched fist.

The shock of this image across *Wisden's* face is as profound as if one were to see HMS *Ark Royal* pushing down the Solent with a giant canvas dangling from the bridge, portraying Noah.

The book itself is sensational. But why, oh why, are newly appointed editors and their publishers so obsessed with change? What are they afraid of? The custodians of *Wisden* have an immense responsibility. The Almanack is one of the important on-going threads in life for so many people. Familiarity is a comforting and precious commodity and we are running out of it at a more frenetic rate than any previous generation.

"It's yours for only a year. Don't tamper with it unduly." That should have been the remit issued by management to their short-term editor. Remarkably, they seem uncertain themselves, for they have insured against this error of judgment by offering a traditional dust-jacket free to anybody who cares to write in for one. A useful consequence of this manoeuvre doubtless will be a sizable addition to *Wisden's* reader mailing list and that will make the marketing men who rule the world purr with anticipation. (A side thought: would there have been any response had it been the other way round? Traditional front cover, but send off for a wrap-around featuring Vaughan.)

A few weeks from now, it being ten times easier to lose readers than to lure them back, the magazine *Wisden Cricket Monthly* together with *The Cricketer*, the rival it shocked with its competitive flair from 1979 onwards, will undergo euthanasia. From the ashes will emerge what is promised to be the greatest cricket magazine ever. The marketing men's favourite word "new" will be splashed everywhere – while long-term readers of both the old magazines will grieve privately.

So, come to think of it, it really is time for change: *counter*-change. For a start, let's see those men in top-hats restored to *Wisden's* frontage**.

* Later revived. ** They returned the following year.

The Times, April 30, 2003

Ross Gregory was the only Australian Test cricketer to die in action in the Second World War. His name meant nothing to modern cricket followers. It was therefore fortuitous that his wartime diary was acquired on 2001, leading to extensive further research in preparation for a full-scale biography which revived his memory:

Diary Discovery Triggers Cricket/War Story

THE RECONSTRUCTION of the life of a special but long-forgotten hero was launched in an auction-room in Melbourne in 2001. Christie's catalogue offered the wartime diary of Ross Gregory (1916-42), "one of the youngest to play Test cricket". The description embraced a reminder that he helped Australia to retain the Ashes in the 1936-37 series, when his 80 in the decisive fifth Test match "overshadowed even the batting of Bradman", an innings, it was noted, that was played on the eve of Gregory's twenty-first birthday. "It was also his last Test as he was killed while serving with the RAAF, aged twenty-six."

In fact, Ross Gregory was the sole Test cricketer from Australia to lose his life in active service during the Second World War.

The summary of the diary's contents was enough to convince me, a hopelessly devoted collector of cricket memorabilia, that a substantial postal bid should be sent, especially since the lot included several other rarities. How many pre-1939 Australia Test sweaters have survived the ravages of time? There was also Gregory's Victoria sweater, and some trophies won at Wesley College.

It is always risky to bid for goods without examining them beforehand but the eighteen-line precis of the diary's contents was sufficient to convince me that I had to go for it. Had I known the full value of the diary I would have taken the precaution of submitting a much higher bid.

Sometimes you have to pretend that you didn't really care all that much that you were outbid. Whoever beat you must also have recognised the great importance of the diary, placed an even higher value on it, and therefore deserved to take it home to read and preserve.

Although I cannot recall exactly how I was informed of the fact (such was my swoon of relief and excitement) my bid was sufficient. It was not for some weeks that I sighted the purchase. It was waiting for me when I arrived in Queensland, where I utilised the middle-of-the-night jet-lag wakefulness to unpack the carton. The frantic rustling of crumpled packing paper as I tore the box open and unwrapped the items caused my half-asleep wife to wonder if a bandicoot or a brush turkey had got in and was rifling the house.

Three-thirty in the morning is hardly the time to be examining an old and slightly shrunken Australia Test sweater and reading a Second World War Australian airman's jottings, but I scanned page after page, greatly moved by young Gregory's penmanship as he described his escapades. Already it seemed like a book in the making.

The test is to ask any keen cricket-lover what he or she knows about a certain player. Gregory? Wasn't he killed in a Spitfire? (No.) Surely he was one of the celebrated Gregory family – Syd, Ned, Jack and the rest? (No.) He was very young when he played Test cricket. (Agreed.) Didn't he score a century in his first Test? (Not quite.) No further questions. No further details known, not even vaguely. Only the most meagre of outlines of his life and career was readily available, and I thought it shameful that his story had been allowed to drift into obscurity. If his life and career were to be brought together in anything resembling a full profile, then pursuit of contacts all over the place as well as some intuition and above-average luck would be required.

Before long, as one contact led to another and the clues multiplied, it began to seem as if a hidden benevolent force was guiding me.

The Ross Gregory Story (Lothian Books, 2003)

The pursuit and the luck paid off handsomely. I made contact with Ross Gregory's fiancee, a cousin, some friends from his teenage years, fellow cricketers, and even some wartime colleagues. The resultant book was recognised with a Cricket Society Book of the Year award.

Ross Gregory, Test batsman and ill-fated RAF/RAAF Wellington bomber navigator.

Dambuster Secret

SIR GEORGE EDWARDS'S unassuming nature was happily conveyed in his obituary. However, in what may have been the only full-length interview this great Englishman ever gave (only a few years ago, for the Imperial War Museum's sound archive) he permitted himself a mild little grumble about the way his contribution to the success of the Dambuster bomb has been overlooked.

As a leg-spin bowler skilful enough to have bowled out the great West Indies batsman Learie Constantine in a wartime match at Guildford, Edwards insisted that back-spin was the key to keeping the bomb bouncing for sufficient time across the surface of the water. Barnes Wallis, he recalled, had believed that top-spin – or perhaps no applied spin at all – was the key.

Successive tests proved Edwards right. He never sought the limelight or disproportionate credit for any of his numerous achievements, but this neglect continued to rankle with him. We should remember him on the forthcoming sixtieth anniversary of the Dambuster raid in May. A realist to the end, he said that his most useful contribution to the war effort was the magnetic minesweeping device affixed beneath the Wellington bombers. These swiftly cleared the Thames Estuary and allowed vital supplies to steam in.

When I asked him what memories he had of the end of the war, he directed that twinkling eagle eye at me and said: "Which war?" He then recalled that as a boy in Essex, he cycled over to the site of a crashed Zeppelin. Pointing to a drawer, he said: "There's a piece of it in there." This incident was the genesis of a truly outstanding career in aerodynamics, for which the nation should be eternally grateful.

The Times, March 21, 2003

My friend George, formerly president of Guildford CC and of Surrey CCC, was accorded countless honours in his later years, the most notable being OM, CBE, FRS and DL. His grave is by St Martha's Church, Chilworth, where also lies General Freyberg, VC, the legendary New Zealander who served in both world wars.

As one of only a handful of people who had attended all seven World Cup finals since the first in 1975, for the eighth final in March 2003, I was Wisden Online's "roving reporter" in Johannesburg:

Australian Slogathon

THE WANDERERS is the most attractive venue of any of the five which have hosted World Cup finals. It's an interesting bowl of a stadium – varied architecture, trees ringing it outside, and a golf-course beyond – and there is no doubting which continent you are in when you spot the patches of zebra-skin pattern which decorate all the balconies.

Although the ground is nowhere near as large as Eden Gardens in Calcutta, there was a distinct Indian feel about the place this morning, with hundreds of flags waving

– a tenner each from the vendors in the street – and many light-blue uniforms on parade, each enhancing the fantasy of it all. Here and there were yellow-clad Australian fans in little clusters. Breaking with convention, one of the cameramen stuck an Australian flag onto his viewfinder.

There had been forecasts of banks of empty seats. South Africa's miserable early exit from the World Cup left thousands of locals shattered and reluctant to attend, but the huge influx of Indian supporters, many of them latecomers, made certain a mass transfer of tickets.

But as Adam Gilchrist played another of his bull-in-a-china-shop innings the Indian masses fell subdued, with the odd rallying chant of "In-dee-ah!"

A hair-dryer had been used to dry any residual moisture on the pitch, and in giving Australia first use of a fast, hard surface, Sourav Ganguly not only handed them the initiative but relinquished any prospect of seeing the match pattern duplicating the famous 1983 World Cup victory at Lord's, when West Indies tripped up badly in chasing India's modest 183.

There was no Duckworth/Lewis system then to frighten everybody. Thoughts of India's greatest day must have lain in every Indian mind, sharpened by Gilchrist's lofted hit to leg, followed by a chase in vain by Zaheer Khan. When he was finally caught – just – in the deep, the Kapil Dev catch to dismiss Viv Richards twenty years

Ponting enjoys one of many joyous moments earned during his career at the top: World Cup triumph at The Wanderers, Johannesburg. (PA Photos)

ago flashed across many minds. The breath was held for several seconds, then as great an explosion of noise as the tournament has known shook the stadium.

And the drums started up. Drinks came as a relief, and then the ground announcer trivialised matters by shrieking a request for everyone to stand on one leg when the score reached 111. It was too early to predict, but if Australia's advance continued there would surely be a few legless Aussie fans by tonight.

The essence of a global cricket tournament was not reflected in the press-box. Over sixty journalists from India were at work, together with a handful from Australia. Some local writers, plus a contingent from British papers, completed the numbers. The English represented the nation that gave cricket to the world, while the camps of the two finalists stood for the new order, the two countries which have put their own forceful stamp on the game.

One Indian journalist, when asked about the interest back home, replied that it was "higher than the sky", and that many grand homecoming receptions were planned. But what if they should fail to win? He smiled softly. With India's poor showings earlier in the tournament taken into account, the more rational fans are simply pleased that Ganguly & Co. made it into the final.

And so, as the wides were called and Ricky Ponting's stratospheric drive fell out of reach and the runs came fifty upon fifty, the majority fell quiet. Some applauded the half-century of Damien Martyn, the quiet achiever, and such was the reduction in tension that some spectators wandered through the corridors down below to inspect the showcases filled with South African cricket memorabilia. Many will have envisaged a photograph of Ponting holding the World Cup aloft joining the collection in the near future. One can only imagine what the applause at the MCG might have amounted to for his century.

This morning I awoke to the sound of thunderclaps and splashing rain. But it passed quickly, and soon this awesomely efficient Australian side were sailing into the last overs of their bombardment. How much must Ganguly have wished that he and his men were making hay under the pale-blue African sky?

For a few precious hours the 27,000 people here, together with the hundreds of millions of television viewers, could distance themselves from the serious events of the world outside. Once again cricket was the exquisite, albeit temporary, escape from reality. And as the South African Airways jumbo-jets' low flypast took place, the distracted Indian supporters must have been praying for Ranjitsinhji, C.K.Nayudu and Duleepsinhji to parachute down into the sunlit Wanderers to help the cause of the response to Australia's incredible slogathon.

Wisden Online, March 25, 2003

Australia eventually won comfortably, after some tension when rain looked like bringing India's revised target within reach. A lot of abandoned Indian flags were to be seen on the footpaths and in the gutters that evening, soaking in the drizzle.

Inescapably one loses good friends as the years pass. Among them was Tony Woodhouse:

My Friend in the North

AROUND THIRTY years ago I ventured to Leeds as a guest of the Northern Cricket Society. I think Ron Yeomans must have been the instigator of my visit. In the question-and-answer session that always follows the speaker's address we all put the world to rights. Then I drove back to Surrey feeling there was something special about Yorkshire people. Ever since, I have felt my strong Australian links to be in parallel with my Yorkshire associations. Captain James Cook and all that . . . .

One of the men I met on that trip was Tony Woodhouse. Needless to say, Audrey was with him. And in the years that followed I scarcely ever visited Yorkshire without seeing him. Tony clearly knew what he was talking about when it came to the county's cricket and its rich history, and we clicked straight away.

At first I thought him a bit too serious – a trait about which I myself am often assumed to be guilty – but then I began to notice that twinkle in his eye. He was simply one of the most contented men I have ever met. And for that, as he would surely have readily admitted, he had not only Audrey but cricket to thank. This bond ties cricket-lovers throughout the world.

My first visit to Audrey and Tony's home illustrated the reality of what others had told me: he had a stupendous collection of cricket books and other material. It was happily spread all over the house, which is better than storing everything in a separate room, for it shows how cricket really is a part of one's life. We talked that special language that cricket students and scholars talk, each learning a little from the other.

The last time I saw him was when I was passing through in 2000 and we had arranged to visit the Lawnswood cemetery to find the final resting places of Hirst and Rhodes. While we were there Tony led me to J.T.Brown's grave and as we stood reverently beside it he produced one of his gems: "Jack Brown had a 'secret' family, you know."

I was speechless, for several seconds anyway. Then he drove us over to Rawdon where we stood by the stream that ran through the garden of remembrance where the ashes of our mutual friend Bill Bowes were scattered. We were both completely at peace in that environment, with the faint sound of birdsong, and a sense that we were engaged in one of cricket history's less familiar but satisfying pursuits.

His love for the game and commitment to it were constantly reiterated. When I took a cricket film show around the country in 1997, I knew instinctively who would be the first people I would see at Headingley that evening. Sure enough, on the pavement outside the flea-pit of a cinema half-an-hour before start of play, there stood Tony and Audrey. I had the beginnings of an audience already.

I've lost a few good mates lately and it's hard. As much as any of them I shall miss Tony Woodhouse, my friend in the North.

The Northern Cricket Society Booklet 2003

India were piling up some gargantuan scores early in the 21ˢᵗ Century. How did their top six rate in cricket's widest perspective?

India's Superb Top Six

AS INDIA handsomely worked their way to a record score (705 for 7 declared, Sydney, January 2004), spoiling Steve Waugh's farewell Test match in the process, it dawned on some of us that this might be as strong a top six in the batting order as ever visited Australia – or perhaps even as strong a top six as the world has seen. At first it seemed a slightly far-fetched conjecture. However, we are here not just talking about a top three (Hobbs, Sutcliffe, Hammond, or Barnes, Morris, Bradman, or Greenidge, Haynes, Richards) but a complete specialist batting order, No.1 to No.6.

The manner in which this India side toyed with the bowling of the world champions (who helped by grassing 15 catches in the four Tests) suggests that it deserves a very high rating indeed. Australia were admittedly without Glenn McGrath and Shane Warne, but the leg-spinner's record against India (29 wickets at 55.44) has been moderate, while the injury-stricken McGrath is nearing the end of his prolific career.

One of the startling achievements of this series was that India's highest individual scores at the four Test venues played have all just been raised (by Ganguly – 144 at Brisbane; Dravid – 233 at Adelaide; Sehwag – 195 at Melbourne; and Tendulkar – 241 not out at Sydney).

When one digs into the annals of Test cricket one finds, of course, several extremely impressive line-ups. Legendary England off-spinner Jim Laker wondered what he had done to deserve a couple of days under a baking Caribbean sun, bowling on a shiny surface to Everton Weekes, Frank Worrell and Clyde Walcott. There have been few to match that West Indies line-up, which also featured the elegant Jeff Stollmeyer and solid Allan Rae opening the innings. Think, too, of Australia's top orders – Victor Trumper, Reg Duff, Clem Hill, Joe Darling. Bill Woodfull, Bill Ponsford, Don Bradman, Stan McCabe. And more recently, Matt Hayden, Justin Langer, Ricky Ponting, Damien Martyn, and the Waughs.

Statistics can mean everything, or nothing. Pitch and weather conditions, opposition strength, freshness or fatigue, the luck of dropped catches, players just past their best or with their best still to come: mix all this into a computer and still there is only the next ball, which could be fatal, or be hit for four, or let go through to the keeper. What really counts is the inherent worth of a player. And in the case of these Indian batsmen, the high quality of Dravid, Tendulkar and Laxman is patently obvious.

It is preposterous to suggest that the Sehwag-Chopra partnership rates (as yet) anywhere near the likes of Hobbs and Sutcliffe, Greenidge and Haynes, Simpson and Lawry, and other pairings. But taken on recent evidence, their potential is quite apparent. I was particularly impressed with the way Chopra, in an inconsequential period of play near the end of the tour match in Hobart, fine-tuned his defensive armoury for over an hour before bothering to open his score. With great mental strength he cocooned himself exactly as Geoff Boycott or Sunil Gavaskar might have done.

We are not merely looking at an outstanding India top six. We are seeing a combination which may yet become even more formidable – abroad as well as at home. Australia may uncharacteristically have given India's batsmen many reprieves in the field, but what if Tendulkar had not been the victim of a bad lbw decision in the opening Test at Brisbane? He might have found his stride much sooner.

The best top six? How can it be proved, even by those confounded statistics? If that is to be the chosen means of deciding, then given another year or two Ganguly's current top six may erase all doubts. I saw the signs on India's last tour of England. Dravid and Ganguly, the young newcomers who had taken Lord's by storm in 1996, were now fully developed. And I recall with great pleasure Tendulkar's maiden Test hundred, at Old Trafford so many years ago. Then, he had the voice of a child and the batting technique of a veteran. He is now comfortably assured of immortality in cricket terms and is recognised as the nearest thing to Bradman since The Great One hung up his bat.

For my money VVS is the most pleasing to watch. Then, controlling the middle order, comes Ganguly, with his penchant for taking the ball on the helmet and for displaying an aloofness that would have delighted England's Golden Age aristocrat A.C.MacLaren. Of the six, Sehwag is the most daring and unpredictable, and therefore exciting. And then there is "Boycott" Chopra.

Some six. Maybe as good as any in the past. I don't really care. They were simply wonderful to watch in this Australian summer, when the balance of power began to shift.

Wisden Asia Cricket, February 2004

The frenzy following England's recapturing of the Ashes in 2005, after a drought lasting sixteen years, ranked with similar occasions in 1926, 1953 and 1981. From my book on the series (the only one that had been scheduled in the spring of 2005, but one of fifteen or so by the end of the summer) comes this description of the final day:

The Day England Won the Ashes

FIFTH DAY, Monday, September 12, 2005

NINETY-EIGHT overs were scheduled to be bowled on this fateful day. While English confidence and brewing excitement were at high levels, there was still a long way to go. I thought of the premature mock obituary published around Manchester in 1902. On the penultimate evening of the 1902 Old Trafford Test, Australia were 122 ahead with two wickets in hand. A Mr Griffiths of Ardwick thought this a strong enough position to guarantee England victory. Beneath a sketch of a horse-drawn funeral carriage he printed the following on his cards:

> *The Australia men, their players feel*
> *The blighting, withering blast,*
> *For full of hope, they thought to steal*
> *The verdict at last:*
> *Twas not to be, so let them lie*
> *Deep in the silent grave,*
> *And shed a tear, o'er their bier,*
> *And the match they tried to save.*

Mr Griffiths was forced to withdraw the cards from sale when Australia were bowled to victory by Trumble and Saunders by three runs.

Forty ahead, nine wickets in hand, up to 98 overs to play. Would England prevail or might Ponting's men roll them over quickly and knock off the runs? The pre-lunch session pointed resoundingly towards the latter course and completely ruined the digestion of millions of England supporters.

For a time it went smoothly. Superstitions were put firmly in their place. While the Aussies must have been praying that Warne would not fall down the stairs and break his right wrist, I merely gave my customary nod towards the grave of Lewis Carroll in the churchyard on the way to the railway station early on this autumnal morning, urging the creator of *Alice* not to spring anything too illogical or bizarre upon the realm of cricket this day.

Again, had there been floodlights at The Oval they might have been switched on at the start. But the sky was clearing gradually as England went about their business. Warne and McGrath, 1132 Test wickets between them to date, began their desperate mission. England's two seniors played them calmly. Vaughan even drove the second ball of the day, from Warne, to the long-on boundary. Lee took over from Warne, but Vaughan took a four backward of point and edged McGrath for another. The fifty came up. Trescothick reached 1000 runs against Australia. It was all too serene.

Then McGrath made a double strike. He found Vaughan's edge and Gilchrist completed a magnificent diving catch low down. A man and a woman clad in scanty swimwear ran uncaringly across the field (until apprehended) between this dismissal and Ian Bell's first ball, which also proved fatal. He edged to Warne at slip, and sloped off, victim of a "pair".

Kevin Pietersen came in on the hat-trick. McGrath slipped him a vicious lifter. He rocked back like a boxer pole-axed and the ball flew high to second slip. The appeals were frenzied, insistent, unreceptive to refusal. But in what was probably the most important decision he'll ever make, umpire Bowden said "Not out!" The ball had struck Pietersen's shoulder and nothing else. So he got down the other end and nicked Warne. The ball touched Gilchrist's glove and eluded Hayden's desperate grasp. It could be said that KP would be lucky to make nought. More jumping and hollering from Warne as a gyrating ball hit Trescothick's pads, but Pietersen hooked McGrath for four and at drinks England had calmed down somewhat at 79 for 3.

The sky was clearing and 85 overs remained, so if anything Australia were in control and might have had strong expectations of yet saving the series. Warne had the usual intimidating box of four close fieldsmen, and when a throw from Clarke plucked a stump out of the ground, nerves jangled.

On 15, Pietersen edged Lee to Warne collarbone-high at first slip. He couldn't hold it. And with that, though it was some time before it became obvious, the Ashes were lost. It was the cruellest stroke of fate against the most powerful bowling agent of the series.

The error seemed to matter little when Trescothick (33) was lbw to a sharply-spinning ball from Warne, reducing England to 109 for 4. This took Shane Warne to 168 wickets against England, passing Dennis Lillee's record, a matter to be savoured later, for battle now was raging full bore. Flintoff's early dismissal, caught for 8 from a return catch to Warne, saw the Australians absolutely exultant. England 126 for 5, a mere 132 ahead with all the top-order men bar Pietersen accounted for, and bags of time remaining.

Just before Trescothick's dismissal, Pietersen had belted two sixes off a Warne over, one over midwicket, the other swept over square, with a crude swipe in between. Now the Hampshire batsman took one in the ribs from Lee and sought attention. He later claimed he was being a bit of a "drama queen", but it must have hurt. When Lee bounced him again, with half a Bodyline field in position, there was booing. Maybe some knew about Larwood's blow to Woodfull's chest at Adelaide in '33, and of how, when he was recovered, he was bounced again, this time to a fully-manned Bodyline field.

By the grace of God, Pietersen made it to lunch (127 for 5) with his head still attached to his neck. He was 35, Collingwood was still with him, having scored no runs, and much of the nationwide cocksuredness had been deflated.

England's aggressive approach was ingrained by now, and upon resumption Pietersen hooked Lee for six, way over the waiting fieldsman. Seventy-one overs were left and England led by 147. Not only were Collingwood's forward defensives being noisily applauded; so were the leaves. Pietersen reached his half-century from 71 balls, but soon Lee was after him again with rockets of close to 100 mph. He hooked him and the ball seemed to be threatening the gas-holder. The next was hooked too, but Tait just failed to make a catch of it in the deep. KP then *hit* a glance for four: not merely letting the ball run off the blade of the bat.

Brett Lee was bowling his heart out and at blistering pace. It was Tom Richardson at Old Trafford all over again, when England tried to stop Australia getting 125 in the 1896 Test match, and he sent down 42.3 consecutive five-ball overs. A vital catch was dropped by England wicketkeeper Lilley (yes, they did it in those days too) and Australia got home by three wickets. The dazed Richardson was led from the field, wrote the fantasist Cardus, "like some fine animal baffled at the uselessness of great strength and effort in this world" (whereas another account states that Tom had sunk a couple of pints before the players had got their boots off). This was the kind of distraction needed to pacify the nerves on this electrifying afternoon at The Oval in 2005. Like Richardson of old, Lee "did bowl and bowl and bowl, and his fury diminished not a jot".

What might Cardus have made of Kevin Pietersen though? Another four under the body of the diving Clarke, another slammed through mid-on, and when the fifty stand came, Collingwood's staunch contribution was a mere four runs. We were seeing fresh folklore under construction.

Katich went off for a while after being struck by a Collingwood pull. While England would have had a super-athletic substitute on in his place, Kasprowicz came on for Australia.

God Save Your Queen rose from the Barmy Army ranks now. They were getting their confidence back after the shocks. "Five-nil! Five-nil!" they taunted Glenn McGrath when he fielded in front of them. Four leg-side byes off Warne were cheered gratefully. Then the next breakthrough: Collingwood (10) fell to Warne, Ponting launching into a dive at short leg: 186 for 6.

Geraint Jones gave his impression of the infamously dogged Trevor Bailey forward defensive as clouds seemed to be gathering again, and the strains of *Jerusalem* once more sent shivers down the spine. The climax was upon us. England led by 195 with 56 overs remaining. Australia, in their desperate position, would surely be capable of lashing anything up to 10 or even 12 runs an over when the time came?

Pietersen slashed Tait for two fours when he bowled for the first time in the 57th over. But the young quickie beat Jones (1) with sheer pace, the ball not rising quite as expected either: 199 for 7. Again an interloper had inspired a wicket, for a large man in a ballerina's tutu had just run across the ground before being carted away by a handful of the hundreds of zealous security men.

Ashley Giles took a calm single to bring up 200, and Pietersen showed he could play copybook as well as kindergarten shots by placing Tait off his toes for four. He was now in the nineties, and Warne teased him with wide balls, one of which was called. Then, just on tea, Pietersen cover-drove Tait for four to raise his first Test century (124 balls, 10 fours, four sixes), an ecstatic moment for him and millions of others. It is hard to see how any hundred he may make in the years ahead could carry such weight of significance.

At tea England were 221 for 7, and close now, surely, to safety?

And so to the final session of the greatest series in 128 years of Test cricket. Giles was the target of bouncers, which he rode well. One from Lee was timed at 96.7mph. He swayed clear. When Lee bounced Pietersen, however, he smote it into the Peter May Enclosure, and in the next over he pounded his sixth six, straight off Warne. That equalled Ian Botham's overall record for an Ashes innings, and it wasn't long before he had the record all to himself, lofting an on-drive off his pal Warne for a seventh six. The audacity and the exuberance of it all took the breath away.

McGrath replaced the exhausted Lee, and Giles looked at ease. Warne was beginning to look slightly slumped. His match effort would be 75 overs, his tally 12 wickets, giving him 40 for the series, a record for Australia against England in a

Telling moment in the great tussle in the Oval Ashes match of 2005: Warne turfs a catch from Pietersen, in retrospect the aberration that contributed most vitally to England's victory. (Philip Brown)

five-Test rubber. He had seen the tantalising hopes of the morning slowly give way to blank despair: the Ashes were lost. And he'd put Pietersen down at 15; here he was 152 not out.

Transfer of the Ashes was not official yet, of course. The new ball was taken at 298 for 7, after 80 overs, and a quick single to cover by Giles raised the hundred stand (143 balls), resistance that made certain of the outcome. The partnership had reached 109 – a new eighth-wicket record for England against Australia at The Oval, passing the 90 by Walter Read and Johnny Briggs in 1886 – when Pietersen's amazing effort came to an end. McGrath knocked his off stump out when he was 158, coincidentally the score made by another South Africa-born England batsman, Basil D'Oliveira, on this ground in 1968, a century that had major political repercussions. It's a team game, but if anybody above all others could be said to have secured the Ashes it was twenty-five-year-old Kevin Peter Pietersen, whose brave assault had saved England's hopes from melting in the white-hot crucible.

Even the stuffiest onlooker forgave him his hair-style and his diamond ear-stud as he saluted the crowd on his way from the arena (using his third bat after breaking two). And to reconfirm the lovely spirit in which this series was played, Warne ran a long way after him to congratulate him. I fancied, too, that the ghosts of F.S.Jackson and his players of 1905 might have been applauding from the balconies – though they might have been difficult to spot midst all the gaudy commercial tack attached to that grand old pavilion. And it so happened that Pietersen's going practically coincided with Richie Benaud's departure from the Channel 4 commentary seat for the last time.

McGrath now plucked Giles's off stump out too, though only jokingly. The batsman had pulled away, unsighted, and the bowler didn't fancy rupturing himself by slamming on the brakes. Giles punched him through the covers then pulled him through mid-on to reach his fifty off 87 balls, an indescribably precious supporting job. And when drinks were summoned by the umpires some spectators mistook it for the end of the match and became very excited.

Shortly after smacking Warne through cover, Giles was bowled by him, having achieved his highest score in Tests in this his fiftieth appearance. Harmison's swift dismissal gave Warne his dozen for the match. But there was little elation about the greatest spin bowler of all time, and the adrenalin had long been replaced by molten concrete in the stomachs of his team-mates.

Eighteen overs now remained and Australia needed an unreachable 342 as England took the field all wearing their navy caps with coronet and three lions. A few bouncers from Harmison, one of which reared well over Jones's upstretched glove, convinced the umpires that there was no future in this light, so off they all trooped. The crowd, unsure as to whether this was it, booed. But the stumps remained in place and it was not until some time later, at 6.15pm, that the anti-climax gave way to a realisation, with the uprooting of the stumps, that the match was over.

After 5886 days, eight series, and forty-four Tests against Australia under seven captains, all unwanted records, England had the Ashes back. Delirium swept across The Oval, across England, across British outposts around the world. It was regrettable that spectators were forbidden from running across the grass to the players' area, as they had done in 1926 and 1953. Instead, the players came to them, doing a slow lap of honour while *Jerusalem* was played, and *Rule Britannia* and *Land of Hope and Glory*. For the multitude, the author included, it was emotionally overwhelming.

Battle for the Ashes (Ebury Press, 2005)

When Kerry Packer, one of the most significant figures in 20th Century cricket, died on Boxing Day 2005, an informal obituary was called for:

Playing with Packer

TO A stranger's eye, there was a threatening air about Kerry Packer. Physically massive, he had a countenance that was never better described than as resembling a man in a stocking mask. Had cricket's 1970s revolution been mounted instead by someone as diminutive and twinkle-eyed as, say, Lindsay Hassett, the sense of assault would never have been so great.

When Packer's plan to hijack international cricket was revealed, it seemed he was acting not only outrageously but irrationally. And few of us believed that he was actually going to play with us in a press cricket match shortly after news of his scheme had exploded worldwide. It was Ian Chappell, one of his lieutenants in the Channel 9 World Series Cricket programme, who lured him into playing.

Equipped at Harrods with shirt, flannels and cricket boots (extra large), Packer took a helicopter to Harrogate, and his grace and charm took us by surprise. Of course, there was a scramble to get an exclusive from him; but he was there to relax, alert at slip after a short not-out innings.

I happened to be batting when he came in. He was jeered by the small Yorkshire gathering, so, after he had tapped the first ball to short cover, I tried to introduce a touch of light relief with the old call of "Yes! No! Wait!" He came down the pitch, menacingly I thought. His response startled me: "I'm in your hands," he sort of growled. If only it were so.

By 1978-79 Packer's plans were well advanced. While his WSC matches (until that extraordinary night in Sydney when, given permission to play at the Sydney Cricket Ground at long last, the Packer match drew a capacity – and very noisy – crowd) were not drawing big crowds, neither was the concurrent official Ashes Test series, and the cricket world was in distracted trauma. This juddering split could not go on. Neither side would win. Cricket was bleeding.

Those of us who had played with KP in that press match were welcome in his VIP enclosure, where I mustered the temerity to point out that Gary Gilmour's name was mis-spelt on the giant screen. He did not caution me not to be so petty. He simply called somebody over, and within seconds the correction was made. That impressed me.

Not that he was getting soft. He glanced at my Australian Cricket Board overnight bag with the sponsor's name all over it. "That won't last the season!" he sneered. He was a master of the sharp put-down, first publicly displayed at Lord's in 1977 after talks with the establishment had irretrievably broken down: "There's a bit of the whore in all of us" and "Let the Devil take the hindmost."

Packer was impressive in the High Court showdown, calm and respectful in the witness-box. The court case having been smartly won by the rebels, cricket had been plucked out of its feudal era and thrust into a time of jangling bells, dancing girls and unbridled commercialism.

The Independent, December 28, 2005

The persecution of umpire Darrell Hair after he had correctly awarded a Test match to England when Pakistan refused to take the field because they resented his accusation of ball-tampering prompted an overall view of the complexities surrounding the men in the white coats:

Muddles in the Middle

JUST OVER a hundred years ago, cricket had another Darrell Hair. His name was Jim Phillips and he was an Australian of strikingly similar physical bulk. A fast bowler for Victoria and Middlesex, Phillips became an umpire in county and Test matches, and was conspicuous for his fearlessness in making decisions that inevitably made headlines, albeit not quite as frenzied as yesterday's.

Throwing was a growing problem as 20th Century cricket developed, and Phillips was the one man with sufficient courage to no-ball the Australian Ernie Jones and the Englishmen C.B.Fry and Arthur Mold. Recently discovered film of Mold shows an action without blemish, but this doesn't prove a thing, for Mold was well aware that he was being filmed. But scores of opposing batsmen had for years been expressing their doubts and their resentment. Phillips was yelled at by the partisan crowds, but it didn't bother him. Like Hair, he would not be deflected from what he knew to be his duty.

As a breed, umpires tend to view criticism of themselves with disproportionate resentment. Some of them, in my experience, feel that umpires should be beyond criticism. They believe that an air of holiness should surround their judicial role. In turn, players have felt that, before respect is forthcoming, an umpire should demonstrate certain qualities: not just friendliness (which is sometimes patronising), but efficiency without officiousness.

This essential commodity, respect, would willingly be extended – and mostly is – by players and by spectators. But it is eroded whenever suspicions of favouritism or incompetence arise, no matter how misguided.

Umpires in the earlier years of county cricket were often from poor backgrounds and often "bent". They would have lost their jobs had they given too many captains out leg-before or caught behind. The troubled story of England v Pakistan may be a book in itself, but Australians have long been suspicious of English umpires, and vice versa. In a 1905 match at Scarborough, F.Stanley Jackson of Yorkshire, a Golden Age figure of stature and distinction, England's then captain and a future chairman of the Tory party, was ruled not out. "Jackson was out by yards," wrote the Australian captain Joe Darling. "The umpire, who was a former player, gave Jackson not out. This was bad enough, but what disgusted all of us was the fact that Jackson turned to the umpire and told him it was a good decision." Still, the Australians didn't lock themselves in their dressing-room at the next interval.

It is only recently that the authorities have given their top umpires reassuring support – with a few glaring exceptions, such as when Hair no-balled Sri Lanka's Muralitharan for throwing.

But that support has not always been there. Frank Chester, an outstanding English umpire (Bradman thought him the best he'd seen), greatly respected by the players (until his last seasons, when his faculties began to fail him), was told not to no-ball South Africa's Cuan McCarthy for throwing during the 1951 tour of England. P.F.Warner, administrator and habitual appeaser, told Chester that it would be wrong to no-ball McCarthy because "these people are our guests".

Such thinking was not unique. Another English bigwig, R.W.V.Robins, forbade the boisterous Lancashire-based Australian umpire Cec Pepper from pursuing his conviction that West Indies fast bowler Charlie Griffith chucked the occasional delivery. Pepper, disgusted by this "umpire-tampering", was not alone on this belief. But yet again, weak governance prevailed.

Umpires were guilty of costly leniency all through the period of four-prong, all-day bouncer attacks by West Indies between 1976 and 1991, an era that made the 1932-33 Bodyline series seem sedate, even though zealots then wanted Australia to secede from the Empire. When Harold Larwood sought to cut Bradman down to size with persistent bouncers and a thick leg-side field, the umpires had no power to intervene under the laws as they stood.

But half-a-century later, in the 1980s, the umpires – if only they had had sufficient strength of character – could have intervened, on grounds of intimidation, against the stultifying four or five bouncers an over.

The West Indians were also fortunate not to forfeit a Test match to New Zealand at Christchurch in 1980, when the tourists sulked in their room long after the tea interval. The same goes for the Sri Lankans, when they staged a walk-off during the 1995-96 series in Australia after Muralitharan was no-balled.

Soon after the Muralitharan sensation, the Australian Cricket Board confidentially told its umpires not to no-ball two other Sri Lanka bowlers who were causing them concern. As in the 1992 rumpus in England, when the Pakistanis were accused of ball-tampering, it is tempting to believe that not only were the umpires leant upon but that – as in the Bodyline series – alarm bells were also ringing in high places.

Although the heavily politicised International Cricket Council scarcely ever gets a favourable press, it has been responsible for a few major developments in recent years that have strengthened the umpires' role – not least the ruling that none of them can stand in a match in which his native country is playing. It is easily forgotten that this was Pakistan's early initiative. While this move could not guarantee greater efficiency among umpires, it did at least lift the burden of suspected home-town decisions.

Sadly, critics of the men in white coats will always be quick to suspect an ulterior motive. When mutterings about the bowling action of Ian Meckiff were finally brought to a head when he was no-balled at Brisbane in 1963, the decision was taken by an Australian umpire, presumed to have been backed by the Australian Cricket Board. Yet still there were cries, especially from Victoria, of "plot!" But, like Darrell Hair, he was only an umpire doing a conscientious job.

Daily Telegraph, August 22, 2006

Writing a book on England's pathetic tour of Australia in 2006-07 led to some byways and diversions:

Nostalgia and Confrontation

THE TEMPTATION was too great. Instead of crossing the road and entering the ground, I needed to stroll in the opposite direction in order to experience the tranquillity that this old part of Sydney infallibly bestows. Leaving early, I walked all the way to Trumper Park, where I'd played for Paddington in the early 1960s. The wide expanse was empty but redolent of times long lost yet still fashioned in a painfully retentive memory bank: a motor-scooter; a pre-match churning stomach; a blow on the head; a late cut; the photo of Victor Trumper on the wall of the ancient (and long gone) wooden pavilion with the splintery floor; the contentment of having a young body; the fear of ageing.

Back through the avenues and boulevards of Paddington I reflectively wound my way, along the terraced lanes built by English immigrants for English settlers well over a hundred years ago, the small scale inimical to the Australian predilection for space, the wrought-iron lacework adding a gentle splendour to the balconies, which are festooned with plants, some colourful and delicate, most with large leaves. The narrow streets are buttressed by enormous trees, Moreton Bay figs, eucalypts, paperbarks. And you never see people . . . only ghosts from the 1890s.

IT WAS a tea interval with a difference. The media centre was suddenly abuzz with all sorts of weird rumours about the Ashes urn. Sir Richard Branson, whose Virgin Airline had been the carrier of the urn on its much-publicised flight from Lord's and all around the capital cities of Australia for public exhibition, had had the temerity to interrupt the flow of this Test match by calling a press conference to announce that he didn't really feel it was right to return the Ashes urn to its regular and rightful home in London now that Australia's cricket team was supreme again.

Some writers (but certainly not this one) had chosen to attend this press conference at the expense of observing a few overs of the Test match. Branson, a master of publicity who clearly has less knowledge and understanding of the history of Ashes Test cricket and its vast ramifications than your average ten-year-old, at one point accused MCC of trying to "rewrite history". One alert journalist instantly charged Sir Richard himself with being guilty of trying to rewrite history, a rebuttal he instantly and graciously accepted. The famous urn, after all, had long been in the legal ownership – and not merely guardianship – of Marylebone Cricket Club.

When word of all this reached the ears of Prime Minister John Howard, he could not resist the temptation to pitch in. Of course, he said, Australia had a kind of moral right to keep the Ashes urn in Australia. As an MCC member for the past thirty-odd years, I felt an urgent need, even a responsibility, to establish some resistance here. Ian Botham and a few other notables were by now lending their voices to the increasingly popular demand that the urn should not go back to its rightful home.

It was therefore important to get some facts on the table, preferably uttered by somebody with authority. Who better than Charles Fry, grandson of the famous C.B.Fry, who had made a century against Australia at The Oval a hundred-and-one years ago? Charles the younger was now chairman of MCC, and an acquaintance of mine. Having spotted him in the VIP area along from us atop the Bradman Stand earlier in the day, I offered to escort a couple of London journalists across the top-deck walkway to find him and obtain a potent quote or two.

The plan went wrong when we discovered that Fry had already left the ground (for all we knew, to hurry to the exhibition site and snatch the urn into his safe keeping before something nasty happened). However, seated in that area was Mr Howard. He smiled benevolently, probably sensing that my companions were cricket writers, and conversation followed.

We are both former pupils of Canterbury Boys' High School, Sydney, the Prime Minister and I, and since I was two or three years ahead of him, I was – or so he had me believe some years ago – among his "heroes", simply because I was in the school cricket first eleven. In fact, quite remarkably, our heads back onto each other in the 1954 edition of the school magazine, his as a member of the debating society group, mine in the cricket team.

Now, as the senior boy, so to speak, I asked him what this was all about. How could he possibly advocate the appropriation of somebody else's legal property? Did he not appreciate that the Ashes urn belonged to that esteemed club in London, NW8?

Aha! Now for his trump card. The PM pointed out that he was a member of MCC! (I'll bet he's an honorary member, free of the burden of paying a sizable subscription each January such as is coughed up by the rest of us.)

Although it was quite warm and it had already been a fairly frantic day, the brain was now in overdrive. Carefully weighing the risk of an unsought charge of insolence against the pressing need of the moment, and with a smiling countenance which I prayed would convey the lightheartedness of the remark, I suggested to John Howard that if he insisted on pressing for Australia's literal retention of the Ashes – that's to say, the hijacking of perhaps the most famous sporting symbol in the world – then he might in due course discover on the agenda for the next AGM at Lord's in May a motion for his suspension by, or even expulsion from, MCC.

Fortunately the smile never left *his* face either. But it was now time to bid the PM adieu, for the Ponting-Flintoff show was about to restart. While this had been an earnest episode which raised the blood pressure and distracted, it was now time to return to the serious business of the day.

The Battle Renewed: the Ashes Regained 2006-2007 (ABC Books, 2007)

Reputations are often established out of smokedrifts. This, perhaps, was one of them:

Nearly the Finest

JOHN ARLOTT has a lot to answer for. In his review in the 1964 *Wisden* he declared *Beyond a Boundary* by C.L.R.James to be "the finest book written about the game of cricket", with only John Nyren's 1833 classic and Hugh de Selincourt's fictional *The Cricket Match* (1924) challenging it.

On the strength of that heady recommendation, and despite all that has joined the market over the past forty years, John's words have prompted hordes of cricket enthusiasts to read the book in one of its several editions. Most will not have been disappointed, especially if their taste is Caribbean cricket, its flavours and its characters.

But an on-going source of amusement derives from meeting people who, having asserted that this is indeed the finest book, confess – when pressed – that they haven't yet quite got around to reading it.

"CLR" was extremely tall and he had the thinnest and most persistent of voices. He was a Marxist, but had been greatly influenced by the writing of William Thackeray, and passages here could have been penned by that most conservative of observers. "A British intellectual long before I was ten," was how he described himself. His friendship with the great all-rounder Learie Constantine served both of them well, and although James travelled widely, and dwelt for many years in England, it is Trinidad that cradles his most tender memories. Well-read from childhood, he was colour-conscious from an early age, and bridled at the apartheid in local club cricket.

Two of the key characters portrayed in loving detail are George John, a superb fast bowler, and Wilton St Hill. The latter was, in James's view, fit to rate alongside Bradman, Sobers, Headley, the three Ws, Hutton, Compton and May. Poor St Hill averaged 19.50 in his three Tests. Romantic stuff.

"What do they know of cricket who only cricket know?" Although there are countless words which might be substituted for "cricket", this aphorism, deserving of digestion, is a trademark slogan tied inextricably to this book.

Cricinfo website, January 26, 2008

In June 2007 I began – under the broad title Frith's Encounters – a series of memoirs in the Wisden Cricketer magazine (the amalgamated title of the merged magazines I had edited some years ago: The Cricketer and Wisden Cricket Monthly) remembering Test cricketers I had known, stretching as far back as Wilfred Rhodes and S.F.Barnes. Here is Number 15 in the series:

Herbert Sutcliffe: Beauty in Duty

AS SURVIVING film testifies, Herbert Sutcliffe was not exactly poetry in motion. He even ran stiff-leggedly. But he was a model of sound technique, control and poise, usually capless, no hair out of place, and he regularly batted for hours at a time. In fact to this day no batsman who has played as many as his 54 Tests touches his average of 60.73.

His suavity and grace were instantly apparent upon first sight of him in person, outside The Oval before that memorable Ashes Test of 1968, forty-two years after a classic in which he had steered England to victory over Australia with a skillful 161 on a damp pitch. I used to carry a big book into which many hundreds of cricketers were persuaded to sign their names. Here was a big one.

Mr Sutcliffe was charming: "I'm sure we've met before?" We had never met and he probably knew it. Out came the fountain pen and into the book went a valued signature, clear and bold. He was encouraged to think back to that 1926 Test match, which he did with modesty, and for the rest of the day – the rest of the year for that matter – I was aglow from that chance encounter with a true immortal.

We corresponded and at his request I was able to locate a few copies of his old book *For England and Yorkshire*. Back came a large photograph of Sutcliffe and his friend Jack Hobbs going out to bat. They seemed then, as they seem now, despite all the later challengers, to be the ultimate in opening partnerships, part of the language.

Herbert Sutcliffe was no sensationalist: "The reason for my two car accidents," he wrote in 1971, "was a burst blood vessel over the left eye which impaired my vision and a black-out followed." Even in old age he allowed nothing to fluster him. The film evidence is still there: a Jack Gregory bouncer, a parry or a sway, a contemplative walk around the crease; elsewhere a sudden break from his stance as somebody moved behind the bowler: an imperious wave of the hand before resumption. As a senior pro during the red-hot Bodyline series, still mindful of the battering dished out by Australia in earlier years, it was often he – ahead of captain Douglas Jardine's instruction – who ushered England's leg-side cordon into position after a few new-ball overs from Larwood and Voce.

This was the man who, in 1924-25, scored three centuries in his first two Ashes Tests and went on piling up runs for Yorkshire and England between the two world wars, one of only seven batsmen to finish with over 50,000.

Late in life he relished his role as man-of-the-match adjudicator at one-day games. At Old Trafford it was my good fortune to be his sponsor's "guide" for the day. It worked out at roughly forty minutes of rich reminiscence for every gin and tonic. He talked about "dear Jack" (Hobbs, not Gregory) and of the gratification in playing for those powerful Yorkshire teams. He was concerned about the hook shot employed by England's latest bright hope Frank Hayes, wanted to discuss the shot with him, but would wait until invited. "I could play the hook," he murmured, without a trace of boastfulness.

Suddenly he disclosed that his wife had just died in a nursing-home, her dress ignited by her cigarette. They had been married for a very long time. He sank into a reflective quiet.

His presentation duties now loomed as a big problem. The pavilion steps were wet and slippery, with a maze of television cables on the ground. With his arthritic knees and walking-sticks it would be far too treacherous for him to attempt to enter the field to announce the match award. I tried hard to persuade him to stay in the pavilion. He would have none of it. He was being paid to perform certain duties and he would carry them out to the letter. We feared a fall and worse.

Mercifully the match was suspended until next day, so no presentations were called for. But I had witnessed the immense grittiness of Herbert Sutcliffe, as brave and unrelenting at eighty as fifty years before.

The Wisden Cricketer, August 2008

Another Encounter spotlights the unwarranted obscurity of a batsman who was not only brilliant but also brave in adversity . . . and somewhat mysterious:

Fred Bakewell: Cavalier Spirit

"HE'S SOMETHING of a wandering minstrel and a sad case," said the Northamptonshire secretary in 1976 when I asked how I might find Fred Bakewell. He was correct on the first count. It took several years of enquiry before the ill-fated old Northants and England batsman was found.

Alfred Harry Bakewell could not understand why somebody would want to place a microphone in front of him after all this time. Yet his tragically brief career had been spectacular and I wanted to know more. "I don't think I missed a match for the county from 1928 to 1936, apart from Test appearances [there were six]," he said softly. Through defeat after defeat he was the spinal column of the county's batting, hammering runs and curtailing the embarrassment of his struggling club. Of their 250 matches in the 1930s, Northants, poor devils, won only 18. From a crab-like stance ("Who worries too much so long as you're hitting the ball?") Bakewell, sharp of reflex, launched into the bowling, once taking five fours off Frank Smailes' opening over in a Championship match at Harrogate.

Four of his 31 centuries were above 200, the last of these an unbeaten 241 at Chesterfield, poignantly only hours before the car crash that ended it all. His skipper, Reggie Northway, who was at the wheel of the open-top sports-car, was killed. Fred's skull and right arm were fractured and the flesh was torn from his hands. He was in hospital for weeks, then tried so hard to overcome the painful physical legacy. Eventually he had to declare "I'm finished". His career as a top cricketer was over and he was only twenty-seven.

The complete absence of regret or bitterness moved me: "Just one of those things that happened," he said with a shrug. "You have to just accept it." He had been seen as the natural successor as an England opener to Herbert Sutcliffe (for whom he sacrificed his wicket in a run-out mix-up in the 1931 Oval Test). That is how good he was. And Bakewell, wearing no protection at all, was as wonderful a short-leg fieldsman as he was a fearless stroke-player.

It was his personality that fascinated. In the shadows of his life story lurked rumours of sleeping rough, snubbing authority, shoplifting charges, a nature that embraced, in Robertson-Glasgow's view, "a dull thread of negligence, even apathy", leaving him "in need of a leader-manager", though Fred would not have been comfortable with the army of supernumeraries in today's England dressing-room. He was, after all, a man who "could have batted with Bradman on not uneven terms".

There was "authority" about his batting.

His Test century came in 1933 against West Indies at The Oval (the surviving film clips convey a sense of defiance and confidence as he steered England from crisis towards innings victory). He made 85 in his next Test that winter at Madras, then 63 and 54 in the 1935 Manchester Test against South Africa, showing that he belonged at the highest level. That Oval hundred? "Just like reaching a century in a county match . . . or even a village match."

While he might have fumbled to recall what he had done the previous day, his memory for cricket past was clear. He and young Alex Snowden were sozzled from birthday champagne when they went out and smashed 199 opening the batting against Kent at Dover. This opening pair also posted a century for the first wicket *twice in one day* at Edgbaston. Bakewell even hooked Larwood for six at Kettering. "That's a short ground," he murmured. But against that bruising Notts attack at Trent Bridge in 1935 he hit 143, winning some money from the Chief Constable of Nottingham in doing so.

As soon as he knew that his time at the top was over he gave away all his cricket gear. He became a village publican, but more grief followed, including another car accident that cost him an eye in 1965. The parallels with another popular Northants and England batsman, Colin Milburn, were chilling.

I shed a quiet tear for Fred Bakewell whenever I catch sight of the MCC tie he was given as an honorary member, passed on to me by his widow.

The Wisden Cricketer, March 2009

Having compiled a biography of Archie Jackson, published in 1974 and updated in 1987, early in the new century I drew attention to the centenary of that tragic cricketer's birth. This is the uncut version as filed to the magazine:

Archie Jackson: the Keats of Cricket

TWO THINGS about Archie Jackson continue to challenge belief. Midst the ranks of eminent Test cricketers, there is no evidence of any personal defect about him. This verges on the unique. Victor Trumper, for all his saintly reputation, attracted criticism with his involvement in the money-making Rugby League breakaway and then in the players' revolt against the Australian Cricket Board in 1911-12.

The other mind-blowing fact is that had Jackson lived beyond his twenty-three years, he would have been celebrating his *100th birthday* on September 5, 2009. This symbol of eternal youth, this John Keats of cricket, Trumper's spiritual successor – a centenarian? It's too much to digest. It conflicts with the sad, veiled, hallowed image.

Had he lived beyond 1933 he must have played many more enchanting innings like his two centuries in a Shield match at the SCG in 1928, when he was still only eighteen. A year later, having charmed his way to six hundreds already, he was capped against one of the strongest sides England have ever sent.

The frail Test debutant, fighting nerves, made a wristy, patient 164 (still second only to Charles Bannerman for an Australian on Test debut against England). It was a lyrical performance that in aesthetic terms overshadowed anything that the nuggety young Don Bradman (a year older) was displaying. In the heaps of celebratory prose was Arthur Mailey's telling remark that it was Bradman's misfortune to have been overshadowed during the partnership with his brilliant pal. Jackson's adventurous and classical strokeplay was capped by a cover-drive to the pickets off a Larwood rocket to reach his hundred. The new Trumper had arrived.

The much-loved Archie Jackson, doomed batting genius.

That 318-minute exertion at Adelaide Oval completely wore him out. "We had to mop him with cold towels, poor little devil," said Stork Hendry years later. This memorable innings, begun tentatively, face white, lips frequently remoistened, sealed Archie Jackson's immortality. His keenness to attack allied to the God-given fluency of his strokeplay won the crowds over in an age of run-*grinding* in Australia, of huge scores in timeless matches on lasting surfaces. This youngster was touched by genius, with a predilection for attack, sometimes over-indulging with risky strokes, especially the late cut, admonishing himself if it mis-fired. And his pleasant nature and readiness to laugh were such that not even his opponents felt other than affection. A stylish dresser and avid reader, he had a pleasant voice and a ready sense of humour.

Ominously, having made a glorious 182 in a Test trial match at Sydney in December 1929, Archie missed the match in which Bradman smashed his world record 452 not out. He was unwell. And although on his customs and immigration document for the tour of England he avowed that he was in good health, the illness which was to kill him was already at work.

Initially the UK papers had hailed Jackson rather than Bradman as the young batsman to watch, and it was he who had drawn the largest crowds to the early net sessions. But he struggled on that 1930 tour, debilitated by cold weather. His sole century came against Somerset, when the sun shone. He did play in two of the Tests however. Caught at short leg in the second over at Headingley (Bradman 334), Archie came back to play a key role in the final contest, the Ashes match when Bradman's discomfort at The Oval against the lifting ball came into sharp focus, leading to the Bodyline strategy when next the two countries met. A few raindrops had freshened the pitch, and when Larwood and Hammond got bounce, The Don's discomfort was exposed. Keen English eyes noticed.

His partner in a stand of 243 was Archie Jackson, who stood his ground, taking some fearful knocks. He scored a patient 73 and Australia went on to win (by an innings) a match which in its score pattern – England 405 and 251; Australia 695 – was similar to the recent Cardiff Test. The 1930 Test, however, was to be played to a finish, so there was no escape. Australia regained the Ashes.

Archie enjoyed his tour of England, or rather Britain, one reason being that he had been born in Rutherglen, Glasgow. (A favourite question: who was the greatest Scots-born cricketer?) He met his cousin James, who was captain of Liverpool FC, and he and several of the Australians enjoyed an afternoon at Wembley Stadium to watch the Cup final.

Archie was only a tot when his mother emigrated to Sydney with her two children to join her shipyard worker husband. There they settled in a small terrace house in the industrial suburb of Balmain, and from his short-pants years the lad stood out as a born batsman. Supported by Arthur Mailey and Labor politician "Doc" Evatt, he played junior cricket with others in the deprived neighbourhood, including Bill Hunt, who was to play in one Test, and Syd Hird, who once made 12th man.

Slim and gifted, Archie was playing first grade at fifteen, bravely facing the thunderbolts of Jack Gregory. NSW skipper Alan Kippax became his chief mentor, and after playing his first State match at 17 years 82 days, in only his second game Jackson became the youngest centurion in Australian first-class cricket. Soon he was fielding out to Victoria's record total of 1107. It was a rigorous apprenticeship.

Tuberculosis first drove him into hospital care in the Blue Mountains, but he refused to stay there. Had he done so he might have lived. Instead he moved up to Brisbane to be near his dancer girlfriend Phyllis. He made heaps of runs there in grade cricket even though he was often close to collapse. Test umpire Col Hoy remembered as a lad seeing him return to the pavilion after one of those innings. Archie signed his book and asked him to help get his pads off, but then a doctor came in and ushered Col out: "Archie was coughing up black stuff – real yukkie. Not long after, Archie Jackson died and I just threw myself on my bed and sobbed my heart out."

He died as the Brisbane Test of the Bodyline series concluded, and Harold Larwood was deeply touched by a congratulatory telegram from him. Archie was among the few who had not condemned Bodyline. Only hours before he died, he and Phyllis became engaged (not married as stated in *Wisden*). His body was taken back to Sydney on the same train which conveyed both Test teams south. Both countries were deeply affected by his passing.

Wherever good film footage exists people are never completely lost to us. There are sequences of a batting exhibition by Archie Jackson at the SCG No.2 ground, and newsreel clips from the 1930 Tests. Had he lived beyond 1933 he must surely have played many more elegant innings to keep the torch of sublime natural style aflame in an age of ruthless marathon innings. Instead it was left chiefly to Stan McCabe and Bill Brown to display the aesthetics of batsmanship on a regular basis in parallel with the dour Ponsford and the piratical, popular Bradman as they rewrote the records.

The Wisden Cricketer, October 2009

In August 2009, England regained the Ashes. Only something like a broken leg would have kept me from being there:

Oval Ecstasy 2009

IT'S GOOD fortune for Kennington Oval, the somewhat soulless fortress that used to be a friendly old cricket ground, that England have won back the Ashes on its turf a remarkable five times since the First World War. As the last two successes have come close together, the nation's delight might not *quite* have matched the level of 2005, when Michael Vaughan's side ended *sixteen* years of frustration and England went almost berserk. But it was still abundantly worth experiencing.

The administrators had done the game a serious disservice by cramming the five Tests into a mere forty-eight days, little enough time to savour fully the exciting and immaculately staged opener at Cardiff, the historic encounter when England threw off the dark seventy-five-year cloak of Ashes failure at Lord's, the damp frustration of the scrap at Edgbaston, and Australia's show of strength to draw level at Headingley. Once more it was all to play for at The Oval.

There was no recall for the prolific and mature Ramprakash. Jonathan Trott was England's surprise selection, the negative reaction of some who resented his inclusion puzzling me. He is of English stock, and he meets all the qualification needs. What is it about the English that they seldom seem to get behind a South Africa-born cricketer (there would have been four of them in this Test had Pietersen played as well as Strauss, Trott and Prior)? Perhaps they suspect that their ancestors were all on the wrong side in the Boer war. And perhaps only a white man can openly be labelled an interloper.

Although Trott's temperament is known to be solid, there he sat, waiting to bat, and every time the cameras picked him up he was chewing his nails. It might have been the wretched C.T.Studd, who shivered with a blanket around him during the famous 1882 Ashes match here as Spofforth was running amok; or Johnny Evans, a hero of the Great War whose knees knocked visibly as he waited to bat against Gregory and McDonald in the 1921 Lord's Test. But we were soon to see that I.J.L.Trott was made of sterner stuff.

England 332, and the pitch far friskier than anyone expected. The elegant Ian Bell balanced his "pair" in the triumph of '05 by top-scoring with 72 and sturdy Strauss (129 here four years ago) made 55 precious runs now. "Australia to make 185" I scribbled in the notepad. When rain brought an early lunch on the second day they were 61 without loss. Cricket's such an unpredictable pastime – as if we didn't know.

There are several umpires who are perceptibly exhibitionist. One of them is Mr Bowden, who, I happen to know, once refused to meet a match referee's request to watch replays of a poor decision, and was now too busy literally pulling up his socks to respond to Shane Watson's request for guard.

Watson soon went anyway, and the bowler, Stuart Broad, then claimed the big wicket, forcing Ponting to play on. In the same over he had Hussey lbw. The English beanpole was cheered like a prizefighter when he returned to the third-man boundary, and he went on to immortalising, blitzing figures of 12-1-37-5. This was Broad's hour of glory. After he trapped Clarke, another English cricketer with character, Graeme Swann, bagged North and Katich (50) at the other end. This bowling pair whisked Australia to nine down before Flintoff waddled in to bowl Hilfenhaus. Ten wickets had fallen for 87: Australia 160, an astounding deficit of 172.

Even during an Ashes Test match the mind is sometimes free to muse. I found myself pondering the lost opportunity of a scorebook entry reading Strauss c Hilfenhaus b Hauritz: something from a match between Munich and Zurich? The omission of Hauritz was a blunder. Ponting confessed as much at one of the evening press conferences.

Attention was never going to wander for long, for later that day England sustained the excitement by losing three wickets for 58 (Collingwood caught off what should have been called a no-ball). This evening session had our nerves twisted tightly until as late as 7.19pm, when the bails were lifted at last.

Stuart Broad enjoyed his press conference, paying compliments to, among others, coach Andy Flower (whisper it softly, another from southern Africa). I asked Broad afterwards if he'd ever seen film of Frank Woolley. He hadn't. It might seem fanciful but it is true: there is a strong resemblance when this youngster swings his bat.

Saturday was the decisive day. It saw England work their way to an impregnable position in the third session. Calm and admirable skipper Strauss made 75 extremely important runs. As Marcus North bowled a marathon spell, I wondered what Jim Laker, the master offie of yesteryear, might have achieved on Bill Gordon's pleasingly responsive surface.

Trott's patient, fighting hundred came after tea, elevating him into the elite list of Ashes debutant centurions. It brought to mind *Melbourne Punch's* subtle verse when *Albert* Trott (apparently, after all, no ancestor of this young man's) burst onto the scene for Australia in 1894-95 with 8 for 43 at Adelaide and 195 runs in his first two Tests:

> *You didn't expect it, my sonny?*
> *Yet truly complain you must not.*
> *You wanted <u>a run</u> for your money.*
> *Complying, I gave you <u>A.Trott</u>.*

All of which left Australia a theoretical target of 546 if the Ashes were to be salvaged after all. A saving draw was almost as unlikely with two further days scheduled, the pitch not exactly bland, and the weather forecast reasonable.

And yet . . . . It was 80 without loss by Saturday night, and the cautious view of the thinking classes seemed to be that it would run into the Monday. What then the weather? And how the hell did we get from those nail-biting last overs in the drawn opening Test at Cardiff to here?

Flintoff was escorted by four heavies this morning as he made his way into the ground: no autographs. Yet it had seldom been all that evident that he was even playing. This afternoon, however, out of nowhere and in a matter of a few seconds, he would steal and seal the event.

Two down at lunch, Australia crept steadily on with Ponting and Hussey.

I had watched an angler last week at our local lake and admired his patience as he teased a huge common carp towards the bank and finally managed to scoop it into his net. But it was as nothing compared to the patience of Graeme Swann and his team-mates today. And when Flintoff tottered in on his creaky million-dollar knees, we winced each time his weight thumped down on the crease.

Yet it was this big bloke from Lancashire who pulled off the most spectacular and significant manoeuvre of all. Somehow getting across and down to intercept a drive from Hussey, he launched a flat throw to the far end and plucked out a stump. Ricky Ponting was a couple of inches short. The Ashes were as good as won. A fair lump of captain Flintoff's Ashes agony of 2006-07 was purged in those few seconds

We were free to ignore the hammy Rocky pose, hands flung high. His team-mates were transformed into little girls all jumping around and hugging at a tea party. And they were not alone. Around the terraces there was wild jubilation – except where several dozen members of Merv Hughes's Australian tour group sat glumly in their yellow caps, like so many paralysed budgies.

Gifts now presented themselves. Michael Clarke was unluckily run out by an inch after a rebound off short leg's boot; negligent North was niftily stumped by Prior. But there was resistance, and the toll of missed chances crept up. Hussey's renascence was confirmed with his hundred. Harmison let loose a nasty lifter, but England wanted more, and the frustration showed.

Then Haddin's crude slog at Swann sent him on his way, and Harmison suddenly accounted for three quick wickets, leaving only one to get. Fittingly it fell to Swann (40.2-8-120-4), whose participation in England's Test ventures this year has been so watchable and refreshing. Hussey stabbed the ball to Cook at short leg, and it was Ashes to England, the margin a handsome 197 runs.

As always there were choice cameos everywhere, if only one had wide enough vision to grasp them all: Brett Lee on the balcony, probably thinking "Now if only *I'd* been playing"(as had the excluded Ernie McCormick on this ground in 1938 when England scored nearly a thousand). And there was room for reflection on England's unlikely triumph *without* the services of K.P.Pietersen. However did they manage it?

Ricky Ponting nursed a raw wound to his upper lip as he handled the press conference with poise, dark brown eyes shaded by the peak of an ageing baggy green cap. Andrew Strauss was characteristically mature and courteous in his responses. There had been fireworks and thousands of rose petals, polite interviews, and so many smiles that it was like The Oval of long ago.

And for this history-conscious nut there was a passing thought about Billy Murdoch, Ponting's only Australian predecessor to have lost the Ashes twice on English soil (in 1884 and 1890). Although he suffered a fatal seizure while watching a Melbourne Test match early in 1911, Murdoch's body was brought all the way to England, where he'd made his home. He was buried at Kensal Green, on the other side of the Thames, a mere five miles from where we were now standing. Not many people knew that.

Previously unpublished, as was the very first item in this anthology

Decisive moment: Hussey caught at short leg by Cook off Swann: Ashes to England.
(David Knapp)

INDEX

305, 341
McCosker, R.B. 73, 78, 79, 80, 81
McDermott, C.J. 178, 212, 216, 256, 257, 271
McDermott, P.D. 249
McDonald, C.C. 247
McDonald, E.A. 34, 139, 194, 219, 315, 339
McDonald, Gary 286
McGilvray, Alan 233, 283
McGlew, D.J. 143, 191
McGrath, G.D. 323, 325, 326, 327, 328
McIntyre, A.J.W. 87
McKenzie, G.D. 19, 23, 49, 61, 66, 190, 192
McLeod, C.E. 107
McNamee, R.L.A. 35
McVicker, N.M. 53
Mead, C.P. 158, 227
Meckiff, I. 78, 190, 331
Menzies, R.G. 12, 40, 65, 79, 241, 252, 253
Mercer, J. 175
Meyer, B.J. 115, 192
Midwinter, W.E. 290
Milburn, C. 22, 24, 31, 47, 61, 62, 336
Milland, Ray 47
Miller, David 127
Miller, G. 127, 161
Miller, Glenn 47
Miller, K.R. 22, 41, 46, 47, 78, 79, 86, 90, 106, 107, 110, 128, 129, 142, 185, 186, 187, 190, 205, 209, 219, 251, 252, 253, 254, 255, 272, 273, 274, 305
Miller, Peggy 253
Milligan, Spike 199
Misson, F.M. 79
Mitchell, A. 244
Mitchell, B. 191
Mitchell, Guy 145
Mitchell, Sandy 279
Mitford, John 27
Mitford, Mary Russell 9
Mix, Tom 36
Mmatli, Eddie 191
Moin Khan 235
Mold, A.W. 330
Monckton, Walter 91
More, K.S. 201, 203
Morris, A.R. 11, 47, 52, 78, 90, 105, 129, 142, 143, 239, 242, 323
Morris, J.E. 211, 212, 213

Mortlock, W. 300
Mosey, Don 122
Moyes, A.G. 283
Mozart, W.A. 145
Mugabe, Robert 156, 236
Muller, K. 239
Mullins, P.J. 110
Muralitharan, M. 330, 331
Murdoch, W.L. 341
Murphy, A.J. 285
Murray, D.L. 53, 238
Murray, J.T. 96, 117, 215
Mushtaq Ali 178
Mushtaq Mohammad 68, 73, 74, 151
Mynn, A. 32, 63

Nabokov, Vladimir 145
Napoleon 144
Nayudu, C.K. 91, 321
Neale, P.A. 217
Newman, J.A. 227
Newman, Thunderclap 221
Nicholas, M.C.J. 246
Nicklaus, Jack 92
Nixon, Richard M. 41
Njokweni 69
Noble, M.A. 27, 35, 84, 102, 107, 111, 253
Nontshinga 69
Norfolk, Duke of 244
Norman, Greg 304
North, M.J. 339, 340, 341
Northway, R.P. 335
Nourse, A.D. 191
Nyren, John 231, 333

Oakman, A.S.M. 52, 53, 54
O'Brien, Barry 178
O'Brien, Edmund 47
O'Brien, L.P.J. 78, 110, 242
O'Brien, T.C. 151
O'Donnell, S.P. 178
O'Keeffe, K.J. 242
Old, C.M. 116, 117, 161
Oldfield, W.A.S. 36, 89, 90, 95, 214, 262, 263, 264, 265, 266, 283, 284
Oliver, Neville 274
Olivier, Laurence 229
Ondaatje, C. 169
O'Neill, N.C. 56, 77, 143, 190, 239
O'Reilly, Jack 241
O'Reilly, Peter 241
O'Reilly, W.J. 59, 78, 79, 89, 101, 103, 104, 105, 127, 128, 143, 144, 154, 178, 179, 204,

206, 233, 240, 241, 242, 243, 246, 255, 271, 272, 305, 306, 313, 315
Orwell, George 138, 227
Oslear, D.O. 238
Owen-Thomas, D.R. 48

Packer, Kerry 89, 91, 92, 114, 148, 151, 195, 211, 234, 268, 278, 281, 329
Page, Michael 306
Paine, Thomas 92
Palance, Jack 47
Palmer, C.H. 121
Palmer, K.E. 238
Palmer, R. 258
Pamensky, J.L. 192
Pardon, C.F. 260
Pardon, S.H. 27
Parfitt, P.H. 49
Parish, R.J. 78
Parker, C.W.L. 27
Parkhouse, W.G.A. 87
Parkinson, Michael 107, 195
Parks, J.H. 204
Parr, Butler 17
Parr, G. 16, 17
Passmore, John 69
Pataudi, Nawab of, snr 244
Patherya, Mudar 178
Patiala, Maharaja 56, 58
Patil, S.M. 134
Patmore, Angela 184
Patten, George 106
Patterson, 'Banjo' 232
Patterson, B.P. 216, 223
Pawson, H.A. 113
Paynter, E. 78, 79, 148, 204
Peate, E. 238
Peel, Mark 235
Peel, R. 118, 238
Pellew, C.E. 42, 78, 104
Pepper, C.G. 274, 331
Perera, S.S. 122
Perrin, P.A. 262
Phillip, Arthur 180
Phillips, Jim 14, 330
Philpott, P.I. 78, 115, 277
Picasso, Pablo 217
Pietersen, K.P. 325, 326, 327, 328, 339, 341
Pigott, A.C.S. 140
Pinder, G. 275
Pithey, D.B. 192
Pitney, Gene 178
Pitt, William 163
Platt, Geoffrey 65
Pocock, P.I. 75, 161